AF736635

JUDICIAL PROTECTION OF FUNDAMENTAL RIGHTS ON THE INTERNET

This book explores how the Internet impacts on the protection of fundamental rights, particularly with regard to freedom of speech and privacy. In doing so, it seeks to bridge the gap between Internet Law and European and Constitutional Law.

The book aims to emancipate the debate on Internet Law and Jurisprudence from the dominant position, with specific reference to European legal regimes. This approach aims to inject a European and constitutional 'soul' into the topic. Moreover, the book addresses the relationship between new technologies and the protection of fundamental rights within the theoretical debate surrounding the process of European integration, with particular emphasis on judicial dialogue.

This innovative book provides a thorough analysis of the forms, models and styles of judicial protection of fundamental rights in the digital era and compares the European vision to that of the United States. The book offers the first comparative analysis in which the notion of (judicial) frame, borrowed from linguistic and cognitive studies, is systematically applied to the theories of interpretation and argumentation.

Judicial Protection of Fundamental Rights on the Internet

A Road Towards Digital Constitutionalism?

Oreste Pollicino

•HART•
OXFORD • LONDON • NEW YORK • NEW DELHI • SYDNEY

HART PUBLISHING

Bloomsbury Publishing Plc

Kemp House, Chawley Park, Cumnor Hill, Oxford, OX2 9PH, UK

1385 Broadway, New York, NY 10018, USA

29 Earlsfort Terrace, Dublin 2, Ireland

HART PUBLISHING, the Hart/Stag logo, BLOOMSBURY and the Diana logo are trademarks of Bloomsbury Publishing Plc

First published in Great Britain 2021

First published in hardback, 2021

Paperback edition, 2022

Copyright © Oreste Pollicino, 2021

Oreste Pollicino has asserted his right under the Copyright, Designs and Patents Act 1988 to be identified as Author of this work.

All rights reserved. No part of this publication may be reproduced or transmitted in any form or by any means, electronic or mechanical, including photocopying, recording, or any information storage or retrieval system, without prior permission in writing from the publishers.

While every care has been taken to ensure the accuracy of this work, no responsibility for loss or damage occasioned to any person acting or refraining from action as a result of any statement in it can be accepted by the authors, editors or publishers.

All UK Government legislation and other public sector information used in the work is Crown Copyright ©. All House of Lords and House of Commons information used in the work is Parliamentary Copyright ©. This information is reused under the terms of the Open Government Licence v3.0 (http://www.nationalarchives.gov.uk/doc/open-government-licence/version/3) except where otherwise stated.

All Eur-lex material used in the work is © European Union, http://eur-lex.europa.eu/, 1998–2022.

A catalogue record for this book is available from the British Library.

Library of Congress Cataloging-in-Publication data

Names: Pollicino, Oreste, author.

Title: Judicial protection of fundamental rights on the internet : a road towards digital constitutionalism? / Oreste Pollicino.

Description: Oxford, UK ; New York, NY : Hart Publishing, an imprint of Bloomsbury Publishing, 2021. | Includes bibliographical references and index.

Identifiers: LCCN 2021000182 (print) | LCCN 2021000183 (ebook) | ISBN 9781849468053 (hardback) | ISBN 9781509947225 (paperback) | ISBN 9781509912711 (pdf) | ISBN 9781509912704 (Epub)

Subjects: LCSH: Internet governance—Law and legislation. | Freedom of expression. | Data protection—Law and legislation. | Political questions and judicial power.

Classification: LCC K4345 .P65 2021 (print) | LCC K4345 (ebook) | DDC 342.08/53—dc23

LC record available at https://lccn.loc.gov/2021000182

LC ebook record available at https://lccn.loc.gov/2021000183

ISBN: PB: 978-1-50994-722-5
ePDF: 978-1-50991-271-1
ePub: 978-1-50991-270-4

Typeset by Compuscript Ltd, Shannon

To find out more about our authors and books visit www.hartpublishing.co.uk. Here you will find extracts, author information, details of forthcoming events and the option to sign up for our newsletters.

FOREWORD

It is my pleasure to be able to introduce this publication, which provides an ambitious analysis across the two sides of the Atlantic of judicial responses to the challenges posed by the digital world. The author takes an in-depth look at the emergence of new technologies and their impact on judicial protection for human rights. More broadly, he also questions the relationship between judicial and political power in this new age.

The book begins with the premise that the information society has amplified the role of judges in the face of what the author calls a certain and inevitable legislative inertia. It then moves on to a comparative analysis of the US and European judicial landscapes, focusing on the topics of freedom of expression, privacy and data protection with a detailed look at the latest case-law of the European Court of Human Rights, the Court of Justice of the European Union and the US Supreme Court. These comparisons provide a unique perspective on intersections and divergences of the three courts.

The work also touches upon the increased power acquired by some business actors in the digital environment and pauses to consider the effect of the COVID-19 pandemic, not just on the impact of the working practices of the courts, but more generally on how the implementation of new technology may interfere or limit fundamental rights.

The reader will particularly appreciate Professor Pollicino's analysis of the conceptual pillars of the judicial frame in adjudicating internet-related cases and jurisdictional issues. I was particularly struck by the author's desire to search for the constitutional 'soul' of digital technology. Ultimately, the digital environment has introduced a multitude of new challenges for lawyers and judges alike and for this reason the book deserves to be widely read.

Robert Spano
President of the European Court of Human Rights

ACKNOWLEDGEMENTS

This book represents the fruits of 10 years of research (2011–2021) exploring a dangerous triangle: the interaction between technology, judicial protection for fundamental rights and the new challenges for constitutional law in the digital era.

I would like first of all to express my gratitude to Róbert Spanó for his very kind words in the Foreword; it is a great privilege to have an introduction from the President of the European Court of Human Rights. I would like to thank as well three great scholars: Luciano Floridi, Woodrwow Hartzog and Frank Pasquale. All of them have been so kind and patient in reading the book and expressing their endorsement so generously.

Since the book has been built, at least methodologically, on work carried out over the previous ten years (2000–10) on the interaction between legal orders and judicial dialogue from a multilevel perspective, I must acknowledge the important intellectual contribution of my friend and colleague Giuseppe Martinico. Without our joint research, as well as the book authored by the two of us on this topic, I am not sure whether this new book would ever have seen the light of day.

I started to engage with the issues addressed in this book in 2011 at the Institute of European and Comparative Law in Oxford, a place which still remains dear to my heart. I have fond memories of my time there and at all of the other institutions I have visited over these past 10 years, as well as the colleagues I have had the pleasure of working with. I am particularly grateful for the time spent at Haifa Law School and for its vibrant and stimulating atmosphere.

Among the many friends and colleagues who have offered generous support and discussed the ideas developed in this book, I would like to thank especially Marco Bassini, Angelo Marcello Cardani, Marta Cartabia, Giovanni De Gregorio, Filippo Donati, Michele Graziadei, Roberto Mastroianni, Laura Montanari, Matteo Monti, Fernanda Nicola, Andras Koltay, Andrea Pin, Giovanni Pitruzzella, Franco Pizzetti, Stefano Rodotà, Antonio Ruggeri, Andras Sajo, Roberto Scarciglia, Andrea Simoncini, Antonio Tizzano, Luciano Violante, Stephen Weatherill and Franz Werro.

I am also indebted to Giovanni De Gregorio and Matteo Monti for their invaluable support in the editing process, to Thomas Roberts for the careful language proofreading and to Roberta Bassi and all of the wonderful team at Hart Publishing for their great professionalism, patience and support.

The book is dedicated to my daughter Teresa.

CONTENTS

LIST OF ABBREVIATIONS

ACPA	Anticybersquatting Consumer Protection Act
AG	Advocate General
Audiovisual Media Services Directive	Directive 2010/13 of the European Parliament and of the Council of 10 March 2010 on the coordination of certain provisions laid down by law, regulation or administrative action in Member States concerning the provision of audiovisual media services
CDA	Commnications Decency Act (1996)
CLOUD Act	Clarifying Lawful Overseas Use of Data Act
CNIL	Commission nationale de l'informatique et des libertés
Convention no 108/1981	Convention on the Protection of Individuals with regard to Automatic Processing of Personal Data (ETS no 108/1981)
COPA	Child Online Protection Act
Copyright Directive	Directive (EU) 2019/790 of the European Parliament and of the Council of 17 April 2019 on copyright and related rights in the Digital Single Market and amending Directives 96/9/EC and 2001/29/EC
CPPA	Child Pornography Prevention Act
CJEU	Court of Justice of the European Union
Data Protection Directive	Directive 95/46/EC of the European Parliament and of the Council of 24 October 1995 on the protection of individuals with regard to the processing of personal data and on the free movement of such data

Data Retention Directive	Directive 2006/24/EC of the European Parliament and of the Council of 15 March 2006 on the retention of data generated or processed in connection with the provision of publicly available electronic communications services or of public communications networks and amending Directive 2002/58/EC
EC	European Community
ECHR or Strasbourg Convention	European Convention on Human Rights
e-Commerce Directive	Directive 2000/31/EC of the European Parliament and of the Council of 8 June 2000 on certain legal aspects of information society services, in particular electronic commerce, in the Internal Market
ECtHR or Strasbourg court	European Court of Human Rights
e-Privacy Directive	Directive 2002/58/EC of the European Parliament and of the Council of 12 July 2002 concerning the processing of personal data and the protection of privacy in the electronic communications sector
EDPB	European Data Protection Board
EEC	European Economic Community
eIDAS Regulation	Regulation (EU) 910/2014 of the European Parliament and of the Council of 23 July 2014 on electronic identification and trust services for electronic transactions in the internal market and repealing Directive 1999/93/EC
EUCFR	Charter of Fundamental Rights of the European Union
European courts	Court of Justice of European Union and European Court of Human Rights
Explanations	Explanations Relating to Charter of Fundamental Rights of the European Union 2007/C 303/02 OJ C 303/17 of 14 December 2007
FAN	Federal Agency of News
FBI	Federal Bureau of Investigation

FCC	Federal Communications Commission
FTC	Federal Trade Commission
GDPR	Regulation (EU) 2016/679 of the European Parliament and of the Council of 27 April 2016 on the protection of natural persons with regard to the processing of personal data and on the free movement of such data, and repealing Directive 95/46/EC (General Data Protection Regulation)
IP	Internet protocol
IPT	Investigatory Powers Tribunal
ISP	Internet service provider
LICRA	Ligue Internationale Contre le Racisme et l'Antisémitisme
MTE	*Magyar Tartalomszolgáltatók Egyesülete and Index.hu Zrt v Hungary*, App no 22947/13
NSA	National Security Agency
SCC	Standard Contractual Clause
Schrems I	Case C-362/14, *Maximillian Schrems v Data Protection Commissioner*
Schrems II	Case C-311/18, *Data Protection Commissioner v. Facebook Ireland Limited and Maximillian Schrems*
TEC or EC Treaty	Treaty establishing the European Community
Terrorism Directive	Directive (EU) 2017/541 of the European Parliament and of the Council of 15 March 2017 on combating terrorism and replacing Council Framework Decision 2002/475/JHA and amending Council Decision 2005/671/JHA
TEU	Treaty on European Union
USA Freedom Act	Uniting and Strengthening America by Fulfilling Rights and Ensuring Effective Discipline Over Monitoring Act of 2015
USA Patriot Act	Uniting and Strengthening America by Providing Appropriate Tools Required to Intercept and Obstruct Terrorism

TABLE OF CASES

Australia

Belgium

Bulgaria

Canada

Cyprus

Czech Republic

European Court of Human Rights

European Union

France

Germany

Israel

Italy

Romania

United Kingdom

United States of America

Introduction

Does a change in the relevant technological environment lead to a significant impact on judicial protection for fundamental rights?

If so, does this impact enhance or reduce the level of protection for fundamental rights?

How does Internet technology affect the models of judicial protection when freedom of expression and data protection are at stake?[1]

More specifically, what are the consequences on the case law of, on the one hand, the European courts (the Court of Justice of European Union (CJEU) and European Court of Human Rights (ECtHR)) and, on the other hand, the case law of the US Supreme Court? What is the relationship between metaphorical language, jurisdiction and judicial protection of fundamental rights on the Internet?

What is the impact of digital technologies on the relationship between judicial power and political power?

More specifically, what are the tangible expressions of this momentum in the age of digital constitutionalism in light of the COVID-19 pandemic?

Those are the main research questions that I shall try to answer in this book.

More than 10 years ago, when I started to study the impact of new technologies on constitutional adjudication and, more broadly, on judicial protection for fundamental rights, my primary aim was in a sense more ambitious. The idea was to provide a humble contribution in order to emancipate the debate around Internet law, which, at that time, was preoccupied with the evidently dominant position of technicians, technocrats, IT experts and intellectual property lawyers.[2]

[1] This book deals with the relationship between law and digital technologies. The primary focus is on the Internet as a communication technology enabling new relationships and services in the so-called digital environment. Besides, the book also looks at algorithmic technologies within the context of the Internet. Indeed, the implementation of such automated technologies is highly interrelated with the Internet and, therefore, it can be considered another layer of complexity that deserves to be analysed when focusing on the judicial protection of fundamental rights online across the Atlantic.

[2] Until the first decades of the twenty-first century, most of the legal studies concerning technologies, especially the Internet, were focused on internet governance, liability of online intermediaries, and intellectual property law and privacy. See, for instance, Lilian Edwards and Charlotte Waelde (eds), *Law and Internet-regulating Cyberspace* (Oxford, Hart Publishing, 1997); Lee A Bygrave and Jon Bing, *Internet Governance: Infrastructure and Institutions* (Oxford, Oxford University Press, 2009); Dan Jerker B Svantesson, *Private International Law and the Internet* (Alphen aan den Rijn, Wolters Kluwer, 2007); Chris Reed, *Internet Law: Text and Materials* (Cambridge, Cambridge University Press, 2004); Graham JH Smith, *Internet Law and Regulation* (London, Sweet and Maxwell, 2002); Mihály J Ficsor, *The Law of Copyright and the Internet: The 1996 WIPO Treaties, Their Interpretation and Implementation* (Oxford, Oxford University Press, 2002); Mark A Lemley, Peter S Menell, Robert P Merges and Pamela Samuelson, *Software and Internet Law* (New York, Aspen Law & Business, 2000); John Dickie, *Internet and Electronic Commerce Law in the European Union* (Oxford, Hart Publishing, 1999).

This idea is still very alive, and even though this dominant position is a little less dominant,[3] the time is ripe to attempt to bridge the gap between the approach of Internet lawyers and the one taken by constitutional and European studies scholars by injecting a European and constitutional 'soul' into the topic under investigation. In doing so, it will be possible to reconcile the analysis of the relationship between new technologies and judicial protection for fundamental rights with the theoretical debate into power in the information society.[4]

In other words, as the interesting debate into digital constitutionalism has been showing,[5] it is time to take one step further in this process of emancipation and reconciliation between constitutional law and technology by trying to answer the research questions mentioned above.

This has become even more compelling in the light of recent experiences during the COVID-19 pandemic.[6] I am not referring here simply to how the virus has impacted on the courts' workflow or to the reliance on new technologies in order to perform judicial activities.[7] Indeed, the pandemic has raised new challenges as regards the relationship between judicial and political power in terms of the implementation of new technology. In particular, the trade-off between the degree of precision within virus maps and the need to respect data protection law has led to new challenges for the principle of the rule of law. The primary concern is the reliance on contact tracing technologies, the implementation of which lacks a legal anchor for interfering with (or even limiting) fundamental rights, even where such measures are used to pursue a public interest such as public health.

[3] In the second decade of the twenty-first century, legal scholars have started to focus on law and technology from a public law perspective. See, in particular, András Koltay, *New Media and Freedom of Expression. Rethinking the Constitutional Foundations of the Public Sphere* (Oxford, Hart Publishing, 2019); Oreste Pollicino and Graziella Romeo (eds), *The Internet and Constitutional Law: The Protection of Fundamental Rights and Constitutional Adjudication in Europe* (London, Routledge, 2016); Ben Wagner, Matthias C Kettemann and Kilian Vieth (eds), *Research Handbook on Human Rights and Digital Technology: Global Politics, Law and International Relations* (Cheltenham, Edward Elgar, 2019); Rikke F Jorgensen (ed), *Human Rights in the Age of Platforms* (Cambridge, MA, MIT Press, 2019); Paul Bernal, *Internet Privacy Rights: Rights to Protect Autonomy* (Cambridge, Cambridge University Press, 2014).

[4] See, in particular, Martin Moore and Damian Tambini (eds), *Digital Dominance: The Power of Google, Amazon, Facebook, and Apple* (Oxford, Oxford University Press, 2018); Eric Brousseau, Meryem Marzouki and Cécile Méadel (eds), *Governance, Regulation and Powers on the Internet* (Cambridge, Cambridge University Press, 2012).

[5] Giovanni De Gregorio, 'The Rise of Digital Constitutionalism in the European Union' (2020) *International Journal of Constitutional Law*, forthcoming; Edoardo Celeste, 'Digital Constitutionalism: A New Systematic Theorization' (2019) 33(1) *International Review of Law, Computers and Technology* 76; Dennis Redeker, Lex Gill and Urs Gasser, 'Towards Digital Constitutionalism? Mapping Attempts to Craft an Internet Bill of Rights' (2018) 80 *International Communication Gazette* 302; Mauro Santaniello, Nicola Palladino, Maria Carmela Catone and Paolo Diana, 'The Language of Digital Constitutionalism and the Role of National Parliaments' (2018) 80 *International Communication Gazette* 320; Nicolas Suzor, 'Digital Constitutionalism: Using the Rule of Law to Evaluate the Legitimacy of Governance by Platforms' (2018) 4(3) *Social Media + Society* 1.

[6] Richard Albert and Yaniv Roznai (eds), *Constitutionalism Under Extreme Conditions* (New York, Springer, 2020); Katharina Pistor, *Law in the Time of COVID-19* (New York, Columbia Law School, 2020).

[7] Adi Robertson, 'The Supreme Court Live-Streamed its First Phone Hearing, and (Almost) Everything Worked' *The Verge* (5 May 2020) at www.theverge.com/2020/5/5/21246566/supreme-court-teleconference-live-stream-hearings-patent-booking-com.

The courts have indeed started to deal with new technological questions,[8] especially in relation to contact tracing apps, without relying on regulation or legislation to determine the usage of and the limits to such instruments. Besides, the lack of legislative anchors has encouraged supreme courts to interpret constitutional safeguards, thus reinforcing that process of judicial amplification in the information society, and this is precisely the issue on which this book will focus.

When writing this book, I have drawn inspiration from the theories of judicial argumentation and interpretation.[9] MacCormick defined argumentation as 'the activity of putting arguments for or against something'.[10] Moreover 'legal argumentation' consists in anchoring such arguments to a certain legal framework. Both legal argumentation and interpretation are part of jurisprudence. Therefore, I have considered the role of judicial arguments in constitutional and European case law as I in fact believe that this standpoint can provide critical insights to explain the reasoning and interpretative path that courts follow when addressing cases involving the digital environment. Whenever judges deal with technological expertise outside the legal domain, judicial interpretation is affected by the contextualisation of a given issue within a legal frame.[11] As Sajó and Ryan put it: 'There is nothing new in this act of judicial framing. The real challenge comes when judges (or legislators) are confronted with unexpected, unpleasant or ambiguous social and economic consequences of technology'.[12]

The role of the judicial frame is not neutral. The frame adopted within any given argumentation is the result of an effort at connecting cognitive structure with context through language, emphasis and other techniques aimed at creating a bridge between knowledge and reality. This approach seeks to highlight the ideological bias of some decisions. For example, the use of the term 'piracy' for online copyright infringement hides a negative approach to such a practice by associating this crime with the sharing of files on the Internet. Likewise, the focus on the frame of 'privacy' in data protection refers to the need to protect against public intrusion and tends to assign prevalence to individual rights rather than public interests.

I am aware of the fact that, although this focus relies on an accurate and systematic analysis of case law, it overstates two drawbacks. First, the cognitive framework

[8] A paradigmatic case is the decision of the Israeli Supreme Court to ban electronic contact tracing without statutory authorisation. Israeli Supreme Court, *Ben Meir v Prime Minister*, HC 2109/20, 19 March 2020. See Elena Chachko, 'The Israeli Supreme Court Checks COVID-19 Electronic Surveillance' *LawfareBlog* (5 May 2020) at www.lawfareblog.com/israeli-supreme-court-checks-covid-19-electronic-surveillance.

[9] Eveline T Feteris (ed), *Fundamentals of Legal Argumentation. A Survey of Theories on the Justification of Judicial Decisions* (Dordrecht, Springer, 2017); Robert Alexy, *A Theory of Legal Argumentation* (Oxford, Oxford University Press, 1989).

[10] Neil MacCormick, 'Argumentation and Interpretation in Law' (1995) 9 *Argumentation* 467, 467.

[11] Chris Riley, 'The Rite of Rhetoric: Cognitive Framing in Technology Law' (2009) 9(3) *Nevada Law Journal* 495.

[12] András Sajó and Clare Ryan, 'Judicial Reasoning and New Technologies: Framing, Newness, Fundamental Rights and the Internet' in Oreste Pollicino and Graziella Romeo (eds), *The Internet and Constitutional Law: The Protection of Fundamental Rights and Constitutional Adjudication in Europe* (London, Routledge, 2016) 3, 3.

of each individual is not the same but tends to a sort of radical subjectivism.[13] Indeed, legal argumentation, like other forms of argumentation, is also shaped by other factors such as the baggage of previous experience of each individual. Secondly, we must not forget that the judges are not the only actors in a trial. Parties' argumentations inevitably contribute, shaping the outcome to decisions and sometimes also obliging courts to adopt certain options.

Despite these challenges, I stress the role of framing in Internet-related case law and connect legal argumentation with judicial frames. In particular, I focus on the extrapolation of judicial frames from legal reasoning in order to understand how (digital) technologies have been contextualised within constitutional adjudication while going beyond the general and formal use of typical words or expressions. This approach shows how the adoption of a certain judicial frame in cases involving digital technologies can lead the courts to outcomes that would have been different had a different frame been applied for the case in question. This is because, as we shall see, words matter. Moreover, the case of the judicial frame shows exactly how judicial activity leads to similar outcomes even in different cases as a result of a particular judicial frame.

However, the role of the judicial frame is not the only way in which this book analyses how courts adjudicate on cases related to the digital environment. The second pillar focuses in fact on the ability of the courts to influence jurisdictional boundaries online. Analysing the courts' approach to jurisdiction is a key issue in understanding how protection for fundamental rights in the digital environment is provided in concrete terms. It is, however, a starting point. Indeed, this book does not simply focus on jurisdiction per se, but also on how the courts have extended the territorial scope of legislation in order to claim jurisdiction. Within this context, the exercise of eradicating jurisdiction is strictly linked to how the claim to digital sovereignty has influenced the reasoning and the ultimate output of US and European courts.

As Floridi stressed, 'The fight for digital sovereignty is an epochal struggle not only of all against all, but also of anyone allied with anyone, with variable alliances changing according to interests and opportunities'.[14] In this case, the role of courts and their judicial frames matter. This is because the courts' ability to define territorial boundaries also results from a particular frame concerning the protection of fundamental rights online.

Within this framework, in order to examine how digital technologies have impacted on forms, models, balancing exercises and the degree of creativity of judicial protection for fundamental rights,[15] judicial frames and jurisdictional issues will be analysed as reasons for amplifying judicial momentum by considering

[13] Richard A Posner, 'The Law of the Beholder', *New Republic* (16 October 2000).

[14] Luciano Floridi, 'The Fight for Digital Sovereignty: What It Is, and Why It Matters, Especially for the EU' (2020) 33 *Philosophy & Technology* 369, 371.

[15] Oreste Pollicino and Mart Susi, 'Internet and Human Rights Law: Introduction' (2019) 25(2) *European Law Journal* 120.

primary fundamental rights in the digital age, namely freedom of speech, privacy and data protection. These fundamental rights have been chosen due to the special relevance of judicial protection for freedom of expression and privacy in the shift from the world of atoms to the world of bits.

Looking at freedom of expression, it can be seen how the Internet has created the perfect environment for individuals to share ideas and opinions.[16] The digital environment has encouraged the dissemination of information between different individuals and communities, who benefit from lower costs compared to traditional media outlets. The positive role of the Internet has already proved its reach. The sharing of ideas and opinions online has resulted in elections being influenced and even led to the consolidation of political movements and parties, thus enhancing political rights. Nonetheless, this positive framework is mediated by how, and especially through whom, information flows online. In the information society, freedom of expression is under major pressure from public and private actors. In authoritarian countries, these fundamental rights have been affected by major censorship measures, leading even to Internet shutdowns.[17] Nonetheless, even democratic countries have implemented other measures to regulate speech as a reaction to the challenges raised by the spread of illegal content online,[18] while the courts have reacted to digital challenges to freedom of expression.[19]

Likewise, the digital environment has also introduced new challenges in the field of privacy and data protection, leading courts to step up to protect these fundamental rights in the information society. Even in this case, in the early days of the Internet, this new digital framework seemed to ensure greater liberty through the promise of anonymity. Nonetheless, the rise of the information society, thanks to the development of new technologies, has increased concerns surrounding protection for privacy and personal data, which are subject to ubiquitous forms of control.[20] At the end of the twentieth century, the development of new processing technologies led to a rise in the positive dimension of privacy, namely data protection; however, at the same time, the new technological framework allowed new business models to develop based on the processing of data. As a result of this process, processing personal data has become critical for the provision of public services or for business to earn profits, thus increasing the scale and scope of risks for these fundamental rights.

[16] Yochai Benkler, *The Wealth of Networks: How Social Production Transforms Markets and Freedom* (New Haven, CT, Yale University Press, 2006).

[17] Giovanni De Gregorio and Nicole Stremlau, 'Internet Shutdowns and the Limits of the Law' (2020) *International Journal of Communication*, forthcoming.

[18] Jonathan L Zittrain, Robert Faris, Helmi Noman, Justin Clark, Casey Tilton and Ryan Morrison-Westphal, 'The Shifting Landscape of Global Internet Censorship', *Berkman Klein Center for Internet & Society Research Publication* (2017) at http://nrs.harvard.edu/urn-3:HUL.InstRepos:33084425.

[19] Róbert Spanó, 'Intermediary Liability for Online User Comments under the European Convention on Human Rights' (2017) 17(4) *Human Rights Law Review* 665.

[20] Shoshana Zuboff, 'Big Other: Surveillance Capitalism and the Prospects of an Information Civilization' (2015) 30(1) *Journal of Information Technology* 75.

Methodologically speaking, I am perfectly aware that these fundamental rights are conceptualised differently across the Atlantic.[21] As we shall see, when looking at European courts, the Internet plays a critical role in the balancing test as an instrument justifying public limitations to fundamental rights, especially freedom of expression. Besides, this is why, when conducting a certain balancing test on the Internet, courts have been shown to pay more attention to misuses. This is not always a sign of judicial activism. It has also resulted from the inescapable need to address contemporary issues. In the US, the US Supreme Court has on the other hand maintained that the Internet opens up new opportunities to exercise traditional freedoms. Therefore, the attitude towards judicial scrutiny within Internet disputes is almost the opposite on the other side of the Atlantic.

Nonetheless, the Internet provides an opportunity to focus on how freedom of expression and the right to privacy and data protection are protected from a transnational point of view. The Internet has in fact provided a powerful bridge for communication between different legal orders, thus setting up courts as the focus for this new transnational legal order. Besides, the choice to focus on these two legal systems was made for two different comparative reasons. On the one hand, it may be based on the 'prototype cases' logic,[22] given that the US and the EU are the two most important actors in the field of Internet regulation. On the other hand, these systems may be considered as heralds of two particularly different approaches to the Internet.[23] The focus on the two sides of the Atlantic enriches the analysis since it allows us to focus on a transnational issue such as the Internet by basing the analysis not only on the European framework, but also on US law, as two consolidated democracies which, however, adopt diverging approaches to judicial protection for fundamental rights online.

[21] Eva Brems (ed), *Conflicts Between Fundamental Rights* (Cambridge, Intersentia, 2008); Lorenzo Zucca, *Constitutional Dilemmas – Conflicts of Fundamental Legal Rights in Europe and the US* (Oxford, Oxford University Press, 2007); Agustín J Menendez and Erik O Eriksen (eds), *Arguing Fundamental Rights* (London, Springer, 2006); Robert Alexy, *A Theory of Constitutional Rights* (Oxford, Oxford University Press, 2002); Jeremy Waldron (ed), *Theories of Rights* (Oxford, Oxford University Press, 1984).

[22] Ran Hirschl, *Comparative Matters: The Renaissance of Comparative Constitutional Law* (Oxford, Oxford University Press, 2014) 256.

[23] Both in Europe and the US constitutional provisions declare freedom of expression as a fundamental right. Nonetheless, some important differences should be observed in this regard. The text of the US First Amendment and those of Articles 10 ECHR and 11 Charter of Fundamental Rights of the European Union (EUCFR) reveal how freedom of expression may enjoy a broader or narrower scope of protection depending on the relevant jurisdiction. See for a more in-depth comparative study, Frederick Schauer, 'Freedom of Expression Adjudication in Europe and America: A Case Study in Comparative Constitutional Architecture' in Georg Nolte (ed), *European and US Constitutionalism* (Cambridge, Cambridge University Press, 2005) 49. Concerning the right to privacy or, better, the right to data protection, while in the US legal system this last right is considered as a fundamental right of citizens in relation to the government's activity (Fourth Amendment), it does not – currently – find general protection online nor against 'private' activities. On the contrary, the EU system has embraced data protection as a fundamental right of EU citizens.

When considering the European system, the analysis will focus on the case law of the CJEU and the ECtHR.[24] I am conscious of the non-national character of the EU compared to the US. However, at the same time I believe that the reasons for comparison mentioned above could legitimate this type of analysis.

It should also be added that, given the power of Internet platforms and the difficulty in making rules effective in the digital world, the US and the EU are the two leading actors among democracies around the world in the specific area of Internet regulation even though, as we will see, they seem to propose two different paradigms when balancing rights on the Internet. This last consideration leads me to explain the second reason for the comparative structure of this book. The rules of these two systems have frequently clashed in the digital environment and have created new challenges in terms of the reasoning followed by supreme courts from a transnational constitutional law perspective.

Therefore, when engaging with this book, readers will encounter three complementary perspectives: the role of judicial frame and the jurisdictional issue as amplifying reasons for judicial momentum in the digital era; the focus on freedom of expression, privacy and data protection as the primary fundamental rights at stake in the information society; and the comparative perspective of judicial protection for fundamental rights in the EU and US. These three standpoints characterise the entire structure of this book in providing a comprehensive overview of the role of judicial power in the information society on both sides of the Atlantic.

Ultimately, if one were to look for a single word that could sum up the spirit of the book, this word would most likely be 'power', considered from multiple perspectives. First of all, the power of courts in the process of adjudication: even if they are often hidden from view, sometimes both from 'winners' and 'losers',[25] the courts in any event always operate, as Cover argues, 'in a field of pain and death'.[26]

As Del Mar has pointed out, 'recognising the power and violence of adjudication, however, does not exclude approaching, with humanity, the difficulties that judges face'.[27] The human, sympathetic interconnecting dimension is capable of revealing the second important power at stake in this book: the poetic power of metaphors,[28] which are more associated with emotions. According to Berger the 'power is thought to arise from metaphor's invitation to see one thing "as another," providing us with a novel perspective and generating new information in the process'.[29] Against this background, the power of metaphors in action will be expressed in showing how legal reasoning in the field of new technology is

[24] This analysis does not focus either on the relationship of the two courts or the systems of rights and freedoms enshrined in the EUCFR.

[25] Maksymilian Del Mar, *Artefacts of Legal Inquiry: The Value of Imagination in Adjudication* (Oxford, Hart Publishing, 2020) 21.

[26] Robert M Cover, 'Violence and the Word' (1986) 95(8) *Yale Law Journal* 1601.

[27] Del Mar (n 25) 21.

[28] Linda L Berger, 'Metaphor and Analogy: The Sun and the Moon of Legal Persuasion' (2013) 22 *Journal of Law and Policy* 147, 176.

[29] ibid 175.

'based on the assumption of particular metaphors that supported the inference made by justice'.[30] A related power is the power of frames. As has been pointed out, 'the facts of certain cases are already presented to judges by reference to certain "frames" within which judges image-schemas, radial categories and metaphors play a central role'.[31] This is a huge power indeed. The third form of power to be analysed is the new private power vested in digital platforms. Here a very important challenge emerges, as will be analysed below, for the new round of constitutional law. Constitutionalism has a congenital mission of limiting power. Until recently, the challenge was to limit public (generally governmental) powers in the classic vertical dimension of frame of state: (public) authority versus individual liberty.[32] The geometry of power (and the resulting challenge for constitutional law) is becoming more complex and articulate: aside from the vertical dimension mentioned there is a growing horizontal one, which, operating within the algorithmic society, connects up individuals with private digital powers, which compete with and often prevail over public powers. As will be shown in the book, the new frontier of digital constitutionalism is precisely to deal with this new challenge of the rise in private powers,[33] bearing in mind the fact that there cannot be any constitutional law if the aim is not to limit power.

Within this framework, Chapter 1 deals with the relationship between *ius dicere* (ie judicial activity) and technology. This chapter introduces two conceptual pillars which are used in this book to reveal how the role of the courts in protecting fundamental rights in the digital age has been amplified: the judicial frame and the jurisdictional issue.

The first part of Chapter 1 deals with the ability of courts to use the judicial frame as an instrument of interpretation in order to adapt constitutional and legislative rules to the new technological scenario, with specific reference to the shift from the 'world of atoms' to the 'world of bits'. This part will outline the emerging importance of the concepts of judicial frame and metaphorical language within judicial reasoning in the light of technological challenges. I look at the relationship between metaphorical language and judicial protection for fundamental rights on the Internet by focusing on how judicial frames impact upon the balance struck between conflicting rights and, in this context, the relevance of the Hartian distinction between internal and external points of view.[34]

The second part of this chapter will examine how the transnational nature of the digital environment has led the judiciary to play a critical role in defining the territorial boundaries to the application of rights and freedoms at local level. I shall

[30] Mark Johnson, *The Aesthetics of Meaning and Thought: The Bodily Roots of Philosophy, Science, Morality, and Art* (Chigago, IL, Chigago University Press, 2018) 176.

[31] Del Mar (n 25) 288.

[32] András Sajó and Renáta Uitz, *The Constitution of Freedom: An Introduction to Legal Constitutionalism* (Oxford, Oxford University Press, 2017).

[33] De Gregorio (n 5).

[34] Herbert LA Hart, *The Concept of Law* (Oxford, Oxford University Press, 1961).

look at how European and US courts have dealt with a global issue from a local standpoint and stress how this process represents the other fundamental characteristic of the amplification of judicial momentum in the digital environment.

The third part of Chapter 1 engages with the constitutional origin of and the consolidation of protection for free speech, privacy and data protection in the EU and the US with a view to providing a normative framework on which the subsequent chapters are built when focusing on judicial protection for fundamental rights online.

Chapter 2 analyses the classic (offline) and new (online) model of judicial protection for freedom of speech, looking to the US and European courts from a comparative perspective. In the light of the issues mentioned above, this chapter will examine how the advent of the Internet has affected the exercise of and the judicial protection for freedom of expression.

The first part of this chapter will deal with the 'holy' nature of the First Amendment in the interpretation of the US Supreme Court and whether the shift from the world of atoms to that of bits has affected judicial argumentation, and subsequently interpretation, in relation to the protection of this fundamental right. The second part of the chapter will instead focus on the European judicial approach to freedom of expression by exploring, first of all, the scope of the relevant constitutional provisions at EU and ECHR levels, and secondly the attempts by the ECtHR and the CJEU to interpret and sometimes manipulate legal provisions in order to adapt constitutional principle to the new challenges thrown up by technology. Then this chapter will analyse the use, misuse and abuse of the metaphor of the free marketplace of ideas in relation to the fight against disinformation online.

After analysing judicial protection for the right to free speech in the shift from the world of atoms to the world of bits across the Atlantic, Chapter 3 will engage with judicial protection for privacy and data protection, once again from a comparative perspective. The amplification of judicial momentum is not specific to the judicial transatlantic narrative on the protection of freedom of expression. Indeed, the analysis focuses, on the one hand, on the crucial role played by judicial frames (and more broadly) judicial imagination relating to the use of metaphoric language and, on the other hand, the jurisdictional issue in relation to the enforcement of privacy and data protection rights in the US and the EU.

As in Chapter 2, the first part of Chapter 3 will examine the relevant case law of the US Supreme Court, underlining its consolidation in the world of atoms and its evolution in the digital environment. In the second part, the focus will move to Europe and in particular the case law of the ECtHR and the CJEU. Here, I have decided to focus on judicial protection for (and the enforcement of) digital privacy by the CJEU. As we shall see, the case law of the CJEU in this field offers a paradigmatic example of the role of the judicial frame and the jurisdictional issue in the information society. Indeed, as far as the frame of protection is concerned, the line between interpretation and manipulation is very thin and, also as regards jurisdiction, the expansion of EU law provides another example of how the CJEU has reinterpreted fundamental rights to adapt their protection to the new technological scenario. After highlighting the two models of judicial protection for privacy and data protection in the EU and US, this chapter will compare the two frames in the digital context. In particular, I shall stress how the European data protection fortress has a lot to teach, but also something to learn from the US Supreme Court's interpretation of the Fourth Amendment as well as, more specifically, the mosaic theory as a way of emancipating that fortress from the slavery of its data-matrix in the era of big data.

After this transatlantic analysis of judicial protection of freedom of expression, privacy and data protection in the digital environment, Chapter 4 will underline how courts have dealt with the extraterritorial reach of these rights. In particular, the information society has highlighted the intimate relationship between privacy and free speech. The linkage between these two rights was already clear from the outset, within the balancing processes proposed by Warren and Brandeis,[35] although now appears to have acquired a broader dimension in the information society. As in the other chapters of this book, this part will also consider the intersection mentioned above from the European and the US perspectives.

The first part of Chapter 4 will focus on the European framework, examining some cases of the ECtHR and CJEU capable of building a drawbridge into the European fortress that can first connect and then reconcile the European frame of privacy and freedom of speech with the global standard of protection.

In the second part, the chapter will focus on the US.[36] While in Europe the data protection fortress is consolidating, the challenge in the US appears to be to identify a way out of the stagnation in which the US system is stuck, as if in quicksand,[37] while granting a right to data protection only in certain specific fields.[38] From a general point of view, it seems that the First Amendment remains the lodestar against which all balancing processes of fundamental rights must be aligned.[39] This initial impression will be examined in this chapter to answer the question about whether the European fortress of data privacy could face up to the castle of freedom of expression in US constitutional law.

[35] Samuel D Warren and Louis D Brandeis, 'The Right to Privacy' (1890) 4 *Harvard Law Review* 193.

[36] Concerning the freedom of expression, see, in particular, Jack M Balkin, 'Free Speech in the Algorithmic Society: Big Data, Private Governance, and New School Speech Regulation' (2018) 51 *UC Davis Law Review* 1149; Frank Pasquale, *The Black Box Society: The Secret Algorithms That Control Money and Information* (Cambridge, MA, Harvard University Press, 2015). For the right to privacy, see, in particular, Woodrow Hartzog, *Privacy's Blueprint: The Battle to Control the Design of New Technologies* (Cambridge, MA, Harvard University Press, 2018).

[37] M Neil Richards, 'The Puzzle of Brandeis, Privacy, and Speech' (2010) 63 *Vanderbilt Law Review* 1295.

[38] Francesca Bignami and Giorgio Resta, 'Transatlantic Privacy Regulation: Conflict and Cooperation' (2015) 8 *Law and Contemporary Problems* 231. On the 'third-party doctrine' and privacy in the US, see Daniel J Solove, 'Fourth Amendment Pragmatism' (2010) 51 *Boston College Law Review* 1511.

[39] See also Eugene Volokh, 'Freedom of Speech, Information Privacy, and the Troubling Implications of a Right to Stop People from Speaking About You' (2000) 52 *Stanford Law Review* 1049.

The final part of the chapter will consider how these two models are related to the conundrum of digital sovereignty in the digital era and how the COVID-19 pandemic season – and in particular the dilemma of reconciling public health and privacy in relation to contact tracing – seems liable to make that conundrum even more problematic.

At this point, Chapter 5 will consider the final research question: what are the tangible expressions of this momentum in the age of digital constitutionalism in light of the COVID-19 pandemic?

After an initial discussion of the balance between judicial and political power in the digital age, this chapter will focus on the delicate issue of how the courts are being confronted with new challenges in relation to the transformation of digital platforms into new private powers. As we shall see, this transformation has been amplified by the pandemic, in which platforms, as digital utilities, have shown their importance for freedom of expression and privacy on a global scale.

The final part of Chapter 5 will seek to identify a possible direction of the role of courts in this phase of digital constitutionalism, also in light of the new challenges raised both during and after the pandemic.

1

Technology and Judges Across the Atlantic

I. The Amplification of Judicial Momentum

Today more than ever, also against the backdrop of the uncertainty triggered by the COVID-19 pandemic, judicial globalisation has placed courts in a privileged position to identify risks of potential collision between interconnected legal regimes in terms of the protection of fundamental rights.[1] Cooperation between courts forges closer ties between different yet interacting orders,[2] while contributing to adapting legal systems to the new global challenges. The importance of this dynamic – and, more generally, the role and the impact of judicial activity – is even greater within the digital domain. This chapter analyses the reasons for and consequences of this 'amplification'.

The increase of the role of judges in the information society can be explained in at least two ways.

The main (substantive) reason focuses on the traditional gap between law and technology, where law lags behind technological advances. The burden of making up for this inevitable legislative inertia – at national and supranational level – falls heavily on the shoulders of the courts. The new factual and legal context created by the Internet has further extended this gap, thus highlighting the lack of judicial expertise to deal with the scenarios thrown up by new technologies. In this context, political inertia (which is not always forced as sometimes power is delegated to

[1] As observed by Slaughter, this is a 'process of judicial interaction across, above, and below borders, exchanging ideas and cooperating in cases involving national as much as international law'. Anne-Marie Slaughter, 'Judicial Globalization' (2000) 40 *Virginia Journal of International Law* 1103, 1104.

[2] Beside the amplification of judicial momentum, there is also a parallel and more worrying process of privatisation of digital justice. The major social network is implementing rules related to the institution of a last instance appeal body, the so-called Facebook Supreme Court (See Kate Klonick, 'The Facebook Oversight Board: Creating an Independent Institution to Adjudicate Online Free Expression' (2020) 129 *Yale Law Journal* 2418) As the President of the European Court of Human Rights Róbert Spanó has recently highlighted that there is 'the ongoing concern with the question of remedies and review mechanism for disputes online and the increasing tendency to privatise or outsource to the platforms the final determination of the scope and the content of free speech and privacy online'. Róbert Spanó, 'Summary of the Issues Discussed during the Seminar: An Aerial View' in *Human Rights Challenges in the Digital Age: Judicial Perspectives* (Strasbourg, Council of Europe Publishing, 2020) 201, 209.

courts with a view to avoiding difficult choices) has fostered judicial imagination within the digital era,[3] along with the resulting use of metaphors and frames to adapt legal systems to the peculiarities of the digital realm.

This new amplification of a well-established process of judicial imagination is not the only reason for the increase in judicial power in the digital age. There is also another (procedural) reason, which is related to the inherently transnational nature of the digital environment. The advent of the World Wide Web has challenged traditional legal categories like sovereignty and territory, thus raising new questions concerning the boundaries of law and jurisdiction. The notion of territory or space has been called into question with respect to the online sphere, where the Internet provides a channel for sharing information, products and services across various jurisdictions. Within this context, courts have been called upon to enforce local law within a transnational environment such as the Internet.

It should indeed come as no surprise that the evolution of the digital environment has been one of the drivers behind this new wave of judicial activism. At the outset, scholars debated for a long time whether the Internet constituted a borderless and anarchic territory, a kind of 'no man's land' immune to any attempts at regulation at national or indeed supranational or transnational level. Other scholars have pointed out that, while it is possible to regulate the Internet, the use of domestic law would be incompatible with the nature of the Internet. More specifically, some authors have described the Internet as a self-regulating platform that is capable of developing its own code;[4] conversely, others have argued that regulation based on geographical boundaries is infeasible, and it is hence impossible to apply national laws to the Internet. Johnson and Post, two champions of this anarchic approach to the web, have stated that 'events on the Net occur everywhere but nowhere in particular … no physical jurisdiction has a more compelling claim than any other to subject events exclusively to its laws'[5] and thus '[e]fforts to determine where the events in question occur are decidedly misguided'.[6] Nonetheless, it is well known that such a libertarian dream has faded away. The courts have played a crucial role in breaking down such utopian views. Both the enforcement of fundamental rights online through the use of new judicial narratives, along with the assertion of jurisdiction,[7] apparently as a simply procedural tool, are two

[3] Lyndsey Stonebridge, *The Judicial Imagination: Writing After Nuremberg* (Edinburgh, Edinburgh University Press, 2011). See also Maksymilian Del Mar, *Artefacts of Legal Inquiry: The Value of Imagination in Adjudication* (Oxford, Hart Publishing, 2020).

[4] Paul Baran, *Communications, Computers and People* (Santa Monica, CA, The RAND Corporation, 1965): the author forecast that new technology would not have required legislation because it would have had the power to self-regulate all its relevant consequences; and Lawrence Lessig, *Code and Other Laws of Cyberspace* (New York, Basic Books, 1999), who argued that the technology would have produced a 'code' more effective than the law to regulate its functioning and consequences.

[5] David R Johnson and David G Post, 'Law and Borders. The Rise of Law in Cyberspace' (1996) 48 *Stanford Law Review* 1367, 1376.

[6] ibid 1378.

[7] Uta Kohl, *Jurisdiction and the Internet. Regulatory Competence over Online Activity* (Cambridge, Cambridge University Press, 2007).

privileged standpoints for understanding the role of courts across the Atlantic in the information society.

This chapter introduces two conceptual pillars, which will be used in this book to reveal how the role of the courts in protecting fundamental rights in the digital age has been amplified. The following sections still stress how the rise of the Internet can be considered as one of the causes of this amplification of judicial momentum.

The first part of this chapter deals with the ability of courts to use the judicial frame as an instrument of interpretation in order to adapt constitutional and legislative rules to the new technological scenario, with specific reference to the shift from the 'world of atoms' to the 'world of bits'. The second part will examine how the transnational nature of the digital environment has led the judiciary to play a critical role in defining the territorial boundaries to the application of rights and freedoms at local level. The third part will then introduce the issue of constitutional protection for these fundamental rights, showing how the (different ages) of codification of fundamental rights within charters and Bills (of rights) have not prevented courts from using new judicial frames and shaping their jurisdiction creatively. Indeed, paradoxically (although only apparently paradoxically), it would appear that the exact opposite has occurred, having resulted in a further amplification of judicial imagination.The fourth part will briefly disclose the constitutional basis of freedom of expression, privacy rights and data protection in the EU and the US, giving an overview of the analysis of the subsequent chapters.

II. Metaphors, Judicial Frames and Cyberspace

One of the principal consequences of the enhanced role of the judiciary in the digital age is the ability for the courts to enjoy broader room for manoeuvre when using metaphorical language and judicial frames in relation to the balancing of fundamental rights. In other words, as mentioned above, the not easy task of adapting 'traditional' legal rules to new technological paradigms implies greater judicial imagination. In some cases, as will be noted in Chapters 4 and 5, such as in relation to enforcement by the Court of Justice of the European Union (CJEU) of digital privacy, outright 'judicial manipulation' has occurred.

In order to fully understand the relevance of metaphors and frames in the new technological context, it is necessary to take a step back and to consider the theoretical backgrounds to the two concepts.

As far as metaphorical language is concerned,[8] the shift from a conception of the metaphor as an exclusively linguistic fact to one that considers it as involving a cognitive process and a conceptual framework occurred with the publication in

[8] Alessandro Morelli and Oreste Pollicino, 'Metaphors, Judicial Frames and Fundamental Right in Cyberspace' (2020) *American Journal of Comparative Law*, forthcoming.

1980 of the volume *Metaphors We Live By*, by Lakoff and Johnson.[9] This is a study that marked a genuine, paradigmatic shift as well as a starting point for research into the role of metaphors within a wide variety of fields (from politics to religion, from economics to the law, etc). Two central theses of modern cognitive linguistics were endorsed: the idea that language is not independent from other human cognitive activities (such as perceiving, reasoning, etc) and the close link between meanings and concepts.

The fundamental theoretical assumption is therefore that a metaphor is more a fact of thinking than language.[10] According to this view, every metaphor has a 'source domain', a 'target domain' and 'source-to-target mapping'.[11] It is claimed that the metaphorical processes developed through the shift from one domain to another reflect the cognitive structures that condition human understanding.

Metaphorical language performs an irreplaceable role within the law. In fact, many legal categories and institutes have been constructed through metaphorical processes. Within that ambit, metaphors perform a constitutive function of legal reality itself: consider, for instance, the categories of 'legal person' or 'sovereignty' in all of its manifestations (state, national, popular, etc). As Blavin and Cohen write:

> Within the law, metaphors mold the framework of discourse, determining the scope of appropriate questions about and answers to various social and legal problems. Courts and commentators employ metaphors as heuristics to generate hypotheses about the application of law to novel, unexplored domains. Metaphors structure the way lawyers conceptualize legal events, as they infiltrate, consciously and unconsciously, legal discourse.[12]

These scholars have analysed three different ways of describing the Internet in metaphorical terms: 'the information superhighway', 'cyberspace' and the Internet as a 'real space'. They have shown how these conceptual metaphors influence the solution to legal problems involving the Internet.[13] However, this aspect is not always fully appreciated and metaphorical language has not always been

[9] George Lakoff and Mark Johnson, *Metaphors We Live By* (Chicago, IL, University of Chicago Press, 1980).

[10] Annamaria Contini, 'La forza cognitiva della metafora' (2016) 1 *I castelli di Yale online* 14.

[11] George Lakoff, *Women, Fire, and Dangerous Things. What Categories Reveal about the Mind* (Chicago, IL, University Chicago Press, 1987) 276.

[12] See Jonathan H Blavin and I Gleen Cohen, 'Gore, Gibson, and Goldsmith: The Evolution of Internet Metaphors in Law and Commentary' (2002) 16 *Harvard Journal of Law & Technology* 265, 266; Thomas W Joo, 'Contract, Property, and the Role of Metaphor in Corporations Law' (2001) 35 *U.C. Davis Law Review* 779. See also Dan Hunter, 'Cyberspace as Place and the Tragedy of the Digital Anticommons' (2003) 91 *California Law Review* 439.

[13] The same idea is behind the book written by Larsson that uses conceptual metaphor theory 'to strengthen the awareness of the strong metaphoricity in contemporary understandings of the Internet'. Stefan Larsson, *Conceptions in the Code. How Metaphors Explain Legal Challenges in Digital Times* (Oxford, Oxford University Press, 2017).

viewed favourably within arguments deployed by legal practitioners (above all in those used by courts). Thus, for example, within the US debate, Posner has asserted that

> [a]nalogies can be suggestive, like metaphors, similes and parallel plots in literature – devices that analogies resemble … But analogies cannot resolve legal disputes intelligently. To say that something is in some respects like something else is to pose questions rather than answer them.[14]

And before him, Cardozo argued – wearing his judge's hat – that 'metaphors in law are to be narrowly watched, for starting as devices to liberate thought, they end often by enslaving it'.[15] It is of singular significance that, in condemning metaphors in this manner, Cardozo did so by recourse to a dual metaphor, namely the liberation of thought and its reduction to slavery. More generally, the creation of new fictions by the courts has been viewed with suspicion by various US scholars as such activity is claimed to jeopardise the 'judicial candor' that should – so the argument goes – characterise the decision-making processes of both judges and courts.[16]

Based on the conceptual and cognitive paradigm of the metaphor, it is also possible to infer a paradigm that is useful for studying some interesting issues arising in relation to judicial protection for fundamental rights in the digital environment: the frame. More specifically, particular attention must be dedicated to the interactive conception and the theory of conceptual metaphors. The interactive conception, which was developed from the 1950s onwards above all by Black,[17] considers a metaphor to be the result of a process of semantic interaction, or more specifically as the product of the combination of an expression used metaphorically (the 'focus') and the enunciative structure within which the expression is framed (the 'frame'). The conceptual and cognitive paradigm of the metaphor presupposes the fundamental concept of 'frame'. Within the specific context of legal argumentation, a 'judicial frame' is the expressive structure and, more broadly, the reference context for the reasoning set out in the judgment.

As Chapter 2 (on judicial protection for freedom of expression from a comparative perspective) will clarify, different balances are struck and diverging solutions are found even in cases that are essentially similar or identical, depending upon the particular judicial frame chosen by a court. In other words, the notion of frame must be shifted from cognitive studies to the theory of interpretation and argumentation. As Sajó and Ryan point out, 'translation of a technology and its

[14] Richard A Posner, *How Judges Think* (Cambridge, MA, Harvard University Press, 2008) 181.

[15] *Berkey v Third Avenue Railway Co* 244 NY 84 (NY 1926) 95.

[16] David L Shapiro, 'In Defense of Judicial Candor' (1986–1987) 100 *Harvard Law Review* 731; Peter J Smith, 'New Legal Fictions' (2006–2007) 95 *Georgetown Law Journal* 1484.

[17] Max Black, *Models and Metaphors. Studies in Languages and Philosophy* (Ithaca, NY, Cornell University Press, 1962) 25; Max Black, 'Metaphor' (1954) 55 *Proceedings of the Aristotelian Society* 273; Ivor A Richards, *The Philosophy of Rhetoric* (Oxford, Oxford University Press, 1936).

consequences into the legal frame is not automatic'.[18] This is where courts play an important role through the judicial process of translating something new into the language of past legal models by means of the judicial framing technique.[19]

It is important to stress how this activity consisting in a 'conceptual transfer' from the world of atoms to the world of bits is not neutral but is rather based on the frame of values on which it is founded. This explains why, for instance, digital privacy gained more protection compared to the non-digital world, most notably in the case law of the CJEU. In particular, we must focus on the impact of the balance struck by the court and, consequently, on the level of protection for the rights at stake. Within this context, the concept of frame proposed by Lakoff helps us to identify a constitutive use of metaphors. The notion of the 'frame' is evident in this context. By transferring this concept from the field of language theory and cognitive science to the theories of interpretation and argumentation, and subsequently identifying the judicial frame as a subcategory of the frame, it will be possible to define the value options that courts can draw on within a specific judicial balancing operation.

In order to reveal the connection between metaphorical language, judicial frames and the protection of fundamental rights within the digital realm, it may be of use to compare two quotes. The first:

> The Court notes that Article 1 of Law no. 47 of 1948 limits itself to expressly defining the concept of the press in its technical sense of reproduction through typographical means or otherwise using mechanical or physical-chemical means. However, the term 'press' also has a figurative meaning and, in that sense, refers to newspapers, which are an instrument of choice for obtaining information, and were so above all at the time when the Constitution and Law no. 47 of 1948 came into force, that is when other forms of mass media, in particular television and online information sites, were not in operation. This concept of press in a figurative sense defines the editorial product that features both the ontological prerequisite (structure) and the teleological prerequisite (purposes of publication) for a newspaper.[20]

The second:

> Now you can see the meaning of my title cyberspace and the Law of the Horse. When asked to talk about Property in Cyberspace, my reaction was, 'Isn't this just the law of the horse?' … This leads directly to my principal conclusion: Develop around law of intellectual property, then just apply it to computer networks.[21]

[18] András Sajó and Clare Ryan, 'Judicial Reasoning and New Technologies: Framing, Newness, Fundamental Rights and the Internet' in Oreste Pollicino and Graziella Romeo (eds), *The Internet and Constitutional Law: The Protection of Fundamental Rights and Constitutional Adjudication in Europe* (London, Routledge, 2016) 3, 7.

[19] ibid 8.

[20] Italian Supreme Court (Joint Session), judgment no 31022, 29 January 2015, 23 (my own translation).

[21] Frank H Easterbrook, 'Cyberspace and the Law of the Horse' (1996) *University of Chicago Legal Forum* 207, 208.

The two quotes apparently have very little in common. The first comes from a ruling of the Italian Supreme Court in January 2015 concerning a specific issue relating to the application to the Internet (and in particular to online newspapers) of rules originally intended for the printed press.[22] The second citation comes from a paper by another judge, Frank Easterbrook, who was, however, writing in his 'academic capacity' for a conference held in Chicago dedicated to the nascent cyberspace.[23] In the early days of the web in 1995, he asked himself ironically whether it would make any sense to speak of the 'law of horses', when it would be sufficient to refer to the more general 'law of animals'. Easterbrook thus proposes that there is no need to adopt any new regulation for the digital world; on the contrary, according to a commonsense approach, it is quite simply sufficient to apply the traditional legal rules from the real world to the new technological realm.

However, despite their different nature, the two quotes highlight the very same dilemma which both practitioners and lawmakers address when they are required to 'transfer' certain categories from the analogue world to the digital world. A choice must be made between shifting and transposing traditional categories *sic et simpliciter* to the new technological context and the need to rethink and reshape those categories due to the need to adapt them to (or to change in light of) a new technological climate.

The choices made in the two quotes would appear to suggest two diametrically opposed options. In the first, the Italian Supreme Court proposes a rethink of the concept of the press, which had previously been defined in a technical sense, so as to open up that concept to technological evolution and, in particular, the impact of the Internet. In the second case, the words of Easterbrook reveal a value frame of resistance to the emerging technology. Indeed, he calls for a mere shift in the application of the traditional legal tool kit to the digital world. However, in both cases, those in charge of interpreting the law, and in particular the courts, cannot refrain from exercising – in the words of White – their 'legal imagination',[24] whether this involves reconsidering existing rules due to changes in technological circumstances, or a shift from the material to the intangible level.

The specific solution that is chosen does not change the role of the courts, especially constitutional (or supreme) courts in performing a highly delicate role as they are required to choose between constitutional 'translation' and constitutional caution.[25] It is for courts to decide whether to translate the values behind the original constitutional principles in order to cover the new technological framework, or whether to adopt an approach characterised by self-restraint, leaving this task to policy makers. In other words, it is necessary to understand whether judicial deference or judicial activism would be the more appropriate approach in such

[22] Italian Supreme Court (Joint Session), judgment no 31022 (n 20).

[23] Easterbrook (n 21).

[24] James B White, *The Legal Imagination* (Chicago, IL, University of Chicago Press, 1985).

[25] Cass R Sunstein, 'Constitutional Caution the Law of Cyberspace' (1996) *University of Chicago Legal Forum* 361.

cases, considering also the important question regarding the relationship between political and judicial power within the context of Internet law.

Although the scenario is much more nuanced, it is possible to identify two alternative options for courts when confronted with new technologies: re-contextualising the relevant parameters by creating new frames in the light of the technological environment, or adopting a position of judicial deference towards political choices. The latter is a solution supported, for example, by Lessig: 'My sense is that, knowing nothing, or at least not very much, terrified by the threats of which they don't know, these judges will defer to democratic authority'.[26]

Still, there is a problem: courts are required to adjudicate on the cases that come before them. They do not have much choice regarding this matter. Justice Kennedy's dissenting opinion in *Denver Area Educational Telecommunications Consortium* on the regulation of cable television is emblematic in this regard.[27] When considering the technological aspect, which was new at the time, he ended up stating that 'we don't know yet, but here's the best we can'.[28] Doubt and caution may be reasons for the US Supreme Court not to take a case, but once taken, it is hard to accept the attitude of the court to not decide.[29] This is why metaphors and analogies to other areas of the First Amendment case law become a responsibility, rather than the luxury the plurality considers them to be. In other words, a decision has to be reached in each case and the technological factor has to be dealt with in some way. Hence, the frame, which is construed by linguistic scientists as a cognitive structure that facilitates comprehension, becomes a *judicial* frame; as such, it is an argumentative technique that can be used to persuade either by metaphors or by analogy, that is by shifting from the familiar archetype to the new technological context.

It is therefore possible to draw a distinction between a frame of resistance to technology on one hand and a frame of openness to technology on the other. These value frames can be encapsulated in the propensity of the courts either to recognise or to reject the technological factor in question. In any case, whichever frame is chosen between continuity and discontinuity with the pre-existing technological framework, the operation will never be neutral as it is conditioned by another important factor, which is often not taken into account in this field. This is specifically the possibility that the juxtaposition between the Hartian external and internal points of view[30] is framed in the more incisive understanding of MacCormick with the result that courts may adopt either a perspective that is internal to the new technology, or one that is external to it.[31]

[26] Lawrence Lessig, 'Reading the Constitution in Cyberspace' (1996) 45 *Emory Law Journal* 869, 874.

[27] *Denver Area Educational Telecommunications Consortium v FCC* 518 US 727 (1996).

[28] Monroe E Price, *Media and Sovereignty: The Global Information Revolution and Its Challenge to State Power* (Cambridge, MA, MIT Press, 2002) 152.

[29] ibid.

[30] Herbert LA Hart, *The Concept of Law* (Oxford, Oxford University Press, 1961).

[31] Neil MacCormick, *Legal Reasoning and Legal Theory* (Oxford, Oxford University Press, 1978).

A juxtaposition of this type between the external and internal points of view vis-à-vis technological developments was already clear before the advent of the Internet within the *Olmstead* judgment, including in particular the dissenting opinion of Justice Brandeis.[32] According to the majority opinion, the use as evidence in a trial of telephone conversations intercepted by federal agents without having previously obtained a court order did not violate the Fourth Amendment because listening to a private telephone conversation did not require a physical search or entry into a person's private space.[33] By contrast, the judicial frame that permeated the dissenting opinion of Brandeis was diametrically opposed in terms of its nature and insisted on the recognition of technological discontinuity between the new technology (at that time) and the status quo. He proposed a teleological interpretation of search and seizure based on the Fourth Amendment.

One might ask why judges sitting at the same time on the same court supported such diametrically opposed approaches. The answer can be found by distinguishing between the internal perspective of the 'player' and the external perspective of the 'outsider'. While the majority in *Olmstead* adopted an external perspective with regard to the person whose telephone conversation was tapped, Brandeis, on the other hand, adopted his own judicial frame as an internal player (and not as an outsider). He considered the new technology at that time from a perspective that was internal, considering the telephone network as a privileged means for creating a virtual closet, in which secrets can be whispered.[34] On the basis of this value frame, which was structurally different from that adopted by the majority, Brandeis did not have any difficulty in concluding that intrusion (albeit not physical but nonetheless an intrusion) had occurred into the private sphere of the person whose conversation was tapped, thereby violating the Fourth Amendment.

While the possible juxtaposition between the external perspective and the internal perspective vis-à-vis the identification of technological developments might have been clear even before the advent of the Internet, the invention of the web has created the fertile soil in which the dialectic between openness and resistance to new technologies has flourished. This should come as no surprise, especially if it is considered that the Internet is the only medium equipped with its own constitutive spatial metaphor: 'cyberspace'. This is because, in contrast to other technologies, the context, or the frame of reference, is so constitutive and self-sufficient in nature that it competes with physical reality and pushes any courts to choose which perspective characterises their judicial frame when addressing Internet law.

Recalling the two quotes cited above, whereas the Italian Supreme Court's preference for the 'figurative meaning'[35] over the 'technical meaning' suggests the adoption of an internal perspective that considers the intangible reality as a place

[32] *Olmstead v United States* 277 US 438 (1928).
[33] ibid.
[34] ibid.
[35] Italian Supreme Court (Joint Session), judgment no 31022 (n 20).

for reconsidering traditional categories, the ironic and provocative reference to the 'law of horses' by Easterbrook[36] is, on the other hand, closer to an external perspective that takes the analogue realm as a point of reference for the application of certain rules. On this view, the digital realm is a mere accessory, to which it is possible, and indeed advisable, to transfer traditional legal categories *sic et simpliciter*.

The cases mentioned point towards the role played by judicial frames in the shift from atoms to bits and the resulting further amplification of judicial momentum. Nonetheless, this represents only one cause of this amplification. The other cause, as noted above, consists in the growing judicial exercise of designing jurisdiction as a reaction to the allegedly anarchic nature of the Internet.

III. Jurisdictions, Territory and Cyberspace

As noted above, one of the first problems the courts had to deal with at the dawn of the Internet was the applicability of state regulation to cyberspace. Within scholarly debate, according to the cyber-anarchic approach, the rise of Internet law has caused state sovereignty to disintegrate within cyberspace. This disintegration, so it is argued, has made it impossible to apply any tool based on the theory of transnational law to the field under investigation. How can sovereignty be shared either horizontally or vertically when it does not exist anymore?[37]

As a reaction to the said approach (which has also been branded as a futility argument, under which laws based on geographic borders are not feasible on the Internet) the US courts have begun to require website operators to configure website architecture in order to recognise or take account of territorial boundaries. In other words, they started to demonstrate that geography and governmental coercion are still of fundamental importance, even for the most revolutionary global communication technologies.

Consequentially, the topic of Internet jurisdiction has become increasingly critical.[38] More specifically, the approach of US courts to the problems raised by

[36] Easterbrook (n 21).

[37] It is indeed quite paradoxical that one of the most famous and drastic assumptions of the new alleged a-national borderless dimension of cyberspace has used, to assert its claim, the constitutional (and then consequently national) rhetoric of the Founding Fathers. Indeed, according to Barlow's notorious cyberspace declaration of independence: 'Governments of the Industrial world, you weary giants of flesh and steel …, the global social space we are building to be naturally independent of the tyrannies you seek to impose on us. You have no moral right to rule us nor do you possess any methods of enforcement we have true reason to fear'. John P Barlow, 'A Declaration of the Independence of Cyberspace', *Electronic Frontier Foundation* (8 February 1996) at projects.eff.org/~barlow/Declaration-Final.html.

[38] Dan Jerker B Svantesson, *Solving the Internet Jurisdiction Puzzle* (Oxford, Oxford University Press, 2017); Tobias Lutzi, 'Internet Cases in EU Private International Law – Developing a Coherent Approach' (2017) 66 *International and Comparative Law Quarterly* 687; Darrel C Menthe, 'Jurisdiction in Cyberspace: A Theory of International Spaces' (1998) 4 *Michigan Telecommunication & Technology Law Review* 69.

the seemingly borderless nature of the Internet has moved from a reconsideration of the criteria for establishing jurisdiction developed over time for disputes involving, either directly or indirectly, two or more legal systems.[39] With regard to certain matters, such as the exercise of freedom of speech, US case law has established the limits to personal jurisdiction in cross-border disputes on the grounds of the 'Due Process' clause enshrined in the Fourteenth Amendment.

It is worth looking at these criteria in order to establish how problems arising out of the nature of the Internet have been solved consistently with previous rulings. In *Pennoyer v Neff*,[40] the US Supreme Court held that

> the authority of every tribunal is necessarily restricted by the territorial limits of the State in which it is established. Any attempt to exercise authority beyond those limits would be deemed in every other forum … an illegitimate assumption of power, and be resisted as mere abuse.[41]

According to the court in *Pennoyer*, each State has jurisdiction 'over persons and property within its territory'.[42]

This decision reflected a concept of personal jurisdiction based exclusively on territorial borders, where the power of national courts to adjudicate lawsuits rests upon a contact between the forum State and the defendant or its property. This approach turned out to be inappropriate as the growth of interstate commerce implied increased litigation, with new technologies facilitating the circulation of people and goods. Thus, harm could be inflicted and suffered in one particular State, even though neither the wrongdoer nor the injured party was physically present there.

In the nineteenth century, in *International Shoe v Washington*,[43] the US Supreme Court overruled *Pennoyer*, albeit not explicitly, and worked out a more flexible test based on the establishment of a minimum contact between the defendant and the forum State. In particular, the court specified that in any case jurisdiction must not 'offend traditional notions of fair play and substantial justice'.[44] The minimum contact test did not provide a fixed rule but rather required a specific and in-depth factual inquiry in every case in which jurisdiction over the defendant was at issue. In addition, in *Hanson v Denckla*,[45] the US Supreme Court further developed the minimum contact test by requiring from the defendant an act that constituted a 'purposeful availment' of the benefits and protections of the forum State.[46]

[39] See Oreste Pollicino and Marco Bassini, 'The Law of the Internet between Globalization and Localization' in Miguel Maduro, Kaarlo Tuori and Suvi Sankari (eds), *Transnational Law – Rethinking Law and Legal Thinking* (Cambridge, Cambridge University Press, 2014) 346.

[40] *Pennoyer v Neff* 95 US 714 (1878).

[41] ibid 720.

[42] ibid 722.

[43] *International Shoe v State of Washington* 326 US 310 (1945).

[44] ibid 326.

[45] *Hanson v Denckla* 357 US 235 (1958).

[46] ibid 253.

An important application of these criteria in the field of tort law is illustrated in *Calder v Jones*,[47] in which the court developed the so-called 'effects test'. The plaintiff had filed suit in California against two reporters, who lived and worked in Florida, and had authored an allegedly defamatory article published in a newspaper distributed in California. The US Supreme Court found that Californian judges had jurisdiction since, under the circumstances, petitioners must '"reasonably anticipate being ha[u]led into court there" to answer for the truth of the statements made in their article'.[48] An individual injured in California need not to go to Florida to seek redress from persons who, though remaining in Florida, knowingly cause injury in California. More specifically, the US Supreme Court set out a three-prong test, pointing to the awareness of the defendant concerning three circumstances: first, the allegedly defamatory article distributed in California; second, the plaintiff resided there; finally, the allegedly defamatory statements would harm the reputation of the plaintiff there.

How did this test affect the emergence of relationships over the Internet? Jurisdiction began to be felt as a key issue since the development of the Internet implied that interactions could apparently take place both everywhere and nowhere.[49] What the American courts did when addressing the emergence of legal relationships over the Internet was to try to adapt their efforts to this new, apparently borderless, environment. Some important 'refinements' were needed.[50] In so doing, courts distanced themselves from the approach of those who had maintained that the Internet could not be subject to legal regulation.[51]

These efforts bore fruit within a series of cases in which the courts considered whether websites should be regarded as foreign entities attempting to enter into the country, or foreign territories that can be visited once users access them. Depending upon the answer, it may be stated that a website is anywhere rather than nowhere, although this seems to be simply a formalistic exercise. Conversely, the courts took account of the type of contact required under the case law in order to establish jurisdiction over defendants situated in other States, with specific reference to the Internet. In this light, they focused mainly on whether the activities

47 *Calder v Jones* 465 US 783 (1984).

48 ibid 789.

49 Jack L Goldsmith, 'Against Cyberanarchy' (1999) 65 *University of Chicago Law Review* 1199.

50 Kohl (n 7).

51 It is worth quoting the concurring opinion delivered by Justice Thomas in *Ashcroft v American Civil Liberties Union* 535 US 564 (2002). In that case, the issue was which 'community standards' content published on websites had to comply with in order not to be prohibited under a national statute. Justice Thomas concluded that '[i]f a publisher chooses to send its material into a particular community, this Court's jurisprudence teaches that it is the publisher's responsibility to abide by that community's standard. The publisher's burden does not change simply because it decides to distribute its material to every community in the Nation. Nor does it change because the publisher may wish to speak only to those in a community where *avant garde* culture is the norm, but nonetheless utilises a medium that transmits its speech from coast to coast. If a publisher wishes for its material to be judged only by the standards of particular communities, then it need only take the simple step of utilising a medium that enables it to target the release of its material into those communities'. Concurring opinion of Justice Thomas, *Ashcroft v American Civil Liberties Union* 535 US 564 (2002) 583.

carried out on the Internet by defendants constituted a 'purposeful availment' and thus met the minimum contact test.[52]

A further development of the criteria listed above was provided in 1997 in the landmark case of *Zippo Manufacturing v Zippo Dot Com*.[53] In *Zippo*, the US District Court for the Western District of Pennsylvania worked out the famous 'sliding scale test' by distinguishing between websites according to three levels of interactivity: 'the likelihood that personal jurisdiction can be constitutionally exercised is directly proportionate to the nature and quality of the commercial activity that an entity conducts over the Internet'.[54]

The court started by focusing on subjects that operate websites for the purpose of doing business: in such cases, 'if the defendant enters into contracts with residents of a foreign jurisdiction that involve the knowing and repeated transmission of computer files over the Internet, personal jurisdiction is proper'.[55] Secondly, the court pointed out that, unlike those mentioned above, passive websites are used only to post information and make it available in other countries, activity which does not constitute a sound basis for personal jurisdiction. Finally, the court held that 'the middle ground is occupied by interactive web sites where a user can exchange information with the host computer. In these cases, the exercise of jurisdiction is determined by examining the level of interactivity and commercial nature of the exchange of information that occurs on the web site'.[56]

On those grounds, the US District Court for the Western District of Pennsylvania concluded that Zippo Dot Com, a Californian corporation, had entered into contact via its website with Pennsylvania residents for the purpose of doing business. Such 'purposeful availment' was sufficient to meet the minimum contact test; thus, the court had jurisdiction and could reject Zippo Dot Com's motion to dismiss the case. However, the sliding scale test has been heavily criticised. Among others, Kohl has noted:

> One may even question why the interactive nature of a site should be at all relevant to whether a court does or does not have jurisdiction over a defendant. Assuming its validity, a site which is highly interactive in its design would appear to subject its provider to the personal jurisdiction of every court, and those which are not, of no court at all.[57]

[52] See *CompuServe, Inc v Patterson* 89 F3d 1257 (6th Cir 1996). In this case, the US Court of Appeals for the Sixth Circuit ruled that the defendant, a Texas resident, purposefully availed himself of the privilege of doing business in Ohio by electronically transmitting shareware software files to CompuServe, which, in turn, advertised and distributed them to its subscribers over the Internet. *Contra* the US Court of Appeals for the Second Circuit in *Bensusan Restaurant v King* 126 F3d 25 (2nd Cir 1997) held that the simple creation of a passive website did not constitute a purposeful availment since it only permitted users located everywhere in the world to access it. See also *Maritz v CyberGold* 947 F Supp 1328 (ED Mo 1996) and *Humphrey v Granite Gate Resorts* 568 NW 2d 715 (Minn 1997).

[53] *Zippo Manufacturing v Zippo Dot Com* 952 F Supp 1119 (WD Pa 1997).

[54] ibid 1124.

[55] ibid.

[56] ibid.

[57] Kohl (n 7) 86.

Hörnle takes the same view as Kohl:

> The Zippo sliding-scale test is only a frequently cited test established by a US District Court. It cannot overrule or replace the minimum contacts test. In fact, it could be argued that the distinction between passive and active websites as a determinative factor is now technologically obsolete, as very few websites are merely passive showcases of information.[58]

Courts have only referred to Zippo's sliding scale test in a few cases. In *ALS Scan v Digital Service Consultants*,[59] the US Court of Appeals for the Fourth Circuit applied both *Zippo* and *Calder* tests in a suit for copyright infringement caused by the defendant's posting of copyrighted materials on the Internet. The court ruled that the infringer could not be subject to the jurisdiction of Maryland (where the plaintiff had filed suit) since its website was at most passive and had not established any contact with the forum State.

Likewise, in *Cybersell v Cybersell*[60] the US Court of Appeals for the Ninth Circuit found that the posting on the website of Cybersell (which was incorporated in California) of an allegedly infringing service mark for which an eponymous Arizona company had filed an application did not establish personal jurisdiction in Arizona as the passive nature of the website (which only advertised the owner's services) did not qualify as purposeful availment of the benefits and protections of Arizona.

On the other hand, the US District Court for the Western District of Wisconsin declined to adopt the sliding scale test in *Hy Cite Corporation v BadBusinessBureau.com* because

> [e]ven a 'passive' website may support a finding of jurisdiction if the defendant used its website intentionally to harm the plaintiff in the forum state … Similarly, an 'interactive' or commercial website may not be sufficient to support jurisdiction if it is not aimed at residents in the forum state.[61]

Additionally, Justice Crabb pointed out that rejecting *Zippo*'s sliding scale test

> does not mean that a website's level of interactivity is irrelevant in deciding whether the exercise of jurisdiction is appropriate. The website's level of interactivity may be one component of a determination whether a defendant has availed itself purposefully of the benefits or privileges of the forum state.[62]

In the field of tort law, in *Amway Corp v The Procter & Gamble Company*,[63] a plaintiff incorporated in Michigan brought a claim against the owner of a website

[58] Julia Hörnle, 'The Jurisdictional Challenge of the Internet' in Lilian Edwards and Charlotte Waelde (eds), *Law and The Internet* (Oxford, Hart Publishing, 2009) 121, 147.

[59] *ALS Scan, Inc v Digital Service Consultants, Inc* 293 F3d 7907 (4th Cir 2002).

[60] *Cybersell, Inc v Cybersell, Inc* 130 F3d 414 (9th Cir 1997).

[61] *Hy Cite Corp v badbusinessbureau.com* 297 F Supp 2d 1154 (WD Wis 2004) 11.

[62] ibid 12.

[63] *Amway Corp v The Procter & Gamble Company* 242 F3d 539 (5th Cir 2000).

that had posted defamatory information concerning it. The US District Court for the Western District of Michigan applied the *Calder* effects test in order to determine whether it had jurisdiction over the defendant, who resided in Oregon. First, it established that the defendant had committed an intentional tort, thus fulfilling the first prong of the *Calder* test. Secondly, the court acknowledged that the brunt of the harm had been felt by the plaintiff in the forum State so that it could be said to be 'the focal point of the harm' suffered by him. Thirdly, the plaintiff had proved that the defendant inflicted the tortious action knowing that the brunt of the harm would be suffered there. Therefore, the court held that it had jurisdiction over the defendant.[64]

American courts have not been the only ones to face problems of jurisdiction over the Internet. Another landmark case regarding a claim for online defamation was considered in 2002 by the High Court of Australia. In *Dow Jones & Company v Gutnick*[65] the plaintiff filed a complaint for defamation against the defendant, a financial information firm, due to an article that had appeared in its online newspaper. Few of its subscribers were located in Australia; however, the High Court of Australia decided to hear the case, holding that

> [i]f people wish to do business in, or indeed travel to, or live in, or utilise the infrastructure of different countries, they can hardly expect to be absolved from compliance with the laws of those countries. The fact that publication might occur everywhere does not mean that it occurs nowhere.[66]

It is worth comparing the arguments used by the High Court of Australia with the criteria adopted within the US case law mentioned above. First, the Australian court found that 'harm to reputation is done when a defamatory publication is comprehended by the reader, the listener, or the observer. Until then, no harm is done by it'.[67] Accordingly, it held:

> Defamation is to be located at the place where the damage to reputation occurs … It is only when the material is in comprehensible form that the damage to reputation is done … In the case of material on the World Wide Web, it is not available in comprehensible form until downloaded on to the computer of a person who has used a web browser to pull the material from the web server. It is where that person downloads the material that the damage to reputation may be done. Ordinarily then, that will be the place where the tort of defamation is committed.[68]

Similarly, a British court heard a libel action brought by an American citizen against the authors of defamatory texts posted on a website based in California.

[64] Conversely, in the above-mentioned case *Cybersell v Cybersell*, the US Court of Appeals for the Ninth Circuit refused to apply the *Calder* test as it found that the test does not apply with the same force as it would to an individual because a corporation does not suffer harm in a particular geographic location in the same way that an individual does.

[65] *Dow Jones & Company v Gutnick* [2002] HCA 56.

[66] ibid para 186.

[67] ibid para 26.

[68] ibid para 44.

In *Lewis v King*[69] the England and Wales Court of Appeal addressed what should be considered as an attempt at 'forum shopping' (which is very similar to the idea of 'regulatory arbitrage').[70] Both the plaintiff and the defendant were resident in the US, and the website on which defamation occurred was 'located' in California. Nonetheless, the plaintiff sued before a British court, assuming that the defamatory content could be accessed in the UK, thereby procuring harm to his reputation there. The court did not consider the forum shopping argument raised by the defendant and held that it had jurisdiction because, as a matter of English law, defamation occurs whenever a libellous statement is posted on the web and becomes accessible in the UK (or specifically England and Wales). Accordingly, since the plaintiff had a reputation in that country, the harmful event was felt in the UK and the domestic court did not lack jurisdiction.[71]

Another remarkable judgment was given in a criminal case. In *R v Perrin*[72] a French operator of a website resident in the UK was convicted of having posted prohibited content under the Obscene Publications Act. He contended that the British court lacked jurisdiction since the server hosting the website was located outside of the UK, and hence UK law was not applicable. However, the court rejected this argument, pointing out that, if domestic laws exclusively were applicable to content posted from the country of origin, then operators would be encouraged to engage in forum shopping, as noted by Kohl.[73]

Courts have also asserted jurisdiction over foreign gambling operators that target users in other countries over the Internet. Gambling regulations vary considerably from country to country since they depend upon a variety of factors such as morality, culture and religion. While many countries have outlawed the practice of gambling, the Internet allows providers to overcome such regulatory barriers. Various rulings concerning this matter have been issued by both national and supranational courts. For instance, the CJEU has sought to strike a balance between the economic freedoms guaranteed by the EU primary law and the right to prohibit or limit online gambling within domestic borders. On the other hand, national courts have sought to assert their jurisdiction over websites that provide cross-border gambling services.

These efforts are illustrated by two leading cases in the US. First, in *People v World Interactive Gaming*[74] the Supreme Court of the State of New York enjoined two companies headquartered in Antigua and legally licensed in that country from offering gambling over the Internet to residents of the State of New York, where such activities were prohibited. The respondents contended that the New York

[69] *Lewis v King* [2004] EWCA Civ 1329.

[70] Michael A Froomkin, 'The Internet as a Source of Regulatory Arbitrage' in Brian Kahin and Charles Nesson (eds), *Borders in Cyberspace* (Cambridge, MA, MIT Press, 1997) 129.

[71] See Amit M Sachdeva, 'International Jurisdiction in Cyberspace: A Comparative Perspective' (2007) 13(8) *Computer and Telecommunication Law Review* 245.

[72] *R v Perrin* [2002] EWCA Crim 747.

[73] Kohl (n 7).

[74] *People v World Interactive Gaming* 714 NYS 2d 844 (1999).

court lacked jurisdiction both *ratione personae* and *ratione materiae*. The court rejected this argument, finding that 'what makes Internet transactions shed their novelty for jurisdictional purposes is that similar to their traditional counterparts, they are all executed by and between individuals or corporate entities which are subject to a court's jurisdiction'.[75]

It first found that it had jurisdiction *ratione personae* on the grounds that both the *International Shoe* 'minimum contact' and the 'purposeful availment' test were met because the respondents were clearly doing business in New York. Responding to the argument that New York law did not apply to operators established in Antigua, the court went on to point out that 'the act of entering the bet and transmitting the information from New York via the Internet is adequate to constitute gambling activity within the New York state'.[76] More specifically, the court held that

> [w]ide range implications would arise if this Court adopted respondents' argument that activities or transaction which may be targeted at New York residents are beyond the state's jurisdiction. Not only would such an approach severely undermine this state's deep-rooted policy against unauthorized gambling, it also would immunize from liability anyone who engages in any activity over the Internet which is otherwise illegal in this state. A computer server cannot be permitted to function as a shield against liability.[77]

Therefore the Supreme Court of the State of New York found that the respondents had violated both domestic law on gambling as well as certain federal statutes aimed at ensuring the enforcement of local laws proscribing gambling with respect to the use of the Internet, even though the companies had complied with Antiguan law.

Similarly, the US Court of Appeals for the Second Circuit upheld the judgment issued by the district court in *United States v Cohen*.[78] The defendant had been convicted of violations under a federal statute which prevented operators involved in the business of betting or wagering from using wire communications facilities (such as the Internet or the telephone) for the transmission in interstate or foreign commerce of bets or wagers. As was the case in *People v World Interactive Gaming*,[79] the company was legally licensed in Antigua, where it had been established, but also targeted residents in the US over the Internet. The case did not concern a violation of the law of the State of New York but rather compliance with the provision of federal laws prohibiting usage of the Internet to circumvent the prohibitions on land-based activities provided for under national laws.

The main issues arising out of the case law analysed here have shown that the Internet environment is atypical in nature from a regulatory point of view. The very idea of the Internet as an anarchic dream completely free from national laws

[75] ibid 849.
[76] ibid.
[77] ibid 850.
[78] *United States v Cohen* 260 F3d 68 (2d Cir 2001).
[79] *People v World Interactive Gaming* 714 NYS 2d 844 (Sup Ct 1999).

has collapsed. Within this perspective, some important remarks concerning jurisdiction over the Internet may be made with reference to the case law cited.

As Reidenberg has highlighted:

> The maturation of the analysis reflects an evolution from a somewhat naïve view of the Internet to a rejection of the Internet activists' simple denial of law. The Internet became popular precisely because of the promise of a global audience. But, this promise could not absolve online activities of legal responsibility. While online technologies were initially designed for geographically indifferent access, nothing fixed the technology in stone. Commercial pressures and the dynamic nature of the Internet have resulted in geolocation and the re-creation of geographic origin and destination.[80]

All of the cases examined above, as well as many others that are also worthy of note, clearly pose at least two types of problem for anyone dealing with the Internet. These problems stem largely from the lack of a common framework of standards that can be shared between countries. Especially in cases involving freedom of speech, for instance an expression that is considered to be defamatory or contrary to public decency in one particular country might be entirely lawful in another country.

First, if the Internet makes websites accessible anywhere and allows jurisdiction wherever harm is caused by their content, two paths are feasible: either the content must comply with all relevant jurisdictions in which the website can be accessed, or access to such content must be limited to countries that have not outlawed it.[81] Both solutions are merely hypothetical: the former would entail the law of the most restrictive country becoming, at least potentially, the law applicable to every form of speech due to the simple fact that the Internet makes it accessible anywhere. It would be paradoxical for a national law to regulate interactions beyond the national borders. This point was highlighted in *American Civil Liberties Union v Reno*,[82] in which the US Court of Appeals for the Third Circuit held:

> Web publishers cannot prevent Internet users in certain geographic locales from accessing their site; and in fact the Web publisher will not even know the geographic location of visitors to its site. Similarly, a Web publisher cannot modify the content of its site so as to restrict different geographic communities to access of only certain portions of their site. Thus, once published on the Web, existing technology does not permit the published materials to be restricted to particular states or jurisdictions … In gravitating toward an effects doctrine, sovereign states promoted submission to the rule of law rather than capitulation to an Internet attack.[83]

[80] Joel R Reidenberg, 'Technology and Internet Jurisdiction' (2005) 153 *University of Pennsylvania Law Review* 1951, 1956.

[81] See also the 1995 German case *CompuServe*. The service provider blocked access to 200 chat groups in order to avoid prosecution under the Bavarian obscenity law. It was unable to ban access only to local customers, so it suspended the groups worldwide. In so doing, it applied the moral standard of Germany in all the countries where the website could be accessed. For further details see Lawrence Lessig, *Code 2.0* (New York, Basic Books, 2006) 39.

[82] *American Civil Liberties Union v Reno* 217 F3d 162 (3rd Cir 2000).

[83] ibid 169.

The second solution, which would lead to an opposite outcome, has long been challenged by operators that dispute the existence of technical instruments to target users according to their place of origin. In addition, it is also asserted that it would not ensure effective protection for constitutional values since technological barriers could also be circumvented under certain conditions.

The second problem is directly related to the first one. Since the Internet enables website content to generate effects across various jurisdictions, courts from countries other than the defendant's could adjudicate claims against such content. In *GlobalSantaFe Corp v Globalsantafe.com*,[84] the plaintiff filed suit under the Anticybersquatting Consumer Protection Act (ACPA)[85] against a Korean citizen who had registered with the local registrar Hangang the domain name globalsantafe.com as soon as Global Marine and Santa Fe announced their merger. The action was brought in Virginia, where the registry authority with control over the .com top-level domains, VeriSign, was headquartered, as the plaintiff was seeking a judicial order directing the Korean and the American authorities to transfer the domain name.

The court first ordered Hangang and VeriSign to take all the necessary steps to transfer the domain name; however, Hangang did not comply because in the meantime the cybersquatter had obtained an injunction from the District Court of Seoul enjoining the registrar from transferring the domain name on the grounds that the US court lacked jurisdiction.[86] The plaintiff thus asked the US District Court for the Eastern District of Virginia for a new order directing VeriSign to cancel the infringing domain name until it was transferred. The US District Court for the Eastern District of Virginia found that the requirements provided under the ACPA were met, and hence could direct the registrar to cancel the domain name. It first held:

> The physical location of the '.com' registry within this district is quite significant, for it is the location of the registry here which establishes the situs of the power to transfer or cancel the domain name within this district, pursuant to the ACPA, even if the registrar has not submitted a registrar certificate granting the court authority over the disputed domain name … if the infringing domain name were registered in a top-level domain whose registry was outside the United States, jurisdiction in the United States might be avoided entirely, provided the registrar is also foreign and the individual registrant lacks sufficient contacts with the forum to meet the due process requirements for personal jurisdiction. In other words, there is a significant gap in the ACPA's trademark enforcement regime for domain names registered under top-level domain names, such as the foreign country code domain names, whose registry is located outside the United States.[87]

[84] *GlobalSantaFe Corp v Globalsantafe.com* 250 F Supp 2d 610 (ED Va 2003).
[85] The Anticybersquatting Consumer Protection Act (ACPA), 15 U.S.C. § 1125(d).
[86] *GlobalSantaFe Corp v Globalsantafe.com* (n 84) 614.
[87] ibid 623.

The court went on to state:

> An aggressive assertion of United States jurisdiction and control over the domain name system based on its essentially arbitrary physical geography may have the unintended consequence of causing a segmentation of the domain name system as other countries seek to assert their own control over the Internet by establishing competing and conflicting systems physically located outside the United States Even absent such segmentation, a desire to avoid United States jurisdiction may cause foreign registrants to choose to use domain names within their respective country code top-level domains, whose registries are located in and operated by the foreign countries, rather than the currently popular 'generic' domain names such as '.com' and '.net.' The result may be an increasing number of domain names registered out of the reach of United States jurisdiction, but accessible to United States users through the universal domain name system, which in turn will pose a serious challenge to the enforcement of United States trademark rights on the Internet.[88]

The court thus held that it had jurisdiction, expressing no significant international comity concerns regarding *in rem* jurisdiction.[89] Since the registries for generic top-level domains such as .com, .org and .edu are situated in the US, disputes arising out of trademark infringements can be adjudicated by US courts under the ACPA.

Moving to consider the EU framework, we can observe how also the CJEU has adapted the EU rules on jurisdiction laid down by the Brussels I Regulation to the digital environment. Article 7(2) of Regulation No 1215/2012,[90] which repealed Regulation 44/2001,[91] on jurisdiction and the recognition and enforcement of judgments in civil and commercial matters, provides that a person domiciled in a Member State may, in another Member State, be sued in matters relating to tort, delict or quasi-delict, in the courts for the place where the harmful event occurred.[92] Even in non-Internet-related cases, the CJEU has consistently

[88] ibid 623–24.

[89] The US District Court for the Eastern District of Virginia (ibid 624) applied the first-in-time rule, according to which 'the first court seized of jurisdiction over property, or asserting jurisdiction in a case requiring jurisdiction over property, may exercise that jurisdiction to the exclusion of any other court'. *Sec and Exch Comm'n v Banner Fund Int'l* 211 F3d 602 (DC Cir 2000) 611. As regards judicial comity, more in-depth remarks will be provided in the analysis of the *Yahoo!* case (see below). However, it is worth reporting the definition of the concept of judicial comity given by the US Supreme Court: '"Comity," in the legal sense, is neither a matter of absolute obligation, nor of mere courtesy and good will. It is a recognition which one nation allows within its territory to the legislative, executive or judicial acts of another nation, having due regard both to international duty and convenience, and to the rights of its own citizens or other persons who are under the protection of its laws. The comity thus extended to other nations is no impeachment of sovereignty. It is the voluntary act of the nation by which it is offered, and is inadmissible when contrary to its policy, or prejudicial to its interests'. See *Hilton v Guyot* 159 US 113 (1895) 163–64.

[90] Regulation (EU) 1215/2012 on jurisdiction and the recognition and enforcement of judgments in civil and commercial matters.

[91] Council Regulation (EC) 44/2001 on jurisdictions and the recognition and enforcement of judgments in civil and commercial matters.

[92] Among others, the Court of Milan recently found proper its jurisdiction in a case against four Google directors concerning the posting of a defamatory video on the grounds of Article 5(3) of Regulation (EC) 44/2001. See Court of Milan, Judgment no 1972, 24 February 2010; Court of Appeals of Milan, Judgment no 8611, 21 December 2012; Italian Supreme Court, Judgment no 5107,

construed this provision as meaning that the 'place where the harmful event occurred' covers both the place where the damage occurred and the location of the event giving rise to the damage.[93]

This was a trend that started in relation to media law cases in the world of atoms, resulting in the so-called 'mosaic approach'. In particular, in *Fiona Shevill*[94] the CJEU stressed that

> the victim of a libel by a newspaper article distributed in several Contracting States may bring an action for damages against the publisher either before the courts of the Contracting State of the place where the publisher of the defamatory publication is established, which have jurisdiction to award damages for all the harm caused by the defamation, or before the courts of each Contracting State in which the publication was distributed and where the victim claims to have suffered injury to his reputation, which have jurisdiction to rule solely in respect of the harm caused in the State of the court seised.[95]

The CJEU recognised that the claimants had two options: suing the offender responsible for defamatory statements and seeking the full amount of damages before the courts of the place of publication, or alternatively at the place where the harm was suffered (including the place of residence). Nonetheless, in the latter eventuality, the claimant can only seek a limited amount of damages, corresponding to the harm suffered in this jurisdiction.

The advent of the Internet has amplified the concerns surrounding this approach. In *eDate*,[96] the CJEU addressed the jurisdictional issue in two cases involving online content on an Internet website that was capable of infringing personality rights. Both cases contributed to enriching the 'mosaic approach' by introducing another basis for bringing an action for damages before domestic courts in the EU. As the CJEU stated:

> [I]n the event of an alleged infringement of personality rights by means of content placed online on an internet website, the person who considers that his rights have been infringed has the option of bringing an action for liability, in respect of all the damage caused, either before the courts of the Member State in which the publisher of

17 December 2013. For a comment on these decisions (the so-called Google-Vivi Down saga) and their implications, see Ernesto Apa and Oreste Pollicino, *Modeling the Liability of Internet Service Providers: Google vs. Vivi Down* (Milan, Egea, 2013).

[93] See Case C-21/76 *Handelskwekerij G J Bier BV v Mines de potasse d'Alsace SA* [1976] ECR 1735; Case C-220/88 *Dumez France and Tracoba v Hessische Landesbank (Helaba) and Othersè* [1990] ECR I-00049; Case C-364/93 *Antonio Marinari v Lloyds Bank plc and Zubaidi Trading Company* [1995] ECR I-02719; Case C-168/02 *Rudolf Kronhofer v Marianne Maier and Others* [2004] ECR I-06009; Case C-18/02 *Danmarks Rederiforening, acting on behalf of DFDS Torline A/S v LO Landsorganisationen i Sverige, acting on behalf of SEKO Sjöfolk Facket för Service och Kommunikation* [2004] ECR I-01417; Case C-27/02 *Petra Engler v Janus Versand GmbH* [2005] ECR I-00481. More recently, see Case C-45/13 *Andreas Kainz v Pantherwerke AG* [2014] ECR I-7, ECLI:EU:C:2014.

[94] Case C-68/93 *Fiona Shevill and Others v Presse Alliance* [1995] ECR I-415.

[95] ibid para 33.

[96] Joined Cases C-509/09 and C-161/10 *eDate Advertising GmbH and Others v X and Société MGN Limited* [2011] ECR I-10269.

> that content is established or before the courts of the Member State in which the centre of his interests is based. That person may also, instead of an action for liability in respect of all the damage caused, bring his action before the courts of each Member State in the territory of which content placed online is or has been accessible. Those courts have jurisdiction only in respect of the damage caused in the territory of the Member State of the court seised.[97]

Assuming that the centre of interests is not necessarily the same as the place of domicile or habitual residence, the CJEU has in fact reinforced its 'mosaic approach' by allowing claimants an even wider choice of forum.

In *Bolagsupplysningen OÜ*[98] the CJEU dealt with another case involving online information across jurisdictions. The case involved requests to rectify information published and the deletion of comments on a website. It is worth noting how the CJEU took account of the technological backdrop. The court held that, considering the ubiquitous nature of the information and content placed online on a website as well as the fact that the scope of their distribution is, in principle, universal, a request to rectify the former and to remove the latter is one single and indivisible application and can, consequently, only be made before a court with jurisdiction to rule on the entirety of a claim seeking compensation for losses under the *Fiona Shevill* and *eDate* case law, and not before a court that does not have jurisdiction to do so.[99] The CJEU held that

> a legal person claiming that its personality rights have been infringed by the publication of incorrect information concerning it on the internet and by a failure to remove comments relating to that person can bring an action for rectification of that information, removal of those comments and compensation in respect of all the damage sustained before the courts of the Member State in which its centre of interests is located.[100]

The CJEU was also called to rule on a case concerning intellectual property law. The *Wintersteiger*[101] case involved the online infringement of a national trademark. The court rejected the argument that jurisdiction should be based on the location of the damage, specifically at the place where the website can be accessed. Instead, the CJEU held that the place of the damage where all losses can be claimed is the place where the national trademark is registered.

Nonetheless, the court has embraced a different interpretation of Article 5(3) in the area of copyright law. In *Pinckney*[102] the case referred to the CJEU involved the unauthorised reproduction and distribution of a French author's songs on CDs in the UK. The national court asked whether under (the former) Article 5(3) of Regulation 44/2001 the court has jurisdiction to hear an action to establish liability

[97] ibid para 52.
[98] Case C-194/16 *Bolagsupplysningen OÜ and Ingrid Ilsjan v Svensk Handel AB*, ECLI:EU:C:2017:766.
[99] ibid para 48.
[100] ibid para 44.
[101] Case C-523/10 *Wintersteiger AG v Products 4U Sondermaschinenbau GmbH*, ECLI:EU:C:2012:220.
[102] Case C-170/12 *Peter Pinckney v KDG Mediatech AG*, ECLI:EU:C:2013:635.

for copyright infringement. The case was brought by the author of a work against a company established in another Member State, which has in the latter state reproduced that work on a physical medium and which has subsequently been marketed by companies established in a third Member State through an Internet site which is also accessible in the Member State of the court seised. Once again, the court drew a clear distinction with cases involving personality rights by observing that

> [i]n applying those principles, for the purposes of identifying the place where damage allegedly caused over the Internet has occurred, the Court has distinguished between infringements of personality rights and infringement of intellectual and industrial property rights. Thus, the alleged victim of an infringement of personality rights by means of content placed online, which is protected in all the Member States may, on the basis that the harmful even occurred there, bring his action before the courts of each Member State in the territory of which content placed online is or has been accessible … Furthermore, given that the impact which material placed online is liable to have on an individual's personality rights might best be assessed by the court of the place where the alleged victim has his centre of interests, the alleged victim may choose to bring an action in one forum in respect of all of the damage caused. However, the allegation of an infringement of an intellectual and industrial property right, in respect of which the protection granted by registration is limited to the territory of the Member State of registration, must be brought before the courts of that State. It is the courts of the Member State of registration which are the best placed to ascertain whether the right at issue has been infringed.[103]

However, unlike trademark law, copyright enjoys harmonised protection throughout the EU and does not depend on national registration. Therefore, the CJEU has recognised that the mere fact that a website is accessible is sufficient to establish jurisdiction for the purposes of Article 5(3) of Regulation 44/2001.

The shift from the world of atoms to the world of bits is evident in another case concerning copyright. The *Hejduk* case involved a violation of copyright involving the publication of photographs on a website.[104] The defendant argued that, since the company was established in Germany and there was no redirection from the German domain name, the German courts should be recognised as having jurisdiction. According to the Advocate General:

> [I]t concerns a divulgation that can hardly be considered as occurring in a specific place that can be defined according to a territoriality criterion. On the contrary, the damage becomes 'dematerialised', ie it becomes diffused and therefore is 'delocalised', thus making it more difficult to determine the place where it occurred pursuant to Article 5(3).[105]

Therefore, considering Article 5(3) of Regulation 44/2001, the Advocate General proposed that only the courts of the state where the event occurred have

[103] ibid para 36.
[104] Case C-441/13 *Pez Hejduk v EnergieAgentur NRW GmbH*, ECLI:EU:C:2015:28.
[105] AG Opinion, Case C-441/13 *Pez Hejduk v EnergieAgentur NRW GmbH*, ECLI:EU:C:2014:2212, para 2.

jurisdiction over the case in question. The CJEU rejected this approach and recalled the 'accessibility approach' previously adopted in *Pinckney*. Therefore, the court recognised that the court of the place where the infringing content can be accessed has jurisdiction solely with regard to loss occurring within that territory.

As the above analysis based on case law demonstrates, courts in fact have rejected the 'futility argument' and, more generally, views sympathetic to cyberanarchy.[106] At least three points seem to have been undervalued by the cyberanarchic approach when commentators have pointed out that 'cyberspace really undermines the relationship between legally significant phenomena and physical location'.[107] The first argument concerns the identification of the relevant concept of sovereignty. The second considers the paradoxical effect of the evolution of technology. The third is related on the other hand to the many facets to the notion of jurisdiction.

First of all, cyberanarchy refers to a solid and static conception of sovereignty that was already old-fashioned at the start of the 1990s, when the Internet took on a commercial dimension, and is even more outdated today. According to this concept, a nation has full enforcement jurisdiction over persons and property within its borders but little, if any, beyond.[108]

This conception could well have been considered valid more than 100 years ago when, in 1895, in the case of *Carrick v Hancock*, Lord Russell of Killowen CJ famously declared that 'the jurisdiction of a court was based upon the principle of territorial dominion, and that all the persons within territorial dominion owe their allegiance to its sovereign power and obedience to all its laws and to the lawful jurisdiction of its courts'.[109]

Since then, however, many things have changed. Such an absolutist concept of sovereignty and the assumptions related to the supposed exclusivity of control by the sovereign state over everything present within its territory have proved to be unsuccessful and inadequate. This happened much earlier than the rise of the Internet, with the evolution of technology, the growth of international trade and a resulting increase in the cross-border movement of persons, goods, capital and services.

In particular, even before the advent of the Internet, problems related to the regulation of, for instance, telephone, television, financial services and pollution pointed to the need for shared sovereignty, or at least agreement between the country of origin and the country of destination concerning the trans-boundary content at issue. In this respect, Internet law does not seem to raise any new problems in qualitative terms as regards the regulation of other transnational activities, but rather more quantitative problems concerning the exploitation of two elements

[106] Jack L Goldsmith and Tim Wu, *Who Controls the Internet? Illusions of a Borderless World* (New York, Oxford University Press, 2008).

[107] Johnson and Post (n 5) 1367.

[108] Jack L Goldsmith, 'The Internet and the Abiding Significance of Territorial Sovereignty' (1998) 5 *Indiana Journal of Global Legal Studies* 475.

[109] *Carryck v Hancock* [1895] 12 TLR 59, 60.

which play a crucial role in the theoretical framework of transnational law: space and time.

As far as space is concerned, the real jurisdictional novelty of Internet law seems to be, first of all, that it will more frequently give rise to effects that are felt in multiple territories at the same time,[110] and secondly that it makes it very easy and inexpensive for individuals outside the regulating jurisdiction to send harmful content into the regulating jurisdiction.[111] As regards the temporal dimension, one of the most peculiar characteristics of the Internet is that it does not seem to raise any new legal issues, but is instead able to rebut the factual assumptions underlying certain already well-known legal regimes.

Copyright law, for example, 'relied upon the factual assumptions that reproduction will lead to a loss of quality and that the marginal cost of reproduction and distribution will outweigh the benefits achieved by infringement. However, in the digital age, an unlimited number of perfect copies can be made and distributed at minimal cost',[112] and with a drastic compression of time. The compression of time in the web is clearly underlined by the High Court of Australia, in the *Dow Jones* case, where it was stated that

> in the past 'The Times' newspaper would have gone to every colony in Australia. It might have got there rather late, but it could have gone … throughout the whole of that part of the world which was coloured red. I do not see the internet as introducing anything particularly novel, you just get it more quickly.[113]

As regards the second aspect mentioned above, at the end of the case law analysis, it could be said that, despite cyberanarchist predictions, Internet technology seems – paradoxically – to have empowered sovereign states to assert their jurisdiction over online activities and conduct.[114]

Indeed, the main concerns about multi-jurisdictional regulatory exposure have been centred on the idea that a content provider or Internet service provider with a multi-jurisdictional presence cannot monitor or control the geographical flow of information over the Internet. As has been correctly stated,[115] this assumption has become steadily weaker with the evolution of digital technologies, most

[110] Joel P Trachtman, 'Cyberspace, Sovereignty, Jurisdiction and Modernism' (1998) 5 *Indiana Journal of Global Legal Studies* 561.

[111] For example, concerning the defamation issues, it has been said that: 'there is nothing very new (about on line defamation) … but the problems of traditional publishing and defamation are so multiplied when applied to a forum as large, as cheap, as transnational as the internet, that is not hard to see why there is a perception that the law of libel has been transformed by its application to new electronic highway'. See Lilian Edwards, 'Defamation and the Internet' in Lilian Edwards and Charlotte Waelde (eds), *Law and Internet-regulating Cyberspace* (Oxford, Hart Publishing, 1997) 183–84.

[112] Kohl (n 7) 38.

[113] See the transcript of proceedings in *Dow Jones & Company, Inc v Gutnick* M3/2002 [2002] HCATrans 253, para 1140.

[114] Reidenberg (n 80) 1956.

[115] Jack L Goldsmith, 'Unilateral Regulation of the Internet: a Modest Defence' (2000) 11 *European Journal of International Law* 135.

notably as a result of the ever more widespread use of geo-localisation, which allows for geographical content discrimination.

Against this backdrop, the key question today is no longer whether content discrimination is technically feasible but, as Goldsmith has noted in this respect,[116] how much it costs and what the desired degree of its effectiveness is. In other words, ironically, the technological infrastructure that has been at the heart of some authors' assault on state regulation has proved to be one of the most powerful engines for making the Internet 'less transnational'.

As regards the third aspect relating to the different facets of jurisdiction, cyberanarchy theorists have overlooked the difference between prospective and enforcement jurisdiction. The former manifests itself in the power of the state to make its law applicable to a particular transaction. It is evident that national law continues to play a crucial role in this context, even if the content source lies beyond the reach of the territorial government. The inability of the relevant government to stop the harmful effects of certain content at the border does not mean that the source lies beyond local regulation.

If it is not possible to intercept the content at the border, a nation can take many steps within its territory to regulate indirectly content that is transmitted from abroad. Generally, this happens through the adoption of legal sanctions against the foreign content provider's local assets or agents. This has worked historically, for example with unwanted radio and television content broadcast from one nation into another. As has been correctly stated, 'the medium by which the harm is transmitted into the regulating jurisdiction – be it economic interdependence, postal mail, wind current or the internet – is not relevant to the justification for regulating it'.[117]

If, in the light of the notion of prospective jurisdiction, the very right of sovereign states to establish rules for online activity is undeniable, such a right would appear to be more problematic as regards the enforcement jurisdiction to enforce all regulatory claims falling under its prospective jurisdiction. While the territorial constraint does not play a decisive role in relation to the former, as is on the other hand apparent from the analysis of the case law, that constraint performs a crucial role in relation to the latter because a state can only enforce its jurisdiction against persons or entities that are present in or have assets within its territory.

This scenario is not merely theoretical. Aside from the issue of internal jurisdiction, there has been an even more critical tension when extending judicial powers overseas. An emblematic case of the difficulties that can arise due to this ontological difference in the protection paradigm when considered in the context of the Internet is that offered by the *Yahoo! LICRA* case.[118] This is one of the oldest and most important cases in this field, which arose out of the creation of a website that held auctions for Nazi relics, which was hosted by Yahoo! and managed by third

[116] ibid.
[117] Goldsmith (n 108) 479.
[118] High Court of Paris, *UEJF et LICRA v Yahoo! Inc. Et Yahoo! France* [2000] no RG:00/0538.

parties in the US. Certain anti-discrimination organisations, including the Ligue Internationale Contre le Racisme et l'Antisémitisme (LICRA), sued to obtain the blocking of the website in France, on the grounds that the activities were expressly prohibited under the French Criminal Code. In May 2000 the High Court of Paris ordered Yahoo! to take the technological steps necessary to prevent the site from being accessed within France. Yahoo! had strongly objected to the requests made by the plaintiffs in this case, and also expressed its intention not to comply with the order issued by the French court, claiming it was immune from that court's jurisdiction. Yahoo! argued in its defence, inter alia, that the servers hosting the site were located in the US, and the site's principal, although not exclusive, target was citizens of the US, a country in which the sale of Nazi relics is not prohibited, but is protected under the broad umbrella of the First Amendment.

Another objection raised by the lawyers for Yahoo! focused on the fact that it was impossible to limit access to the website to visitors residing in a specific State in which the sale of Nazi relics was not prohibited. In actual fact, however, while such a limitation might have been costly at the time, it was certainly not impossible. The strongest criticism of the request to block the website was related to the refusal to extend to a site operated by a US provider a more restrictive conception of freedom of expression at odds with the 'absolutist' vision incorporated into the First Amendment. According to Yahoo!, this decision unjustifiably gave priority to the European understanding of freedom of expression, which embraced a lower standard of protection, thus de facto making this protection applicable at global level. This is another aspect to a problem that has arisen more recently in relation to the enforcement of the right to privacy in the digital sphere (on which see also the ad hoc chapter below): a right in relation to which the EU stands out as the most protective legal order, whereas the US (along with many other non-European countries) endorses a narrower view. It is no coincidence that the right to privacy has been labelled as the 'Europe First Amendment'.[119]

The dispute had additional legal repercussions, as Yahoo! took action before the US courts to challenge the decision of the High Court of Paris, questioning whether a 'foreign' judge had the right to impose a duty to respect a conception of freedom of expression that conflicted with the First Amendment. While the US District Court for the Northern District of California recognised Yahoo!'s arguments, finding that the decision by the French court did not follow the First Amendment rules and claiming that the French decision was thus inapplicable and not subject to enforcement,[120] the US Court of Appeals for the Ninth Circuit subsequently reversed the ruling at first instance, underlining that the district court did not have jurisdiction over the appellants.[121]

[119] Bilyana Petkova, 'Privacy as Europe's First Amendment' (2019) 25(2) *European Law Journal* 140.

[120] *Yahoo!, Inc v La Ligue Contre le Racisme et L'Antisemitisme* 169 F Supp 2d 1182 (ND Cal 2001).

[121] *Yahoo! Inc a Delaware Corporation v La Ligue Contre Le Racisme et l'antisemitisme, a French Association; L'union Des Etudiants Juifs De France, a French Association* 433 F3d 1199 (9th Cir 2006).

The case brings out at least two critical aspects: on the one hand, it highlights the latent conflict within the conceptions of freedom of expression between the constitutional paradigms of Europe and the US (not to mention other countries). On the other, it shows that – absent a 'common' standard for the Internet or international conventions establishing what level of protection should apply to online speech – the decision is de facto left to the discretion of the courts; and although the courts certainly have greater 'proximity' to the questions raised from time to time, they do, however, risk concentrating quasi-legislative power within their own hands and generating uncertainty as to the legal consequences of the online conduct of individuals and of the exercise of freedom of speech.

The case mentioned above is one which involves a head-on clash and probably an unresolvable rift between US and European cultures of freedom of expression. On this basis, the divide widened even further as a result of the emergence of new information technologies, which, as we have seen, have provoked opposite reactions when courts have interpreted constitutional guarantees: a more suspicious attitude by the European courts, which tend to confirm restrictions on free speech that are necessary to protect other rights; on the other hand, a more favourable and 'expansive' view on the part of the US Supreme Court.

We have seen that courts have already found their role in defining jurisdiction in the information society. However, there is still more to be said concerning the extension of judicial power across the Atlantic, as we shall see in Chapter 3. Specifically, CJEU decisions in *Google Spain* and the Schrems saga offer clear examples of how the field of privacy and data protection could be a privileged standpoint for examining the jurisdictional issue and the resulting amplification of judicial momentum in the digital age.[122] This will become clearer in Chapter 4, which will focus on the issue of extraterritoriality and how the General Data Protection Regulation deals with the issue of jurisdiction.

IV. Freedom of Expression, Privacy and Data Protection Across the Atlantic

Together with metaphorical language and judicial frames, the jurisdictional issue provides a crucial element within the account of judicial power in the information society. Nonetheless, the amplification of judicial momentum in the information society is not neutral and obviously has implications for the protection of fundamental rights in the new digital environment.[123]

[122] Case C-362/14 *Maximillian Schrems v Data Protection Commissioner*, ECLI:EU:C:2015:650; Case C-131/12 *Google Spain SL and Google Inc v Agencia Española de Protectión de Datos (AEPD) and Mario Costeja Conzález*, ECLI:EU:C:2014:317.

[123] See András Koltay, *New Media and Freedom of Expression. Rethinking the Constitutional Foundations of the Public Sphere* (Oxford, Hart Publishing, 2019); Mart Susi (ed), *Human Rights, Digital Society and the Law. A Research Companion* (London, Routledge, 2019); Council of Europe,

The aim of the following chapters is to focus on two fundamental rights which are under pressure in the digital era: freedom of expression and the right to privacy and data protection.[124] Judicial protection for these fundamental rights is analysed respectively in Chapters 2 and 3. Before moving on to this analysis, it is worth setting out the constitutional basis for guaranteeing freedom of expression, privacy rights and data protection in both the EU and the US.

If the US constitutional framework is considered, it can be observed how the succinct wording of the First Amendment gives rise to very extensive protection for free speech:

> Congress shall make no law respecting an establishment of religion, or prohibiting the free exercise thereof; or abridging the freedom of speech, or of the press; or the right of the people peaceably to assemble, and to petition the Government for a redress of grievances.

This provision imposes a prohibition on Congress from adopting any law that may entail a restriction on freedom of speech. The US Supreme Court has clarified that the ban also applies to States and, therefore, to their respective governments. In fact, although the First Amendment only refers to 'Congress' as regards the prohibition on enacting laws restricting free speech, under the equal protection clause in the Fourteenth Amendment,[125] even individual State governments must refrain from interfering with the exercise of this right.[126] It is worth noting that there is no mention, in the text of the First Amendment, of any restrictions necessary in order to protect other fundamental rights that may be balanced against freedom of expression. The First Amendment thus seems to protect free speech as an absolute right that does not tolerate any restriction or interference.[127]

Human Rights Challenges in the Digital Age: Judicial Perspectives (Strasbourg, Council of Europe Publishing, 2020); Marco Bassini, *Internet e libertà di espressione. Prospettive costituzionali e sovranazionali* (Roma, Aracne, forthcoming 2020); Oreste Pollicino and Graziella Romeo (eds), *The Internet and Constitutional Law: The Protection of Fundamental Rights and Constitutional Adjudication in Europe* (London, Routledge, 2016).

[124] The prematurely deceased European Data Protection Supervisor, Giovanni Buttarelli, was very conscious, as stressed in many speeches and interviews, that in the digital world the freedom of expression and the right to privacy are two sides of the same coin. See Giovanni Buttarelli, 'Privacy in an age of hyperconnectivity, Keynote speech to the Privacy and Security Conference 2016' at https://edps.europa.eu/sites/edp/files/publication/16-11-07_speech_gb_austria_en.pdf.

[125] Section 1 of the Fourteenth Amendment reads as follows: 'All persons born or naturalized in the United States, and subject to the jurisdiction thereof, are citizens of the United States and of the State wherein they reside. No State shall make or enforce any law which shall abridge the privileges or immunities of citizens of the United States; nor shall any State deprive any person of life, liberty, or property, without due process of law; nor deny to any person within its jurisdiction the equal protection of the laws'.

[126] See *Gitlow v New York* 268 US 652 (1925) and *Stromberg v California* 283 US 359 (1931). These are regarded as landmark cases since the US Supreme Court forced a State to comply with the First Amendment to the US Constitution on the grounds of the equal protection clause contained in the Fourteenth Amendment. See also *De Jonge v Oregon* 299 US 353 (1937); *Wolf v Colorado* 338 US (1949) and *Gideon v Wainwright* 372 US 335 (1963).

[127] The reasons why, in 1791, such an extensive protection was granted to free speech, deal with, at first glance, the historical background of the emergence of the US. Since some of the States had refused to sign the US Constitution in the absence of appropriate guarantees of civil liberties, the Bill of Rights entered into force. The First Amendment, in particular, was supposed to meet the 'Anti-Federalist' States' expectation of freedom to express (political, first of all) opinions. Then, the right in question was

If this is the constitutional framework of the balancing process between free speech and other rights – embracing the First Amendment as a super fundamental right – it may be asserted that the US Supreme Court has adopted a very similar stance in relation to the digital world, as we shall see in Chapter 2. Leaving aside the new phenomenon of the Internet, at the present time the courts seem to have adopted a stance that considers free speech as an absolute right. Considering this issue from the perspective of the dichotomy between external and internal perspective, it may be concluded that the courts have adopted an external perspective, applying the same regime to online speech.

On the other hand, while in Bollinger's words free speech is 'the paramount right within the American constellation of constitutional rights',[128] the same cannot be said with regard to European law, especially when considering the case law of European courts, including in particular the CJEU and the ECtHR. The metaphor of the marketplace of ideas does not seem to fit very well with the EU framework of rights protection. Article 10 ECHR, as opposed to the First Amendment, is very clear in rejecting the view that free speech is an absolute right.[129] By contrast, this provision has a bipartite structure. On the one hand, it attaches to freedom of expression the value of a human right:

> Everyone has the right to freedom of expression. This right shall include freedom to hold opinions and to receive and impart information and ideas without interference by public authority and regardless of frontiers. This article shall not prevent States from requiring the licensing of broadcasting, television or cinema enterprises.[130]

On the other hand, unlike the First Amendment, Article 10 ECHR tolerates interferences that are necessary, in a democratic society, to meet certain social pressing needs:

> The exercise of these freedoms, since it carries with it duties and responsibilities, may be subject to such formalities, conditions, restrictions or penalties as are prescribed by law and are necessary in a democratic society, in the interests of national security, territorial integrity or public safety, for the prevention of disorder or crime, for the protection of health or morals, for the protection of the reputation or rights of others, for preventing the disclosure of information received in confidence, or for maintaining the authority and impartiality of the judiciary.[131]

Contracting States can thus legitimately impose restrictions on freedom of expression, provided that the criteria set forth under Article 10(2) ECHR are respected.[132] It is worth noting that the scope of freedom of expression encompasses a broad

meant to be, at least in its original consideration, a freedom from any undue interference from public bodies in the enjoyment of free speech. Then, a provision intended to produce 'vertical effects'.

[128] Lee C Bollinger, *The Tolerant Society: Freedom of Speech and Extremist Speech in America* (New York, Oxford University Press, 1988) 7.

[129] See, for a comment on Article 10 ECHR, Jean-François Flauss, 'The European Court of Human Rights and the Freedom of Expression' (2009) 84 *Indiana Law Journal* 809.

[130] ECHR, Art 10.

[131] ibid.

[132] As noted by Voorhoof, the ECtHR came to the conclusion in only a limited number of cases that the condition 'prescribed by law' was not fulfilled. This condition requires foreseeability, precision,

range of rights applicable both to passive acts (holding opinions and ideas, receiving information) as well as active subjects (imparting information). As has been noted by commentators, Article 10 ECHR protects 'several freedoms of speech', not just one.[133] A large number of decisions have been taken concerning complaints based on Article 10 ECHR. In these decisions, the ECtHR has introduced a distinction between political and commercial speech. Whereas Contracting States enjoy a broader margin of appreciation for the former, restrictions are less tolerable, in the court's view, when rights to political speech are at stake.

Moreover, Article 10(2) ECHR provides that restrictions to freedom of expression are necessary in a 'democratic society'. From this viewpoint, the ECtHR has focused on the possible restrictions envisaged by Contracting States, which can give rise to so-called 'chilling effects', ie possible imbalances resulting from the adoption of measures that excessively circumscribe the legitimate exercise of rights protected by Constitutions and by the ECHR. It is worth pointing out that Article 10 ECHR entails both the freedom to disseminate information as well as the freedom to receive it. Under Article 10 it is not enough just to protect the right to receive information but there is also the need to ensure information quality to the public opinion.

Likewise, Article 11 of the EU Charter of Fundamental Rights protects freedom of expression under EU law. In contrast to the ECHR, Article 11 EUCFR does not incorporate any limitations, which are instead provided for under Article 52(1) EUCFR, according to which

> [a]ny limitation on the exercise of the rights and freedoms recognised by this Charter must be provided for by law and respect the essence of those rights and freedoms. Subject to the principle of proportionality, limitations may be made only if they are necessary and genuinely meet objectives of general interest recognised by the Union or the need to protect the rights and freedoms of others.

This scenario is in fact different from the US system for at least two reasons. The first concerns the degree of protection. The reach of constitutional protection for freedom of expression is more limited in Europe as there is no provision carving out a sphere of protection as broad as that provided by the First Amendment. Europe is also so different due to the lack of a unique constitutional architecture. Whereas in the US the First Amendment is the sole and 'sacred' point of reference, the European model cannot be explained or understood unless the EU system is combined with that of the ECHR, and unless the decisions of the respective courts are read in light of the reciprocal influence and integration between the relevant principles under each system.

publicity or accessibility of the restriction. See Dirk Voorhoof, 'Freedom of Expression under the European Human Rights System. From Sunday Times (n° 1) v. U.K. (1979) to Hachette Filipacchi Associés ("Ici Paris") v. France (2009)' (2009) 1–2 *Inter-American and European Human Rights Journal/Revista Interamericana y Europa de Derechos Humanos* 3.

[133] Flauss (n 129) 810.

Against this backdrop, it is worth recalling a difference in the balancing process operated by the ECtHR and the CJEU: in particular, since the EU – at least at the outset – was intended as an economic community only, the constitutional backdrop has been provided by the ECHR system and the ECtHR. A common feature of the two courts is that, according to the European approach to freedom of expression, its exercise must be balanced with protection for other fundamental rights. Besides, Article 10 ECHR is closely mirrored by the EUCFR,[134] where the fundamental tenets of media freedom and pluralism are explicitly enshrined within the design of freedom.[135] This freedom has been developed by the CJEU in a manner consistent with its framework of fundamental rights, which is broadly fashioned according to the rule of interpretation of the ECtHR in consonance with Article 52(3) EUCFR.[136]

Turning to the ECtHR decisions in which the court has been called upon to rule on applications concerning alleged violations of freedom of expression on the Internet, the court has shown an inclination to moderate the expansive scope that characterised its previous case law on the application of Article 10 ECHR within the analogue world. In this way, it can be asserted that the European system has taken on an 'internal perspective', modifying its approach in the digital world and changing some of the parameters used in its balancing operations, as will be highlighted in the next chapter.[137]

The shifting paradigm becomes more evident if the focus is placed on the right to privacy and the right to data protection, as is also the difference between the US and EU approaches. Although the right to privacy has been enshrined within a Bill of Rights at European level, it is inextricably linked in terms of its conceptual origins to the corresponding US right. Over the decades, an increasingly complex right to privacy has emerged in line with social developments, ie the right to exclude interference in one's private life by others.

It may be observed that this claim, which was elaborated in detail by Warren and Brandeis and described as the right to be left alone, 'the right to be left in peace', was directly related to sensationalist news and tabloid activities.[138] In a famous article published in the *Harvard Law Review*, the authors stressed the need for the common law system to put in place adequate protection for individuals against new forms of interference offered by technology, such as – at that time – photography and the printed press. And it is no coincidence that, when weighing up rights, the right to privacy is 'defeated' in most cases by the free speech clause.[139]

[134] EUCFR, Art 11.

[135] ibid Art 11(2).

[136] For instance, Case C-274/99 P *Connolly v Commission* [2001] ECR I-1611, para 39, quoting *Handyside v United Kingdom*, App no 5493/72, Decision of 7 December 1976, para 49.

[137] See for a comparative overview Oreste Pollicino and Marco Bassini, 'Free Speech, Defamation and the Limits to Freedom of Expression in the EU: A Comparative Analysis' in Andrej Savin and Jan Trzaskowski (eds), *Research Handbook On EU Internet Law* (Cheltenham, Edward Elgar, 2014) 508.

[138] Samuel D Warren and Louis D Brandeis, 'The Right to Privacy' (1890) 4 *Harvard Law Review* 193.

[139] 'Accordingly, in cases where the freedom of speech conflicts with the interest related to privacy, generally the former prevails', Koltay (n 123) 33.

It is also no coincidence that the focus of Warren and Brandeis was to establish whether there was any foundation for protecting the right to privacy. This has been effectively identified in a series of judicial decisions in which rules designed to protect private rights were applied. In order to illustrate this perspective in better detail, the authors offered the example of a letter received in error. It is clear, in this regard, that none of the rules designed to protect property rights could be validly invoked, for instance in order to prevent the content from being published; on the contrary, it is the right to privacy that lays the foundation for the protection of the private sphere.

Within the boundaries set out by Warren and Brandeis, the right to privacy started to be taken into account by the US judges in a variety of cases.[140] In particular, the lack of any clear stipulation within legislation or the Constitution has allowed the US Supreme Court to identify the most appropriate principle for protecting privacy. Indeed, it may be observed that the nature of privacy protection under the US Constitution is diffuse, or in other words decentralised. For example, both the First Amendment, which protects the privacy of beliefs, and the Fourteenth Amendment, which sets out the due process of law clause, have been used as sources in order to recognise an adequate right to privacy. The expansive nature of the right to privacy has thus been directly proportional to the ability of the courts to identify its foundation in principles – including even principles of constitutional law – that are very different from one another. In particular, the relevance of the Fourth Amendment in this field deserves further consideration. According to the US Constitution:

> The right of the people to be secure in their persons, houses, papers, and effects, against unreasonable searches and seizures, shall not be violated, and no warrants shall issue, but upon probable cause, supported by oath or affirmation, and particularly describing the place to be searched, and the persons or things to be seized.

This Amendment concerns, in particular, law enforcement and restrictions on the rights of individuals, and hence the relationship with the right to privacy and data protection is evident. Specifically, it only applies to individuals who are physically present in the US and to US citizens abroad. As discussed in Chapter 3, the US Supreme Court has considered the issue of privacy above all in relation to new technologies in the offline world.[141] Within this context, the digital world appears to have paralysed the evolution of the right to privacy in the US, which has remained stuck in the quicksand of the definition of the right to privacy and data protection on the Internet, and has suffered from the hyperactivity of the CJEU. As we will see in Chapter 3, in this regard, it may be asserted that an external

[140] See, among the older decisions, *Meyer v Nebraska* 262 US 390 (1923); *Griswold v Connecticut* 381 US 479 (1965); *Stanley v Georgia* 394 US 557 (1969); *Roe v Wade* 410 US 113 (1973); *Kelley v Johnson* 425 US 238 (1976); *Moore v City of East Cleveland* 431 US 494 (1977); *Cruzan v Director, Missouri Department of Health* 497 US 261 (1990).

[141] *Olmstead* (n 32); *Katz v United States* 389 US 347 (1967); *Smith v Maryland* 442 US 735 (1979).

perspective has prevailed in the US within the process of balancing this right in the online world, as the US Supreme Court has not pursued an innovative approach within its case law, in contrast to the European system.

The right to privacy and data protection have undergone an incredible metamorphosis within the European system. The legal basis for the right to privacy in Europe was originally the second paragraph of Article 8 ECHR, which associates the right to respect for private and family life with the traditional guarantees afforded to fundamental rights in legal systems governed by the rule of law: the prohibition on interference by public authorities that is not provided for by law and justified by the need to pursue specified purposes. It was thus that the right to privacy came to Europe and was subsequently fully incorporated into the first European Bill of Rights (which was the only one, until the EUCFR was adopted). The task of adequately protecting the right to privacy naturally lies primarily with the Contracting States. However, ensuring that such protection is effective is the responsibility of the ECtHR, a body ad hoc established within the Council of Europe as a court of fundamental rights.

As is the case under US constitutional law, in Europe the right to privacy has been recognised in 'negative' terms as a right to respect for private life. However, technological evolution has enabled the negative dimension to privacy to be enriched by a 'positive' element, which is no longer reduced simply to the right to be left alone. The transition from a purely negative and static matrix to a positive and dynamic matrix was tangibly achieved, once again, thanks to the Council of Europe. This occurred in particular through the Convention on the Protection of Individuals with regard to Automatic Processing of Personal Data, also known as Convention no 108/1981. The purpose of this Convention is specifically to guarantee 'in the territory of each Party for every individual, whatever his nationality or residence, respect for his rights and fundamental freedoms, and in particular his right to privacy, with regard to automatic processing of personal data relating to him ("data protection")'.[142] The provisions of the Convention are predominantly programmatic in nature and charge Contracting States with the task of identifying suitable measures to ensure an adequate level of protection, in addition to the necessary procedures and sanctions.

However, the ECHR was the first legal text to introduce a group of principles that have been crucial in regulating the processing of personal data. It is worth pointing out that, under the Convention, the need to adopt a nuanced approach within the general overall category of personal data is already emerging, discriminating within it between special categories of data and the ordinary categories. In this regard, in fact, the Convention requires that such data should only be processed automatically if this is subject to appropriate guarantees.

[142] Convention for the Protection of Individuals with regard to Automatic Processing of Personal Data (1981) Art 1.

Against this backdrop, the institutions of the then European Community were slower to codify a right to data protection or digital privacy due to their original focus on trade. For a long time, individual rights were recognised under EC law almost exclusively in order to ensure economic fundamental freedoms. Consequently, within this context it was difficult to turn data protection into an issue that could capture the attention of European institutions owing to its direct impact on certain fundamental rights. On this view, the paradigm of the right to privacy in the EU has paralleled the rise of the Internet, and consequently has been heavily influenced by the web, rapidly adapting the right to privacy to new technologies. In light of these considerations, it can be asserted that the internal point of view was the preferred approach of the European courts, which developed a different balancing process for the digital environment.

This analysis has set out only the constitutional basis on which Chapters 2 and 3 will focus as regards the role of the judiciary within the information society in relation to freedom of expression, privacy and data protection. The focus on the EU and US will make it possible to emphasise how, despite the different constitutional framework, courts have been called upon to balance fundamental rights online by adapting their judicial frames and addressing the issue of jurisdiction.

V. Conclusions

In the light of this comparative analysis, the reasons for amplifying the role of courts in the information society cannot simply be dismissed as a rhetorical and argumentative contrivance to persuade the audience of the soundness of the decision reached. On the contrary, it has been seen how that choice has immediate repercussions on the way in which the courts engage with new technologies, and ultimately on the outcome of the balancing operation between the rights and freedoms at stake online.

However, also metaphors such as those that describe the Internet as a 'new free marketplace of ideas' and Internet law as the 'Law of the Horse' are expressions of a particular worldview. Thanks to their explanatory and imaginative capacity, they are capable of impinging significantly on the frame of reference, inevitably conditioning the scope of the value frame that is used by the courts or by the decision-making body in the particular case. As has been noted above, the reference to the 'free marketplace of ideas' in order to define the expansive scope of digital technology reflects a view of the US Supreme Court that – if this is possible at all – amplifies the unbridled freedom of expression under the First Amendment beyond its scope in the real world when that freedom is exercised online; however, the provocative reference made by Easterbrook to the Law of the Horse reveals an opposing stance of incomplete acceptance (if not the refusal) of the new technology, which is typical of someone who considers the Internet from the external point of view of the analogue reality. Against this background, quoting another judge, the President of the ECtHR Robert Ragnar Spanó, the European approach to new technologies seems to embrace an internal point of view:

> [I]t is for the Court to be very clear that it interprets and applies the Convention not in a static manner not in a retrogressive manner but in a manner which takes account of every expanding understandings of the reality of human life and the way in which human rights guarantees within the Convention ... have to be applied to novel realities for example, now, the digital age ... the Court must be at the forefront of understanding and conceptualizing the way in which the Convention should be interpreted in the future.[143]

The de facto freedom enjoyed by the courts within the digital domain in choosing the metaphorical universe that is capable of offering the decisive parameters for resolving jurisdictional disputes that come before them has for some time triggered further debate in both North America and in Europe concerning the institutional role of the courts.[144] These are familiar questions, which need not therefore be considered further here, and may be largely countered by an objection, which has been raised from various quarters, concerning the supposed lack of democratic legitimacy for a decision-making body with such broad and fluid boundaries. It cannot be denied that the courts currently occupy a privileged position within their respective legal systems in identifying the risks of constitutionally relevant collisions between rights, both internally and externally. This is in particular the case as regards the identification of the highest standard of protection for the particular rights in play as well as their intervention – through dialogue – in order to avoid the risk of an inter- and extra-constitutional 'collision' between different legal systems. The centrality of judicial momentum has been further enhanced first of all by the fact that jurisdiction is particularly important due to the cross-border nature of the web. Its significance has also increased as the issue of the applicable law – a question which is logically related to (even if conceptually autonomous from) the jurisdiction of the relevant court – has very far-reaching implications for the standard of protection for the fundamental rights in play.

All of this – and this is the most significant aspect for our present purposes – appears to be all the more applicable to the specific interaction between courts that occurs in relation to the Internet. The continuous and dizzying changes in the world of technology, coupled with the transnational nature of the web, considerably magnify the difficulties, which are already apparent in other areas, that national (although also supranational) legislatures encounter in providing even minimum

[143] Mikael R Madsen, 'Judicial Independence: Online Public Talk by Robert Spano, President of the ECtHR' *Københavns Universitet Video Portal* (2 June 2020) at https://video.ku.dk/judicial-independence-online-public, minute 47.03 (my own transcription).

[144] On this topic see Allan Rosas, 'The European Court of Justice in Context: Forms and Patterns of Judicial Dialogue' (2007) 1 *European Journal of Legal Studies* 1; Ran Hirschl, *Towards Juristocracy: The Origins and Consequences of the New Constitutionalism* (Cambridge, MA, Harvard University Press, 2004); Julie Allard and Antoine Garapon, *Les juges dans le mondialisation. La nouvelle révolution du droit* (Paris, Seuil, 2005).

normative protection capable of addressing the most significant questions. It is evident that an immediate consequence of that inertia or inadequacy on the legislative side is the amplification of the creative, substitutive role of the courts.

Against this backdrop, it should be pointed out that, as ingredients of judicial imagination, metaphors should be taken seriously, as will be seen in Chapter 2 on the metaphor of the free marketplace of ideas. Words and definitions should be selected with care in order to avoid causing a distortive effect on debates concerning the identification of the right legal tools.

The same could be said in relation to the term 'digital platform', in which the image of a neutral and passive hosting basis entirely masks the consistently more active and non-impartial role of such platforms. More specifically, as we shall see in Chapter 5, the combination of the economic strength of the major Internet giants and the introduction of algorithm technology has resulted in a very significant shift for constitutional law. It is in fact precisely because of algorithms that the freedom to conduct business has turned into a power. Digital firms are no longer market participants: rather, they are market makers, which are capable of exerting quasi-regulatory control over the terms on which others can sell goods and services.[145] In addition, they 'aspire to displace more government roles over time, replacing the logic of territorial sovereignty with functional sovereignty'.[146] Taking the example of Amazon, Pasquale observes that 'as artificial intelligence improves, the tracking of shopping into the Amazon groove will tend to become ever more rational for both buyers and sellers. Like a path through a forest trod ever clearer of debris, it becomes the natural default'.[147]

It is no coincidence that commentators have fine-tuned this category by replacing the term 'digital platforms' with references to 'gatekeepers' in order to stress how the implications of the control exerted by them over infrastructure and users is no longer limited to the economy and competition. Secondly, it is necessary to stress how the shift in power towards private actors also implies that they are performing functions and tasks that are normally vested in public authorities, such as courts or other judicial bodies. These dynamics have also led to a privatisation of the protection of individuals' rights. In this respect, Van Loo has framed the fascinating metaphor of 'corporation as courthouse' to describe the platforms that implement dispute resolution schemes in order to settle disputes between buyers and sellers.[148]

While public enforcement has long been the default option, based on the role of public authorities as monopolists within the context of human rights adjudication, private enforcement has recently emerged as a new trend for protecting digital rights, ie fundamental rights in the digital realm. This privatisation of the

[145] Frank Pasquale, 'From Territorial to Functional Sovereignty: The Case of Amazon, Law and Political Economy', *Law and Political Economy blog* (6 December 2017) at https://lpeblog.org/2017/12/06/from-territorial-to-functional-sovereignty-the-case-of-amazon/.

[146] ibid.

[147] ibid.

[148] Rory Van Loo, 'The Corporation as Courthouse' (2016) 33 *Yale Journal on Regulation* 548.

protection of rights is just one of the many and countless processes occurring within the context of a trend by which judicial discretion is increasingly being replaced by the incorporation of algorithms or algorithmic techniques into online platforms.

These are only some examples of the role performed by courts in the information society. Other recent trends (such as Executive Order 13925 signed by US President Donald Trump on 28 May 2020)[149] confirms that the role of digital platforms stands at the intersection of political and legal considerations, which are easy to predict.

Moreover, the judiciary is also likely to become more proactively involved due to the outbreak of the COVID-19 pandemic, which has led governments to adopt new technologies in order to counter or contain the spread of the virus, which have entailed significant effects on human rights (for example, there has been a flourishing of contact tracing apps). The lack of 'emergency clauses' in some jurisdictions or other constitutional provisions to regulate how and to what extent governments can limit human rights in times of emergency will perhaps induce some courts to take action and result in new cases. For instance, the Israeli Supreme Court has recently held that there is no proper legal basis for the implementation of the national contact tracing system.[150]

Therefore, it is possible to point to judicial imagination as one of the leading factors that has enabled states and national authorities to assert their power to uphold fundamental rights also in the digital realm, contrary to the views expressed by cyberanarchy theorists. This premise accurately reflects the process that has led courts in various jurisdictions to 'find some way' to ensure that the Internet is not a complete 'free-for-all', or rather a promised land of liberty without responsibility.

The next chapters will reveal how specifically courts have accomplished this task as regards the protection of freedom of expression and the right to privacy, applying different frames and metaphors from case to case in order to determine the most appropriate solution. This interpretive process will become increasingly sophisticated considering the engagement of digital platforms as what are now commonly referred to as 'private powers' and the consequent need, as we will see in the next chapter, to rethink the original scope of constitutionalism (namely limiting government).[151]

[149] This Executive Order was adopted as a consequence of Twitter's activity concerning content relating to disinformation. It came at a time of strong debate about the regulation of social media after more than 20 years since the adoption of the legal framework of liability of online intermediaries as developed at the end of the twentieth century. See Giovanni De Gregorio and Roxana Radu, 'Trump's Executive Order: Another Tile in the Mosaic of Governing Online Speech' *MediaLaws* (6 June 2020) at www.medialaws.eu/trumps-executive-order-another-tile-in-the-mosaic-of-governing-online-speech/.

[150] Israeli Supreme Court, *Ben Meir v Prime Minister*, HC 2109/20, 19 March 2020.

[151] András Sajó, *Limiting Government. An Introduction to Constitutionalism* (Budapest, Central European University Press, 1999).

As the analysis concerning judicial protection of freedom of expression and the right to privacy will make clear, platforms lie at the heart of the current challenges concerning the protection of fundamental rights in the information society.[152] They are therefore subject to special responsibilities,[153] which are not limited to liability in strictly legal terms.[154]

Two examples appear to be quite telling in this respect: consider, for instance, the role that digital platforms perform in relation to expressions and data. Similarly, one might also consider the role that certain digital utilities such as Google and Apple might perform in the context of the pandemic, by operating, eg, contact tracing apps, which may have the ability to retain very significant amounts of information.[155] These recent trends that have emerged during the pandemic will most likely give rise to new waves of judicial activism reflecting new frames. It is therefore necessary to consider from a comparative perspective what courts have done so far to safeguard human rights in the digital sphere, also with a view to understanding what is most likely to happen in future. The comparative analysis will focus, as mentioned in the Introduction, in Chapter 2 on judicial protection of freedom of speech, in Chapter 3 on privacy (and data protection) and in Chapter 4 on the relationship between the two mentioned rights from a transatlantic perspective.

[152] Luciano Floridi, *The Fourth Revolution: How the Infosphere Is Reshaping Human Reality* (Oxford, Oxford University Press, 2014).

[153] In antitrust terms, dominant position per se is not problematic but, because of the aforementioned 'appreciable' influence, the CJEU has argued (in *Michelin*) that the undertaking in this situation has a special responsibility, not shared by other companies that are not in a dominant position. Case C-322/81 *NV Nederlandsche Banden Industrie Michelin v Commission of the European Communities* [1983] ECR 03461.

[154] See for a comprehensive picture of the role of Internet service providers in modern societies Mariarosaria Taddeo and Luciano Floridi (eds), *The Responsibilities of Online Service Providers* (Berlin, Springer Verlag, 2017).

[155] The model proposed by Apple and Google for contact tracing has attracted the attention of states around the world dealing with the spread of the virus. Greig Paul, 'Contact-tracing apps: Apple dictating policies to nations won't help its EU anti-trust probe', *The Conversation* (24 June 2020) at https://theconversation.com/contact-tracing-apps-apple-dictating-policies-to-nations-wont-help-its-eu-anti-trust-probe-141304; Zak Doffman, 'Forget Apple and Google: Contact-Tracing Apps Just Dealt Serious New Blow', *Forbes* (12 May 2020) at www.forbes.com/sites/zakdoffman/2020/05/12/forget-apple-and-google-contact-tracing-apps-just-dealt-serious-new-blow/#2b82c2342172.

2

Judges and Freedom of Expression: From Atoms to Bits Across the Atlantic

I. Freedom of Expression in Action

The previous chapter shed some light on two of the driving forces triggering the amplification of judicial momentum in the transition from the world of atoms to that of bits across the Atlantic: the use of metaphorical language and judicial frames and the definition of jurisdictional boundaries online.

A few, very well-known cases illustrate how these two drivers can represent the two sides of judicial power in the digital domain. More than others, *Yahoo! v Licra* has been referred to as one of the leading cases in this area. This case involves by no means simply jurisdictional concerns as described in Chapter 1. Indeed, it is also relevant in terms of enforcement as well as the difficulty in striking a balance between freedom of speech and the protection of other fundamental rights on the Internet. Indeed, when two French anti-racist organisations sought an order directing Yahoo! to disable the website in France, the problem concerned not only jurisdiction, but also the different scope of protection for freedom of expression across the Atlantic.

This case showed that any difference between the degree of fundamental rights protection can produce conflicts between jurisdictions and problems of enforcement. Different approaches to freedom of speech, as well as to other fundamental rights such as public order, ultimately result in problems in the enforcement of judgments issued by courts belonging to different jurisdictions, even though the legal orders concerned are becoming increasingly interconnected.

The differences between the extent to which freedom of expression can be exercised are not limited solely to the level of protection afforded by the relevant constitutional parameters. They are also dependent on the scope of protection afforded to other contrasting fundamental rights with, at least in theory, the same constitutional *status*, which must accordingly be balanced with freedom of expression. In this context, the judicial frame becomes crucially important. Depending on the values that a court considers to prevail in any specific case as well as the point of view (external or internal, in Hartian terms)[1] adopted as regards

[1] See Herbert LA Hart, *The Concept of Law* (Oxford, Oxford University Press, 1961).

the newness of technology,[2] the balancing exercise can give rise to an entirely different result.

Returning to the *Yahoo!* case, it provides a powerful example of how judicial frames and jurisdiction are inevitably intertwined in the exercise of judicial power in cases concerning digital matters. In that case, the French judicial frame concerning the protection of dignity contrasted with freedom of expression under the US legal system. It was noted in Chapter 1 how courts have addressed the issue of jurisdiction in cases concerning online defamation. Likewise, this chapter will argue that judicial frames play a more critical role in influencing the way in which courts consider protection for freedom of expression across the Atlantic.

In fact, whereas in Europe free speech is conceived of as a right that can be limited when other constitutional freedoms have to be safeguarded (eg, public order, national security), in the US it is likely to prevail in the vast majority of cases, unless any very limited exceptions apply. In the area of free speech, an additional reason why adopting a comparative perspective is essential is that the advent of the Internet has exacerbated and over-amplified certain problems related to jurisdiction that were already familiar to scholars of freedom of speech, albeit to a lesser degree. The differences between the US and EU approaches to freedom of expression become apparent, for instance, when it is considered how the law treats matters such as defamation, hate speech or the protection of minors from violent or sexually explicit content.[3]

Within this scenario, this chapter will first examine the position on freedom of expression in the US, with specific reference to the case law of the US Supreme Court. It will then focus on the European judicial context, considering how the CJEU and ECtHR protect freedom of expression in the shift from the world of atoms to the world of bits.[4]

II. The US Judicial Landscape of Freedom of Expression

Chapter 1 has already examined the US liberal roots to freedom of expression. In fact, the First Amendment guarantees broad protection for these fundamental rights, the importance of which has been significantly extended over two centuries of case law. Nonetheless, the core essence of this fundamental right is described in

[2] Monroe E Price, 'The Newness of New Technology' (2001) 22(5–6) *Cardozo Law Review* 1885.

[3] In this respect see Michel Ronsenfeld and András Sajó, 'Spreading Liberal Constitutionalism: An Inquiry into the Fate of Free Speech in New Democracies' in Sujit Choudhry (ed), *The Migration of Constitutional Ideas* (Cambridge, Cambridge University Press, 2006) 142, 146. See also Oreste Pollicino and Marco Bassini, 'Free Speech, Defamation and the Limits to Freedom of Expression in the EU: A Comparative Analysis' in Andrej Savin and Jan Trzaskowski (eds), *Research Handbook on EU Internet Law* (Cheltenham, Edward Elgar, 2014) 508. See also the *LICRA v Yahoo!* saga (Chapter 1) and the judgment of the US Supreme Court in *Reno v American Civil Liberties Union* 521 US 844 (1997).

[4] Nicholas Negroponte, *Being Digital* (New York, Alfred A Knopf Inc, 1995).

a few landmark cases.[5] In *Schenck v United States*[6] Justice Holmes developed the 'clear and present danger' doctrine for the first time, which has so far been the test for assessing public powers' ability to restrict freedom of expression. In Holmes's words:

> The question in every case is whether the words used are used in such circumstances and are of such a nature as to create a clear and present danger that they will bring about the substantive evils that the United States Congress has a right to prevent. It is a question of proximity and degree. When a nation is at war, many things that might be said in time of peace are such a hindrance to its effort that their utterance will not be endured so long as men fight, and that no Court could regard them as protected by any constitutional right.[7]

On the other hand, Justice Holmes dissented, in a famous opinion joined by Justice Brandeis, in *Abrams v United States*. The US Supreme Court has embraced the very well-known metaphor of the free marketplace of ideas.[8] This metaphor is in some way deeply linked to a particular concept of liberal democracy, in which the role of the state is minimal.[9] According to Justice Holmes:

> Persecution for the expression of opinions seems to me perfectly logical. If you have no doubt of your premises or your power, and want a certain result with all your heart, you naturally express your wishes in law, and sweep away all opposition. To allow opposition by speech seems to indicate that you think the speech impotent, as when a man says that he has squared the circle, or that you do not care wholeheartedly for the result, or that you doubt either your power or your premises. But when men have realized that time has upset many fighting faiths, they may come to believe even more than they believe the very foundations of their own conduct that the ultimate good desired is better reached by free trade in ideas – that the best test of truth is the power of the thought to get itself accepted in the competition of the market, and that truth is the only ground upon which their wishes safely can be carried out.[10]

These cases concerned the constitutional review under the First Amendment of the provisions of the Espionage Act 1917 and the Sedition Act 1918, which provided for the prosecution of certain conduct constituting the exercise of freedom of expression during World War I. The most important heritage of these opinions is the assumption that freedom of expression can only be limited when its exercise is likely to create a clear and present danger. Outside this scope, there is a 'marketplace of ideas' where opinions and thoughts may achieve consensus by virtue of their true or authoritative content.

[5] See Elisabeth Zoller, 'The United States Supreme Court and the Freedom of Expression' (2009) 84 *Indiana Law Journal* 885.

[6] *Schenck v United States* 249 US 47 (1919).

[7] ibid 52.

[8] On the metaphor of the 'free marketplace of ideas' see Haig Bosmajian, *Metaphor and Reason in Judicial Opinions* (Carbondale, IL, Southern Illinois University Press, 1992).

[9] *Abrams v United States* 250 US 616 (1919).

[10] ibid 630.

A picture of the US approach to free speech can be obtained by applying these principles to certain specific areas of the law: defamation, hate speech and sexually explicit speech.[11] It is only once these principles have been observed 'in action' that it is possible to understand how the Internet has affected traditional categories and doctrines of law.

As far as defamation law is concerned, the decision taken in *New York Times v Sullivan* is one of the leading cases in this area.[12] The core issue in the case was whether the use of false or defamatory statements by the press against public figures was protected by freedom of expression. The US Supreme Court pointed out that statements made with actual malice or reckless disregard are beyond the protection of freedom of speech (more specifically, freedom of the press) and can therefore trigger liability for the author. Otherwise, where these criteria are not met, no limit can be imposed on public debate. This standard is based on the assumption that no advancement in public opinion can be achieved through the dissemination of false statements.

The area of law that more than the others brings to the fore the broad scope of the protection guaranteed to freedom of expression in the US is hate speech.[13] The common denominator for the three leading cases concerning racial and religious hatred is that only those expressions that are likely to result in incitement to violence lie beyond the constitutional protection guaranteed under the First Amendment.[14] The adoption of this standard has led the US courts to tolerate conduct that would most likely be prohibited under the corresponding European provisions. In so doing, the US Supreme Court has set a very high threshold for punishing hate speech: incitement to hatred does not suffice. Only incitement to violence justifies a restriction of freedom of expression.

For instance, it should be stressed in relation to hate speech and terrorism that the fight against international terrorism and the enactment of 18 U.S. Code §§ 2339A–2339B have potentially restricted this kind of speech when supporting international terrorist groups as defined by the US government. The US Supreme Court has analysed whether this measure could constitute a violation of the First Amendment.[15] In a very ambiguous decision, the court observed that a difference must be drawn between the independent advocacy and the material support to terrorist groups.[16] In this respect, the US Supreme Court held: 'In particular, we in no way suggest that a regulation of independent speech would pass constitutional

[11] See Ronsenfeld and Sajó (n 3).

[12] *New York Times v Sullivan* 376 US 254 (1964).

[13] For an analysis of the hate speech issue and its relationship with freedom of expression see Alisdair Gillespie, 'Hate and Harm: The Law on Hate Speech' in Andrej Savin and Jan Trzaskowski (eds), *Research Handbook on EU Internet Law* (Cheltenham, Edward Elgar, 2014) 488.

[14] See *Brandeburg v Ohio* 343 US 250 (1969); *RAV v City of St Paul* 505 US 377 (1992); *Virginia v Black* 538 US 343 (2003).

[15] *Holder v Humanitarian Law Project* 561 US 1 (2010).

[16] 'Even assuming that a heightened standard applies because the material support statute potentially implicates speech, the statutory terms are not vague as applied to plaintiffs', ibid 16.

muster, even if the Government were to show that such speech benefits foreign terrorist organizations'.[17]

Even with respect to sexually explicit and violent content, the approach of the US courts has been consistent with the purpose of granting extensive protection to freedom of speech. In *Miller v California*[18] the US Supreme Court established a three-prong test for defining content as obscene: a work goes beyond the scope of protection of free speech and can therefore be regulated where that work, taken as a whole, appeals to prurient interest in sex; portrays, in a patently offensive way, sexual conduct specifically defined by applicable State law; and which, taken as a whole, does not have serious literary, artistic, political or scientific value. Another landmark decision in *New York v Ferber* excluded child pornography from free speech protection.[19]

A very recent judgment concerned a California statute that had made it a criminal offence to sell to anyone under the age of 18 video games portraying killing, maiming, dismembering or sexually assaulting an image of a human being. In *Brown v EMA*[20] the US Supreme Court struck down the law, finding that video games qualify for First Amendment protection in the same way as films, music and other forms of literary or artistic expression. In this decision, the US Supreme Court focused on a crucial aspect: the degree of protection of freedom of speech does not vary depending upon the medium and legislation cannot create categories of unprotected speech, even for the purpose of protecting minors.

Even when focusing on the issue of fake news, the American legal system does not distinguish between political speech and freedom of information,[21] applying the same limits to the free speech clause and the press clause. As a consequence, unlike in Europe,[22] the balancing process does not consider the passive aspect to freedom of information, ie the right to be informed. As was clearly asserted in *United States v Alvarez*: 'Even when considering some instances of defamation and fraud … falsity alone may not suffice to bring the speech outside the First Amendment. The statement must be a knowing or reckless falsehood'.[23] Within the media system, this approach has been confirmed by *Gertz v Robert Welch* as well as *New York Times v Sullivan*, mentioned above.[24]

[17] ibid 34.

[18] *Miller v California* 413 US 15 (1973). See also *Roth v United States* 354 US 476 (1957) and *Ginsberg v New York* 390 US 629 (1968).

[19] *New York v Ferber* 458 US 747 (1982).

[20] *Brown v Entertainment Merchants Association et al* 564 US 1 (2011).

[21] Sonja R West, 'Press Exceptionalism' (2014) 127 *Harvard Law Review* 2434.

[22] The EU is currently dealing with the fake news issue with a soft-law tool, the EU Code of Practice on Disinformation: Matteo Monti, 'The EU Code of Practice on Disinformation and the Risk of the Privatisation of Censorship' in Serena Giusti and Elisa Piras (eds), *Democracy and Fake News – Information Manipulation and Post-Truth Politics* (Abingdon, Routledge, forthcoming 2020).

[23] *United States v Alvarez* 567 US 7 (2012). For further details about the legal status of lies in the US legal system, see Catherine J Ross, 'Incredible Lies' (2018) 89 *University of Colorado Law Review* 377.

[24] *Gertz v Robert Welch Inc* 418 US 323 (1974).

In order to answer the question whether the advent of the Internet has further extended the scope of freedom of expression as protected in the 'world of atoms', a few US cases should be mentioned. The most important decision of the US Supreme Court, which is nowadays regarded as a landmark ruling for freedom of expression online, is *Reno v ACLU*.[25] The US Supreme Court found the provisions contained in the Communication Decency Act (CDA), which criminalised the online distribution of obscene or indecent materials to any person under 18, to be unconstitutional. In the US Supreme Court's view, the restrictions imposed by the CDA were too vague and lacked the precision required to limit free speech only to the extent necessary for the protection of minors, in particular by failing to properly define 'indecent' and 'patently offensive' content.

It is worth noting that the decision expressly took account of the difference between the nature of the Internet and that of other media such as radio and television:

> [R]adio and television, unlike the Internet, have, as a matter of history … received the most limited First Amendment protection, … in large part because warnings could not adequately protect the listener from unexpected program content. … [On the Internet], the risk of encountering indecent material by accident is remote because a series of affirmative steps is required to access specific material.[26]

Similar nuances characterised another attempt by the US government to regulate protection of minors online. In 1998, after the US Supreme Court had struck down the most relevant part of the CDA, the Child Online Protection Act (COPA) came into force with similar purposes. This Act was also reviewed by the US Supreme Court, which ruled that it violated the First Amendment. Specifically, COPA classified as 'material harmful to minors' any obscene material or material that, based on community standards, an average person would consider appealing to prurient interest. According to the US Supreme Court, even this definition failed to meet the standards required to circumscribe free speech limitations.[27]

Another decision concerning protection for freedom of speech on the Internet was taken in *Ashcroft v Free Speech Coalition*.[28] The case concerned the final effort to protect minors from the dissemination of explicit content, specifically the Child Pornography Prevention Act (CPPA) adopted in 1996. The US Supreme Court found that the restrictions introduced by the CPPA to freedom of expression were disproportionate and over-broad. Most notably, the decision focused on provisions that prohibited, first of all, the diffusion of images that appeared to be minors engaged in sexual activity and, secondly, any form of speech conveying the impression that the images represented minors involved in sexual conduct. Free speech activists complained that these provisions gave rise to chilling effects. The US Supreme Court found that Congress, of course, has the power to pass laws with

[25] *Reno v American Civil Liberties Union* (n 3).
[26] ibid 868.
[27] *Ashcroft v American Civil Liberties Union* 535 US 564 (2002)
[28] *Ashcroft v Free Speech Coalition* 535 US 234 (2002).

the aim of preventing child pornography and the circulation of obscene content. However, since the provisions contained in the CPPA went beyond the admissible scope, the restriction on freedom of speech was over-broad and violated the First Amendment.

All of these cases would appear to suggest that the advent of the Internet has not weakened the protection afforded to freedom of expression, in spite of the possible threats to other interests caused by its use. On the contrary, the US Supreme Court has supported the idea that advances in the effectiveness of freedom of speech have been made, in particular by applying strict scrutiny to the conditions that might constitute legal grounds for restricting this fundamental right.

If, in the world of atoms, courts have proved to be suspicious of any potential restriction on free speech but have admitted that other interests may prevail under certain circumstances, the advent of the Internet has instead prospected another path. As the decisions mentioned above concerning the publication of obscene content online demonstrate, even where another primary constitutional interest is at stake (eg the protection of minors), limitations on freedom of speech must be strictly proportionate to the aim pursued by the regulation concerned. In all these cases, in fact, the US Supreme Court has never denied the nature of the legal interest of protecting minors from dissemination of obscene content; however, it has always required that restrictions based on this equally protected interest must not excessively impair freedom of expression.

Recently, the US Supreme Court has issued two decisions, which are important in understanding how the internal and external perspective of judges influence the balancing of fundamental rights and, therefore, the outcome of cases.

In *Elonis v United States*,[29] the US Supreme Court considered a case concerning threats posted on Facebook by Mr Elonis during divorce proceedings against his soon-to-be ex-wife and other people. The case concerned the use of symbolic speech and indirect threats made through modified rap songs, quotations of artistic works, photographs and personal monologues. Mr Elonis was unsuccessful before the lower courts and decided to appeal to the US Supreme Court. While the court's opinion focused exclusively on the required mental state for criminal sanctions, the risk of serious harm etc, in his concurring opinion, Justice Alito underscored the importance of the context and the role played by social networks:

> 'Taken in context', lyrics in songs that are performed for an audience or sold in recorded form are unlikely to be interpreted as a real threat to a real person … Statements on social media that are pointedly directed at their victims, by contrast, are much more likely to be taken seriously.[30]

Justice Alito was even careful in considering the new technologies, looking at the operation of social networks and taking into account that aspect. On the other

[29] *Elonis v United States* 575 US ___ (2015).
[30] ibid 6.

hand, it is evident that the majority of the court embraced an external perspective as regards threats on Facebook. The US Supreme Court did not consider how new technologies affect fundamental rights in the digital environment. Analysing the rationale of the decision, it should be stressed that no references were made to the new aspects and innovation which the Internet has introduced into society. As a result, the US Supreme Court's reasoning in balancing fundamental rights does not depart from its precedents.

The second important decision for understanding the internal and external judicial perspective is *Packingham v North Carolina*.[31] The decision concerned a North Carolina statute, which banned the use of commercial social networking websites by registered sex offenders. Following a police investigation, Mr Packingham was convicted by the Supreme Court of North Carolina,[32] which upheld the constitutionality of the contested provision, holding that the State had a sufficient interest in 'forestalling the illicit lurking and contact' of registered sex offenders and in protecting their potential future victims, thereby facilitating 'the legitimate and important aim of the protection of minors'.[33]

On the one hand, in this case, the US Supreme Court adopted a kind of external perspective, asserting that courts should exercise 'extreme caution' before limiting the application of the First Amendment to the Internet.[34] On the other hand, it widened the application of the First Amendment online. In other words, the US Supreme Court has not made any effort to 'downgrade' its sensitivity to this issue, specifically by focusing on the possible critical implications of the Internet. However, it has confirmed its own liberal vision, even recognising scope for an expansion of freedom of speech in view of the characteristics of an entirely new instrument. Once the US Supreme Court considered the very important role of social networks within a democratic society, it applied an external perspective, which neither expanded nor restricted the scope of the First Amendment:

> The better analogy to this case is Board of Airport Comm'rs of Los Angeles v Jews for Jesus, Inc. … where the Court struck down an ordinance prohibiting any 'First Amendment activities' at Los Angeles International Airport because the ordinance covered all manner of protected, nondisruptive behavior including 'talking and reading, or the wearing of campaign buttons or symbolic clothing,' … If a law prohibiting 'all protected expression' at a single airport is not constitutional, … it follows with even greater force that the State may not enact this complete bar to the exercise of First Amendment rights on websites integral to the fabric of our modern society and culture.[35]

As a consequence, it is quite clear that the US Supreme Court has transposed the offline balancing of fundamental rights into the online domain. This case makes

[31] *Packingham v North Carolina* 582 US ___ (2017).
[32] *State v Packingham* 368 NC 380 (2015).
[33] ibid.
[34] *Packingham v North Carolina* (n 31) 6.
[35] ibid 9.

it possible to investigate how the external vision of the US Supreme Court has affected the case law of the lower courts, which is quite important in a federal legal system where access to the Supreme Court is limited (ie by the writ of certiorari). The new trends that may be triggered by this decision are also analysed in Chapter 4, with specific reference to the decision in *Manhattan Community Access Corp v Halleck*.[36]

By considering the decisions of the national courts and federal circuits, it is possible to explore how the external perspective has influenced the lower courts, even before *Packingham*. The first case which may be considered is the *Baidu* case.[37] The US District Court for the Southern District of New York ruled on the censorship by the Baidu search engine of content critical of the Chinese government, thus preventing content from appearing in the American version of the search engine. Applying the categories previously developed by the US Supreme Court for newspapers and thus embracing an external perspective, the court claimed that

> [a]lthough the [US] Supreme Court has not addressed the precise question at issue, its First Amendment jurisprudence all but compels the conclusion that Plaintiffs' suit must be dismissed. The starting point for analysis is *Miami Herald Publishing Co. v. Tornillo* … in which the Court held that a Florida statute requiring newspapers to provide political candidates with a right of reply to editorials critical of them violated the First Amendment.[38]

In this way, after analysing other cases concerning the offline world in which the US Supreme Court has ruled on the protection of 'editorial choices' under the First Amendment, the US District Court for the Southern District of New York disregarded the significance of the technological aspect (eg the algorithmic one) and adopted an external perspective. In this way, ignoring the hybrid nature of the search engine and the new Internet environment, the court affirmed that 'For that reason, the First Amendment protects Baidu's right to advocate for systems of government other than democracy (in China or elsewhere) just as surely as it protects Plaintiffs' rights to advocate for democracy'.[39] This vision based on a strict application to the online world of the First Amendment as developed offline has implications from a technological point of view and, according to some scholars, should involve different considerations concerning the use of data and the relationship between those private companies and governments.[40]

[36] *Manhattan Community Access Corp v Halleck* 587 US __ (2019).

[37] *Jian Zhang v Baidu.Com Inc* 10 F Supp 3d 433 (SDNY 2014).

[38] ibid 436.

[39] ibid 443. See Eugene Volokh and Donald Falk, 'First Amendment Protection for Search Engine Search Results: White Paper Commissioned by Google' (2012) *UCLA School of Law Research Paper* no 12–22; Oren Bracha, 'The Folklore of Informationalism: The Case of Search Engine Speech' (2014) 82 *Fordham Law Review* 1630; Michael Ballanco, 'Searching for the First Amendment: An Inquisitive Free Speech Approach to Search Engine Rankings' (2013) 24 *George Mason University Civil Rights Law Journal* 89.

[40] Lisa M Austin, 'Technological Tattletales and Constitutional Black Holes: Communications Intermediaries and Constitutional Constraints' (2016) 17 *Theoretical Inquiries in Law* 451.

Another very interesting case of the federal courts is *Jane Doe No 1 v Backpage.com.*[41] The case concerned the application of Section 230(c) of the Communications Decency Act, ie the provision which regulates intermediaries' liability for third-party content in the US (and providing for almost blanket immunity).[42] The Backpage.com company offered online classified advertising through certain categories, including 'Adult Entertainment', which had a subcategory named 'Escorts'. The US Court of Appeals for the First Circuit, assuming an external perspective, held as follows:

> We begin with the appellants' assertion that Backpage's activities do not involve traditional publishing or editorial functions, and are therefore outside the protective carapace of section 230(c)(1). In support, the complaint describes choices that Backpage has made about the posting standards for advertisements – for example, rules about which terms are permitted or not permitted in a posting, the lack of controls on the display of phone numbers, the option to anonymize e-mail addresses, the stripping of metadata from photographs uploaded to the website, the website's reaction after a forbidden term is entered into an advertisement, and Backpage's acceptance of anonymous payments. The appellants submit that these choices are distinguishable from publisher functions. We disagree.[43]

In this sense, all of the choices that have favoured the spread of sex trafficking are considered by the court as 'editorial choices that fall within the purview of traditional publisher functions'.[44] As a consequence:

> Although the appellants try to distinguish *Doe* by claiming Backpage's decisions about what measures to implement deliberately attempt to make sex trafficking easier, this is a distinction without a difference. Whatever Backpage's motivations, those motivations do not alter the fact that the complaint premises liability on the decisions that Backpage is making as a publisher with respect to third-party content.[45]

Finally, even if a website facilitates illegal conduct through its own editorial rules, the operator's choices fall under the protection established by Section 230 CDA.

The external perspective can also be found in *Caraccioli v Facebook.*[46] Mr Caraccioli sued Facebook for damages because it did not remove content

[41] *Jane Doe No 1 v Backpage.com LLC* 817 F3d 12 (1st Cir 2016). Some precedent cases, however, seemed not to extend the freedom of Internet websites widely (eg *Fair Housing Council of San Fernando Valley v Roommates.com LLC* 521 F3d 1157 (9th Cir 2008)). Nevertheless, it is possible to affirm that this case law is actually overruled by the majority of decisions by federal circuits. See Danielle K Citron and Benjamin Wittes, 'The Internet Will Not Break: Denying Bad Samaritans § 230 Immunity' (2017) 86 *Fordham Law Review* 401.

[42] On which see Jeff Kosseff, *The Twenty-Six Words That Created the Internet* (Ithaca, NY, Cornell University Press, 2019); see also, for an overview of the most influential judgments enforcing S 230 CDA, Eric Goldman, 'The Ten Most Important Section 230 Rulings' (2017) 20 *Tulane Journal of Technology & Intellectual Property* 1.

[43] *Jane Doe No 1 v Backpage.Com LLC* (n 41) 20.

[44] ibid 21.

[45] ibid.

[46] With the decision *Franco Caraccioli v Facebook Inc* no 16-15610 (9th Cir 2017) the US Court of Appeals for the Ninth Circuit confirmed the District Court's decision, dismissing the case.

posted by an unknown third-party account named 'Franco Caracciolijerkingman', which, after connecting with Caraccioli's friends, disseminated pictures and videos of Mr Caraccioli 'sexually arousing or pleasuring himself'. Although Facebook initially refused to take down the fake profile, it eventually decided to remove it. The US District Court for the Northern District of California stressed that:

> Facebook contends the court should disregard one particular allegation critical to Plaintiff's theory; that Facebook 'recreated, sponsored, republished, and/or acted as a speaker of the content' of the suspect account 'by deciding to continue displaying it as opposed to deleting it.' The court agrees this allegation should be disregarded under well-established rules applicable in this context.[47]

In addition, the US District Court for the Northern District of California ruled on an attempt to demonstrate that a breach of contract had been committed, considering the proof submitted by the plaintiff. The district court's decision, upheld by the US Court of Appeals for the Ninth Circuit, established another important point concerning the liability regime:

> Plaintiff proposes that this case is distinct from others to which §230(c) has applied because, according to him, the content on the suspect account was 'facially objectionable' which Facebook 'should have and could have easily deleted.' In other words, he classifies this case as one involving editorial inaction rather than affirmative editorial action. But the Ninth Circuit has already explained why this distinction makes no difference.[48]

Cases concerning the material support for terrorism can provide other interesting insights. While decisions concerning the liability of online platforms seem to apply an external perspective that does not change the balancing of fundamental rights and does not alter the reasoning applied with reference to the nature of the Internet, the decision concerning terrorist hate speech appears to involve the application of an internal perspective.

The *Cohen* case concerned an action brought by Israeli citizens against Facebook, which was accused of having given material support to jihadist terrorists.[49] The US District Court for the Eastern District of New York applied Section 230 of the CDA in order to dismiss any form of liability for Facebook:

> While the Force Plaintiffs attempt to cast their claims as content-neutral, even the most generous reading of their allegations places them squarely within the coverage of Section 230(c)(l)'s grant of immunity. In their opposition to the present motion, the Force Plaintiffs argue that their claims seek to hold Facebook liable for 'provision of services' to Hamas in the form of account access 'coupled with Facebook's refusal to use available resources. to identify and shut down Hamas accounts.' … While superficially content-neutral, this attempt to draw a narrow distinction between policing accounts

[47] *Caraccioli v Facebook Inc* WL 859863 (ND Cal 2016) 6.
[48] ibid 11.
[49] *Cohen v Facebook Inc* 252 F Supp 3d 140 (EDNY 2017).

> and policing content must ultimately be rejected. Facebook's choices as to who may use its platform are inherently bound up in its decisions as to what may be said on its platform, and so liability imposed based on its failure to remove users would equally 'derive from [Facebook's] status or conduct as a "publisher or speaker"'. … Section 230(c)(1) prevents courts from entertaining civil actions that seek to impose liability on defendants like Facebook for allowing third parties to post offensive or harmful content or failing to remove such content once posted.[50]

The decision in *Force v Facebook* concerning Hamas propaganda dispelled any doubts about the application of Section 230 CDA[51] and also about the relationship between the use of algorithms and the editorial role of the publisher. According to the US Court of Appeals for the Second Circuit:

> We disagree with plaintiffs' contention that Facebook's use of algorithms renders it a non-publisher. First, we find no basis in the ordinary meaning of 'publisher,' the other text of Section 230, or decisions interpreting Section 230, for concluding that an interactive computer service is not the 'publisher' of third-party information when it uses tools such as algorithms that are designed to match that information with a consumer's interests … Indeed, arranging and distributing third-party information inherently forms 'connections' and 'matches' among speakers, content, and viewers of content, whether in interactive Internet forums or in more traditional media. That is an essential result of publishing. Accepting plaintiffs' argument would eviscerate Section 230(c)(1); a defendant interactive computer service would be ineligible for Section 230(c)(1) immunity by virtue of simply organizing and displaying content exclusively provided by third parties.[52]

The US Court of Appeals for the Second Circuit confirmed the balancing between the First Amendment and other interests as enshrined in the traditional application of Section 230 CDA. In addition, it held that the algorithm did not create any content as it is neutral.[53] Favouring certain content is typical of an editorial choice.[54] From this perspective, the dissenting opinion is interesting in that it attempts to criticise the exceptionalism of Section 230 CDA by stating that

> [i]t would be one thing if congressional intent compelled us to adopt the majority's reading. It does not. Instead, we today extend a provision that was designed to encourage computer service providers to shield minors from obscene material so that it now

[50] ibid 157.

[51] *Force v Facebook Inc* No 18-397 (2d Cir 2019).

[52] ibid 32. Affirming also that 'plaintiffs argue, in effect, that Facebook's use of algorithms is outside the scope of publishing because the algorithms *automate* Facebook's editorial decision-making. That argument, too, fails because "so long as a third party willingly provides the essential published content, the interactive service provider receives full immunity regardless of the specific edit[orial] or selection process"', ibid 38.

[53] 'The algorithms take the information provided by Facebook users and "match" it to other users – again, materially unaltered – based on objective factors applicable to any content, whether it concerns soccer, Picasso, or plumbers', ibid 47.

[54] 'We do not mean that Section 230 requires algorithms to treat all types of content the same. To the contrary, Section 230 would plainly allow Facebook's algorithms to, for example, de-promote or block content it deemed objectionable', ibid 47, note 24.

> immunizes those same providers for allegedly connecting terrorists to one another. Neither the impetus for nor the text of § 230(c)(1) requires such a result. When a plaintiff brings a claim that is based not on the content of the information shown but rather on the connections Facebook's algorithms make between individuals, the CDA does not and should not bar relief.[55]

The paradox inherent within the dissenting opinion, which criticises the mainstream interpretation of Section 230 CDA by formulating a kind of distinction between an Internet platform and an editor, is that the dissent makes use of a metaphor based on the offline world. Judge Katzmann's argument is that whoever brings two people into contact by calling them together cannot be classified as an editor; similarly, Facebook cannot be classified as a publisher for having brought people into contact.[56]

Following this trend, the US Court of Appeals for the Ninth Circuit has confirmed the interpretation as well as the external perspective in relation to material support in the *Fields v Twitter case*.[57] The US Court of Appeals for the Ninth Circuit dismissed the plaintiffs' requests on the grounds that the requirement for the application of the legislation to terrorist crimes is proximate causation and not simple causation or foreseeability. According to the court:

> Communication services and equipment are highly interconnected with modern economic and social life, such that the provision of these services and equipment to terrorists could be expected to cause ripples of harm to flow far beyond the defendant's misconduct. Nothing in § 2333 indicates that Congress intended to provide a remedy to every person reached by these ripples; instead, Congress intentionally used the 'by reason of' language to limit recovery. Moreover, we are troubled by the seemingly boundless litigation risks that would be posed by extending the ATA's bounds as far as foreseeability may reach.[58]

As regards material support for a terrorist organisation, it is also possible to identify a decision which appears to apply an internal perspective. Indeed, there is probably one case – which was not, however, considered by the US Supreme Court, certiorari having been refused – that follows an opposite trend: the *Mehanna* case.[59] This case involved an American citizen who provided assistance in relation to jihadist propaganda by translating certain Al-Qaida material into English and was also involved in other activities such as a failed attempt to locate an Al-Qaida training camp in Yemen. As already seen, terrorist propaganda is punishable only if it is coordinated with a terrorist group. Otherwise, it can be considered as independent advocacy and, thus, falls within the category of hate speech.

[55] Dissenting and concurring opinion of Justice Katzmann, *Force v Facebook Inc* No 18-397 (2d Cir 2019) 3.

[56] ibid 2.

[57] *Fields v Twitter Inc* 881 F3d 739 (9th Cir 2018).

[58] ibid 749.

[59] *United States v Mehanna* 735 F3d 32 (1st Cir 2013).

The *Mehanna* case is relevant since it shows how the digital environment influences not only the balancing process, but also the internal perspective of the US Court of Appeals for the First Circuit. In fact, coordination was proved not by direct contact but by virtue of the fact that a translation was provided to a website considered to be close to Al-Qaida as well as a range of other elements.[60] What is important in this decision is the relevance given to Internet innovation. The court observed that '[t]he government claimed that Mehanna had direct contact with al Qaeda because he responded to al Qaeda's public call for support'.[61] This element was considered to be relevant because the terrorist organisation had made a call for Internet support and online propaganda.[62] It should be stressed that the partial change in the attitude towards hate speech online is evident within a legal system where hate speech such as that indulged in by the Ku Klux Klan (albeit domestic) is considered to constitute speech protected by the First Amendment. This could amount to the first case involving an internal perspective, which highlights the need for a different balancing of rights in the online world. However, the denial of the writ of certiorari by the US Supreme Court leaves the matter open to different interpretations.[63]

In this sense, it should be recalled that the federal courts have applied an external perspective and extended the rules and guarantees of the First Amendment to all online conduct, even in relation to the most atypical ones such as the use of 'like' on Facebook. Translating the categories of free speech into the online world, the US Court of Appeals for the Fourth Circuit has claimed that the 'like' on Facebook constitutes symbolic speech: 'it is the Internet equivalent of displaying a political sign in one's front yard, which the Supreme Court has held is substantive speech'.[64]

Last but not least, a recent trend has been that of censorship of free speech on social networks, which confirms the same balancing process described above, ie the vesting of a right to free speech in Internet corporations and the prohibition on governmental enforcement of users' First Amendment rights online. One notable decision is that given in *Knight First Amendment Inst. at Columbia Univ. v Trump*.[65] In this case, certain social media users were prevented from accessing

[60] Christopher Pochon, 'Applying the Holder Standard to Speech That Provides Material Support to Terrorism in United States v. Mehanna, No. 09-10017-GAO (D. MASS. 2012)' (2013) 36 *Harvard Journal of Law & Public Policy* 375, 378; David Cole, '39 Ways to Limit Free Speech' *The New York Review of Books* (2012) at www.nybooks.com/blogs/nyrblog/2012/apr/19/39-ways-limit-free-speech/.

[61] Nikolas Abel, 'United States vs. Mehanna, the First Amendment, and Material Support in the War on Terror' (2013) 54 *Boston College Law Review* 711, 734.

[62] ibid 724.

[63] Vittoria Barsotti, *L'arte di tacere. Strumenti e tecniche di non decisione della Corte suprema degli Stati Uniti* (Turin, Giappichelli, 1999).

[64] *Bland v Roberts* 730 F3d 368 (4th Cir 2013) 386.

[65] *Knight First Amendment Inst at Columbia Univ v Trump* No 18-1691-cv (2nd Cir 2019). See for some remarks also Marco Bassini, *Internet e libertà di espressione. Prospettive costituzionali e sovranazionali* (Rome, Aracne, forthcoming 2020), who notes that these developments show the controversial qualification of digital platforms in terms of an essential facility for the exercise of freedom of speech, which accordingly could be equalised to state actors and thus subjected to the same obligations applicable to public authorities. See also Tim Wu, 'Is the First Amendment Obsolete?' (2018) 547 *Michigan Law Review* 117.

and interacting with the Twitter account *@realDonaldTrump* – the private account of President Donald Trump – by President Trump himself or his staff due to comments they had made when replying to Trump's tweets. The plaintiff alleged that the block violated the First Amendment. The US Court of Appeals for the Second Circuit held:

> We do not consider or decide whether an elected official violates the Constitution by excluding persons from a wholly private social media account. Nor do we consider or decide whether private social media companies are bound by the First Amendment when policing their platforms. We do conclude, however, that the First Amendment does not permit a public official who utilizes a social media account for all manner of official purposes to exclude persons from an otherwise-open online dialogue because they expressed views with which the official disagrees.[66]

In this case, the US Court of Appeals for the Second Circuit adopted an external perspective. Although the decision takes into account every individual aspect of the mode of operation of Twitter and reflects a profound knowledge of how the social network concerned operates, it applies the doctrine of the public forum simply because the President used the account as one of the most effective ways of disseminating his political agenda. The innovative aspect of the decision consists in the fact that it frames the virtual space of a Twitter account as a public forum. However, it is important to draw a distinction between the framework of the social network overall and Donald Trump's individual account. It is only the latter that could be considered as a public forum, and its censorship should be regarded as equivalent to offline governmental restrictions. Indeed, as was stressed by the US Court of Appeals for the Second Circuit, it is the use made by a public and governmental figure – such as the President – that transforms a private space into a public one:

> The Account was intentionally opened for public discussion when the President, upon assuming office, repeatedly used the Account as an official vehicle for governance and made its interactive features accessible to the public without limitation. We hold that this conduct created a public forum.[67]

And, in consequence: 'By blocking the Individual Plaintiffs and preventing them from viewing, retweeting, replying to, and liking his tweets, the President excluded the Individual Plaintiffs from a public forum, something the First Amendment prohibits'.[68]

This decision has not changed the established case law on the status of online platforms – social networks *in primis* – as private forums and their self-standing right to free speech, which allows them to censor their users.[69] In this

[66] *Knight First Amendment Inst at Columbia Univ v Trump* (n 65) 4.

[67] ibid 23.

[68] ibid 24.

[69] In recent years (from 2018) the numbers of decisions applying this rationale have been increasing in the federal circuits, see *ex pluribus*: *Brittain v Twitter Inc* WL 2423375 (ND Cal 2019); *Fyk v Facebook Inc* no C 18-05159 JSW (ND Cal 2019); explicitly about the refusal of the application of the state

way, the courts have held that the state action doctrine does not apply to online platforms.[70] For example, the case of *Dipp-Paz v Facebook*,[71] in which the plaintiff sued Facebook, alleging an infringement of his right to free speech, shows how the courts are now spilling less ink when justifying the dismissal of actions of this type. According to the US District Court for the Southern District of New York, 'Facebook is a private corporation, and Plaintiff does not allege any facts suggesting that Facebook's actions are attributable to the state'.[72]

It is clear that the perspective offered by this case is close to the decision in *Baidu* case as regards search engines and is consistent with the 'traditional' and broad interpretation of Section 230 CDA, which has recently been called into question by the executive order 13925 issued on 28 May 2020 by President Donald Trump, as we shall see in Chapter 4. This traditionally highly protective approach also has an effect on the fight against fake news and information disorder (it is no coincidence that the decision to undermine the application of Section 230 CDA was taken after a specific fact-checking feature had been rolled out by Twitter). Even if fake news is protected by the First Amendment, Facebook has started a campaign to take down fake news factories, especially those linked to foreign propaganda (ie from Russia). It took this action for the Federal Agency of News (FAN), which was taken down by Facebook because it was controlled by a Russian agency.[73] According to the US District Court for the Northern District of California's reasoning when dismissing the case with prejudice, it is clear that Facebook meets all the requirements of Section 230 CDA:

> Plaintiffs again argue that Section 230 does not immunize Facebook because the instant case 'does not concern obscenity or any other form of unprotected speech; it concerns political speech that strikes at the heart of the First Amendment.' … It is telling that Plaintiffs fail to cite any authority for this argument. Immunity under the Section 230 does not contain a political speech exception.[74]

In conclusion, by ruling that Facebook does not have the status of a public forum and that the First Amendment need not be respected on Internet platforms, the US District Court for the Northern District of California legitimised the possibility for online platforms to engage in a deeper battle against fake news. Specifically, it confirmed the applicability of an external perspective, which does not fully consider the vast impact of new technologies.

action doctrine: *Johnson v Twitter Inc* no 18ECG00078 (Cal Superior Ct 2018) and *Williby v Zuckerberg* 3:18-cv-06295-JD (ND Cal 2019).

[70] Kate Klonick, 'The New Governors: The People, Rules, and Processes Governing Online Speech' (2018) 131 *Harvard Law Review* 1599; *contra*: Jonathan Peters, 'The "Sovereigns of Cyberspace" and State Action: The First Amendment's Application (or Lack Thereof) to Third-Party Platforms' (2017) 32 *Berkeley Technology Law Journal* 989.

[71] *Dipp-Paz v Facebook Inc* WL 3205842 (SDNY 2019).

[72] ibid 3.

[73] *Federal Agency of News LLC v Facebook Inc* WL 137154 (ND Cal 2020). See also *Federal Agency of News LLC v Facebook Inc* WL 3254208 (ND Cal 2019).

[74] *Federal Agency of News LLC v Facebook Inc* WL 137154 (n 73) 14.

In this sense, it must be recalled that most of the case law concerning new technologies and free speech online has been developed in the federal circuit, and that a decision by the US Supreme Court could reverse the established process for balancing free speech and other rights online. As noted above, the US Supreme Court's decision in *Manhattan Community Access Corp v Halleck* has not paved the way for new tendencies or a new balancing process, as many commentators thought it might.[75] The developments that this decision might have triggered, as well as new trends and scholars' theories, will be explored in Chapter 4.

In conclusion, the picture painted with regard to the US proves that the advent of the Internet has resulted in a further enhancement of the already vast protection enjoyed by freedom of speech in the world of atoms. The First Amendment has not only retained, but has also increased its value in the new digital context, at least until President Trump's Executive Order 13925, the consequences of which are nevertheless still to be appreciated. The US Supreme Court may also wade into this debate, which could certainly provide it with a good opportunity to confirm this protective stance, or to revisit it. Bearing this reservation in mind as regards potential developments in the near future, the next section will demonstrate that the position in Europe seems to be the opposite.

III. The European Judicial Landscape of Freedom of Expression

As shown in the previous section, US courts have preserved the very broad protection granted to freedom of expression under the First Amendment, in spite of the fact that First Amendment rights are now more likely to enter into conflict with other rights or interests in the digital domain. Nonetheless, the US courts have adopted a quite broad frame of protection for free speech, even when it clashes with other fundamental rights. We must now consider the impact which the Internet has had on this side of the Atlantic.

As already mentioned in Chapter 1, the European approach to freedom of expression is more cautious. The exercise of this fundamental right must be balanced against the protection of other interests. This is not a merely theoretical point, but is also clearly apparent from the approach taken by the European courts in the field of freedom of expression online. The courts within the ECHR and EU systems have interpreted respectively Article 10 ECHR and Article 11 EUCFR as the key provisions on which protection for freedom of expression in Europe is based. Through their judgments they have clarified the scope of the protection afforded to free speech in Europe. It was initially the task of the ECtHR to scrutinise the legislation of Contracting States alleged to be in breach of Article 10 ECHR. However, the CJEU has now also progressively developed case law on

[75] *Manhattan Community Access Corp v Halleck* (n 36).

freedom of expression, according to a trend that is consistent with the emancipation of the EU from its original economic nature.

It is worth stressing that, unlike the Council of Europe framework, the CJEU is competent to handle matters involving EU secondary legislation on freedom of expression. The amendments to the Audiovisual Media Services Directive,[76] the Terrorism Directive or the Copyright Directive provide just some examples of how regulation has influenced freedom of expression online.[77] With specific regard to the Internet, the primary legal framework concerns information society services. Directive 2000/31, in particular, introduced certain provisions which exempt Internet service providers from liability, provided that certain conditions are met.[78] The basic assumption is that a service provider has no control over the content transmitted and, provided that it does not carry out any editorial activity, it does not bear any responsibility for illegal content posted by individuals when using its services. These principles are enshrined in Articles 12 to 14 of the e-Commerce Directive, together with Article 15 of the e-Commerce Directive, which provides that Internet service providers (ISPs) are not generally obliged to monitor online third-party content. As we will see, the most important decisions of the CJEU have been based on this principle.

Having stressed this non-exhaustive framework, it is essential to focus on how the European courts have balanced freedom of expression online. The next subsections will demonstrate the significance of the judicial frame adopted by the Strasbourg court and the CJEU in the shift from atoms to bits.

A. The Jurisprudence of the Strasbourg Court

Starting with an analysis of the case law on Article 10 ECHR, it is worth noting that the scope of the protection guaranteed under this provision has been defined with reference to the real world, and hence offline.

In *Handyside*[79] the ECtHR rejected a complaint brought by an editor who had been convicted of having published a schoolbook containing sexually explicit content. The court found that the restrictions to freedom of expression imposed in the case, including the seizure of copies of the book, met the criteria set forth

[76] Directive (EU) 2018/1808 of the European Parliament and of the Council of 14 November 2018 amending Directive 2010/13/EU on the coordination of certain provisions laid down by law, regulation or administrative action in Member States concerning the provision of audiovisual media services (Audiovisual Media Services Directive) in view of changing market realities.

[77] Directive (EU) 2017/541 of the European Parliament and of the Council of 15 March 2017 on combating terrorism and replacing Council Framework Decision 2002/475/JHA and amending Council Decision 2005/671/JHA; Directive (EU) 2019/790 of the European Parliament and of the Council of 17 April 2019 on copyright and related rights in the Digital Single Market and amending Directives 96/9/EC and 2001/29/EC.

[78] Directive 2000/31/EC on certain legal aspects of information society services, in particular electronic commerce, in the internal market (e-commerce Directive).

[79] *Handyside v United Kingdom*, App no 5493/72, judgment of 7 December 1976.

under Article 10(2) ECHR. However, what is notable in this decision is an obiter dictum where the court stressed that

> [f]reedom of expression constitutes one of the essential foundations of such a society, one of the basic conditions for its progress and for the development of every man. Subject to paragraph 2 of Article 10, it is applicable not only to 'information' or 'ideas' that are favourably received or regarded as inoffensive or as a matter of indifference, but also to those that offend, shock or disturb the State or any sector of the population. Such are the demands of that pluralism, tolerance and broadmindedness without which there is no 'democratic society'.[80]

According to the ECHR, freedom of expression also extends to offensive, shocking or disturbing expressions with respect to the State or to any part of the population and this is necessary in order to meet the demand for pluralism, tolerance and openness necessary in a democratic society. Indeed, this ruling considerably widens the boundaries of freedom of expression, stating that even content that would be considered by society as shocking or offensive cannot be deprived of protection as free speech. Therefore, the level of social approval for an expression cannot be regarded as a criterion justifying protection for it. As a result, this approach would seem to support the idea that the more the panorama of ideas and opinions are varied, the more the democratic character of a democracy will benefit.

The case of *Jersild*[81] is of particular importance in the field of freedom of expression. With regard to hate speech,[82] it should be noted that the ECtHR has often referred to the 'abuse clause' enshrined in Article 17 ECHR, preventing the exercise of the fundamental rights protected under the Convention in a way that is likely to undermine the enjoyment of other freedoms established therein.[83] In other words, the ECtHR has pointed out that to dispute the existence of 'clearly established historical events' amounts to an abuse of freedom of expression that Contracting States may legitimately restrict – upon certain conditions – when it is necessary to preserve other fundamental values underlying the Convention.[84] This has allowed some Contracting States, including Austria, France and Germany, to enact laws against hate speech.[85]

[80] ibid para 49.

[81] *Jersild v Denmark*, App no 15890/89, judgment of 23 September 1994.

[82] On this issue see also Françoise Tulkens, 'Freedom of Expression and Hate Speech in the Case-law of the European Court of Human Rights' in Josep Casadevall, Egbert Myjer and Michael O'Boyle (eds), *Freedom of Expression. Essays in Honour of Nicolas Bratza* (Oisterwijk, Wolf Legal Publishers, 2012) 349.

[83] For a deeper analysis of the abuse clause, see Hannes Cannie and Dirk Voorhoof, 'The Abuse Clause and Freedom of Expression in the European Human Rights Convention: An Added Value for Democracy and Human Rights Protection?' (2011) 29 *Netherlands Quarterly of Human Rights* 54.

[84] *Garaudy v France*, App no 65831/01, admissibility decision, 24 June 2003. See also *Peta Deutschland v Germany*, App no 43481/09, judgment of 8 November 2012.

[85] *Lehideux and Isorni v France*, App no 24662/94, judgment of 23 September 1998. In this regard, see Robert A Kahn, 'Why Do Europeans Ban Hate Speech? A Debate Between Karl Lowenstein and Robert Post' (2013) 41 *Hofstra Law Review* 545.

Returning to *Jersild*, the ECtHR paid particular attention to the place where offensive expressions were formulated. The applicant was a journalist sentenced in Denmark for having interviewed several members of a young racist organisation in which offensive and insulting expressions were used. Although Mr Jersild had clearly dissociated himself from these statements and rebutted some of them, he was convicted of aiding and abetting the youths interviewed. The ECtHR said that, under the circumstances of the case, interference with the enjoyment of freedom of expression was not necessary in a democratic society and that, in particular, the means employed were disproportionate to the aim of protecting the reputation or rights of others.

In the leading case of *Sunday Times*,[86] the ECtHR found for the first time that Article 10 ECHR had been violated. The case concerned a court order preventing the publication by a newspaper of an article concerning drugs. The court held that the restriction was not 'necessary in a democratic society'. It is thus clear how review under Article 10 ECHR operates as an additional layer of control over protection for freedom of expression in Europe.

Having regard to these cases, there are clear indications that the scope of protection should be broad, covering even those expressions that do not make a significant contribution to public opinion or that have disturbing content.[87] However, it must be stressed that the 'flexible' approach of the Strasbourg court in respect of the possible limitations to freedom of expression does not constitute a new approach. The cases handled by the ECtHR prior to the development of new technologies prove that the Strasbourg court was ready to enforce Article 10(2) ECHR. However, in contrast to the trend within the US Supreme Court, it appears that the advent of the Internet has further extended the scope for limiting freedom of expression, provided that the conditions laid down in Article 10(2) ECHR have been met by the national legislation.

Although the court has repeatedly held that Article 10(2) ECHR must be construed narrowly, the Internet has resulted in an increase in cases involving restrictions on the right to freedom of expression. Considering the decisions in which the ECtHR has been asked to rule on complaints involving alleged violations of freedom of expression online, it is possible to discern an opposite trend to the expansive scope that had previously characterised that court's case law on the application of Article 10 ECHR in the world of atoms. While the 'relative' status of

[86] *The Sunday Times v United Kingdom*, App no 6538/74, judgment of 26 April 1979.

[87] However, it is necessary to observe that the application of Article 17 ECHR by the Strasbourg court, which prohibits the abuse of a right understood as a constraint on other rights or freedoms or limitation of the same in a more severe manner than that provided by the Convention has led to exclude the balancing process among fundamental rights in case of abuse of rights. See *Garaudy* (n 84); *Ivanov v Russia*, App no 40450/04, judgment of 15 October 2009; *Norwood v United Kingdom*, App no 23131/03, admissibility decision, 16 November 2004. In other cases of hate speech, however, the ECtHR focused on the possible impact on Art 10 of the ECHR. See *Perinçek v Switzerland*, App no 27510/08, judgment of 15 October 2015; *Lehideux and Isorni* (n 85).

the fundamental rights protected by the Convention is nothing new, this element has been particularly stressed in cases involving the Internet.[88] In particular, in the view of the European courts, the Internet has contributed to amplifying the threats posed by the exercise of freedom of expression. In other words, owing to the risks relating to the use of digital technologies, the approach to freedom of expression online is more restrictive.

Although the use of the Internet had already come into play, albeit indirectly, in previous judgments such as *Editions Plon v France*,[89] *Ovchinnikov v Russia*[90] and *Perrin v UK*,[91] this specific point emerged, for the first time, in *Editorial Board of Pravoye Delo and Shtekel v Ukraina*,[92] which concerned the particular aspect of freedom of expression relating to freedom of the press:

> The risk of harm posed by content and communications on the Internet to the exercise and enjoyment of human rights and freedoms, particularly the right to respect for private life, is certainly higher than that posed by the press. Therefore, the policies governing reproduction of material from the printed media and the Internet may differ. The latter undeniably have to be adjusted according to technology's specific features in order to secure the protection and promotion of the rights and freedoms concerned.[93]

The assumptions behind the reasoning of the ECtHR are that the Internet is likely to give rise to new problems for the protection of fundamental rights and also that the measures applicable to traditional media will not work effectively in the new digital environment. A new balance must therefore be sought between freedom of expression and other human rights. In a nutshell, since the Internet has given rise to unprecedented legal issues, restrictions to freedom of expression should be more broadly accepted.

Unlike the US Supreme Court which, as previously explained, in *Reno* immediately highlighted the potential of the digital environment for an expansion (defined as 'phenomenal') of scope for freedom of thought, the European court appeared to be concerned by the risks associated with the use of the Internet for other fundamental rights.[94] The following remark could per se be sufficient to describe how different the approach of the ECtHR has been from that of the US

[88] For a very comprehensive overview of the case law of the Strasbourg court on Art 10 ECHR in the digital age, see Dirk Voorhoof, 'Same Standards, Different Tools? The ECtHR and the Protection and Limitations of Freedom of Expression in the Digital Environment' in Council of Europe, *Human Rights Challenges in the Digital Age: Judicial Perspectives* (Strasbourg, Council of Europe Publishing, 2020) 11. In this respect, see also Róbert Spanó, 'Summary of the Issues Discussed During the Seminar: An Aerial View' in Council of Europe, *Human Rights Challenges in the Digital Age: Judicial Perspectives* (Strasbourg, Council of Europe Publishing, 2020) 201.

[89] *Editions Plon v France*, App no 58148/2000, judgment of 18 August 2004.

[90] *Ovchinnikov v Russia*, App no 24061/04, judgment of 16 March 2011.

[91] *Perrin v UK*, App no 5446/03, judgment of 18 October 2005.

[92] *Editorial Board of Pravoye Delo and Shtekel v Ukraine*, App no 33014/05, judgment of 05 August 2011

[93] ibid para 63.

[94] Pollicino and Bassini (n 3).

Supreme Court, which, in the decision mentioned above, expressed a diametrically opposite viewpoint:

> The record demonstrates that the growth of the Internet has been and continues to be phenomenal. As a matter of constitutional tradition, in the absence of evidence to the contrary, we presume that governmental regulation of the content of speech is more likely to interfere with the free exchange of ideas than to encourage it. The interest in encouraging freedom of expression in a democratic society outweighs any theoretical but unproven benefit of censorship.[95]

The two courts seem to be focused on different approaches: the US Supreme Court presumes that content regulation, and hence control over expression, does not result in greater benefits than freedom. On the other hand, the European approach is more sceptical as it takes into consideration dangers for other rights and, therefore, assumes the need to apply corrective measures that may limit the exercise of free speech. It should also be remembered that, as highlighted above, the European court has always considered freedom of expression, and in particular freedom of the press, to perform a watchdog function as regards the level of democracy.

This is confirmed, first of all, by considering how the ECtHR has responded to the use of the Internet with respect to freedom of the press, which is regarded as an essential part of freedom of speech and a pillar of democracy. In *Stoll*,[96] the assumption behind the reasoning of the ECtHR is that, by virtue of the new technologies, journalists' duties have become more demanding:

> [T]he safeguard afforded by Article 10 to journalists in relation to reporting on issues of general interest is subject to the proviso that they are acting in good faith and on an accurate factual basis and provide 'reliable and precise' information in accordance with the ethics of journalism … These considerations play a particularly important role nowadays, given the influence wielded by the media in contemporary society: not only do they inform, they can also suggest by the way in which they present the information how it is to be assessed. In a world in which the individual is confronted with vast quantities of information circulated via traditional and electronic media and involving an ever-growing number of players, monitoring compliance with journalistic ethics takes on added importance.[97]

In *KU v Finland*[98] the ECtHR highlighted the non-absolute nature of protection for certain fundamental rights on the Internet. The case concerned the dissemination of the personal data of a minor by an anonymous individual who had posted an online advertisement in which he claimed to be interested in starting a sexual relationship. When the applicant filed a complaint with the local court, there were no legal grounds under domestic law to force an ISP to disclose personal data in a case involving criminal conduct such as that at issue. The domestic legislation had

[95] *Reno v American Civil Liberties Union* (n 3) 885.
[96] *Stoll v Switzerland*, App no 69698/01, judgment of 10 December 2007.
[97] ibid paras 103–4.
[98] *KU v Finland*, App no 2872/02, judgment of 02 March 2009.

also failed to strike a balance between the right to data protection and other interests. Although the complaint was not based on Article 10 ECHR, the ECtHR made significant comments concerning freedom of speech on the Internet:

> Although freedom of expression and confidentiality of communications are primary considerations and users of telecommunications and Internet services must have a guarantee that their own privacy and freedom of expression will be respected, such guarantee cannot be absolute and must yield on occasion to other legitimate imperatives, such as the prevention of disorder or crime or the protection of the rights and freedoms of others … [I]t is nonetheless the task of the legislator to provide the framework for reconciling the various claims which compete for protection in this context.[99]

This vision was also confirmed in *Perrin v United Kingdom*.[100] The applicant contested his conviction, claiming a lack of jurisdiction since the website was based in the US, and also objected that the measures adopted by the court were disproportionate due to the nature of the Internet.[101] The applicant suggested that the balancing process on the Internet should be different compared to that applied offline. The ECtHR dismissed the case, holding that domestic law should be interpreted broadly. However, what is more relevant in that decision is the approach of the court to the new media as well as the fact that the process for balancing rights may have been transformed owing to the nature of the Internet. However, the applicant did not take the action necessary in order to avoid criminal punishment, as required by the English courts:

> The Court further observes that it would have been possible for the applicant to have avoided the harm and, consequently, the conviction, while still carrying on his business, by ensuring that none of the photographs were available on the free preview page (where there were no age checks). He chose not to do so, no doubt because he hoped to attract more customers by leaving the photographs on the free preview page.[102]

This case shows how the court's approach to new media is flexible and has paved the way for changes to the process for balancing fundamental rights where certain conditions are met. In this case, the Strasbourg court seems to have endorsed the stance adopted by the English court concerning the nature of the Internet – where 'people are able to make very substantial profits',[103] and this type of content is available 'to anyone surfing the Internet and that, in any event, the material was, as pointed out by the Court of Appeal, the very type of material which might be sought out by young persons whom the national authorities were trying to protect'.[104]

[99] ibid para 49.

[100] *Perrin v UK* (n 91), Reports of Judgments and Decisions 2005-XI 323.

[101] 'As to proportionality, he pointed out that similar material was readily available on the internet and that there were better means of inhibiting access, such as industry self-regulation, blockage by service providers and steps taken at home', ibid 328.

[102] ibid 334.

[103] ibid 329.

[104] ibid 333.

The influence of new media in the reasoning of the court and in the balancing process between fundamental rights is evident also in *Willem v France.*[105] The case concerned a call by a French mayor to boycott Israeli products, which was classified as hate speech by the French Supreme Court. The call for a boycott was made both orally, as reported in a newspaper, and through the website of the municipality. According to the French Supreme Court, the message posted on the Internet 'aggravated' the conduct:

> La Cour note que la Cour de cassation a non seulement pris en compte l'annonce du boycott faite oralement lors du conseil municipal mais également le message diffusé sur le site Internet de la commune. A cet égard, ce message a aggravé le caractère discriminatoire de la position du requérant, confortée ainsi par l'utilisation de termes polémiques.[106]

In this regard, it is important to stress that the ECtHR did not express any view as to whether a message posted online is stronger than an offline message, and appeared to accept the stance of the French Supreme Court, legitimising the action under the margin of appreciation.

In the case of *Times Newspapers v United Kingdom*,[107] concerning defamation online caused by news items initially published by *The Times* both offline and online, the Strasbourg court had the opportunity to clarify several principles related to the right to freedom of expression online. Under domestic law, the action was brought specifically against the digital version of the articles published in *The Times*. The plaintiffs contested in particular the action taken by English courts against online archives, arguing that Article 10 ECHR had been violated. The court thus upheld the importance of the Internet in the spread of news and the protection of archives under Article 10:

> In the light of its accessibility and its capacity to store and communicate vast amounts of information, the Internet plays an important role in enhancing the public's access to news and facilitating the dissemination of information in general. The maintenance of Internet archives is a critical aspect of this role and the Court therefore considers that such archives fall within the ambit of the protection afforded by Article 10.[108]

Although the applicant stressed the importance of the integrity of historical sources for a democratic society, the ECtHR recognised the States' margin of appreciation in restricting online archives:

> The Court agrees at the outset with the applicant's submissions as to the substantial contribution made by Internet archives to preserving and making available news and information. Such archives constitute an important source for education and historical research, particularly as they are readily accessible to the public and are generally free.

[105] *Willem v France*, App no 10883/05, judgment of 10 December 2009.

[106] ibid para 36.

[107] *Case of Times Newspapers Ltd (nos 1 and 2) v The United Kingdom*, App nos 3002/03 and 23676/03, judgment of 10 June 2009.

[108] ibid para 27.

> The Court therefore considers that, while the primary function of the press in a democracy is to act as a 'public watchdog', it has a valuable secondary role in maintaining and making available to the public archives containing news which has previously been reported. However, the margin of appreciation afforded to States in striking the balance between the competing rights is likely to be greater where news archives of past events, rather than news reporting of current affairs, are concerned. In particular, the duty of the press to act in accordance with the principles of responsible journalism by ensuring the accuracy of historical, rather than perishable, information published is likely to be more stringent in the absence of any urgency in publishing the material.[109]

On these bases, the Strasbourg court held that the requirement to publish a 'notice' on newspaper articles contained in the archives regarding the fact that they are subject to litigation for defamation does not constitute a violation of Article 10 ECHR.[110] In this way, the court considered the particular nature of digital archives, thus assuming an internal perspective. This approach has influenced the balancing of fundamental rights – from the proportionality viewpoint – in consideration of new technological innovations.

The ECtHR has only adopted a stricter approach when the limitations imposed on freedom of expression are excessive compared to the aim pursued. For instance, this was the case in *Ahmet Yıldırım v Turkey*,[111] where the Strasbourg court concluded that Turkey had violated Article 10 ECHR by imposing a disproportionate restriction on Internet access. With reference to criminal proceedings against the owner of a website on which expressions insulting Atatürk's memory had been posted, an administrative authority imposed a block on the entire Google Sites service in order to prevent access to the site in question, without first considering whether a less far-reaching measure could have been ordered. The applicant, who owned a website on which his academic works were published and which was affected by the extension of the blocking order, alleged a violation of his right to freedom of expression. The Strasbourg court noted that the blocking of a website falls within the legitimate restrictions that Contracting States may adopt in accordance with Article 10(2) ECHR, but only on condition that such a restriction meets the requirements referenced therein. In this case, a strict legal framework defining the scope of the ban was lacking, and there was no provision for judicial review. Of particular interest in this decision is the attempt to broaden the rules applicable

[109] ibid para 45.

[110] 'The Court notes the conclusion of the Court of Appeal that the attachment of a notice to archive copies of material which it is known may be defamatory would "normally remove any sting from the material". To the extent that the applicant maintains that such an obligation is excessive, the Court observes that the Internet archive in question is managed by the applicant itself. It is also noteworthy that the Court of Appeal did not suggest that potentially defamatory articles should be removed from archives altogether. In the circumstances, the Court, like the Court of Appeal, does not consider that the requirement to publish an appropriate qualification to an article contained in an Internet archive, where it has been brought to the notice of a newspaper that a libel action has been initiated in respect of that same article published in the written press, constitutes a disproportionate interference with the right to freedom of expression', ibid para 47.

[111] *Ahmet Yıldırım v Turkey*, App no 3111/10, judgment of 18 March 2013.

to the press on the new phenomenon of the Internet, including in particular the limits of prior restrictions, which also have to be applied to publications other than newspapers that deal with a topical issue. Considering the risk as well as the actual collateral censorship that was a direct consequence of the measure adopted, and the absence of any guarantees, the ECtHR further observed that

> the measure in question produced arbitrary effects and could not be said to have been aimed solely at blocking access to the offending website, since it consisted in the wholesale blocking of all the sites hosted by Google Sites. Furthermore, the judicial review procedures concerning the blocking of Internet sites are insufficient to meet the criteria for avoiding abuse, as domestic law does not provide for any safeguards to ensure that a blocking order in respect of a specific site is not used as a means of blocking access in general.[112]

The approach of the ECtHR has proved to be very cautious. On the one hand, it has held that Article 10 ECHR is violated whenever the restrictions to freedom of expression do not fulfil the conditions set forth under Article 10(2) ECHR. On the other hand, however, the Strasbourg court has conceded that free speech is not an absolute right, or a right to which a greater protection is attached compared to other fundamental rights. In addition, given the risks that the Internet entails, there is more scope for limiting the right to freedom of expression online than that there is in the non-digital context.

A very similar case is *Cengiz and Others v Turkey* in which Turkish authorities blocked access to YouTube because of the presence of certain videos which were considered to insult the memory of Atatürk.[113] The ECtHR took care in distinguishing this case, concerning the free speech of YouTube users, from cases in which a blocking order affects only the possibility to use a platform.[114] After restating the importance of the Internet for free speech, the Strasbourg court considered the particular nature of YouTube:

> In this connection, the Court observes that YouTube is a video-hosting website on which users can upload, view and share videos and is undoubtedly an important means of exercising the freedom to receive and impart information and ideas. In particular, as the applicants rightly noted, political content ignored by the traditional media is often shared via YouTube, thus fostering the emergence of citizen journalism. From that perspective, the Court accepts that YouTube is a unique platform on account of its characteristics, its accessibility and above all its potential impact, and that no alternatives were available to the applicants.[115]

[112] ibid para 68.

[113] *Cengiz and Others v Turkey*, App nos 48226/10 and 14027/11, judgment of 01 March 2016.

[114] 'The present case also differs in another respect from that in Akdeniz, where the Court had regard, inter alia, to the fact that the applicant could easily have had access to a whole range of musical works by a variety of means without infringing copyright rules (ibid § 25). YouTube, however, not only hosts artistic and musical works, but is also a very popular platform for political speeches and political and social activities', ibid para 51.

[115] ibid para 52.

As a consequence, the ECtHR found that Article 10 ECHR had been violated due to the collateral effects of blocking YouTube:[116]

> Indeed, as is apparent from the Government's observations and the practice of the Turkish authorities, URL filtering technology for foreign-based websites is not available in Turkey. In practice, therefore, to implement court decisions concerning specific content, an administrative authority – the TİB – decided to block all access to the entire website in question. As the Court has already held in Ahmet Yıldırım, the authorities should have taken into consideration, among other aspects, the fact that such a measure, by rendering large quantities of information inaccessible, was bound to substantially restrict the rights of Internet users and to have a significant collateral effect.[117]

This paragraph is particularly interesting because it takes account of the different technologies available when striking a balance between fundamental rights online, which seems to suggest that it will be necessary to develop more advanced technologies in order to ensure a better balance of the various interests online.

More recently,[118] the ECtHR had to decide a case related to Mr Kharitonov, the owner and administrator of the website 'Electronic Publishing News', which features a compilation of news, articles and reviews about electronic publishing. The website is hosted by DreamHost, a service which hosts multiple websites, all with the same Internet protocol (IP) address but different domain names. In late 2012 the applicant became aware that access to his website had been blocked by a number of Russian ISPs as a result of an order of the Russian telecoms regulator (*Roskomnadzor*), which, in turn, had given effect to a decision of the Federal Drug Control Service. The order was directed at blocking another website, rastaman.tales.ru ('a collection of cannabis-themed folk stories'), also hosted by DreamHost and sharing the same IP address as Electronic Publishing News. In March 2013 the blocking of the IP address ceased. Mr Kharitonov brought a claim to the Taganskiy District Court in Moscow, arguing that the decision to block the entire IP address had resulted in the undue blocking of his website, which did not contain any illegal information.

The action at both first instance and on appeal failed. In 2014 the Russian Constitutional Court also refused to consider a separate application filed by Kharitonov, who eventually decided to bring his case against Russia to the ECtHR. The Strasbourg court began its assessment by referring to its prior decision in the already mentioned *Ahmet Yıldırım v Turkey*. Having noted the importance of the Internet to the exercise of freedom of expression and information, the ECtHR

[116] 'Having regard to the foregoing and to the need for flexible application of the criteria for acknowledging victim status, the Court accepts that, in the particular circumstances of the case, the applicants may legitimately claim that the decision to block access to YouTube affected their right to receive and impart information and ideas even though they were not directly targeted by it. It therefore dismisses the Government's preliminary objection as to victim status', ibid para 55. In this passage is it possible to identify an internal perspective in the recalled need for flexibility of the legal category in looking at Internet phenomena.

[117] ibid para 65.

[118] *Kharitonov v Russia*, App no 10795/14, judgment of 23 June 2020.

recalled that 'measures blocking access to websites are bound to have an influence on the accessibility of the Internet and, accordingly, engage the responsibility of the respondent State under Article 10'.[119] In the present case, the applicant had been prevented from sharing the latest developments and news about electronic publishing (ie exercising his freedom to impart information), while visitors to his website had had their freedom to receive information limited. Hence, such interference will constitute a breach of Article 10 ECHR unless it is 'prescribed by law', pursues one or more of the legitimate aims referred to in Article 10(2) ECHR and is 'necessary in a democratic society' to achieve those aims.

Under domestic law, the legal basis for the blocking had been section 15.1 of the Russian Information Act, which – noted the ECtHR 'with concern' – allows targeting of an entire website without distinguishing between the legal and illegal content that it may contain:

> Reiterating that the wholesale blocking of access to an entire website is an extreme measure which has been compared to banning a newspaper or television station, the Court considers that a legal provision giving an executive agency so broad a discretion carries a risk of content being blocked arbitrarily and excessively.[120]

This said, the requirement of 'prescribed by law' is not only fulfilled when the relevant authority acts in accordance with the letter of the law; rather, 'the Court must also ascertain whether the quality of the law in question enabled the applicant to regulate his conduct and protected him against arbitrary interference'.[121] This, concluded the ECtHR, was not the case in the present instance.

The cautious approach of the Strasbourg court can also be examined in the field of copyright. In the *Pirate Bay* case,[122] the applicants were the owners of a well-known online platform on which users were provided with links to download copyrighted materials illegally through the use of peer-to-peer systems. They had been convicted under a Swedish law which criminalised copyright infringements, but objected that this constituted a violation of their right to freedom of expression. The court ruled the complaint inadmissible as the restriction imposed on free speech fulfilled the conditions laid down by Article 10(2) ECHR, and in particular was proportionate to the legitimate aim pursued. Thus, the view taken by the Strasbourg court is that the advent of new technologies, and the Internet in particular, has not generally expanded the scope of freedom of expression. On the contrary, it has created more scope for this right to enter into conflict with other constitutional interests.

Similarly, in *Ashby Donald*[123] the ECtHR found that the applicants' conviction for copyright infringement committed by unlawfully reposting photographs on

[119] ibid para 35.
[120] ibid para 38.
[121] ibid para 40.
[122] *Fredrik Neij and Peter Sunde Kolmisoppi (The Pirate Bay) v Sweden*, App no 40397/12, judgment of 19 February 2013.
[123] *Ashby Donald and others v France*, App no 36769/08, judgment of 10 April 2013.

the Internet for commercial purposes did not amount to a violation of Article 10 ECHR. As has been noted by Voorhoof,

> [b]oth in *Ashby Donald and Others* and in *Neij and Sunde Kolmisoppi* [ie the *Pirate Bay* case] the Court is of the opinion that there were reasons to afford the State authorities a 'wide' margin of appreciation justifying the inference with the applicants' right of freedom of expression and information as guaranteed under the ECHR, being necessary in the interest of protecting the rights of the copyright-holders.[124]

Furthermore, these observations are still valid even where similar conduct occurs in the non-digital domain. Recalling the case of *Yıldırım v Turkey*, the broad limitation of freedom of expression implemented by the Turkish authorities would not have been necessary. In fact, Turkey was found to have violated Article 10 ECHR on the grounds that the blocking of all the sites hosted by Google was completely disproportionate. The measure was found to be general and, even if it was intended to block only the individual website concerned, its effect was to impede access to a large number of websites that were not committing the offence in question. If a single publication is found to be defamatory and there are legal grounds to prevent its circulation, the measures to be taken by the relevant authorities in the 'non-digital' world must concern only that publication, and not others as well. In other words, there will be no reason to block multiple online content instead of the content that is deemed to constitute an unlawful exercise of freedom of expression. The problem of proportionality, which is a key factor in this respect, is related to the nature of the technical means used and is one of the leading factors when addressing protection for freedom of expression online.

This argument applies, for example, to the case of *Delfi AS v Estonia*,[125] a landmark decision of the Grand Chamber of the ECtHR from 2015, which confirmed the approach towards limitations to freedom of expression online. In particular, 'defamatory and other types of clearly unlawful speech, including hate speech and speech inciting violence, can be disseminated like never before, worldwide, in a matter of seconds, and sometimes remain persistently available online'.[126] In this case, the ECtHR was asked for the first time to examine a complaint concerning liability for comments published by third parties on an online news portal. The Strasbourg court ruled that the finding by the Estonian courts that Delfi was liable had amounted to a justified and proportionate restriction on the portal's freedom of expression. Indeed, the order to pay a sum (in this case 320 euros) as compensation for the damage suffered by an individual as a consequence of certain defamatory comments which remained accessible for around six weeks alongside an article published on an online news portal did not constitute a disproportionate restriction on freedom of expression due to the need to balance it with the protection to be afforded to the other personality rights (such as honour and

[124] Voorhoof (n 88) 21.
[125] *Delfi AS v Estonia*, App no 64569/09, judgment of 16 June 2015.
[126] ibid para 110.

reputation) of the victim. It is important to stress the ECtHR's attitude in considering how the nature of the balancing of fundamental rights online might change as a result of new technological tools:

> On this basis, and in particular considering that this is the first case in which the Court has been called upon to examine a complaint of this type in an evolving field of technological innovation, the Court considers it necessary to delineate the scope of its inquiry in the light of the facts of the present case.[127]

This is quite evident within the reasons provided in relation to prior checks of comments, in contrast to the position for printed media publications.[128] Consequently, the court stressed how the balancing process must be changed with regard to the Internet, which constitutes a new medium:

> Therefore, the Court considers that because of the particular nature of the Internet, the 'duties and responsibilities' that are to be conferred on an Internet news portal for the purposes of Article 10 may differ to some degree from those of a traditional publisher as regards third-party content.[129]

Recalling the case of *Editorial Board of Pravoye Delo and Shtekel v Ukraine*, the Strasbourg court stressed that

> [i]n this particular context the Court takes into account the fact that some countries have recognised that the importance and the complexity of the subject matter, involving the need to ensure proper balancing of different interests and fundamental rights, call for the enactment of specific regulations for situations such as that pertaining in the present case.[130]

As already explained, Article 10 ECHR does not afford absolute protection to freedom of expression. While the legislation at stake did impose a significant restriction, it was nevertheless held that it did not amount to a violation of Article 10 ECHR. According to the Strasbourg court, protecting an individual's reputation is one of the reasons that may justify a restriction of freedom of expression; as a result, the ECtHR held that there had been no infringement of Article 10 ECHR.

It must not be forgotten that the decisions of the ECtHR are based on a case-by-case assessment. This aspect makes it possible to consider radical rulings or statements in a manner which focuses on the specific case. However, a line of cases after *Delfi* seems to establish some form of scrutiny as regards the balancing of fundamental rights online. In fact, this case allows extrapolation of a

[127] ibid para 111.
[128] The ECtHR recognised that '[a]t the same time, because of the nature of Internet media, it cannot reasonably be required of a portal operator to edit comments before publishing them in the same manner as applies for a printed media publication. While the publisher [of a printed media publication] is, through editing, the initiator of the publication of a comment, on the Internet portal the initiator of publication is the author of the comment, who makes it accessible to the general public through the portal', ibid para 112.
[129] ibid para 113.
[130] ibid para 128.

multi-factor test for scrutinising the proportionality of national authorities' actions in similar cases.

In a similar case, the ECtHR reached different conclusions. In *MTE v Hungary*[131] the facts of the case were not substantially different as the complaint concerned the proportionality of a ruling against an online information portal due to defamatory comments published anonymously by third parties.[132] The court was thus considering defamatory comments posted by the readers of the website against certain companies. The Hungarian courts had found the owner of the website liable for the comments posted by readers. Even the Hungarian Constitutional Court did not consider the laws applied by the courts to be unconstitutional in any way. As was observed by the Strasbourg court:

> At this juncture the Court would add that the outcome of such a balancing performed by the domestic courts will be acceptable in so far as those courts applied the appropriate criteria and, moreover, weighed the relative importance of each criterion with due respect paid to the particular circumstances of the case. In the case of Delfi AS, the Grand Chamber identified the following specific aspects of freedom of expression in terms of protagonists playing an intermediary role on the Internet, as being relevant for the concrete assessment of the interference in question: the context of the comments, the measures applied by the applicant company in order to prevent or remove defamatory comments, the liability of the actual authors of the comments as an alternative to the intermediary's liability, and the consequences of the domestic proceedings for the applicant company.[133]

According to the ECtHR, the difference between the two cases in question concerns the nature of the offensive comments and their different disvalue. In *Delfi*, the content published by third parties amounted to a form of hate speech, being characterised by incitement to engage in violence and racial hatred, while in the case before it the absence of such a characteristic of manifest illegality justified a different approach towards the Internet service provider. In particular, according to the court:

> [I]n the case of Delfi AS, the Court found that if accompanied by effective procedures allowing for rapid response, the notice-and-take-down-system could function in many cases as an appropriate tool for balancing the rights and interests of all those involved. The Court sees no reason to hold that such a system could not have provided a viable avenue to protect the commercial reputation of the plaintiff. It is true that, in cases

[131] *Magyar Tartalomszolgáltatók Egyesülete and Index.hu Zrt v Hungary*, App no 22947/13, judgment of 02 May 2016.

[132] 'This is the first post-Delfi judgment, but, of course, it will not be the last. It is confined to the individual circumstances of this particular case. There will inevitably be other cases dealing with liability for the content of Internet messages and the administration thereof. Today, it is too early to draw generalising conclusions. One should look forward to these future cases, with the hope that the present judgment, although it may now appear to some as a step back from Delfi AS, will prove to be merely further evidence that the balance to be achieved in cases of this type is a very subtle one'. Concurring opinion of Judge Kūris, ibid, para 4.

[133] ibid paras 68–69.

> where third-party user comments take the form of hate speech and direct threats to the physical integrity of individuals, the rights and interests of others and of the society as a whole might entitle Contracting States to impose liability on Internet news portals if they failed to take measures to remove clearly unlawful comments without delay, even without notice from the alleged victim or from third parties. However, the present case did not involve such utterances.[134]

As mentioned above, the *Delfi* case led to a standard of scrutiny that allows for a particular balancing process to be applied in relation to freedom of expression online.[135] Consequently, the court considered whether the national courts had respected the standard developed by *Delfi*. Since this test was not met and the case did not concern hate speech, the court found that Article 10 ECHR had been violated. This decision illustrates that, as pointed out by Judge Spanó, compared to *MTE* the *Delfi* case retains greater value as a precedent,[136] although this does not necessarily depend on its status as a Grand Chamber judgment, but rather on the fact that it was the first case of this type to be decided in Strasbourg.[137]

From a not-dissimilar perspective, in *Phil v Sweden*,[138] while declaring the application inadmissible, the ECtHR explored another dimension to the standard developed in relation to the status and nature of comments. Once the Strasbourg court had found that the comment did not constitute hate speech, it dismissed the case by applying the standard developed in *MTE* and *Delfi*, finding that

> [i]n relation thereto, the Court attaches importance to the fact that the association is a small non-profit association, unknown to the wider public, and it was thus unlikely that it would attract a large number of comments or that the comment about the applicant would be widely read … As the Court found in Magyar Tartalomszolgáltatók

[134] ibid para 91.

[135] 'These latter criteria were established so as to assess the liability of large Internet news portals for not having removed from their websites, without delay after publication, comments that amounted to hate speech and incitement to violence. However, for the Court, they are also relevant for the assessment of the proportionality of the interference in the present case, free of the pivotal element of hate speech. It is therefore convenient to examine the balancing, if any, performed by the domestic courts and the extent to which the relevant criteria … were applied in that process, with regard to the specific aspects dictated by the applicants' respective positions', ibid para 70.

[136] Róbert Spanó, 'Intermediary Liability for Online User Comments under the European Convention on Human Rights' (2017) 17(4) *Human Rights Law Review* 665, 675.

[137] ibid 676 and 679. In the view of Spanó: 'the case is to some extent unique and unsuitable as a basis for broad interpretive conclusions over and above the facts presented by the case', so that the ECtHR itself circumscribed the scope of the decision, having regard to (a) the nature and the structure of the web portal where users had posted the relevant comments; (b) the content and the context of the comments, including the gravity of the same. Regarding the differences between the two cases and the comments pointing to the alleged difference in the applicable standard of protection, according to Spanó: 'in Delfi AS, by in some sense encouraging Contracting States to consider the beneficial value of the notice-and-take-down system as a suitable mechanism for balancing the relevant conflicting interests, the Court adopted a middle ground between two diametrically opposing viewpoints on the regulation of the Internet, one advocating for an environment relatively free from regulation of online conduct and the other campaigning for a regulated Internet where the same legal principles apply both online and offline'; on these grounds, in *MTE* the ECtHR developed its ruling.

[138] *Pihl v Sweden*, App no 74742/14, admissibility decision, 9 March 2017.

> Egyesülete and Index.hu Zrt …, expecting the association to assume that some unfiltered comments might be in breach of the law would amount to requiring excessive and impractical forethought capable of undermining the right to impart information via internet.[139]

In *Høiness v Norway*[140] the Strasbourg court addressed a case concerning comments in a forum associated with an online newspaper. The ECtHR took the opportunity to affirm once again the standard developed in *Delfi*. Starting from the assumption that Articles 8 and 10 ECHR deserve equal respect, the Strasbourg court recalled the test in *Delfi*:

> In making this proportionality assessment, the Court has also identified the following specific aspects of freedom of expression as being relevant for the concrete assessment of the interference in question: the context of the comments, the measures applied by the company in order to prevent or remove defamatory comments, the liability of the actual authors of the comments as an alternative to the intermediary's liability, and the consequences of the domestic proceedings for the company … The question is thus whether, in the present case, the State has struck a fair balance between the applicant's right to respect for her private life under Article 8 and the online news agency and forum host's right to freedom of expression guaranteed by Article 10 of the Convention.[141]

Reviewing the decisions of the national courts and using *Phil v Sweden* as a parameter, the ECtHR held that the balance proposed by the national courts was consistent with ECtHR case law and dismissed the case by applying the doctrine of the margin of appreciation.

In addition, in *Tamiz v UK*[142] the Strasbourg court distinguished cases similar to *Delfi* from other cases:

> [A]lthough the applicant relied heavily on Delfi …, the Court finds nothing in the judgment of the Grand Chamber that would cast doubt on that position. In Delfi the Grand Chamber was concerned with a large, professionally managed Internet news portal run on a commercial basis which published news articles of its own and invited its readers to comment on them; it expressly stated that it did not concern other Internet fora, such as a social media platform where the platform provider does not offer any content and where the content provider may be a private person running a website or blog as a hobby.[143]

What could be considered to be of interest in this decision is an obiter dictum, which apparently defines an autonomous right of Google to free speech,[144] which

[139] ibid para 31.
[140] *Høiness v Norway*, App no 43624/14, judgment of 19 June 2019.
[141] ibid paras 67–68.
[142] *Tamiz v United Kingdom*, App no 3877/14, admissibility decision, 12 October 2017.
[143] ibid para 85.
[144] 'It is true that the national courts did not expressly balance the applicant's right to respect for his reputation against the right to freedom of expression of both Google Inc. and its end users', ibid para 86.

was used as part of the rationale developed in order to declare the application inadmissible:

> [I]n other words, in applying this test the national courts were, in fact, ensuring that there would be no interference with Google Inc.'s right to freedom of expression in a case where the interference with the applicant's reputation was 'trivial'. Furthermore, while the domestic proceedings in the present case preceded delivery of the Grand Chamber judgment in Delfi, in substance the national courts addressed the specific aspects of freedom of expression identified therein as relevant for the concrete assessment of the interference in question …: namely, the nature of the comments and the context in which they were made …, the action taken by Google Inc. following notification …, the potential liability of the actual authors of the comments …, and the consequences of the domestic proceedings for both the applicant's reputation and for Google Inc.'s role as the provider of a platform for the free exchange of information and ideas.[145]

More recent cases have shown how the process of balancing fundamental rights online takes place. In the case of *Kablis v Russia*[146] the applicant organised a 'picket' to discuss local government corruption. He publicised the proposal on his personal blog, proposing that a 'people's assembly' be held if authorisation were to be refused by local authorities. The refusal of the picket in that place led the applicant to convene a 'people's assembly' through the blog, which did require authorisation. He then published another post on his blog inviting people to this rally. The last post was blocked by order of the Russian authorities. After the block was imposed, the plaintiff criticised the government's policy, and also the fact that the post was blocked by the website administrator on the instructions of the prosecutor. In addition, even his social network account was blocked. Within this scenario, the ECtHR stressed the importance of the Internet within the public debate and noted as follows:

> The Court finds that the blocking by a deputy Prosecutor General of the applicant's social networking account and of three entries on his blog on the grounds that they contained calls to participate in a public event the location of which had not been approved by the town administration amounted to 'interference by a public authority' with the applicant's right to freedom of expression, of which the freedom to receive and impart information and ideas is an integral part … That the applicant could create a new social networking account or publish new entries on his blog has no incidence on this finding.[147]

The violation of Article 10 ECHR was caused by the disproportionate nature of the measures taken, given also the fact that there was no risk of public disorder or criminal actions, and prior restraints must be accompanied by adequate judicial review (which was not available in this case).

[145] ibid para 87.
[146] *Kablis v Russia*, App nos 48310/16 and 59663/17, judgment of 09 September 2019.
[147] ibid para 84.

Finally, another very interesting case concerned threats and hate speech posted under a photo on Facebook of a gay couple kissing each other.[148] The applicants sought to obtain a conviction for the hate speech posted under the picture; however, all attempts failed and in some cases absurd arguments were adopted by the national courts.[149] Dismissing the national courts' argument concerning the publicity regime applicable to a post that is not shared only with Facebook friends,[150] coupled with the fact that different people were responsible for the hate speech and the incitement to violence,[151] the ECtHR stressed that

> [a]ccordingly, the Court does not find it unreasonable to hold that even the posting of a single hateful comment, let alone that such persons should be 'killed', on the first applicant's Facebook page was sufficient to be taken seriously. This is further supported by the fact that the photograph had 'gone viral' online and received more than 800 comments.[152]

In this sense, the Strasbourg court asserted the importance of the Internet in communicating hate speech and even the virality of the Facebook post, showing a keen eye for new online phenomena. Moreover, regarding the conduct on Facebook, it concluded as follows:

> The Court therefore also rejects the Government's argument that comments on Facebook are less dangerous than those on the Internet news portals .... Neither can it see as pertinent the Government's argument that the people who commented negatively on the Facebook page of the first applicant had not outnumbered the applicants and their supporters.[153]

In conclusion, the ECtHR held that the applicants' rights under Articles 8, 13 and 14 ECHR had been violated due to the failure by the public authorities to intervene.

Two other areas of the case law of the ECtHR deserve some analysis as regards the attitude to interpreting freedom of expression on the Internet.

[148] *Beizaras and Levickas v Lithuania*, App no 41288/15, judgment of 14 May 2020.

[149] 'The district court also pointed out that the first applicant's Facebook page, where the picture of the two men kissing had been posted, had been public, visible and accessible not only to his acquaintances and friends, but also to individuals who were completely unknown to him. Therefore, a person who posted in the public space (viešoje erdvėje) a picture "of two men kissing" should and must have foreseen that such "eccentric behaviour really did not contribute to the cohesion of those within society who had different views or to the promotion of tolerance"', ibid para 21.

[150] 'The Court thus recalls that the Klaipėda District Court considered that the picture of two men kissing did not contribute to social cohesion and the promotion of tolerance ... That view was fully endorsed by the Klaipėda Regional Court, which also found that it would have been preferable if the applicants had only shared such pictures among "like-minded people", since the Facebook social network allowed such a possibility', ibid 121.

[151] 'In this context the Court, whilst acknowledging that it is not its task to take the place of the domestic courts to resolve problems of interpretation of domestic legislation ..., does not disregard the argument that the LGL Association put forward in the domestic proceedings ..., namely that the number of the comments could constitute a circumstance determining the gravity of the crime or the extent of the culprit's criminal liability, but that it did not constitute an indispensable element of the crime under the aforementioned provision of the Criminal Code', ibid para 126.

[152] ibid para 127.

[153] ibid.

The first segment of case law concerns the conceptualisation of the right to access the Internet as an element of freedom of speech. The court delivered two judgments in *Kalda v Estonia*[154] and *Jankovskis v Lithuania*[155] in which the applicants were prisoners who claimed that Article 10 ECHR had been violated because they had been refused access to the Internet. To start with, the court made it clear that a general obligation binding for Contracting States to provide individuals with access to the Internet cannot be inferred from Article 10 ECHR. Nonetheless, in both judgments the Strasbourg court found that the national authorities had violated this provision as they had failed to consider the possibility of granting prisoners limited access to websites from which they could retrieve information concerning legal proceedings and the protection of their rights.[156]

The second area of the ECtHR case which is also worth noting concerns the balance between freedom of expression and the right to private and family life, protected under the umbrella of Article 8 ECHR. In some sense, the case law of the ECtHR seems to have paralleled that of the CJEU in three judgments concerning protection for the right to be forgotten. The common feature of these three decisions of the ECtHR was the fact that the contested requests to remove information (which were rejected by the national authorities) did not concern the search engine but rather the website from which the information had been retrieved.[157] Therefore, unlike mere delisting from a search engine, the protection of privacy rights supposedly interfered more significantly with freedom of expression. It is no coincidence that the Strasbourg court struck a balance between the two competing rights in finding that the national authorities had not violated Article 8 ECHR for the purpose of protecting free speech, in the light of the sensitive and valuable role of Internet archives. The ECtHR referred to the well-established criteria already present within its case law prior to the rise of the Internet, which consider factors such as the contribution to a debate of public interest; the degree of notoriety of the person affected; the subject of the news report; the prior conduct of the person concerned; the content, form and consequences of the publication; the way in which the information was obtained and its veracity; and the gravity of the penalty imposed on the journalists or publishers.

Despite the apparently solid case law on the right to be forgotten, the Strasbourg court's case law also includes cases in which freedom of expression has been legitimately restricted for the purpose of protecting privacy rights. Among others, in *Satakunnan Markkinapörssi Oy and Satamedia Oy v Finland*[158] the ECtHR found that the exercise of journalistic freedom could not constitute justification for a

[154] *Kalda v Estonia*, App no 17429/10, judgment of 06 June 2016.
[155] *Jankovskis v Lithuania*, App no 21575/08, judgment of 17 April 2017.
[156] Voorhoof (n 88) 28.
[157] *Węgrzynowski and Smolczewski v Poland*, App no 33846/07, judgment of 16 October 2013; *Fuchsmann v Germany*, App no 71233/13, judgment of 19 January 2018; *ML and WW v Germany*, App nos 60798/10 and 65599/10, judgment of 28 September 2018.
[158] *Satakunnan Markkinapörssi Oy and Satamedia Oy v Finland*, App no 931/13, judgment of 27 June 2017.

disproportionate dissemination of large quantities of information concerning the private life of the applicant.[159]

Having regard to such a complex framework, it must be stressed that the 'relative' (rather than 'absolute') consideration paid to the fundamental rights enshrined in the ECHR does not constitute an invention by the ECtHR fostered by the impact of the new technologies. Indeed, balancing fundamental rights has been the task of the ECtHR since it was created. However, the digital environment where fundamental rights can be enjoyed has led the Strasbourg court to adopt a judicial frame that underscores the relative nature of fundamental rights protection, justifying restrictions that they most likely would not have been tolerated in the 'world of atoms'.

B. The Jurisprudence of the CJEU

We have discussed the cases of *Delfi* and *MTE*. How would the CJEU have ruled on these cases? This question is crucial in introducing the EU judicial framework for freedom of expression online.

As noted above, these cases arose out of proceedings brought by the owner of an Internet news portal, who had lost a defamation action in relation to statements posted by users. If we consider this case in the EU context, it is apparent that the CJEU would have followed a different judicial path. The CJEU would have applied the e-Commerce Directive to review whether the Estonian legislation was compatible with the obligations imposed on, and the liability exemptions of, ISPs, including in light of Article 11 EUCFR.

This brief comparison offers the opportunity to stress the differences between the ECHR and EU law systems, as well as the tasks of the respective courts.

It has been noted above that, as far as freedom of expression is concerned, the Strasbourg court handles complaints based on Article 10 ECHR, with which the relevant provisions of national constitutions concerning freedom of expression should comply. The ECtHR acts as constitutional court of fundamental rights in the context of the Council of Europe. However, the Convention provision was adopted in 1950, when the Convention entered into force. Thus, when tackling cases involving new technologies, the Strasbourg court has been required to conduct its review on the basis of a dated parameter, which was designed to apply to a different scenario. At the same time, however, Article 10 ECHR (as well as the other provisions of the Convention) does lend itself to a very flexible interpretation.

It is no coincidence that the EU parameters, and particularly the e-Commerce Directive, seem to be more obsolete than Article 10 ECHR. The CJEU, in fact, normally issues its decisions within the context of preliminary proceedings. Since it is for Member State courts to make a reference for a preliminary ruling,

[159] Voorhoof (n 88) 19–20.

the CJEU is bound by the terms of the question referred, thus preventing it from carrying out any broader scrutiny. In other words, this prevents the CJEU – unlike the Strasbourg court – from acting as a constitutional court of fundamental rights, despite the recent incorporation of the EUCFR into EU primary law. The parameters on the basis of which the CJEU issues preliminary rulings are less flexible than Article 10 ECHR. The rise of user-generated content platforms or peer-to-peer systems has represented a challenge to the system of the e-Commerce Directive, which, unlike Article 10 ECHR, does not always ensure flexibility in dealing with new digital challenges.[160]

To return to our question, the *Delfi* and *MTE* cases would most likely have been resolved on the basis of the liability exemptions. Rather than examining whether a ruling against the news portal concerning offensive comments constitutes a violation of freedom of expression, the CJEU would have focused on the absence of control by the owner of the website over the (unlawful) activity of users. No consideration would have been given, in all likelihood, to freedom of speech since the task of the court is not to ascertain whether a violation has occurred, but rather whether the provider could be responsible for the conduct of those users who posted defamatory comments.

This does not mean, however, that freedom of expression has not been considered in some CJEU judgments. It has only been by incorporating the EUCFR into the EU primary law that freedom of expression, as well as other fundamental rights, has been provided with a 'constitutional footing' within EU law. This fact is reflected by the approach of the CJEU, which for a long time was unable to identify a parameter for enforcing freedom of expression under EU law. In fact, the scope of the CJEU's scrutiny, which is essentially conducted within preliminary proceedings, has been limited to acts adopted within the competence of the EU in the economic domain, such as the e-Commerce Directive.

The relevant EU parameter, enshrined in Article 11 EUCFR, constitutes a constitutional point of reference, which binds the European institutions when adopting secondary legislation. Moreover, as a binding document focused on the protection of fundamental rights, the EUCFR is the basis for recognising the constitutional dimension to the EU. In other words, a legal Bill of Rights is not only binding on the law-making activity of the EU legislator, but also allows the CJEU to review acts of Union law and to balance fundamental rights. Until the Lisbon Treaty, the development of the European Community (and Union, since 1992) was based on economic considerations rather than the protection of fundamental rights, in contrast to the ECHR system. The field of fundamental rights has therefore for a long time amounted to an exceptional space, which the CJEU could take

[160] See, in this respect, Joined Cases C-236/08, C-237/08 and C-238/08 *Google France SARL and Google Inc v Louis Vuitton Malletier SA, Google France SARL v Viaticum SA and Luteciel SARL, and Google France SARL v Centre national de recherche en relations humaines (CNRRH) SARL and others* [2010] ECR I-02417. See also Case C-324/09 *L'Oréal SA and Others v eBay International AG and Others* [2011] ECR I-06011.

into consideration only insofar as linked to the economic freedoms enshrined in the treaties. Indeed, the CJEU could be seised in order to examine whether any limitations of these freedoms provided for by the Member States in the name of protection of fundamental rights could be justified. Consequently, it should come as no surprise that the decisions taken by the CJEU when dealing with the protection of freedom of expression have been exceptional.

In any case, the effects of the adoption of the EUCFR should not be overestimated. Indeed, the legal situations that are now protected by the EUCFR already received protection indirectly through the general principles and constitutional traditions of the Member States. Clearly, the choice to vest the EUCFR with binding force has given rise to systemic and constitutional implications over and above the original economic matrix. This became clear in *Omega*,[161] where the CJEU was called on to rule on the compatibility of a German national gambling provision which prohibited the playing of certain games (eg those involving murder and violence) in the name of protecting human dignity. According to the CJEU, economic activity can certainly be prohibited in accordance with the law of the EU where the purpose of the provision seeks to protect public order. Here, the protection of fundamental rights, in particular human dignity, emerged within case law concerning EU economic freedoms.

However, in some cases, the CJEU has indirectly acknowledged the status of freedom of expression as a fundamental right. For instance, this occurred in the *Schmidberger* case.[162] The CJEU was asked to determine whether the domestic legislation at stake was compatible with the free movement of goods insofar as it permitted the temporary closure of a motorway for a demonstration that sought to draw public attention to environmental issues. Then, the purpose of the proceedings was to establish whether the fundamental economic freedoms established in the EU had been respected and whether the restrictions imposed on them were legitimate. The judgment expressly referred to Article 10 ECHR:

> [U]nlike other fundamental rights enshrined in that Convention, such as the right to life or the prohibition of torture and inhuman or degrading treatment or punishment, which admit of no restriction, neither the freedom of expression nor the freedom of assembly guaranteed by the ECHR appears to be absolute but must be viewed in relation to its social purpose. Consequently, the exercise of those rights may be restricted, provided that the restrictions in fact correspond to objectives of general interest and do not, taking account of the aim of the restrictions, constitute disproportionate and unacceptable interference, impairing the very substance of the rights guaranteed.[163]

However, taking account of the circumstances of the case, the CJEU held that various interests had to be weighed and noted that an outright ban on the

[161] Case C-36/02 *Omega Spielhallen- und Automatenaufstellungs-GmbH v Oberbürgermeisterin der Bundesstadt Bonn* [2004] ECR I-9609.
[162] See Case C-112/00 *Eugen Schmidberger, Internationale Transporte und Planzüge v Republik Österreich* [2003] ECR I-05659.
[163] ibid para 80.

demonstration would have constituted 'unacceptable interference with the fundamental rights of the demonstrators to gather and express peacefully their opinion in public'.[164]

Even in the absence of any specific substantive regulation, it is possible to assess how freedom of expression has been balanced with other fundamental rights within some recent decisions involving the digital domain.

First of all, the case law shows that freedom of expression has been at issue within copyright cases. This is also a result of the incorporation into EU primary law of the EUCFR, which expressly affords protection to intellectual property as a fundamental right under Article 17(2). The fact that intellectual property, as an essential element of the right to property, ranks among the rights protected under the Charter means that copyright is a competing interest with freedom of expression, thus entering into the balance of fundamental rights.

This factor has one important consequence: whereas in the past freedom of expression as an individual fundamental right by no means competed with copyright, which was regarded as a property right and subsequently as an economic interest, the position has now changed. The digital revolution has led to some important rulings concerning the relationship between freedom of expression and other rights, including, in particular, the protection of personal data and copyright. The development of a judicial frame concerning the balancing of freedom of expression with the right to protection of personal data and copyright demonstrates the relevance of the paradigm of freedom of expression online.

As will be seen in Chapter 3, one of the most important decisions of the CJEU in the field of privacy was that delivered in *Google Spain*.[165] Despite the focus on privacy and data protection, *Google Spain* is also relevant for freedom of expression. In his Opinion, Advocate General Jääskinen focused, inter alia, on whether EU law protects the individual's right to be forgotten.[166] The question here was whether an ISP operating as a search engine could be required to remove links to dated or non-accurate personal data without prior consultation with the owner of the pertinent website from which the data are indexed. The answer given by AG Jääskinen in his Opinion was that it could not. However, this position was based on the interpretation of the Data Protection Directive as in force at that time,[167] and not on the other possible grounds engaged, for instance, by free speech claims. The reason why Google could not be required to remove personal data is that ISPs do not generally operate as data controllers and therefore bear no responsibility for the processing of personal data, which is entirely automatic and is operated by the

[164] ibid para 89.

[165] Case C-131/12 *Google Spain SL, Google Inc. v Agencia Española de Protección de Datos, Mario Costeja González*, ECLI:EU:C:2014:317.

[166] AG Opinion, Case C-131/12 *Google Spain SL and Google Inc v Agencia Española de Protección de Datos, Mario Costeja González*, ECLI:EU:C:2013:424.

[167] Directive 95/46/EC on the protection of individuals with regard to the processing of personal data and on the free movement of such data.

owner of the website. The same question may, however, be addressed from a different perspective: is the right to have certain personal data available on a website covered by free speech, and does it fall under the right to information?

Advocate General Jääskinen made several remarks concerning this issue:

> Making content available on the Internet counts as such as use of freedom of expression, even more so when the publisher has linked his page to other pages and has not limited its indexing or archiving by search engines, thereby indicating his wish for wide dissemination of content.[168]

In any case, AG Jääskinen concluded that none of the fundamental rights established under the EUCFR enjoys absolute protection, thus leaving room for a solution concerning the balance between freedom of expression and other rights.

It is worth also mentioning another point, where it seems that AG Jääskinen considered the problem of protecting freedom of expression. Specifically, with regard to the possible implementation of a notice and take-down procedure based upon individuals' subject data complaints, AG Jääskinen clearly noted that the imposition of such a system for the removal of the indexed content would undermine the freedom of expression of the owners of websites as it would amount to a private form of censorship. Thus, even if these assumptions do not resolve the balance between rights over personal data and freedom of expression, it seems that the freedom to carry out business is no longer the only aspect that is considered when assessing the impact of the Internet on the protection of fundamental rights.

The CJEU held that EU law provides a sound basis for the right to delist personal data and also specified that it is up to search engines to assess whether the conditions for the exercise of this right are met as well as its compatibility with freedom of information. In reaching this conclusion, the CJEU followed a multi-step route, the outcome of which was to recognise the possibility of applying the same obligations to search engines as those applicable to entities that handle 'personal data' (such as, for example, a newspaper); such obligations may include a requirement to erase personal information (in this case, links to news reported by third-party sites) when they are no longer accurate, up to date, or relevant.

As was stressed in Chapter 3, the *Google Spain* decision proposed a balance between the right to be informed and the protection of an asymmetric privacy. The latter would prevail over the former, as confirmed by the references to Articles 7 and 8 EUCFR and the lack of any reference to Article 11 EUCFR, which deals, as said several times, with the protection of freedom of expression.

This should not be considered a novelty within the European framework. The case law of the Strasbourg court has shown that the new technological context has resulted in an increase in situations in which the protection of fundamental rights is in jeopardy. Therefore, freedom of expression could be defined as a 'yielding'

[168] AG Opinion, *Google Spain* (n 166) para 122.

fundamental right because, within the world of bits, it is a weapon which is considered to be more dangerous than it could be in the world of atoms.

The second analysis focuses on the balance struck with copyright. Along with the advent of the Internet, this factor has escalated the conflict between copyright protection and freedom of expression. Indeed, both the CJEU and the ECtHR have been confronted with an increase in cases in which these rights are in conflict.

In two almost identical cases, specifically *Scarlet v Sabam* and *Sabam v Netlog*,[169] the issue was whether EU law allowed the courts to impose an obligation on ISPs to adopt a filtering system aimed at detecting possible copyright infringements, on the assumption that the use of a large volume of Internet data traffic implied illegal downloading. In particular, the CJEU objected to a requirement imposed by the Belgian authorities on ISPs to adopt a filtering system, at their own cost, in order to determine the presence of unlawfully disseminated content and to prevent it from being shared. The manner in which this mechanism was structured was such as to constitute genuine surveillance by operators, which is prohibited by the e-Commerce Directive. In addition, the characteristics of this filtering system resulted in an unjustified pre-eminence of copyright over other fundamental rights, including not only freedom of economic initiative and the protection of personal data, but also freedom of expression.

Surprisingly, the CJEU only considered the claim concerning freedom of expression to be residual. First, the court examined the question with reference to the other two aspects. The CJEU held that the imposition of a requirement to adopt a filtering system such as that in question was not proportionate to the objective of copyright protection as it resulted in a restriction, first of all, on the ISP's right to engage in economic activity, which is protected under Article 16 EUCFR. Secondly, the CJEU addressed the framework of the EUCFR, finding that Articles 8 and 11, which refer respectively to the rights to personal data and freedom of expression, had been violated.

It is indeed true that copyright also enjoys protection as a fundamental right under the EUCFR. However, it is significant that the compatibility of measures aimed at ensuring copyright protection was reviewed on a subsidiary basis with respect to individual rights.

These decisions seem to downgrade the role assigned to freedom of expression, which is considered as a fundamental right like any other, especially compared to the freedom to engage in economic activity. The fact that no particular prominence has been given to this right can perhaps be considered in relation to the as-yet incomplete emancipation of the EU from a prevalent economic dimension.

In the wake of the *Sabam* case an Opinion was delivered by Advocate General Cruz Villalón in a case pending before the CJEU.[170] This case concerned the

[169] Case C-70/10 *Scarlet Extended SA v SABAM* [2011] ECR I-11959; Case C-360/10 *Belgische Vereniging van Auteurs, Componisten en Uitgevers CVBA (SABAM) v Netlog NV* [2012] ECR I-0000.

[170] AG Opinion, Case C-314/12 *UPC Telekabel Wien GmbH v Constantin Film Verleih GmbH and Wega Filmproduktionsgesellschaft GmbH*, ECLI:EU:C:2013:781.

compatibility with EU law of injunctions ordering an ISP to block a website providing illegal access to copyrighted materials. Advocate General Cruz Villalón – who found that an ISP may be required to prevent access to a website, provided that such measures are proportionate – argued that copyright protection must be balanced, as far as ISPs are concerned, against freedom of expression and the freedom of economic initiative. The Opinion seems to attach greater importance to freedom of speech, conceived of as the right of ISPs to disseminate information and to provide users with access to it; however, the analysis does prevalently focus on the possible infringement of Article 16 EUCFR. In any case, AG Cruz Villalón focused on the 'social role' of ISPs, in order to bring to light how operators are now playing a crucial role in access to information (from both an active and a passive perspective).

In *Telekabel*[171] the CJEU recognised that

> [t]he fundamental rights recognised by EU law must be interpreted as not precluding a court injunction prohibiting an internet service provider from allowing its customers access to a website placing protected subject-matter online without the agreement of the rightholders when that injunction does not specify the measures which that access provider must take and when that access provider can avoid incurring coercive penalties for breach of that injunction by showing that it has taken all reasonable measures, provided that (i) the measures taken do not unnecessarily deprive internet users of the possibility of lawfully accessing the information available and (ii) that those measures have the effect of preventing unauthorised access to the protected subject-matter or, at least, of making it difficult to achieve and of seriously discouraging internet users who are using the services of the addressee of that injunction from accessing the subject-matter that has been made available to them in breach of the intellectual property right, that being a matter for the national authorities and courts to establish.[172]

This decision indicates the approach to freedom of expression taken by the CJEU, which appears to be not as careful as that of the Strasbourg court, as the former has not been fully able to emancipate itself from the original economic dimension to the EU in granting protection to fundamental rights. For example, in *Telekabel*, although freedom of expression played a fundamental role, it did not lie at the heart of the court's reasoning, even though the ruling referred to the 'fundamental rights recognised by EU law', which also include freedom of expression.

This conduct is, however, also consistent with the lack of content regulation at EU level, given that Member States seem to have retained the power to determine the extent to which content is free to circulate, subject to the exceptions laid down in the Audiovisual Media Service Directive and, more recently, the Copyright Directive. The common framework adopted by the EU under the e-Commerce Directive deals only with ISP liability. The core rules stipulate that operators that do not exercise any editorial control over content do not bear any responsibility for

[171] Case C-314/12 *UPC Telekabel Wien GmbH v Constantin Film Verleih GmbH and Wega Filmproduktionsgesellschaft GmbH*, ECLI:EU:C:2014:192.

[172] ibid para 64.

any unlawful conduct that may occur. Thus, the advent of the Internet has probably caused a downgrading of the consideration afforded to freedom of expression.

As will be noted in Chapter 5, the relevance afforded to freedom of expression is slowly changing within the EU context under the Digital Single Market strategy. Nonetheless, judicial protection for freedom of expression in the EU is still characterised by a frame of distrust vis-à-vis new technologies, while the US continues along its path towards fostering judicial protection for freedom of expression online.

IV. Concluding Remarks: Transatlantic Frames Compared and the Need for Care when Handling Metaphors

To conclude this analysis, it can be argued that the use of a particular value frame is capable not only of influencing the argumentative structure of a decision and the balance struck by the courts, but also, consequently, of impinging upon the level of protection for the fundamental rights in play. This has been clear when considering the different judicial outcomes in the US and Europe.

Let us return for a moment to the *Reno* judgment, in which the US Supreme Court held that

> [a]s a matter of constitutional tradition, in the absence of evidence to the contrary, we presume that governmental regulation of the content of speech is more likely to interfere with the free exchange of ideas than to encourage it. The interest in encouraging freedom of expression in a democratic society outweighs any theoretical but unproven benefit of censorship.[173]

The judicial frame adopted by the US Supreme Court not only enables protection for freedom of expression to be extended to the digital domain, but also fosters its scope as a new channel for promoting the free marketplace of ideas.

When comparing this passage to the findings reached in the decisions of the ECtHR on compatibility with Article 10 ECHR, it is possible to identify a European judicial frame that seeks to re-moderate the expansive scope of freedom of expression in the digital domain. The perhaps most complete manifestation of this cautious approach may be found in 2011 when the ECtHR in the *Editorial Board of Pravoye Delo and Shtekel v Ukraine* case held that

> [t]he Internet is an information and communication tool particularly distinct from the printed media, especially as regards the capacity to store and transmit information. The electronic network, serving billions of users worldwide, is not and potentially will never be subject to the same regulations and control. The risk of harm posed by content and

[173] *Reno v American Civil Liberties Union* (n 3) 885.

> communications on the Internet to the exercise and enjoyment of human rights and freedoms, particularly the right to respect for private life, is certainly higher than that posed by the press. Therefore, the policies governing reproduction of material from the printed media and the Internet may differ. The latter undeniably have to be adjusted according to technology's specific features in order to secure the protection and promotion of the rights and freedoms concerned.[174]

It is evident that the European Court of Human Rights, without ever neglecting the added value of the digital technology,[175] placed the emphasis less on the benefits of a further expansion in the exercise of freedom of expression online, and more on the risks that such an expansion could have on effective protection for the rights and freedoms that may come into conflict. In other words, the two courts seem to be working on the basis of opposite presumptions. While the US Supreme Court presumes that content regulation does not give rise to greater benefits for freedom, the ECtHR, which is more suspicious, considers the digital environment as a threat to rights and freedoms, thus stressing the need for proportionate and necessary actions to limit the exercise of free speech.

In contrast to the digital distrust in the new technology displayed by European courts, it is clear that the frame underlying the case law of the Supreme Court is one of unconditional trust in the (digital) instrument, which is considered to be capable of further expanding the reach of the First Amendment. The US Supreme Court has indeed acted in accordance with that value frame characterised by trust in the 'novelty' of the web. The original nature of the technology is claimed to support the need for reducing regulatory intrusion on the web compared to the regulatory framework applicable to television. For the European courts, on the other hand, the new digital channel is used as a reason for justifying greater restrictions on freedom of expression when exercised online. This is due to a judicial frame that is characterised by substantial mistrust in new technologies and concerns about the potential expansion of other competing rights that are liable to affect freedom of expression more online than in the real world.

That said, as a final consideration on the need to handle metaphors with care when moving them from their original context, let us take the example of the free marketplace of ideas, and in particular the version of the metaphor used by the US Supreme Court in *Reno*. 'Internet is a new free marketplace of ideas'.[176] This is the preferred metaphor used by scholars and within public debate in support

[174] See *Editorial Board of Pravoye Delo and Shtekel v Ukraine* (n 92) para 63.

[175] See for instance *Cengiz* (n 113) paras 49 and 52: '[T]he Internet has now become one of the principal means by which individuals exercise their right to freedom to receive and impart information and ideas, providing as it does essential tools for participation in activities and discussions concerning political issues and issues of general interest. Moreover, as to the importance of Internet sites in the exercise of freedom of expression, "in the light of its accessibility and its capacity to store and communicate vast amounts of information, the Internet plays an important role in enhancing the public's access to news and facilitating the dissemination of information in general". User-generated expressive activity on the Internet provides an unprecedented platform for the exercise of freedom of expression'.

[176] *Reno v American Civil Liberties Union* (n 3). See Bosmajian (n 8).

of the claim that the issue of fake news should not be addressed (and confronted) by public authorities (and public law). The main idea behind such an assertion is that, if in the world of atoms, as Justice Holmes wrote in 1919, the 'best test of truth is the power of the thought to get itself accepted in the competition of the market',[177] this is even more true in the world of bits because the Internet amplifies the free exchange of and competition between ideas and opinions. Consequently, according to the marketplace of ideas paradigm, if 'under the First Amendment there is no such thing as a false idea'[178] in the material world, this is even truer in the digital world thanks to the enhanced scope for expressing thoughts. In other words, public powers should not perform any role in dealing with the increasingly prevalent phenomenon of fake news on the Internet. This is because web users are (optimistically) supposed to have all the tools necessary to select the most convincing ideas, ie true news, and to disregard any unconvincing fake news. This reflects the complete trust in the self-corrective capacity of the market for information.

Against this background, according to the European champions of the free marketplace of ideas metaphor, since by definition scarcity of resources is an analogical and not a digital limit, and consequently there is no need for the EU to protect pluralism of information on the Internet, legal rules (and especially public law) should take a step back in the name of the alleged self-corrective capacity of the market for information. The consequence, from a policy-making perspective, is to consider self regulation as the only feasible solution and to state that, also in Europe, hard regulation, as considered from a US perspective, is absolutely not suitable for dealing with the fight against disinformation. In other words, according to such perspective, the metaphor of the free marketplace of ideas could be excised neutrally from the context in which it was created and transferred to the European legal system. It is reasonable to ask whether such a transfer would really be so neutral and whether the metaphor of the free marketplace of ideas is well suited to the scope (and limits) of the protection of free speech according to the European constitutional paradigm.

There are least two elements which might mitigate against a legal transplant of this type.[179]

First of all, as noted above, protection for freedom of expression is more limited in Europe than in the US. One need only compare the wording of the US First Amendment with Article 10 ECHR. However, it is not simply a question of difference in scope, but also of difference in focus. While the First Amendment focuses mainly on the active dimension related to the right to express thoughts freely, Article 10 ECHR (and also Article 11 EUCFR)[180] stresses the passive dimension

[177] Dissenting opinion of Justice Holmes, *Abrams v United States* (n 9) 624, 630.

[178] *Gertz* (n 24) 339.

[179] Rodolfo Sacco, 'Legal Formants: A Dynamic Approach To Comparative Law' (1991) 39(1) *The American Journal of Comparative Law* 1.

[180] On which see Lorna Woods, 'Article 11 Freedom of Expression and Information' in Steve Peers, Tamara Hervey, Jeff Kenner and Angela Ward (eds), *The EU Charter of Fundamental Rights A Commentary* (Oxford, Hart Publishing, 2014) 311. See also Monti (n 22).

to the right to be informed pluralistically. In this respect, it could be argued that fake news does not fall within the constitutional purview under the European vision of free speech. Alternatively, the European courts would at the very least have difficulty in accepting the view of the US Supreme Court that 'Under the First Amendment there is no such thing as a false idea. However pernicious an opinion may seem, we depend for its correction not on the conscience of judges and juries but on the competition of other ideas'.[181]

Secondly, as noted above, metaphorical language fits very well with legal reasoning; however, it must be handled properly (and with care). Metaphor implies knowledge transfer across domains (from the Greek *meta pherein*, to 'carry over'). This means that we have two relevant constitutive domains: the source domain and the target domain. The free marketplace of ideas metaphor carries over from the source domain of economic activity to the target domain of speech a systematic set of entailments that supersedes the limitations of the older free speech model. In order to understand it fully, it is important not to forget the features of the source 'market' domain when Holmes made use of the metaphor in 1919 and the US Supreme Court then adapted it to the Internet in 1997. Holmes was writing during a period of *laissez-faire* capitalism, in which the liberal state and competition on the market were at their pinnacle. Holmes was sceptical about any external verification of the truth and the removal of proven false news, and the concept of a free market provided a meaningful alternative model for the notion that truth, just like economic well-being, could result from the competition of (true and false) ideas and information. Similarly, when the US Supreme Court borrowed the metaphor, referring to the Internet as the 'new marketplace of ideas', the online economic market was, at the outset, absolutely free and not in any way affected by dominant positions or, worse still, monopolies and oligopolies. In this context, the metaphor of the free marketplace of ideas and the proposed test for truth (competition in the absence of any control by public authorities) made perfect sense.

By contrast, today, the same metaphor seems to have been entirely decontextualised when the economic market (as the source domain from which the metaphor has transferred) is far from free, as is well known by Directorate General (DG) Competition in Brussels along with every other national competition authority, being characterised by huge market failures, which call for *ex post* intervention by public authorities.

The risks of the misleading use of a metaphor (as the one of the free marketplace of ideas) is due not only to its decontextualisation, but also neglecting the 'diacronicity' of metaphors and their dynamic nature. As has been written, 'metaphors cannot be understood as having the same static effect over the time. The way they work, and what effect they have, having the change over the time'.[182]

[181] *Gertz* (n 24) 339.
[182] Maksymilian Del Mar, *Artefacts of Legal Inquiry: The Value of Imagination in Adjudication* (Oxford, Hart Publishing, 2020) 280.

In our specific case, contrary to the claims of the US Supreme Court, which, in 1997, defined the Internet as the 'new free marketplace of ideas', today almost 20 years after that judgment the web is anything but a free market. It is in fact characterised by financial concentration and, as will be discussed in the final chapter, the economic and sometimes even political dominance by (a limited number of) private operators that dominate algorithmic technology.

The rise of the new private digital powers is in fact, as will be seen in the next chapters, the principal challenge to European constitutional law in the digital era.

3

Judges, Privacy and Data Protection: From Atoms to Bits Across the Atlantic

I. Privacy and Data Protection in Action

The amplification of judicial momentum in the shift from the world of atoms to the world of bits is not specific to the judicial transatlantic narrative on protection for freedom of expression. The crucial role played by judicial frames and (more broadly) judicial imagination as well as the relevance of the jurisdictional issue are also apparent within transatlantic judicial practice in relation to privacy and data protection.

Without data transfers across national borders, it would not be easy to allow a globalised digital economy to flourish, or even to carry out public tasks involving the cross-border exchange of information between administrations or supranational authorities. The flow of data around the globe is not a neutral phenomenon from a constitutional point of view. Although different legal regimes and territories are involved in this process, the courts must still adjudicate on disputes and take decisions in order to safeguard the right to privacy and data protection within the respective jurisdictions involved. Very often, the primary decision concerning jurisdiction over data within the 'onlife' dimension falls to them.[1] In other words, judicial activism in this field can be regarded as the natural consequence of the role of data and new technologies in the information society,[2] and the inherent obsolescence of the law when capturing the relevant legal issues.[3]

Nonetheless, this is not quite the end of the story. The jurisdictional issue has emerged after a long process of emancipation and constitutionalisation of the right to privacy and data protection, which has been driven also by judicial frames. As this chapter shows, even in this case, courts across the Atlantic have played a key role in adapting (or rather interpreting) the protection of rights and freedoms in

[1] Luciano Floridi (ed), *The Onlife Manifesto: Being Human in a Hyperconnected Era* (Cham, Springer, 2015).

[2] For further insight into the necessity to focus on, in the author's terms, the three privacy-related values affected by design – trust, obscurity and autonomy – see Woodrow Hartzog, *Privacy's Blueprint: The Battle to Control the Design of New Technologies* (Cambridge, MA, Harvard University Press, 2018) 94.

[3] Frank Pasquale, *The Black Box Society: The Secret Algorithms That Control Money and Information* (Cambridge, MA, Harvard University Press, 2015).

the transition from atoms to bits. While the right to privacy was initially considered only in its negative dimension, the scenario changed due to the rise, first, of welfare states and, more recently, of the information society. Both phenomena have resulted in an increase in the circulation and processing of personal data. For example, in order to provide services to citizens, public administrations need to collect large amounts of data concerning various aspects of individuals' lives.

At least in the European framework, the focus on 'personal data' has constituted a critical premise for the consolidation of a frame of protection that is linked to individuals, the movements of whom directly engage the concept of privacy. In fact, if personal data are not processed correctly, the protection of that essential core of the person, which lies at the heart of the concept of personal identity, will be put at risk. Thus, the need for personal data to be processed in accordance with a body of principles and rules is necessary in order to ensure protection for the individual and his or her personality. It is thus no longer simply privacy but also data protection that is a constitutional pillar of the information society. On the other hand, the protection of privacy in the US is not linked to the individual but rather a mosaic theory where the individual per se is not relevant without the other parts of the mosaic.[4] In other words, while under the EU framework the focus is on the individual and the protection of personal data, the US approach instead focuses more on the aggregated effects that certain processing can produce over society.[5]

However, even though the right to privacy has been recognised within international documents such as the Universal Declaration of Human Rights adopted by the UN General Assembly on 10 December 1948, it should not be forgotten that privacy and data protection do not enjoy the same legal status around the globe. These two rights are not protected in the same way, as was shown by the comparison of the European and US experiences in this field in Chapter 1. Although the right to privacy has been the result of a progressive maturation in North America, it has followed its own path in Europe. Even in the European framework, the way in which this right has emerged has not been homogeneous. During the initial stages the Council of Europe adopted a proactive approach towards the development of the positive dimension of the right to privacy; the EU, on the other hand, first perceived personal data as a resource for ensuring the broad circulation of personal data and, therefore, a guarantee of EU fundamental freedoms.

[4] Orin S Kerr, 'The Mosaic Theory of the Fourth Amendment' (2012) 111 *Michigan Law Review* 311.

[5] Schwartz and Peifer have recently analysed the respective constitutional identities constructed around data privacy in the EU and the US. According to the authors, 'the EU has created a privacy culture around "rights talk" that serves to protect data subjects. In the EU, rights talk forms a critical part of the postwar European project of creating the identity of a European citizen. In the United States, by contrast, data privacy law is based on the idea of consumers whose interests merit governmental protection in a marketplace marked by deception and unfairness. In the United States, the focus is on "marketplace discourse" about personal information and the safeguarding of "privacy consumers"', see Paul M Schwartz and Karl-Nikolaus Peifer, *Transatlantic Data Privacy Law* (2017) 106 *Georgetown Law Journal* 115, 118.

It was only at a later stage, evidently due to the acceleration of technological development, that the 'negative' dimension inherent in the right to privacy was enriched by the 'positive' dimension of the right to the protection of personal data, marking the expansion of a concept that had initially been limited to privacy. At this time, alongside the European institutions, the role of the European courts become predominant in shaping and enlarging the boundaries of protection for personal data, even beyond the jurisdiction of the EU, as was made clear in the cases concerning EU judicial enforcement of digital privacy.

Within this framework, this chapter will examine how the rights to privacy and data protection have developed along two different paths. First, it will discuss the landmark decisions of the US Supreme Court concerning the right to privacy, while examining the consolidation of a new right to data protection in Europe as the result of the evolution and adaptation of the right to privacy in line with the new technological scenario. The second part will focus on the role of the CJEU in emancipating and consolidating a new frame of protection for the right to privacy and personal data, even beyond the borders of Europe.

II. Stagnation in the US and the European Metamorphosis

Within the US framework, judicial protection for the right to privacy has had different bases in constitutional law. As already pointed out in Chapter 1, constitutional protection for this right may be considered to be diffuse. Nonetheless, the case law in the field of the Fourth Amendment, specifically on protection against unreasonable searches and seizures, appears to show how the US Supreme Court adapted its frame for protection in response to the development of new digital technologies.

In order to understand the evolution of the judicial frame of the US Supreme Court in the field of privacy, it is worth starting with the decision in *Olmstead*.[6] In this judgment, the US Supreme Court considered whether the use of wiretapped private telephone conversations, obtained by federal agents without prior judicial authorisation and subsequently used as evidence, constituted a violation of the defendant's rights under the Fourth and Fifth Amendments. The US Supreme Court held that neither the Fourth nor the Fifth Amendment rights of the recorded parties had been violated:

> The United States takes no such care of telegraph or telephone messages as of mailed sealed letters. The Amendment does not forbid what was done here. There was no searching. There was no seizure. The evidence was secured by the use of the sense of hearing, and that only. There was no entry of the houses or offices of the defendants.

[6] *Olmstead v United States* 277 US 438 (1928).

> By the invention of the telephone fifty years ago and its application for the purpose of extending communications, one can talk with another at a far distant place. The language of the Amendment cannot be extended and expanded to include telephone wires reaching to the whole world from the defendant's house or office. The intervening wires are not part of his house or office any more than are the highways along which they are stretched.[7]

According to the US Supreme Court, the use of wiretapped conversations as incriminating evidence was, first of all, not a violation of the Fifth Amendment since the conversations were conducted voluntarily between the parties and other individuals.

Secondly, as far as the Fourth Amendment was concerned, this was not infringed because wiretapping does not constitute a 'search and seizure' within the meaning of the Fourth Amendment:

> The reasonable view is that one who installs in his house a telephone instrument with connecting wires intends to project his voice to those quite outside, and that the wires beyond his house and messages while passing over them are not within the protection of the Fourth Amendment. Here, those who intercepted the projected voices were not in the house of either party to the conversation … We think, therefore, that the wiretapping here disclosed did not amount to a search or seizure within the meaning of the Fourth Amendment.[8]

A search or seizure involves an 'actual physical examination of one's person, papers, tangible material effects, or home'.[9] As a result, by adopting an external perspective, the US Supreme Court did not consider the right to privacy to have been violated in relation to the use by public actors of technology that was new at that time.

This case was reversed by *Katz v US*,[10] where the US Supreme Court departed from the property-based approach to the Fourth Amendment chosen in *Olmstead*. In this case, the US Supreme Court considered a situation involving the transmission of gambling information over the telephone to clients in other states. Federal agents used an eavesdropping device situated close to a public phone booth specifically in order to gather such information. Based on the recordings, Katz was convicted of the illegal transmission of wagering information through different states. In particular, it is interesting to note first of all the approach of the US Supreme Court to the right to privacy, which shows its truly fragmented nature as described above:

> [T]he Fourth Amendment cannot be translated into a general constitutional 'right to privacy'. That Amendment protects individual privacy against certain kinds of governmental intrusion, but its protections go further, and often have nothing to do with privacy at all. Other provisions of the Constitution protect personal privacy from

[7] ibid 464.
[8] ibid 466.
[9] ibid.
[10] *Katz v United States* 389 US 347 (1967).

> other forms of governmental invasion. But the protection of a person's *general* right to privacy – his right to be let alone by other people – is, like the protection of his property and of his very life, left largely to the law of the individual States … For the Fourth Amendment protects people, not places. What a person knowingly exposes to the public, even in his own home or office, is not a subject of Fourth Amendment protection.[11]

This last point enables us to understand why the US Supreme Court departed from *Olmstead*, thus emancipating individual privacy from property rights through the adoption of an internal perspective. According to the US Supreme Court:

> [A]lthough a closely divided Court supposed in *Olmstead* that surveillance without any trespass and without the seizure of any material object fell outside the ambit of the Constitution, we have since departed from the narrow view on which that decision rested … Once this much is acknowledged, and once it is recognized that the Fourth Amendment protects people – and not simply 'areas' – against unreasonable searches and seizures, it becomes clear that the reach of that Amendment cannot turn upon the presence or absence of a physical intrusion into any given enclosure … The Government's activities in electronically listening to and recording the petitioner's words violated the privacy upon which he justifiably relied while using the telephone booth, and thus constituted a 'search and seizure' within the meaning of the Fourth Amendment. The fact that the electronic device employed to achieve that end did not happen to penetrate the wall of the booth can have no constitutional significance.[12]

Another interesting feature in *Katz* was the third-party doctrine according to which, once information has been exposed to the public, it is no longer protected under the Fourth Amendment. According to Justice Harland's concurring opinion:

> My understanding of the rule that has emerged from prior decisions is that there is a twofold requirement, first that a person have exhibited an actual (subjective) expectation of privacy and, second, that the expectation be one that society is prepared to recognize as 'reasonable.' Thus, a man's home is, for most purposes, a place where he expects privacy, but objects, activities, or statements that he exposes to the 'plain view' of outsiders are not 'protected,' because no intention to keep them to himself has been exhibited. On the other hand, conversations in the open would not be protected against being overheard, for the expectation of privacy under the circumstances would be unreasonable.[13]

The US Supreme Court applied the criterion of 'reasonability' on different occasions, including in particular the case *Smith v Maryland*, which deserves further attention.[14] The case involved the use of a pen register at a telephone company's office with the aim of recording the numbers dialled from a criminal suspect's home telephone. The US Supreme Court held that this conduct did not constitute a 'search' within the meaning of the Fourth Amendment. This is because, by

[11] ibid 350.
[12] ibid 353.
[13] ibid 361.
[14] *Smith v Maryland* 442 US 735 (1979).

placing calls, individuals expose the telephone numbers they dial to the telephone company and, therefore, assume the risk that the company may reveal the numbers dialled to the police.

These decisions are examples of how technologies can alter expectations of privacy. On the one hand, the expectation in *Katz* would amount to nothing when compared with the technology used in the information society. As a result, this is particularly significant since it shows how the technological dimension has a strong influence on judicial protection of fundamental rights, resulting in a change in the case law of the US Supreme Court from an external to an internal perspective.

It should be stressed that the role of the US Supreme Court in the balancing of privacy rights seems to be stuck in a rut as the US Supreme Court did not propose any move towards enshrining a positive dimension to the right to privacy in the digital world, at least until the *Jones* and *Carpenter* cases addressed in Chapter 4. The silence of the US Supreme Court concerning this matter suggests that it has adopted an external 'view' in relation to the issue of digital privacy.

On the other side of the Atlantic, the ECHR was the first document to introduce a right to private and family life at the European level. However, this document is not directly applicable by the CJEU, even though the principles contained in it have undoubtedly exerted an important influence on its arguments and on the results of its rulings, including in the guise of general principles of EU law. Besides, even given the lack of clear codification within the constitutions of European countries, it is clear that the right to privacy enjoys privileged status.[15] Although Article 8 ECHR refers exclusively to the right to private and family life, the ECtHR has contributed to the evolution of this parameter. The transition from a static to a dynamic dimension as well as a certain manipulative approach have followed the evolution of new technologies. It was by interpreting Article 8 ECHR, which protects the right to private and family life as an obligation of non-interference by public authorities, in a positive way that it was possible to adopt a dynamic standpoint vis-à-vis the emergence of the right to data protection.

The first technological case that stimulated the creativity of the ECtHR occurred at the end of the 1980s. In *Klass*[16] the ECtHR acknowledged that telephone conversations fall within the scope of Article 8 ECHR. As technology evolved, 10 years later, when computers become ubiquitous, albeit offline, the ECtHR was encouraged to interpret this provision as also covering the collection of personal data. This happened for the first time in 1987, when the ECtHR clarified that the collection and processing of personal data must be included within the scope of Article 8 ECHR:

> It is uncontested that the secret police-register contained information relating to Mr. Leander's private life. Both the storing and the release of such information, which

[15] Taking Italy as an example, Art 117 of the Italian Constitution, as interpreted by the Italian Constitutional Court, requires the legislator to comply with the restrictions deriving from international and EU law, thus making the provisions of the ECHR, as well as those contained in other documents in force at the international level and the EU, an interposed parameter of constitutional legitimacy. See Italian Constitutional Court decisions nos 348 and 349 (2007).

[16] *Klass and Others v Germany*, App no 5029/71, judgment of 6 September 1978.

> were coupled with a refusal to allow Mr. Leander an opportunity to refute it, amounted to an interference with his right to respect for private life as guaranteed by Article 8(1).[17]

This assertion was explained *ex post* in two main stages. In the first step, in 1992, the ECtHR questioned the expansive scope of Article 8 ECHR for the first time although, in that case, the issue was not new technologies. In particular:

> The Court does not consider it possible or necessary to attempt an exhaustive definition of the notion of 'private life'. However, it would be too restrictive to limit the notion to an 'inner circle' in which the individual may live his own personal life as he chooses and to exclude therefrom entirely the outside world not encompassed within that circle. Respect for private life must also comprise to a certain degree the right to establish and develop relationships with other human beings. There appears, furthermore, to be no reason of principle why this understanding of the notion of 'private life' should be taken to exclude activities of a professional or business nature since it is, after all, in the course of their working lives that the majority of people have a significant, if not the greatest, opportunity of developing relationships with the outside world.[18]

The ECtHR later applied this extensive interpretation in 2002. However, at that time, it linked the interpretation with the new technological aspect to data processing and the requirement for the protection of personal data, relying on a source external to the ECHR, which was not Directive 95/46 but rather the instrument that served as inspiration for its adoption, namely Council of Europe Convention 108/1981. In particular, according to the ECtHR:

> That broad interpretation corresponds with that of the Council of Europe's Convention of 28 January 1981 for the Protection of Individuals with regard to Automatic Processing of Personal Data, which came into force on 1 October 1985 and whose purpose is 'to secure in the territory of each Party for every individual … respect for his rights and fundamental freedoms, and in particular his right to privacy, with regard to automatic processing of personal data relating to him' (Article 1), such personal data being defined as 'any information relating to an identified or identifiable individual' (Article 2).[19]

Unsurprisingly, the ECtHR acknowledged that the protection of personal data also contributes to the protection of private and family life, which enjoys express protection in the ECHR.

In the case of *S and Marprer v UK*[20] the Grand Chamber of the ECtHR recognised that the protection of personal data is of fundamental importance for an individual to fully enjoy the right to respect for private and family life. In this case, the ECtHR made broad references to a set of principles in EU law. Thus, in a case originating from the retention of fingerprints, tissues samples and DNA

[17] *Leander v Sweden*, App no 9248/81, judgment of 26 March 1987, para 48.
[18] *Niemietz v Germany*, App no 13710/88, judgment of 16 December 1992, para 29.
[19] *Amann v Switzerland*, App no 27798/95, judgment of 16 February 2000, para 65.
[20] *S and Marper v The United Kingdom*, App nos 30562/04 and 30566/04, judgment of 4 December 2008.

profiles of the applicant for an indefinite period of time after a criminal trial, which was concluded with the acquittal of the applicant, the ECtHR held that Article 8 ECHR had been violated on the grounds that a disproportionate interference had occurred with the right to private and family life that was not necessary in a democratic society. In particular, the ECtHR referred to the need for a balance to be struck between the public interest and individual rights, although also to those principles that allow for the storage of personal data, provided that this is relevant and not excessive compared to the purposes for which the data were collected:

> The mere storing of data relating to the private life of an individual amounts to an interference within the meaning of Article 8. The subsequent use of the stored information has no bearing on that finding. However, in determining whether the personal information retained by the authorities involves any of the private-life aspects mentioned above, the Court will have due regard to the specific context in which the information at issue has been recorded and retained, the nature of the records, the way in which these records are used and processed and the results that may be obtained.[21]

Within this framework, the processing of personal data for judicial purposes has been privileged terrain for the ECtHR, which on several occasions has had the opportunity to rule on violations of Article 8 ECHR, as it did in the case of *MM v UK* on the excessive duration of data collection in relation to the applicant's criminal record.[22]

Another issue addressed by the ECtHR has been access to personal data in cases involving the absence of mechanisms for obtaining details about incidents that may have caused harm to health,[23] or concerning the existence of parental relationships.[24] In an even more recent case, the ECtHR found against the government of Romania for not having analytically regulated information concerning conversations obtained by the national security services, on the basis of which the appellant had been convicted without having had the opportunity to prove that the content was inaccurate.[25] In other cases, Article 8 ECHR has been found to have been violated due to the disclosure of personal data, where a decision was reported to the press along with details such as the applicant's HIV positive status, even though it did not have any relevance to the case,[26] or where certain information concerning the mental and psychological health of the applicant had been disseminated without any evidence during a public hearing.[27]

As is the case in the US, one of the most significant trends in the case law of the ECtHR in this field has concerned the interception of communications and surveillance. Many decisions have been adopted in this area by the ECtHR

[21] ibid para 67.
[22] *MM v UK*, App no 24029/07, judgment of 29 April 2013.
[23] *Roche v United Kingdom*, App no 32555/96, judgment of 19 October 2005.
[24] *Odièvre v France*, App no 42326/98, judgment of 13 February 2003.
[25] *Rotaru v Romania*, App no 28341/95, judgment of 4 May 2000.
[26] *Z v Finland*, App no 22009/93, judgment of 25 February 1997.
[27] *Panteleyenko v Ukraine*, App no 11901/02, judgment of 12 February 2007.

as national legal rules usually do not provide for clear and precise limits to the scope as well as type of restrictions affecting freedom of communication.[28] In the past, the ECtHR held Article 8 ECHR to have been violated by national measures that allowed the judicial authorities to monitor the content of correspondence and telephone conversations without any obligation to inform the interested parties concerning the measures adopted.[29] The ECtHR's reasoning has focused on exceptions that, according to Article 8(2) ECHR, legitimise interference with the right to private and family life.

In the same field, aside from the *Big Brother* case,[30] which we shall focus on in Chapter 4, there are at least two cases that describe an interesting change of approach to surveillance and interception systems.

In *Kennedy v UK*[31] the ECtHR rejected an application filed by a citizen complaining about the general implementation of communications capture measures by police, although he had not been directly affected. The ECtHR held that Article 8 ECHR had not been violated, relying on the arguments in favour of the lawfulness in practice of the measures adopted in the UK. These measures were justified according to the conditions established by Article 8(2) ECHR, even though their application to the applicant was unproven, thus evoking the perspective of individual justice, namely the need for a specific, and not merely general, violation of the rights established by the ECHR.

However, this trend changed with the ruling in *Zakharov v Russia*.[32] This case addressed the compatibility with Article 8 ECHR of a mobile communications interception system. The ECtHR concluded that Article 8 had been breached since national law did not establish adequate safeguards against the risk of abuse and arbitrary interference in the private lives of citizens. The Strasbourg court also noted that a risk also resulted from the limitation to the right to challenge the legitimacy of these measures only to applicants who were able to demonstrate an actual interception. It was not possible to meet this condition given the lack of a notification system or any possibility of access to data relating to the operations carried out in any given case. In this ruling, the ECtHR held that a violation had occurred, irrespective of the allegation of any specific breach of the rights of the applicant, who had not submitted any evidence that interception activities had actually taken place.

Leaving aside the arguments that allowed the ECtHR to embrace protection of personal data within the framework of Article 8 ECHR, it is worth focusing on another interpretative phase based on the shift from offline data processing to

[28] *Malone v United Kingdom*, App no 8691/79, judgment of 2 August 1984; *Kruslin v France*, App no 11801/85, judgment of 24 April 1990; *Kopp v Switzerland*, App no 23224/94, judgment of 25 March 1998; *Wisse v France*, App no 71611/01, judgment of 20 March 2006.

[29] *Klass* (n 16).

[30] *Big Brother Watch and Others v The United Kingdom*, App nos 58170/13, 62322/14 and 24960/15, judgment of 13 September 2018, Referral to the Grand Chamber 04 February 2019.

[31] *Kennedy v UK*, App no 26839/05, judgment of 18 August 2010.

[32] *Zakharov v Russia*, App no 47143/06, judgment of 4 December 2015.

online data processing. In 2007 the web was formally included within the scope of Article 8 by the ECtHR:

> According to the Court's case-law, telephone calls from business premises are prima facie covered by the notions of 'private life' and 'correspondence' for the purposes of Article 8 § 1 ... It follows logically that e-mails sent from work should be similarly protected under Article 8, as should information derived from the monitoring of personal Internet usage.[33]

As previously observed in relation to judicial protection for freedom of expression in Chapter 2, the Strasbourg court interpreted the new digital scenario as a source of greater danger, even for the rights protected by Article 8 ECHR. This has resulted in the adoption of an approach that reinforces the dimension of confidentiality and the protection of personal data in comparison with other rights. It would be sufficient to recall the decision in *Editorial Board of Pravoye Delo and Shtekel v Ukraine* examined in Chapter 2.[34]

The frame of distrust in new technologies has also led the ECtHR to hold states responsible not only for having violated the fundamental rights at stake, but also for the failure to implement adequate safeguards to protect the right to privacy. While respecting the margin of appreciation of Contracting States,[35] the reliance on the doctrine of positive obligations requiring states to ensure protection for fundamental rights has increasingly shifted the attention from the relationship between states and individuals (ie vertical relations) to the relationship between private actors (ie horizontal relations).[36] This step is critical when considering the digital environment since it leads network operators, which are private subjects, to be involved in the protection of privacy and data through the legal measures that states are required to implement in order to safeguard these fundamental rights. This evolution is apparent in *KU v Finland*.[37] The ECtHR held that Article 8 ECHR had been violated, arguing that

> [w]ithout prejudice to the question whether the conduct of the person who placed the offending advertisement on the Internet can attract the protection of Articles 8 and 10, having regard to its reprehensible nature, it is nonetheless the task of the legislator to provide the framework for reconciling the various claims which compete for protection in this context. Such framework was not however in place at the material time, with the result that Finland's positive obligation with respect to the applicant could not be discharged.[38]

[33] *Copland v UK*, App no 62617/00, judgment of 3 July 2007, para 41.

[34] *Editorial Board of Pravoye Delo and Shtekel v Ukraine*, App no 33014/05, judgment of 5 August 2011.

[35] Róbert Spanó, 'Universality or Diversity of Human Rights? Strasbourg in the Age of Subsidiarity' (2014) 14(3) *Human Rights Law Review* 487.

[36] Mattias Kumm and Victor Ferreres Comella, 'What Is So Special about Constitutional Rights in Private Litigation? A Comparative Analysis of the Function of State Action Requirements and Indirect Horizontal Effect' in András Sajó and Renata Uitz (eds), *The Constitution in Private Relations: Expanding Constitutionalism* (The Hague, Eleven International Publishing, 2005) 241; John H Knox, 'Horizontal Human Rights Law' (2008) 102(1) *American Journal of International Law* 1.

[37] *KU v Finland*, App no 2872/02, judgment of 2 March 2009.

[38] ibid para 49.

In the case in question, the ECtHR held that the Contracting State had infringed Article 8 ECHR on the grounds that it had not established any legal basis that could allow a judicial authority to order an ISP to disclose the details of the author of defamatory statements that had violated the right to private and family life of the interested party.

In *Copland v UK*[39] the Strasbourg court held that Article 8 ECHR had been violated by an employer which monitored telephone calls, emails and websites visited by an employee. According to the ECtHR, the fact that that information had not been used on disciplinary grounds or disclosed to third parties did not mean that no infringement had occurred. The court held that

> [s]toring of personal data relating to the private life of an individual also falls within the application of Article 8(1) … Thus, it is irrelevant that the data held by the college were not disclosed or used against the applicant in disciplinary or other proceedings. Accordingly, the Court considers that the collection and storage of personal information relating to the applicant's telephone, as well as to her e-mail and Internet usage, without her knowledge, amounted to an interference with her right to respect for her private life and correspondence within the meaning of Article 8.[40]

Even in this case, it is worth noting a broad frame of protection for the right to privacy and personal data. However, no violation of Article 8 ECHR was found to have occurred in *Węgrzynowski and Smolczewski v Poland*.[41] In particular, news already considered to be defamatory at the time of publication in a physical newspaper had also been published on the web. By balancing the interests protected by Articles 8 and 10 ECHR, the Strasbourg court concluded that the publication of an explanatory note concerning the defamatory nature of the news constituted a sufficient remedy to guarantee the reputation of the individuals defamed and did not entail a disproportionate interference with freedom of information. The ECtHR observed:

> In this respect, it is noteworthy that in the present case the Warsaw Court of Appeal observed that it would be desirable to add a comment to the article on the website informing the public of the outcome of the civil proceedings in which the courts had allowed the applicants' claim for the protection of their personal rights claim … The Court is therefore satisfied that the domestic courts were aware of the significance which publications available to the general public on the Internet could have for the effective protection of individual rights. In addition, the courts showed that they appreciated the value of the availability on the newspaper's website of full information about the judicial decisions concerning the article for the effective protection of the applicant's rights and reputation.[42]

Here, the primary difference was the result of a balance between fundamental rights and not simply the prevalence of the right to privacy over a public legitimate interest. The focus on the interference with individuals' privacy rights by

[39] *Copland v UK* (n 33).
[40] ibid paras 43–44.
[41] *Węgrzynowski and Smolczewski v Poland*, App no 33846/07, judgment of 16 October 2013.
[42] ibid para 66.

private actors seems to be clearer in the decision in *Bărbulescu v Romania*.[43] In this case, the Grand Chamber of the ECtHR reversed the ruling of the Fourth Section holding that the monitoring of an employee's Yahoo Messenger account violated the applicant's right to respect for private life as prescribed by Article 8 ECHR. Therefore, Romania was held responsible for its failure to act positively in order to protect an individual's right to privacy. In particular, according to the ECtHR:

> [I]t appears that the domestic courts failed to determine, in particular, whether the applicant had received prior notice from his employer of the possibility that his communications on Yahoo Messenger might be monitored; nor did they have regard either to the fact that he had not been informed of the nature or the extent of the monitoring, or to the degree of intrusion into his private life and correspondence. In addition, they failed to determine, firstly, the specific reasons justifying the introduction of the monitoring measures; secondly, whether the employer could have used measures entailing less intrusion into the applicant's private life and correspondence; and thirdly, whether the communications might have been accessed without his knowledge.[44]

The role of the ECtHR is just one aspect of the evolution of the right to privacy and data protection in Europe. If the ECtHR case law could be considered as the first steps towards protecting the right to privacy and personal data in Europe, in the last few years the role of the EU, and especially the CJEU, has resulted in the consolidation and adaptation of these fundamental rights in the digital domain. In the next section, this framework will be supplemented by the CJEU case law, the judicial activism of which has paved the way for the creation of the European personal data fortress.

III. The EU Judicial Enforcement of Digital Privacy: A New Frame?

The attention afforded by the ECtHR to the right to privacy, as well as to the right to the protection of personal data, certainly leaves no doubt concerning the relevance of these rights within the European framework. However, unlike the Council of Europe, the (former) European Economic Community (EEC) has not followed the same path, even though before 1995, at the time Directive 95/46 ('Data Protection Directive') was adopted, some Member States had already enacted legislation on data protection (eg France). The EEC approach was driven mainly by economic considerations relating to the harmonisation of the rules on the free flow of data in the internal market.[45] In fact, the Data Protection Directive focused on the free movement of personal data, considered as a crucial asset for the internal market.

[43] *Bărbulescu v Romania*, App no 61496/08, judgment of 12 January 2016.

[44] ibid para 140.

[45] In the European Community (EC) system, for a long time, rights have been recognised almost exclusively to ensure economic fundamental freedoms. This does not mean that the fundamental rights

Therefore, the protection of personal data did not immediately capture the attention of the European institutions as a fundamental right.

However, these considerations should not lead us to believe that the EU had entirely undermined fundamental rights, including the right to privacy and the protection of personal data, for the sake of the fundamental economic freedoms enshrined in the EU Treaties. In particular, the influence of the Council of Europe's framework is certainly not extraneous, at least in the reasoning of the CJEU before the adoption of the EUCFR. Although, as already explained, the Data Protection Directive was inspired by the economic dimension to the European Community, it was the first instrument to harmonise data protection rules at EU level by establishing general principles applicable to the processing of personal data.

Among the first cases involving the digital dimension and the application of the Data Protection Directive, it is worth mentioning the *Lindqvist* decision.[46] The case arose out of an online publication by a Swedish citizen which disclosed, without having acquired any prior consent, the personal data of certain parishioners along with details of their private and family lives. The individual received a criminal conviction on the grounds that her conduct constituted unlawful data processing. In particular, the CJEU observed without any scope for doubt that

> the act of referring, on an internet page, to various persons and identifying them by name or by other means, for instance by giving their telephone number or information regarding their working conditions and hobbies, constitutes the processing of personal data wholly or partly by automatic means within the meaning of Article 3(1) of Directive 95/46.[47]

Thus, the CJEU was asked to clarify whether the limitations laid down by the Data Protection Directive were compatible with protection for freedom of expression. The CJEU was aware of the conflict that can arise between the right to privacy and other fundamental rights, including especially freedom of expression. In particular, according to the CJEU:

> In that context, fundamental rights have a particular importance, as demonstrated by the case in the main proceedings, in which, in essence, Mrs Lindqvist's freedom of expression in her work preparing people for Communion and her freedom to carry out activities contributing to religious life have to be weighed against the protection of the private life of the individuals about whom Mrs Lindqvist has placed data on her internet site.[48]

have not played any role, but many of the issues that regard the protection of the fundamental rights have been – above all – considered in the community context as rights functional to economic freedoms. Concerning the evolution of fundamental rights in the EU framework, see, in particular, Case C-29/69 *Erich Stauder v City of Ulm – Sozialamt* [1969] ECR 00419; Case C-11/70 *Internationale Handelsgesellschaft mbH v Einfuhr- und Vorratsstelle für Getreide und Futtermittel* [1970] ECR 1125; Case C-4/73 *J Nold, Kohlen- und Baustoffgroßhandlung v Ruhrkohle Aktiengesellschaft* [1977] ECR 985. For instance, the CJEU has turned its attention to issues that seriously affect the protection of fundamental rights, such as abortion, through the prism of the free provision of services. See Case C-159/90 *Society for the Protection of Unborn Children Ireland Ltd v Stephen Grogan and Others* [1991] ECR I-04685.

[46] Case C-101/01 *Bodil Lindqvist* [2003] ECR I-12971.

[47] ibid para 27.

[48] ibid para 86.

This approach shows how the CJEU played a fundamental role in building the path towards the legal recognition of the right to privacy and data protection under EU law, even before the entry into force of the EUCFR. Through the set of principles introduced by the Data Protection Directive, the right to data protection found tangible expression within EU law. Those principles and rules are set within a framework that has been implemented in a generally uniform manner throughout the Member States, thus shifting the content of the right to privacy from a negative to a positive dimension.

Likewise, in *Promusicae*,[49] a collecting society representing producers and publishers of musical and audiovisual recordings asked Telefonica, as the access provider, to disclose personal data relating to its users due to alleged access to the IP-protected works of the collecting society's clients without having obtained prior authorisation from the rights holders. The question referred to the CJEU sought to establish whether an access provider could be obliged to provide this information to the collecting society. The CJEU held that Member States are not obliged to impose an obligation requiring intermediaries to disclose personal data in order to ensure effective protection of copyright within the context of civil proceedings. Even more importantly, in this case, the CJEU paved the way for a shift in the paradigm of an autonomous concept of data protection, albeit still inherently linked to the right to privacy. The CJEU held:

> It should be recalled that the fundamental right to property, which includes intellectual property rights such as copyright …, and the fundamental right to effective judicial protection constitute general principles of Community law … However, the situation in respect of which the national court puts that question involves, in addition to those two rights, a further fundamental right, namely the right that guarantees protection of personal data and hence of private life.[50]

These were only the first steps. The path towards the constitutionalisation of the protection of personal data has been closely linked to the evolution of the EU's own identity also in more recent times. As noted above, in the last decade, thanks to the proclamation of the EUCFR in 2000 and its entry into force in 2009, the EU has been progressively yet decisively emancipated from the economic vocation that characterised the first 50 years of its life. At the same time, the Treaty of Lisbon revolutionised the EU architecture as a precursor to its adherence to the ECHR, thus bringing the EU closer to a 'constitutional-like' system.

Hence, the right to privacy that Warren and Brandeis imagined as the right to be left alone initially migrated from the US to Europe. Since then, this right has progressively evolved, not only protecting the individual's expectation of privacy, but also going beyond an exclusive negative and static dimension (right to be left alone) and extending its reach to the positive and dynamic one related to data protection.

[49] Case C-275/06 *Productores de Música de España (Promusicae) v Telefónica de España SAU* [2008] ECR I-271.

[50] ibid 62–63.

As was stressed in Chapter 1, the EUCFR protects not only the right to privacy under Article 7, but also the protection of personal data as enshrined in Article 8.[51] Despite the attempt in the explanatory notes of the EUCFR to restrict the purpose of this provision to merely reiterating the existing *acquis*,[52] the contribution of Article 8 EUCFR is quite significant. This provision has not only recognised the constitutional status of the right to data protection, but has also resulted in this right being emancipated from the economic dimension that characterised Directive 95/46, at least at the outset.[53]

Within this framework, the CJEU has played a crucial role in the evolution of the right to data protection in EU law. A fairly emblematic example can be identified in the *Volker* case,[54] in which the CJEU held:

> The right to respect for private life with regard to the processing of personal data, recognised by Articles 7 and 8 of the Charter, concerns any information relating to an identified or identifiable individual … and the limitations which may lawfully be imposed on the right to the protection of personal data correspond to those tolerated in relation to Article 8 of the Convention.[55]

It is apparent from the reference in that decision to Article 8 ECHR that the right to data protection is considered simply as an implication of the right to respect for private life under Article 7 EUCFR corresponding to a right to informational

[51] This is confirmed, inter alia, by the Explanations Relating to Charter of Fundamental Rights of the European Union 2007/C 303/02 OJ C 303/17 of 14 December 2007. The Explanations regarding Art 7 of the EUCFR say: 'The rights guaranteed in Article 7 correspond to those guaranteed by Article 8 of the ECHR. To take account of developments in technology the word "correspondence" has been replaced by "communications". In accordance with Article 52(3), the meaning and scope of this right are the same as those of the corresponding article of the ECHR. Consequently, the limitations which may legitimately be imposed on this right are the same as those allowed by Article 8 of the ECHR'.

[52] ibid. According to the Explanations regarding Art 8 of the EUCFR: 'This Article has been based on Article 286 of the Treaty establishing the European Community and Directive 95/46/EC of the European Parliament and of the Council on the protection of individuals with regard to the processing of personal data and on the free movement of such data … as well as on Article 8 of the ECHR and on the Council of Europe Convention of 28 January 1981 for the Protection of Individuals with regard to Automatic Processing of Personal Data, which has been ratified by all the Member States'. However, as has been noted, the drafters of the EUCFR have not managed to provide a reasonable justification to the encapsulation in Art 8 of the EUCFR of a very fundamental right to personal data protection.

[53] As is confirmed, inter alia, first of all by the crucial circumstance that the legal basis for the adoption of the Directive was found in Art 100 EC Treaty, a provision introduced by the Single European Act and which then became Art 95 of the TEC, which provides the grounds for all EU acts that aim at harmonising national measures related to the implementation and the functioning of the internal market. Additionally, it is confirmed by the third recital of the Data Protection Directive, which reads as follows: 'Whereas the establishment and functioning of an internal market in which, in accordance with Article 7a of the Treaty, the free movement of goods, persons, services and capital is ensured require not only that personal data should be able to flow freely from one Member State to another, but also that the fundamental rights of individuals should be safeguarded'.

[54] Joined Cases C-92/09 and C-93/09 *Volker und Markus Schecke GbR and Hartmut Eifert v Land Hessen* [2010] ECR I-11063.

[55] ibid para 52.

self-determination reminiscent of the German *informationelle Selbstbestimmung* (informational self-determination).[56]

However, this approach does not seem to reflect the intentions of the framers of the EUCFR. While, in fact, the concept of self-determination with respect to personal data is based on the request for consent to data processing, when Article 8 EUCFR was introduced the aim of the framers was to emancipate data processing from initial consent by the data subject.[57] As has been noted, Article 8 EUCFR reflects the *acquis communitaire* in the field of data protection, which 'looks beyond consent and only created a system of checks and balances which ensures lawful processing also without asking the consent of the person involved'.[58]

This was stressed in particular in a case involving digital privacy. As will be illustrated below, in the case *Digital Rights Ireland*[59] the CJEU invalidated the EU directive on the retention of data on the grounds that it violated certain provisions of the EUCFR.[60] In *Google Spain*[61] the CJEU held that, under certain conditions, Internet search engine service providers are under an obligation, following a complaint by the data subject, to remove links to websites containing information that could harm the applicant's right to be forgotten,[62] where personal data have been available for a significant period of time on the Internet.

These decisions, and in particular the approach taken by the CJEU in both cases, reveal a judicial frame that is focused on modelling a new right to privacy and data protection as a consequence of the legal implications of the Internet. In fact, this dynamic is backed up by a complex process of deterritorialisation, denationalisation and dematerialisation that reflects, inter alia, the jurisdictional issue characterising the digital revolution, as will be seen in Chapter 4.

[56] This right to informational self-determination was first and organically articulated by the German Constitutional Court, judgment of 15 December 1983, 1 BvR 209/83.

[57] This is also confirmed by the reference that the Explanations regarding Art 8 of the EUCFR make to Convention no. 108 of 1981 of the Council of Europe, which does not rank the consent of the data subject among its basic principles.

[58] Herke Kranenborg, 'Article 8 Protection of Personal Data' in Steve Peers, Tamara Hervey, Jeff Kenner and Angela Ward (eds), *The EU Charter of Fundamental Rights: A Commentary* (Oxford, Hart Publishing, 2014) 223, 229.

[59] Joined Cases C-293/12 and C-594/12 *Digital Rights Ireland Ltd v Minister for Communications, Marine and Natural Resources, Minister for Justice, Equality and Law Reform, The Commissioner of the Garda Síochána, Ireland and the Attorney General and Kärntner Landesregierung, Michael Seitlinger, Christof Tschohl and Others* [2014] ECR I-238.

[60] For some comments on the decision, see Franziska Boehm and Mark D Cole, 'Data retention after the Judgement of the Court of Justice of the European Union' (2014) report commissioned by Greens/EFA, European Parliament, at www.janalbrecht.eu; Federico Fabbrini, 'The European Court of Justice Ruling in the Data Retention Case and its Lessons for Privacy and Surveillance in the U.S.' (2015) 28 *Harvard Human Rights Journal* 65.

[61] Case C-131/12 *Google Spain SL and Google Inc v Agencia Española de Protección de Datos, Mario Costeja González*, ECLI:EU:C:2014:317.

[62] For some comments, see, among others, Orla Lynskey, 'Deconstructing Data Protection: The "Added-Value" of a Right to Data Protection in the EU Legal Order' (2014) 63 *International & Comparative Law Quarterly* 569; Oreste Pollicino and Marco Bassini, 'Reconciling Right to Be Forgotten and Freedom of Information: Past and Future of Personal Data Protection in Europe' (2014) 2 *Diritto pubblico comparato ed europeo* 641.

Moreover, both decisions show the common approach adopted by the CJEU to exploring the impact of technological changes on the level of protection for fundamental rights. The crucial aspect in this respect is not whether limitations are legitimate. Rather, these decisions deal with how new technology affects fundamental rights across jurisdictions. The new right to digital privacy is the result of the attempt made by the CJEU to adopt a judicial frame that is capable of protecting fundamental rights in the world of bits. As will be stressed in Chapter 5, the primary question is still whether the existing rules, including but not limited to those with constitutional standing, should constitute an appropriate legal basis for protecting the 'new' rights emerging on the Internet, or whether alternatively they should be replaced by new provisions adopted on an ad hoc basis to regulate the consequences of the Internet.

In order to understand the evolution of the right to digital privacy, it is necessary to focus once again on the role of the courts and, specifically, the judicial activism on the part of the CJEU in interpreting (or, as noted below, sometimes even manipulating) the legal framework for data protection in order to deal with the new technological scenario.

A. *Digital Rights Ireland*

The first case in the field of digital privacy is *Digital Rights Ireland*, which already unveils the inquisitive spirit of the European courts (or their judicial frame), most notably in relation to new technologies. In the decision invalidating the Data Retention Directive (Directive 2006/24/EC) the CJEU appeared to consider the fundamental rights established by Articles 7 and 8 EUCFR as independent parameters, overcoming the functional approach in *Promusicae*. In addition, this decision draws a clear distinction between the violation of the essence of fundamental rights and the assessment of proportionality in the light of the objectives of protecting public order and combating terrorism. The hard core of the constitutional backbone to this case is captured in the words of Advocate General Cruz Villalòn:

> In the present cases, the Court has before it two references for a preliminary ruling on the validity of Directive 2006/24/EC, offering it the opportunity to rule on the circumstances in which it is constitutionally possible for the European Union to impose a limitation on the exercise of fundamental rights within the specific meaning of Article 52(1) of the Charter of Fundamental Rights of the European Union, by means of a directive and the national measures transposing it.[63]

[63] AG Opinion, Joined Cases C-293/12 and C-594/12 *Digital Rights Ireland Ltd v Minister for Communications, Marine and Natural Resources, Minister for Justice, Equality and Law Reform, The Commissioner of the Garda Síochána, Ireland and the Attorney General and Kärntner Landesregierung, Michael Seitlinger, Christof Tschohl and Others*, ECLI:EU:C:2013:845, para 1.

And the CJEU did not pass up on this opportunity. For the first time in the history of the European integration process, the CJEU decided to invalidate an act of EU secondary law on the grounds that it violated the EUCFR.

The preliminary reference proceedings had been launched by the references by the High Court of Ireland and the Austrian Constitutional Court. The High Court of Ireland was considering a dispute involving Digital Rights Ireland and local authorities concerning national measures on the retention of data in relation to electronic communication. On the other hand, the Austrian Constitutional Court had received a number of constitutional complaints by which the applicants sought to annul the domestic legislation implementing the Data Retention Directive.

The legal issues raised by this case originated from the fact that the Data Retention Directive allowed national authorities to collect intrusive information concerning multiple aspects of the private life of subscribers of telecommunications service providers, such as the identities of those involved as well as the time and place where the communications took place. Taken as a whole, this information could provide precise details concerning the private lives of the individuals whose data had been retained. Numerous claims had therefore been made in respect of both the Data Retention Directive and the domestic provisions transposing it since the conditions under which interference with the private life of individuals could be justified were not established in a clear and precise manner.

Therefore, the CJEU enforced the EUCFR as a constitutional principle, thus revealing its vocation as a quasi-constitutional court and the guardian of fundamental rights in Europe. Indeed, it is no coincidence that a historic chapter in the case law of the CJEU was written in relation to substantive legislation such as the Data Retention Directive. Its provisions had already been brought before the CJEU, although to no avail as in that previous case the reference had been based on allegedly erroneous legal grounds for the act and not on insufficient protection for the fundamental rights at stake.[64]

The Data Retention Directive resulted from the *security ethos*, as an immediate response to the attacks of 11 September 2001. This objective became apparent, in the first instance, as a functional requirement for the efficient implementation of the four fundamental freedoms established by the EU Treaties, and subsequently, following the entry into force of the Treaty of Maastricht, as an independent *telos* of the EU. Imbued with a logic of preventive control and widespread suspicion, the Data Retention Directive has carved out some exceptions to the protection of the right to respect for private life laid down in Directives 95/46 and 2002/58, as was noted by AG Cruz Villalòn.[65] In fact, these instruments were intended to guarantee

[64] It is worth noting that in the mentioned decision the CJEU had been asked to invalidate Directive 2006/24 on the basis (solely) of alleged inappropriate legal basis. The CJEU then pointed out that '[t]he action brought by Ireland relate[d] solely to the choice of legal basis and not to any possible infringement of fundamental rights arising from interference with the exercise of the right to privacy contained in Directive 2006/24'. Case C-301/16 *Ireland v European Parliament and Council of the European Union* [2009] ECR I-00593, para 57.

[65] AG Opinion, *Digital Rights Ireland* (n 63) paras 39–40.

the confidential status of communications and traffic data and, in order to do so, established an obligation for telecommunication operators to delete or anonymise data where they were no longer required for the transmission of a communication, unless necessary for billing purposes.

Against this background, the Data Retention Directive stipulated that Member States must establish an obligation to retain data for a period no shorter than six months and no longer than two years for the purposes of the investigation, detection and prosecution of serious crime. The issue came as no surprise for the supreme and constitutional courts of the Member States, which were asked to review the legality of national legislation implementing the Data Retention Directive.[66] Since 2008, national courts had raised concerns concerning the insufficient protection afforded to the rights to privacy and data protection. Advocate General Cruz Villalòn also contributed to clarifying the independent scope of Articles 7 and 8 EUCFR:

> Article 8 of the Charter enshrines the right to the protection of personal data as a right which is distinct from the right to privacy. Although data protection seeks to ensure respect for privacy, it is, in particular, subject to an autonomous regime.[67]

The reasoning of AG Cruz Villalòn sought to stress that there may be cases in which legislation restricting the right to protection of personal data according to Article 8 EUCFR may nevertheless be regarded as a disproportionate restriction on Article 7 EUCFR. In order to achieve this, AG Cruz Villalòn drew a distinction between 'personal data' per se and data 'more than personal'.[68] In his view, the former category concerns data that exclusively have the function of identifying a person and have neutral character, being as such 'personal data and nothing more'. These are the personal data for which the structure and the guarantees of Article 8 EUCFR are the most appropriate.[69] Data that are 'more than personal' relate essentially to private life and its confidential status, including intimacy. According to AG Cruz Villalòn,

> in such cases, the issue raised by personal data commences, so to speak, further 'upstream'. The issue which arises in such cases is not yet that of the guarantees relating to data processing but, at an earlier stage, that of the data as such, that is to say, the fact that it has been possible to record the circumstances of a person's private life in the form of data, data which can consequently be subject to electronic processing.[70]

[66] See, in particular, Supreme Administrative Court of Bulgaria, judgment no 13627, 11 December 2008; Supreme Court of Cyprus, App nos 65/2009, 78/2009, 82/2009 and 15/2010–22/2010, judgment of 1 February 2011; Romanian Constitutional Court, judgment no 1258, 8 October 2009; Constitutional Court of Czech Republic App no 24/2010, judgment of 22 March 2011; German Constitutional Court, judgment of 11 March 2008, 1 BvR 256/08.

[67] AG Opinion, *Digital Rights Ireland* (n 63) para 55.

[68] ibid para 65.

[69] ibid para 64.

[70] ibid para 65.

A second distinction emerged in the reasoning of the CJEU and constituted an innovative departure from its previous case law. This distinction is based on the wording of Article 52(1) EUCFR and concerns the assessment of possible violations of the essence of the rights under Articles 7 and 8 EUCFR as well as the proportionality of the measures specified under the Data Retention Directive in order to achieve the objectives of safeguarding public order and preventing terrorism, which were considered to be legitimate by the CJEU.

Before this decision, the CJEU had focused on the first paragraph of Article 52 EUCFR as a 'single block', without considering the possibility that, even though a restriction of fundamental rights might not affect their essence, it could nevertheless be found to be disproportionate with respect to the goals pursued by the relevant legislation. By contrast, in the decision in question, the CJEU not only held that 'the interference caused by Directive 2006/24 with the fundamental rights laid down in Articles 7 and 8 of the Charter' was 'wide-ranging', but also separately addressed the Article 52(1) EUCFR aspects. With regard to the first aspect, the CJEU held that no violation had occurred of the essence of both the right to privacy and the right to data protection for two reasons. First, Article 5(2) of the Data Retention Directive prohibited operators from accessing electronic communications, thus granting a minimum level of protection at least to the content thereof, which is the most sensitive aspect of the data at issue. Secondly, according to the CJEU, 'Member States are to ensure that appropriate technical and organisational measures are adopted against accidental or unlawful destruction, accidental loss or alteration of the data'.[71] In this way, the CJEU held that the measures for retaining data and communicating that data to the national authorities were per se admissible. In the view of the CJEU, these mechanisms pursued objectives of general interest for the EU such as the prevention of terrorism, the maintenance of international peace and security, and, more generally, combating serious crime and, thus, protecting public safety.

However, the CJEU held that EU primary law had been breached when considering the proportionality of the collection and storage of data as provided for under the Data Retention Directive.[72] Once the CJEU had established the wide-ranging interference with the rights protected under Articles 7 and 8 EUCFR, the CJEU focused on the proportionality of such interference with regard to the objectives pursued by the Data Retention Directive. The CJEU thus analysed whether appropriate and necessary safeguards were in place in order to justify the proposed limitations on the relevant fundamental rights guaranteed by the EUCFR.

The CJEU provided an in-depth analysis of the critical aspects of the Data Retention Directive. The CJEU first noted that interference with the fundamental

[71] *Digital Rights Ireland* (n 59) para 40.

[72] For general comments on Directive 2006/24/EC see Francesca Bignami, 'Protecting Privacy Against the Police in the European Union: The Data Retention Directive' (2007) 8 *Chicago Journal of International Law* 233; Eleni Kosta, 'The Way to Luxembourg: National Court Decisions on the Compatibility of the Data Retention Directive with the Right to Privacy and Data Protection' (2013) 10 *scritpted* 339.

right to private life could affect the entire EU population, without any distinction. In this light, the CJEU pointed out that the collection of data affected individuals who were not necessarily suspected of having committed any crime. According to the CJEU, this processing was carried out regardless of any direct or indirect connection with the commission of a serious crime. In other words, the collection of data was neither limited to a certain group of individuals nor circumscribed to a particular geographical area or a specific period of time.

The CJEU held that the reference to the 'serious crimes' was not proper and generic and, thus, incompatible with the principle of proportionality. According to the CJEU, while allowing each Member State to set its own definition of 'serious crimes', the effect of the Data Retention Directive was that this notion was unlikely to be properly defined. The CJEU also stressed the lack of any substantive and procedural guarantee concerning access to data by domestic authorities. Moreover, it was not clear who within the respective authorities of each Member State had access to the data retained. Indeed, access to the data was not subject to prior scrutiny by any judicial or independent administrative authority. As regards the retention period, the critical issues concerned the lack of any distinction between the various categories of data and the relevant duration of retention. This period should in any case be limited to the time necessary in order for the purposes of retention to be fulfilled.

On these grounds, the CJEU held that the Data Retention Directive did not establish clear and specific provisions, and thus violated the fundamental rights enshrined in Articles 7 and 8 EUCFR. Such wide-ranging interference could not be based on the principle of necessity, which could be seen as ancillary and supplementary to the principle of proportionality.[73]

It is particularly important to stress that this decision entails not only the recognition of a high standard under EU law for protecting the fundamental rights of privacy and data protection, but also the starting point for the adoption of a judicial frame focused on ensuring a high level of protection for digital privacy. This can also be regarded as the starting point for another phase in the process of constitutionalising the right to data protection, which, especially in this case, has been considered separately from the right to privacy.

B. *Google Spain*

The path towards the recognition of the right to digital privacy, which was first embarked upon by the CJEU in the decision invalidating the Data Retention Directive, reached its climax in the decision issued a few weeks later in the *Google Spain* case, in which – in the words of Post – the court had the opportunity to

[73] *Digital Rights Ireland* (n 59) para 65.

consider the difference between 'dignitary privacy' and 'data privacy'.[74] In this case, the CJEU adopted a judicial frame that extended the protection recognised under Articles 7 and 8 EUCFR by granting almost absolute protection to the right to privacy in the digital domain. In fact, the CJEU interpreted the relevant legislation having been inspired by the purpose of granting the widest possible protection to the rights to privacy and data protection. This loose interpretation (or even manipulation) was probably supported by the fact that the Data Protection Directive entered into force during the transition from the analogue to the digital domain.

At the national level, the Spanish Data Protection Authority ordered Google to remove certain links generated by the complainant's name as a keyword. Specifically, the complainant requested the removal of links to news published by a legal bulletin (which was obliged to publish this information) concerning a procedure involving him, which had been completed many years before. Google refused to comply with the complainant's request, stating that, as a US-based company, it was not subject to EU law and, accordingly, to domestic legislation implementing the Data Protection Directive. According to Google, such an injunction would most likely restrict the freedom of expression of website owners. By contrast, only an injunction against the websites concerned (and not the search engine) to delete specific content could remove any prejudicial effects for the plaintiff.

During the appeal proceedings against the injunction issued by the Spanish Data Protection Authority, the *Audiencia Nacional* raised a preliminary reference to the CJEU concerning, inter alia, the possibility of enforcing the individuals' right to be forgotten against Internet search engine service providers. According to AG Jääskinen:

> The particularly complex and difficult constellation of fundamental rights that this case presents prevents justification for reinforcing the data subjects' legal position under the directive, and imbuing it with a right to be forgotten. This would entail sacrificing pivotal rights such as freedom of expression and information. I would also discourage the Court from concluding that these conflicting interests could satisfactorily be balanced in individual cases on a case-by-case basis, with the judgment to be left to the internet search engine service provider. Such 'notice and take down procedures', if required by the Court, are likely either to lead to the automatic withdrawal of links to any objected contents or to an unmanageable number of requests handled by the most popular and important internet search engine service providers.[75]

This is the view expressed by AG Jääskinen in the concluding remarks of his opinion. The 'balance' proposed by AG Jääskinen between the fundamental rights involved in the 'particularly complex and difficult constellation' was nevertheless rejected by the CJEU. Indeed, it is hard to think of any case in which the judgment of the CJEU has departed so significantly from the Opinion of AG Jääskinen.

[74] See Robert C Post, 'Data Privacy and Dignitary Privacy: Google Spain, the Right To Be Forgotten, and the Construction of the Public Sphere' (2018) 67 *Duke Law Journal* 981.

[75] AG Opinion, Case C-131/12, *Google Spain SL and Google Inc v Agencia Española de Protección de Datos, Mario Costeja González*, ECLI:EU:C:2013:424, para 133.

Not only were conclusions reached by the CJEU very different from the Opinion of AG Jääskinen, but the court in actual fact largely rejected it.

It is therefore important to focus on the choice made by the CJEU to base the judgment almost exclusively on Articles 7 and 8 EUCFR. This approach, however, did not prevent the CJEU from addressing certain anomalies and, to a certain degree, interpreting the relevant provisions loosely. For instance, unlike AG Jääskinen, the CJEU did not mention Articles 11 and 16 EUCFR as anomalies which protect respectively freedom of expression and the freedom to conduct business. In the Opinion delivered by AG Jääskinen, there is on the other hand almost an equivalence in the references to Articles 7 and 8 EUCFR on the one hand and Articles 11 and 16 EUCFR on the other. By contrast, the decision simply focused on protection of the right to privacy and personal data.

Some parts of the judgment show how the CJEU has promoted protection for the right to digital privacy.[76] Specifically, the CJEU stressed this aspect in finding that, when striking a balance between the right to information and the right to privacy, the latter is generally assumed to prevail, except where the removal of the information concerned might undermine the legitimate interest of Internet users in receiving it. In fact, the CJEU held, on one hand, that 'in situations such as that at issue in the main proceedings a fair balance should be sought in particular between that interest and the data subject's fundamental rights under Articles 7 and 8 of the Charter'.[77] However, at the same time it noted that

> [w]hilst it is true that the data subject's rights protected by those articles also override, as a general rule, that interest of internet users, that balance may however depend, in specific cases, on the nature of the information in question and its sensitivity for the data subject's private life and on the interest of the public in having that information, an interest which may vary, in particular, according to the role played by the data subject in public life.[78]

In other words, the right to access information is limited to safeguarding other rights relating to the private sphere and the personal data of users. The former would only prevail over the latter as an exception, under certain circumstances and subject to certain specific conditions.

There is no support for construing this relationship as a general rule in the reasoning of AG Jääskinen, and this position was moreover expressly refused also by AG Kokott in the *Satamedia* case.[79] In particular:

> Strict application of the data protection rules could substantially limit freedom of expression. Investigative journalism would to a large extent be ruled out if the media could process and publish personal data only with the consent of, or in conformity

[76] *Google Spain* (n 61) paras 81 and 96.

[77] ibid para 81.

[78] ibid.

[79] AG Opinion, Case C-73/07 *Tietosuojavaltuutettu v Satakunnan Markkinapörssi Oy and Satamedia Oy*, ECLI:EU:C:2008:266, para 43; Case C-73/07 *Tietosuojavaltuutettu v Satakunnan Markkinapörssi Oy and Satamedia Oy* [2008] ECR I-09831.

> with information provided by, the person concerned. On the other hand, it is obvious that the media may violate the right of individuals to respect for their private life. Consequently a balance must be found.[80]

This approach is not even consistent with the relevant case law of the ECtHR. In *Węgrzynowski and Smolczewski*, mentioned above (as well as in subsequent decisions),[81] the court indicated that freedom of expression should prevail as the general rule, whereas restrictions on it can only be allowed as exceptions, and are subject to strict interpretation. Moreover, this should be the rule even where the conflict involves the right to access information online and any claim brought by an individual seeking the removal of information harmful to his or her reputation.[82]

The relevance of Articles 7 and 8 EUCFR was also crucial when the CJEU focused on the interpretation of the Data Protection Directive. It is possible to identify at least four respects in which the CJEU adopted a loose interpretation: the relevance of the case for EU law; the definition of the Internet search engine provider as a controller for data processing purposes; the application of Article 12(b) of the Data Protection Directive on the right to obtain the erasure, blocking and rectification of personal data; and the application of Article 9 of the Data Protection Directive on the exemption to the general rules laid down by the same directive in the event that personal data are processed for the purposes of journalism.

With regard to the first point, the CJEU reached the same conclusion as AG Jääskinen regarding the applicability of the Data Protection Directive to Internet search engine service providers. However, the CJEU went beyond the arguments provided by the Advocate General. By adopting an expansive interpretation of the notion of 'context of the activities of an establishment' under Article 4(a) of the Data Protection Directive, the CJEU dealt with the jurisdictional issue by observing that

> [i]n the light of that objective of Directive 95/46 and of the wording of Article 4(1)(a), it must be held that the processing of personal data for the purposes of the service of a search engine such as Google Search, which is operated by an undertaking that has its seat in a third State but has an establishment in a Member State, is carried out 'in the context of the activities' of that establishment if the latter is intended to promote and sell, in that Member State, advertising space offered by the search engine which serves to make the service offered by that engine profitable. In such circumstances, the activities of the operator of the search engine and those of its establishment situated in the Member State concerned are inextricably linked since the activities relating to the

[80] AG Opinion, *Tietosuojavaltuutettu v Satakunnan* (n 79) para 43.

[81] *Węgrzynowski and Smolczewski v Poland* (n 41).

[82] For a comparison between the approach of the ECtHR and the CJEU on the right to be forgotten, see John F Larkin, 'Strasbourg or Luxembourg: A Right to Truth or *Suppressio Veri*?' in *Human Rights Challenges in the Digital Age: Judicial Perspective* (Strasbourg, Council of Europe Publishing, 2020) 79. See also, for a recent overview on the right to erasure in Europe, Jef Ausloos, *The Right to Erasure in EU Data Protection Law. From Individual Rights to Effective Protection* (Oxford, Oxford University Press, 2020).

> advertising space constitute the means of rendering the search engine at issue economically profitable and that engine is, at the same time, the means enabling those activities to be performed.[83]

Again, the right to private life became the relevant parameter for the purposes of granting protection. In this respect, the CJEU attempted to justify this approach by mentioning some paragraphs (notably 62 and 63) from its judgment in the *L'Oréal* case.[84] However, these points were of very limited relevance for the case in question. The only aspect that is of any relevance for the decision concerns the establishment of the servers on which personal data are stored outside the EU.[85] In particular:

> As the Advocate General observed at point 127 of his Opinion and as the Commission pointed out in its written observations, the effectiveness of those rules would be undermined if they were not to apply to the use, in an internet offer for sale or advertisement targeted at consumers within the EU, of a sign identical with or similar to a trade mark registered in the EU merely because the third party behind that offer or advertisement is established in a third State, because the server of the internet site used by the third party is located in such a State or because the product that is the subject of the offer or the advertisement is located in a third State.[86]

As regards the definition of Google as controller, it must be pointed out that the CJEU drew inspiration, when reaching that conclusion, from Articles 7 and 8 EUCFR as the only relevant legal provisions. Turning to the scope of Article 2(d) of the Data Protection Directive, which sets out the definition of controller, the CJEU in *Google Spain* specified that

> it would be contrary not only to the clear wording of that provision but also to its objective – which is to ensure, through a broad definition of the concept of 'controller', effective and complete protection of data subjects – to exclude the operator of a search engine from that definition on the ground that it does not exercise control over the personal data published on the web pages of third parties.[87]

Here, the interpretation of the relevant provisions, duly 'lightened' by Articles 7 and 8EUCFR, contrary to expectations, makes the reasoning of the CJEU weaker and more ambiguous. In fact, the CJEU made use of a clear *excusatio non petita*, an unnecessary argument to justify the 'enlarged' notion of controller. The purpose of adopting such a broad definition of controller was to grant as much protection as possible to the subjects. This statement is inappropriate and raises a number of issues. In fact, classifying an entity as a data controller entails some obligations under the Data Protection Directive, which, if applied to an Internet service

[83] *Google Spain* (n 61) paras 55–56.
[84] Case C-324/09 *L'Oréal SA v eBay International AG and Others* [2011] ECR I-06011.
[85] ibid para 63.
[86] ibid.
[87] *Google Spain* (n 61) para 34.

provider, are likely to conflict with the regime established by the e-Commerce Directive and, accordingly, the business model of search engine operators.

Furthermore, the CJEU failed to clarify a crucial aspect: what is the purpose of the processing of personal data by search engines? The CJEU noted that the processing of personal data by the Internet search engine service provider is separate and independent from processing by the owners of the websites from which information is retrieved and indexed. Moreover, the question that may arise is whether the search engine provider itself must obtain the consent of the data subject, at least assuming that processing is carried out for business purposes.

Should any doubts persist concerning the role of Articles 7 and 8 EUCFR in extending the scope of the relevant provisions of the Data Protection Directive through this loose interpretation, the CJEU further stressed the point that

> [i]nasmuch as the activity of a search engine is therefore liable to affect significantly, and additionally compared with that of the publishers of websites, the fundamental rights to privacy and to the protection of personal data, the operator of the search engine as the person determining the purposes and means of that activity must ensure, within the framework of its responsibilities, powers and capabilities, that the activity meets the requirements of Directive 95/46 in order that the guarantees laid down by the directive may have full effect and that effective and complete protection of data subjects, in particular of their right to privacy, may actually be achieved.[88]

Furthermore, the court was asked to assess whether Articles 12(b) and 14(1)(b) of Directive 95/46 confer data subjects with the right to obtain from search engines the removal of search results including links to web pages containing personal data or information, without prior consultation of the website owner, and with no requirement that the information being processed is unlawful. Here, a balance has to be struck between the freedom of expression of website owners and, on the other hand, data protection.

Once again, in order to grant as much protection as possible to the right to digital privacy of data subjects, the CJEU acknowledged that, according to Article 12(b) of Directive 95/46, the data subject may ask for the erasure, rectification or blocking of the data when they are not being processed in accordance with the principles laid down by the Data Protection Directive and, in particular, on the grounds that the data are inaccurate or incomplete. In this way, the CJEU established a basis for making any breach of the general principles set forth by the Data Protection Directive grounds for the data subject to take action to enforce his or her rights against the controller.

There is still one last point which shows, once again, how the CJEU's interpretation sought to ensure protection for the right to digital privacy. The aspect concerns Article 9 of the Data Protection Directive, which exempted the processing of personal data, either for journalistic purposes or for purposes of artistic or literary expression, from the general rules. According to the CJEU, recital 37 of the Data Protection

[88] ibid para 38.

Directive states that Article 9 of the same directive aims to balance two fundamental rights: the right to private life and the right to freedom of expression. In addition, recital 37 stresses that, according to Article 9 of the Data Protection Directive, derogations are only allowed where they are necessary to ensure that the right to private life is enjoyed by individuals in accordance with the law on freedom of expression. However, the CJEU reached the following conclusion:

> [T]he processing by the publisher of a web page consisting in the publication of information relating to an individual may, in some circumstances, be carried out 'solely for journalistic purposes' and thus benefit, by virtue of Article 9 of Directive 95/46, from derogations from the requirements laid down by the directive, whereas that does not appear to be so in the case of the processing carried out by the operator of a search engine.[89]

In other words, the CJEU held that an Internet search engine service provider cannot avail itself of the derogation established by Article 9 of the Data Protection Directive. However, while the CJEU quoted the decision in the *Satamedia* case in support of this position, it failed to mention the part of that decision that specifies that the reference to the processing of personal data for journalistic purposes must be interpreted broadly as including any activities whose 'object is the disclosure to the public of information, opinions or ideas, irrespective of the medium which is used to transmit them'.[90] In the light of this definition, one could question whether the distinction drawn by the CJEU with respect to the application of Article 9 of Directive 95/46 between the owner of a website and the Internet search engine service provider may actually be reasonable.

These are the most important consequences of the judicial frame adopted by the CJEU, which resulted in EU law being interpreted loosely in the light of Articles 7 and 8 EUCFR. There is, however, something paradoxical in the conclusions reached by the CJEU at the end of this fundamentally rights-based reasoning. Burdening a search engine provider with an obligation to remove links, regardless of the activities carried out by the owner of the website concerned, is likely to result in reduced liability for those exercising editorial control and increased liability (perhaps excessively so) for the search engine.

The CJEU did not take this requirement into account. On the contrary, the CJEU delegated to search engines, as private actors, with the task of carrying out activities in the public interest, including specifically the striking of a balance between the right to information and the right to privacy. It is worth quoting in this respect the words used by the ECtHR in the *Węgrzynowski* case:

> [It] is not the role of judicial authorities to engage in rewriting history by ordering the removal from the public domain of all traces of publications which have in the past been found, by final judicial decisions, to amount to unjustified attacks on individual reputations.[91]

[89] ibid para 85.
[90] *Tietosuojavaltuutettu v Satakunnan* (n 79) para 61.
[91] *Węgrzynowski and Smolczewski v Poland* (n 41) para 65.

Having explored the reasoning of the CJEU in the decisions on the Data Retention Directive and in the *Google Spain* case, it should go without saying that the CJEU has taken the protection of a new right to digital privacy seriously. In particular, the CJEU has attempted to model a right to privacy, which Warren and Brandeis previously described with reference to the world of atoms, according to the characteristics of the digital world. In addition, it should be pointed out that, in the *Digital Rights Ireland* and *Google Spain* cases, the CJEU engaged with the issue of the definition and protection of the right to privacy in the digital age so seriously as to overlook the consequences of this approach. Two negative consequences in particular should be taken into account carefully. The first is the underestimating of the implications of enhancing to an extreme degree the protection afforded to personal data over the protection granted to other values with constitutional standing and which are ranked as fundamental rights, including, first and foremost, freedom of expression. Furthermore, there is a risk that such an extreme way of engaging with protection for personal data may result in an excess of Europeanisation, related to the balkanisation, of Internet regulation.

With regard to the former risk, the absence of any express reference to Article 11 EUCFR at any point in the judgment in the *Google Spain* case is only one of the various signals that confirms that the balance struck by the CJEU seems to be skewed towards the right to digital privacy. Another consequence of this overbalancing is the reduced level of protection for freedom of expression online. Such a trend is also apparent in relation to the ECtHR, which, despite using different arguments, seems to reach the same conclusions as the CJEU: downgrading protection for freedom of expression when it is exercised online.

Returning to the cases in question, it is possible to observe that Articles 7 and 8 EUCFR did not operate solely as the relevant applicable legal provisions. On the contrary, the CJEU seems to some extent to assume that these provisions have horizontal effects. One of the most significant statements in this respect was made in the *Google Spain* decision:

> In the light of the foregoing, when appraising such requests made in order to oppose processing such as that at issue in the main proceedings, it should in particular be examined whether the data subject has a right that the information relating to him personally should, at this point in time, no longer be linked to his name by a list of results displayed following a search made on the basis of his name. In this connection, it must be pointed out that it is not necessary in order to find such a right that the inclusion of the information in question in the list of results causes prejudice to the data subject.[92]

This seems to be a crucial point. On the one hand in fact, vesting the fundamental rights enshrined in the EUCFR with direct horizontal effects is the only viable option for removing the obstacles to involving private actors in the protection of fundamental rights on the Internet. On the other hand, however, the CJEU recently stressed the importance of horizontal application in its annual report for 2013.

[92] ibid para 96.

In the *Åklagaren* case,[93] a key passage in understanding this approach by the CJEU is that in which it held that

> European Union law precludes a judicial practice which makes the obligation for a national court to disapply any provision contrary to a fundamental right guaranteed by the Charter conditional upon that infringement being clear from the text of the Charter or the case-law relating to it, since it withholds from the national court the power to assess fully, with, as the case may be, the cooperation of the Court of Justice, whether that provision is compatible with the Charter.[94]

With respect to the latter risk, ie the adoption of an extreme data-based or data-oriented approach by the CJEU, at least two factors suggest that it is likely to entail detrimental consequences, especially in terms of the excessive Europeanisation of Internet regulation.

The first is the stance that EU data protection law should apply at all times in relation to European citizens, or rather persons resident in the EU, regardless first of all of the location of the servers used to process personal data, and secondly of whether or not the personal data are processed in Europe, considering also where the controller is established – and not only the place where the relevant equipment is located. The broad (or 'loose') interpretation given to the expression 'context of the activities' of an establishment brings the CJEU to the same conclusion that it would have most likely reached by applying the criterion provided for under Article 3(2) of the General Data Protection Regulation (GDPR).

The second aspect concerns the issue of the 'physical' location at which personal data are stored. This is a further stage within an alarming trend towards an excessive Europeanisation of the Internet by the European courts. This approach became apparent in the decision invalidating the Data Retention Directive in which, redirecting its attention from the problem of the applicable law to the physical infrastructure, the CJEU specified that

> [the] directive does not require the data in question to be retained within the European Union … it cannot be held that the control, explicitly required by Article 8(3) of the Charter, by an independent authority of compliance with the requirements of protection and security … is fully ensured.[95]

In this case, the CJEU referred to Article 8(3) EUCFR in order to justify the requirement that personal data of individuals resident in Europe that are processed in order to prevent attacks on national security must be stored within the territory of Member States. The problems of determining the applicable law and the place where data are stored are two elements within the same project of the European courts of building a data protection fortress in the Old Continent. While this fortress may be 'impregnable', it is likely to lack the necessary flexibility to ensure the actual extraterritorial application of EU law, protecting the right to digital privacy, as Chapter 4 will bring to light.

[93] Case C-617/10 *Åklagaren v Hans Åkerberg Fransson*, ECLI:EU:C:2013:280.
[94] ibid para 48.
[95] *Digital Rights Ireland* (n 59) para 68.

C. *Schrems*

There is another landmark decision which shows the role of judicial frames and the jurisdiction issue along the path towards digital privacy. The *Schrems I* decision followed along the lines of *Digital Rights Ireland* and *Google Spain*. This approach arose at several points in the decision, most notably when the court addressed certain issues. At the very outset, as a preliminary remark, the CJEU stressed that

> the provisions of Directive 95/46, inasmuch as they govern the processing of personal data liable to infringe fundamental freedoms, in particular, the right to respect for private life, must necessarily be interpreted in the light of the fundamental rights guaranteed by the Charter.[96]

This methodological premise paved the way for the CJEU to rely on a flexible and broad interpretation of the legal framework that was compatible with its purpose of a loose interpretation of the law. Another aspect that shows how the *Schrems I* decision reflects this goal is the enhancement of the powers vested in national data protection authorities. In particular, one of the questions raised by the national court was whether national regulators have *marge de manouvre* to challenge an EU Commission decision by assessing the adequacy of the level of protection ensured by third countries' legal systems. According to the CJEU, although the decision adopted pursuant to Article 25 of the Data Protection Directive is binding on all the Member States,[97] the existence of such an act does not deprive individuals of the right to appeal to the competent authorities according to Article 28(4) of Directive 95/46 in order to protect their fundamental rights. In this respect, it was Article 47 EUCFR that was considered by the CJEU.[98]

However, the court stressed that the EU Commission's decision may not undermine the powers of the national regulatory authorities to protect individuals' rights. In this respect therefore, the justification for manipulating the applicable legal framework took root when the CJEU provided a broad interpretation of the powers of these authorities to provide individuals with appropriate means to protect their personal data.[99] According to the CJEU:

> [I]t would be contrary to the system set up by Directive 95/46 and to the objective of Articles 25 and 28 thereof for a Commission decision adopted pursuant to Article 25(6) to have the effect of preventing a national supervisory authority from examining a

[96] Case C-362/14, *Maximillian Schrems v Data Protection Commissioner*, ECLI:EU:C:2015:650, para 38 (*Schrems I*).

[97] ibid para 51.

[98] ibid para 52. In particular: 'until such time as the Commission decision is declared invalid by the Court, the Member States and their organs, which include their independent supervisory authorities, admittedly cannot adopt measures contrary to that decision, such as acts intended to determine with binding effect that the third country covered by it does not ensure an adequate level of protection. Measures of the EU institutions are in principle presumed to be lawful and accordingly produce legal effects until such time as they are withdrawn, annulled in an action for annulment or declared invalid following a reference for a preliminary ruling or a plea of illegality'.

[99] ibid para 54.

> person's claim concerning the protection of his rights and freedoms in regard to the processing of his personal data which has been or could be transferred from a Member State to the third country covered by that decision.[100]

Thus, by interpreting the applicable legal framework in the light of Article 47 EUCFR, the CJEU enhanced individuals' rights under Articles 7 and 8 EUCFR, thus paving the way for enhancing the extent of protection for fundamental rights.

However, the most important point that brings out the loose interpretative approach of the CJEU can be found in the part of the decision that considers whether Decision 2000/520 met with the conditions laid down by Article 25 of the Data Protection Directive, which required an adequate level of protection for personal data transferred to third countries. This led the CJEU to consider whether the US legal system, and notably the safe harbour principles, afforded the personal data of European residents 'an adequate level of protection'. It is only if this requirement is fulfilled that the transfer of personal data to third countries is lawful under the EU legislative framework (at the time, the Data Protection Directive, now the GDPR).

The CJEU pointed out that the Data Protection Directive assumed a relatively flexible notion of 'adequate level of protection'. A rather significant degree of ambiguity and vagueness thus surrounds this parameter. The Data Protection Directive did not in fact set out in an exhaustive and systematic way the criteria to be applied by the competent European authorities when carrying out such an assessment. Nor did it provide a specific definition of the concept of 'adequacy'. Article 25(2) of Directive 95/46 only established that: 'The adequacy of the level of protection afforded by a third country shall be assessed in the light of all the circumstances surrounding a data transfer operation or set of data transfer operations'. In addition, it also suggested that

> particular consideration shall be given to the nature of the data, the purpose and duration of the proposed processing operation or operations, the country of origin and country of final destination, the rules of law, both general and sectoral, in force in the third country in question and the professional rules and security measures which are complied with in that country.

Indeed, in order to reduce this ambiguity and vagueness, the Data Protection Directive spelled out some factors that should be considered when assessing whether the level of protection offered by a third country is actually 'adequate'. Nonetheless, Article 25 of Directive 95/46 did not clarify whether these parameters are binding and exhaustive, thus preventing any evaluation from relying on different criteria.

On the one hand, the CJEU pointed out that Article 25(6) of the Data Protection Directive required (and the GDPR still requires) that a third country 'ensures' an adequate level of protection by reason of its domestic law or its international commitments. On the other hand, according to the CJEU, the adequacy

[100] ibid para 56.

of protection must be assessed 'for the protection of the private lives and basic freedoms and rights of individuals'. The assessment is thus not purely normative but is more demanding, being rooted in fundamental rights.

In order to assess the compatibility of the Decision on the safe harbour agreement with the Data Protection Directive, also in this case the CJEU acted as a fundamental rights adjudicator with a view to enforcing Articles 7 and 8 EUCFR. In the subsequent parts of the judgment,[101] the CJEU provided arguments that confirm its judicial frame focused on protecting fundamental rights through a strict interpretation of the notion of 'adequate level of protection'. The CJEU converted this parameter into a standard requiring that there be some kind of equivalence between the legal orders compared. In this respect, the CJEU referred back to the goal behind Article 25 of the Data Protection Directive, ie 'to ensure that the high level of that protection continues where personal data is transferred to a third country'. This was clear when the CJEU stated that

> [t]he word 'adequate' in Article 25(6) of Directive 95/46 admittedly signifies that a third country cannot be required to ensure a level of protection identical to that guaranteed in the EU legal order. However, as the Advocate General has observed in point 141 of his Opinion, the term 'adequate level of protection' must be understood as requiring the third country in fact to ensure, by reason of its domestic law or its international commitments, a level of protection of fundamental rights and freedoms that is essentially equivalent to that guaranteed within the European Union by virtue of Directive 95/46 read in the light of the Charter. If there were no such requirement, the objective referred to in the previous paragraph of the present judgment would be disregarded. Furthermore, the high level of protection guaranteed by Directive 95/46 read in the light of the Charter could easily be circumvented by transfers of personal data from the European Union to third countries for the purpose of being processed in those countries.[102]

Even though an adequate level of protection does not require third countries to adopt an identical standard, individuals may nevertheless enjoy a degree of protection that is 'substantially equivalent' to that offered by EU law.[103] The equivalence of the degree of protection is required, according to the court, 'by virtue of an interpretation of the Data Protection Directive in light of the Charter'.

[101] ibid para 72.
[102] ibid para 73.
[103] AG Opinion, Case C-498/16 *Maximillian Schrems v Data Protection Commissioner*, ECLI:EU:C:2015:627. In particular, paragraph 141 states: 'a third country ensures an adequate level of protection only where, following a global assessment of the law and practice in the third country in question, it is able to establish that that third country offers a level of protection that is essentially equivalent to that afforded by the Directive, even though the manner in which that protection is implemented may differ from that generally encountered within the European Union'. Therefore, it has been primarily the Advocate General who has manipulated the interpretation of the Directive. After having taken this crucial point, however, he has pointed out (para 142) that 'Although the English word "adequate" may be understood, from a linguistic viewpoint, as designating a level of protection that is just satisfactory or sufficient, and thus as having a different semantic scope from the French word "adéquat" ("appropriate"), the only criterion that must guide the interpretation of that word is the objective of attaining a high level of protection of fundamental rights, as required by Directive 95/46'.

The EUCFR thus becomes the judicial device for the advancement of the level of protection required by EU law through a loose interpretation of the parameter of 'adequacy'. This approach is anything but rhetorical since the CJEU was inspired by the entry into force of the EUCFR to revisit the provisions enshrined in the Data Protection Directive and to renew its interpretation of it. Therefore, the meaning of the provisions of the Data Protection Directive changed and, accordingly, the level of protection provided to personal data was much broader even before the adoption of the GDPR.

Moreover, the judgment seems to pay attention to the dynamic nature of the level of protection, which may vary in line with a number of factors. This is essentially why the CJEU urged the EU Commission to carry out regular checks into whether the finding concerning the adequacy of the level of protection offered by third countries is still factually and legally justified. In addition, 'such a check is required, in any event, when evidence gives rise to a doubt in that regard'.[104] To this end, the European institutions should take into account all factually and legally relevant circumstances occurring once this assessment was carried out. This approach mirrors a revisited interpretation of the standard of adequacy according to which a kind of 'continuity' in the level of protection should be guaranteed not only from a geographical, but also from a temporal viewpoint.[105] This dynamic view of the concept of adequacy arose when the CJEU pointed out that

> even though the means to which that third country has recourse, in this connection, for the purpose of ensuring such a level of protection may differ from those employed within the European Union in order to ensure that the requirements stemming from Directive 95/46 read in the light of the Charter are complied with, those means must nevertheless prove, in practice, effective in order to ensure protection essentially equivalent to that guaranteed within the European Union.[106]

Therefore, the Data Protection Directive no longer constituted the sole basis on which the legitimacy of the Decision on the safe harbour was based.

[104] *Schrems I* (n 96) para 76.

[105] AG Opinion, *Schrems I* (n 103). This approach reflects the influence of the Advocate General's opinion, particularly at paragraphs 146–48: '[I]n order to ensure that Article 25(1) to (3) of Directive 95/46 is effective, account should be taken of the fact that the adequacy of the level of protection afforded by a third country involves a developing situation that may change with the passage of time, depending on a series of factors. The Member States and the Commission must therefore be constantly alert to any change of circumstances that may necessitate a reassessment of whether the level of protection afforded by a third country is adequate. An assessment of the adequacy of that level of protection cannot be fixed at a specific time and then be maintained indefinitely, irrespective of any change in circumstances showing that in reality the level of protection afforded is no longer adequate. The obligation for the third country to ensure an adequate level of protection is thus an ongoing obligation. While the assessment is made at a specific time, retention of the adequacy decision presupposes that no circumstance that has since arisen is such as to call into question the initial assessment made by the Commission. Indeed, it must not be forgotten that the objective of Article 25 of Directive 95/46 is to prevent personal data from being transferred to a third country that does not ensure an adequate level of protection, in breach of the fundamental right to protection of personal data guaranteed by Article 8 of the Charter'.

[106] *Schrems I* (n 96) para 74.

Indeed, the parameter that the CJEU used to review the EU Commission's decision was the EUCFR, the entry into force of which shifted the judicial perspective from a mainly market-oriented to a fundamental rights approach.

On the one hand, the CJEU stressed that such an adequate level of protection can be achieved through the implementation of measures that may not necessarily correspond to those practised within the EU and provided for under Member States' domestic legislation. The CJEU seemed to step back by adopting an approach marked by self-restraint when recognising that the goal of guaranteeing appropriate protection may be pursued by different means, tailored to the relevant specific legal context. On the other hand, the CJEU did not take this path. The CJEU examined the US legal instruments for determining whether these measures were compatible with the purpose of granting an adequate level of protection to personal data. The CJEU challenged the safe harbour system by adopting reasoning that is quite uncommon when it comes to protecting fundamental rights. In particular, the judgment is remarkable for its rather unambiguously pragmatic view, which is reflected by the efforts made by the CJEU to determine whether the objective of ensuring adequate protection is actually met.

These remarks constituted the premise for the analysis carried out by the CJEU of the compliance of the safe harbour principles with EU law. The CJEU reached the conclusion that the US measures did not provide personal data with adequate protection compared to the EU standard. Although the review was formally conducted by comparing the Data Protection Directive with the content of the safe harbour principles, from a substantive standpoint, the decision of the CJEU found that the US legal system was not compatible with the protection of the fundamental rights enshrined in Articles 7 and 8 EUCFR.

The reasoning behind this decision deserves to be analysed in the light of the precedent established by the CJEU in *Digital Rights Ireland*. First, while in *Schrems I* the CJEU focused on annulling Decision 2000/520 based on the adequacy of the level of protection offered by the US legal order, in *Digital Rights Ireland* the CJEU applied exclusively an internal perspective based on the EU paradigm of protection for fundamental rights, especially Articles 7 and 8 EUCFR. In other words, in *Schrems I* the US framework operated as the parameter for assessing compliance with fundamental rights by an act from the EU legal order. Indeed, the interpretation of 'adequacy' was reviewed by focusing on the compatibility between the US approach and the EUCFR since, as was recognised by the CJEU, personal data of EU individuals were not properly protected by the US standard. Moreover, a factual element needs to be included in such an assessment. Indeed, it is necessary to refer to the influence of the National Security Agency (NSA) scandal in the US, which at the time had largely captured the attention of the international community in the area of state surveillance.[107]

[107] For a comparative overview, see, in particular, Francesca Bignami and Giorgio Resta, 'Transatlantic Privacy Regulation: Conflict and Cooperation' (2015) 8 *Law and Contemporary Problems* 231.

However, it is necessary to also take into consideration the effects that the *Schrems I* case produced on the US system in the aftermath of the decision. In particular, in the case *ACLU v Clapper*,[108] the US Court of Appeals for the Second Circuit ruled that Section 215 of the USA Patriot Act did not authorise the NSA to conduct bulk surveillance and to mass harvest metadata. In particular:

> [T]he bulk collection of data as to essentially the entire population of the United States, something inconceivable before the advent of high-speed computers, permits the development of a government database with a potential for invasions of privacy unimaginable in the past. Thus, appellants argue, the program cannot simply be sustained on the reasoning that permits the government to obtain, for a limited period of time as applied to persons suspected of wrongdoing, a simple record of the phone numbers contained in their service providers' billing records.[109]

Moreover, Section 215 of the USA Patriot Act contained an expiration clause, which was not renewed by the US Senate. Therefore, the USA Freedom Act did not extend the validity of this provision.[110]

Also, another important point concerns the protection of personal data in relation to national security, an interest which is generally evaluated under the discretion of the Member States. Protection of national security is not in fact subject to harmonisation at EU level. Member States can thus adopt different solutions, which may also impinge upon the protection of personal data, despite the existence of a harmonised data protection legal framework (in contrast to events following the recent pandemic, where a common European approach to the implementation of contact tracing technologies was possible under the umbrella of the GDPR, thus fostering the development of various apps according to common guidelines). Here, the EU constitutional system can mitigate such asymmetry by harmonising protection for such fundamental rights. In particular, Article 6(2) Treaty on European Union (TEU) considers ECHR rights as general principles of EU law and, thus, Article 52(3) EUCFR clarifies that protection for the rights enshrined in the EUCFR shall be equal to the meaning and the scope of ECHR rights.[111] As a result, the ECHR can be considered as another (even implicit) parameter within the decision in question.

[108] *ACLU v Clapper* 785 F3d 787 (2d Cir 2015).

[109] ibid 824.

[110] Alan Yuhas, 'NSA reform: USA Freedom Act passes first surveillance reform in decade – as it happened', *The Guardian* (2 June 2015) at www.theguardian.com/us-news/live/2015/jun/02/senate-nsa-surveillance-usa-freedom-act-congress-live; Cindy Cohn and Rainey Reitman, 'USA Freedom Act Passes: What We Celebrate, What We Mourn, and Where We Go From Here', *Electronic Frontier Foundation* (2 June 2015) at www.eff.org/it/deeplinks/2015/05/usa-freedom-act-passes-what-we-celebrate-what-we-mourn-and-where-we-go-here.

[111] Case C-399/11 *Stefano Melloni v Ministerio Fiscal*, ECLI:EU:C:2013:107; *Åklagaren* (n 93). Among others, see Leonard FM Besselink, 'The Parameters of Constitutional Conflict after Melloni' (2014) 39 *European Law Review* 531; Maartje De Visser, 'Dealing with Divergences in Fundamental Rights Standards' (2013) 20 *Maastricht Journal of European and Comparative Law* 576; Giulia Cavallone, 'European Arrest Warrant and Fundamental Rights in Decisions Rendered in Absentia: The Extent of Union Law in the Case C-399/11 Melloni v Ministerio Fiscal' (2014) 4 *European Criminal Law Review* 19.

This can be demonstrated by focusing on the following decisions of the ECtHR, with the case of *Zakharov v Russia* (mentioned above) being considered as a sequel to the *Schrems I* case.[112] In that case, the applicant – a journalist – complained that his telephone conversations had been intercepted by the Russian authorities in order to prevent terrorist attacks. The issue was that the telecommunications service providers had been obliged to set up devices for interception of private communications without a prior court order. The domestic courts rejected the journalist's claim due to a lack of evidence.

However, the Grand Chamber of the ECtHR recognised that the right to private life had been violated.[113] In this case, the ECtHR followed a path which is very similar to that of the CJEU in the *Schrems I* case, granting broad protection to the right enshrined in Article 8 ECHR, even given the absence of any strong evidence regarding the harm suffered by the complainant. According to the ECtHR:

> Russian legal provisions governing interceptions of communications do not provide for adequate and effective guarantees against arbitrariness and the risk of abuse which is inherent in any system of secret surveillance, and which is particularly high in a system where the secret services and the police have direct access, by technical means, to all mobile telephone communications. In particular, the circumstances in which public authorities are empowered to resort to secret surveillance measures are not defined with sufficient clarity. Provisions on discontinuation of secret surveillance measures do not provide sufficient guarantees against arbitrary interference. The domestic law permits automatic storage of clearly irrelevant data and is not sufficiently clear as to the circumstances in which the intercept material will be stored and destroyed after the end of a trial. The authorisation procedures are not capable of ensuring that secret surveillance measures are ordered only when 'necessary in a democratic society'. The supervision of interceptions, as it is currently organised, does not comply with the requirements of independence, powers and competence which are sufficient to exercise an effective and continuous control, public scrutiny and effectiveness in practice. The effectiveness of the remedies is undermined by the absence of notification at any point of interceptions, or adequate access to documents relating to interceptions.[114]

In this case, the court based its decision on the threat to the rights of the journalist according to the standard developed in the *Klass* case and the *Kennedy* case, where it had found that a threat can amount to a violation of the ECHR if two cumulative conditions are met: the applicant must be among the individuals potentially affected by the implementation of the mass surveillance systems at hand; and the absence of any legal remedies available to the applicant. According to the *Kennedy* decision, it is sufficient that the applicant's right to a private life has potentially

[112] Paul De Hert and Pedro C Bocos, 'Case of Roman Zakharov v Russia: The Strasbourg follow up to the Luxembourg Court's Schrems judgment', *Strasbourg Observers* (23 December 2015) at https://strasbourgobservers.com/2015/12/23/case-of-roman-zakharov-v-russia-the-strasbourg-follow-up-to-the-luxembourg-courts-schrems-judgment/.

[113] Lorna Woods, 'Zakharov v Russia: Mass Surveillance and the European Court of Human Rights', *EU Law Analysis* (16 December 2015) at http://eulawanalysis.blogspot.com/2015/12/zakharov-v-russia-mass-surveillance-and.html.

[114] *Zakharov* (n 32) para 302.

been put at risk in order for his application to be lodged before the court. For this reason, the *Zakharov* case mirrors the *Schrems I* judgment. In both cases, the violation of fundamental rights was only based *in abstracto* on a finding that the legal environment was liable to jeopardise the essence of those rights and not on a specific threat or on the degree of likelihood.

Turning back to the EU framework, it is possible also to consider the *Schrems I* case with reference to the principle of equivalence for the protection of fundamental rights in Europe. As noted above, adequacy was the main parameter according to which the CJEU reviewed the compatibility of the decision on the safe harbour agreement with the EUCFR. The first case which should be mentioned is the *Kadi* saga.[115] In particular, the CJEU specified that the EU is grounded on the rule of law when clarifying that all acts of its institutions are subject to a review of their compatibility with, in particular, the EU Treaties, general principles of law and fundamental rights.

Connecting the *Schrems I* decision with this view in the *Kadi* judgment,[116] the existence of an autonomous model of protection for fundamental rights emerged. This is an example of how, since the adoption of the EUCFR, the EU has started to abandon its mainly economic view of constitutionalisation, most notably in the area of fundamental rights. As already explained at the start of this chapter, while at the very outset EU protection for fundamental rights was mainly justified by the need to protect the economic freedoms established by the EU Treaties, nowadays the situation has changed since the level of protection for fundamental rights determines the degree of protection for other interests and any act of EU law must be compatible with the EUCFR as primary source of law.

However, an important difference which deserves to be underlined was the perspective adopted in the two cases. Indeed, in *Kadi*, the perspective was external since the threat to fundamental rights lay with an act of international law, specifically a resolution of the United Nations Security Council. In *Schrems I*, on the other hand, the challenges to fundamental rights that EU law had to face were not posed by an act of international law but rather by the US legal system, and in particular by the safe harbour principle. In this case, it was not international law that was at stake but rather the legal order of a third country which posed certain threats to EU fundamental rights.

[115] Case T-315/01 *Kadi v Council and Commission* [2005] ECR II-3649; Joined Cases C-402/05 P and C-415/05 P *Yassin Abdullah Kadi and Al Barakaat International Foundation v Council of the European Union and Commission of the European Communities* [2008] ECR I-6351; Case T-85/09 *Yassin Abdullah Kadi v European Commission* [2010] II-5177; Joined Cases C-584/10 P, C-593/10 P and C-595/10 P *European Commission and others v Yassin Abdullah Kadi* [2013] ECR II-518.

[116] See, in particular, Juliane Kokott and Christoph Sobotta, 'The Kadi Case – Constitutional Core Values and International Law – Finding the Balance?' (2012) 23 *European Journal of International Law* 1015; Matej Avbelj, Filippo Fontanelli and Giuseppe Martinico (eds), *Kadi on Trial: A Multifaceted Analysis of the Kadi Trial* (Abingdon-New York, Routledge, 2014); Christian Tomuschat, 'Primacy of the United Nations Law. Innovation Features in the Community Legal Order' (2006) 43 *Common Market Law Review* 537.

As regards the principle of equivalence, another significant reference comes once again from the ECHR framework, in particular from the case of *Bosphorus v Ireland*.[117] In this case, the ECtHR refused to review the compatibility of a regulation with the ECHR by arguing that, as secondary sources of EU law which do not require implementation by the Member States, the presumption of ECHR compliance applies. The ECtHR had already addressed these cases, ruling that Contracting States are not liable for obligations established by EU law where such acts do not leave states any room for discretion. In the *Bosphorus* case, the ECtHR specified that the principle of equivalence must be interpreted by taking into account the comparability of the orders at stake:

> [B]y 'equivalent' the Court means 'comparable'; any requirement that the organisation's protection be 'identical' could run counter to the interest of international cooperation pursued … However, any such finding of equivalence could not be final and would be susceptible to review in the light of any relevant change in fundamental rights protection.[118]

Hence, Member States cannot be held liable for violations of the ECHR when they act in accordance with provisions of EU law that are directly applicable. Such a presumption that Member States guarantee an equivalent level of protection can be rebutted only if the protection of the rights covered by the ECHR is manifestly insufficient.

As a result, the *Schrems I* decision provided a new perspective in terms of adequacy. While the above examples consider the issue of granting an equivalent level of protection respectively between the EU legal order and international law (ie *Kadi*) or between the EU legal order and the ECtHR framework (ie *Bosphorus*), in *Schrems I* the CJEU addressed the relationship between the EU legal order and the level of protection guaranteed to fundamental rights by a national legal order of a third country.

Besides, in this case the CJEU also pointed out that it is for the EU Commission to regularly check whether the legal orders of the third countries concerned provide personal data with an adequate level of protection, in the light of any legal and factual circumstances that may affect it. This statement reflects a dynamic, more practical and changing understanding of the standard of adequacy.[119]

[117] *Bosphorus Hava Jollari Turizm ve Ticaret v Ireland*, App no 45036/98, judgment of 30 June 2005. See, in particular, Cathryn Costello, 'The Bosphorus Ruling of the European Court of Human Rights: Fundamental Rights and Blurred Boundaries in Europe' (2006) 6 *Human Rights Law Review* 87; Frank Schorkopf, 'The European Court of Human Rights' Judgment in the Case of Bosphorus Hava Yollari Turizm v Ireland' (2005) 6 *German Law Journal* 1255; Steve Peers, 'Bosphorus – European Court of Human Rights: Limited Responsibility of European Union Member States for Actions within the Scope of Community Law Judgment of 30 June 2005, Bosphorus Airways v Ireland, Application No. 45036/98' (2006) 2 *European Constitutional Law Review* 443.

[118] *Bosphorus* (n 117) para 155.

[119] See among others, taking account of the post-*Schrems* scenario, Christopher Kuner, 'Reality and Illusion in EU Data Transfer Regulation Post Schrems' (2017) 18(4) *German Law Journal* 881, who notes that the *Schrems I* decision has brought to light the (wrong) attitude of EU data protection law that looks only at legalistic mechanisms in order to guarantee the data transfers rather than at effective protection of data transferred.

It must, however, be considered whether the CJEU was affected by a decrease in the level of protection ensured by the US legal system, compared to the standard in force when the safe harbour agreement was concluded, or whether the judgment was instead a reaction to the risk of reduced protection for European residents in the light of purely internal factors. In a nutshell, the question is whether the CJEU's decision reflects an evolution of the relevant background or rather an involution that urged Europe to raise its defences.

These considerations might contribute to defining a dynamic level of protection for privacy and personal data from at least two different perspectives. First, the range of factors that must be considered by the EU Commission when evaluating the adequacy of the protection offered by third countries becomes broader. Indeed, the EU Commission would not limit its assessment to the status quo, but rather regularly check whether any assessment previously carried out still corresponds to the standard of adequate protection in light of the relevant factual and legal circumstances. Secondly, the CJEU recognised that the EU Commission's discretion in evaluating the protection offered by non-EU countries is narrow and that it is necessary to adopt a strict scrutiny in relation to Article 25 of the Data Protection Directive (and now the corresponding provisions of the GDPR) in order to safeguard the right to privacy and data protection. The adoption of the strict scrutiny test reflects the revisited understanding of Directive 95/46. This act was intended, at the very beginning, to regulate purely economic matters, while it has been regarded more recently as the cornerstone for affording a high degree of protection to the fundamental rights to privacy and personal data. Finally, the CJEU, as mentioned, basically rewrote the relevant criteria: from adequacy to essential equivalence. This constitutes further important evidence of the 'manipulation through interpretation' which the CJEU engaged in through this decision.

In Chapter 4 we will focus on how this approach has been followed even in *Schrems II*.[120]

As already addressed, the high level of protection for fundamental rights to privacy and data protection in the EU is a hot topic, especially as the GDPR entered into force only a few months after the resolution of this court case. Indeed, the EU personal data fortress would most likely reinforce the transnational nature of data, underlining the jurisdictional issue and therefore, once again, the role of courts.

IV. The European Personal Data Fortress

The extensive interpretation of the scope of the right to privacy and data protection no longer represents a novelty within the case law of the European courts. As examined above, the CJEU has played a critical role in underlining the relevance

[120] Case C-311/18 *Data Protection Commissioner v Facebook Ireland Limited and Maximillian Schrems*, ECLI:EU:C:2020:559. Marc Rotenberg, 'Schrems II: From Snowden to China, the Evolution of Data Protection as a Fundamental Right' (2020) *European Law Journal*, forthcoming.

of data protection in the European framework.[121] This has been done by adopting a judicial frame that sought to ensure broad protection to Articles 7 and 8 EUCFR which, in *Google Spain*, should in principle prevail over the economic interest of search engine service providers.

In addition, the same 'data privacy-oriented' approach is confirmed by the lack of any reference to other conflicting interests such as freedom of information. Therefore, starting from the judgment on the invalidation of the Data Retention Directive, the CJEU started to build a European personal data fortress through the emphatic enforcement of Articles 7 and 8 EUCFR. In fact, there does not appear to be any difference in terms of the ranking of fundamental rights, if one considers the catalogue encapsulated by the EUCFR. Against this background, it goes without saying that fundamental rights may conflict with one another under certain circumstances: it is up to the courts, in such cases, to strike a balance in order to ensure that the substantial essence of the rights at stake is respected or that any restrictions are necessary for and proportionate to the aim pursued.

A similar judicial frame lies behind the judgment of the CJEU in *Digital Rights Ireland* and *Schrems*. In *Digital Rights Ireland* the technological factor led the CJEU to adopt a frame of protection in order to invalidate an EU legal instrument for the first time in European history. Indeed, in order to ensure effective protection for the fundamental rights enshrined in the EUCFR, the CJEU balanced privacy and data protection against legitimate interests, thus emancipating data protection from its linkage with the right to privacy.

In *Schrems I* the CJEU noted that, while regulating the transfer of personal data from the EU to third countries, the Data Protection Directive assumed that such transfers were necessary for the expansion of international trade.[122] In addition, the judgment took account of the fact that transfers are strategic within the international context and also impact upon the economic fundamental freedoms provided for under the EU Treaties. When exploring how the safe harbour principles did actually protect personal data, the CJEU scrutinised how these principles operate in practical terms under US law and how they actually safeguard the protection of personal data as well as other relevant freedoms, including the freedom to conduct business. Nonetheless, the court imposed an important requirement: transfers of personal data must only occur when an essentially equivalent level of protection is ensured. On this view, the freedom to conduct business, as well as any other interests related to organisations that process personal data, must never prevail over data protection except under very exceptional circumstances. By adopting such a judicial frame, the CJEU followed in the wake of the *Google Spain* decision, relying once again on an expansive view of data privacy in the digital context.

The CJEU thus revisited its well-established traditional approach as guardian of the fundamental economic freedoms established under the EU Treaties.

[121] Fernanda Nicola and Oreste Pollicino, 'The Balkanization of Data Privacy Regulation' (2020) *West Virginia Law Review*, forthcoming.

[122] *Schrems I* (n 96) para 48.

While in the past fundamental rights represented legitimate exceptions that, in situations involving compelling reasons, could be enforced in order to justify restrictions on economic freedoms, now the protection of economic freedoms must not prevail over individuals' fundamental rights. However, in this way, the CJEU introduced a difference among rights and freedoms covered by the EUCFR, which by contrast protects fundamental rights equally. This new interpretation of the catalogue of fundamental rights protected by the EUCFR has indirectly paved the way for transforming the standard of adequate protection for personal data into a standard of substantial equivalence.

The effects of the CJEU's judicial activism are not limited to these considerations. The CJEU has also reversed the legal significance of the Data Protection Directive and the Charter from a chronological point of view. By following a trend that was already apparent in *Google Spain*, the court pointed out that Article 25(6) of the Data Protection Directive implemented the obligation to provide personal data with a high degree of protection enshrined in Article 8 EUCFR. Likewise, in *Google Spain* the CJEU observed that certain provisions of the Data Protection Directive sought to transpose and render enforceable the obligations stemming from Articles 7 and 8 EUCFR.

According to this view, the Data Protection Directive, which entered into force in 1995, is intended to implement the rights enshrined in the EUCFR, which was drafted in 2001 and formally ranked among primary sources of EU law only in 2007. By reversing the chronological order of the acts at hand, the CJEU reaffirmed the natural relationship between primary sources and secondary acts of EU law, and most notably between the EUCFR and the relevant EU directives.

This argument does not undermine the assumption that the EUCFR only reaffirms, as is stated in its preamble, the rights and freedoms already protected under EU law, for instance through the category of general principles or by reference to the ECHR. However, in order to understand the approach of the CJEU to ensuring the maximum degree of protection for personal data, it is necessary to consider the case law in the area of digital privacy as an attempt to adopt a judicial frame, adapting privacy and data protection to the new technological scenario. Furthermore, it should not be forgotten that the same values have been shielded since 1950 in relation to Article 8 ECHR. In these years, the ECHR has influenced EU law, affecting de facto the content of Member States' constitutional traditions and playing a significant role as part of the general principles of EU law pursuant to Article 6(2) TEU.

However, even assuming that the provisions of the Data Protection Directive were 'indirectly' implementing the obligations stemming from the Convention, which were encapsulated in the EUCFR more than half a century later, there are two objections that cannot be overcome. First, the CJEU has not referred to the ECHR but only to the relationship between the EUCFR and the relevant provisions of the Data Protection Directive. The interpretation of the CJEU, in other words, seems to be a very formal one and focused only on the enforceable sources of EU law. A second critical point arises with regard to the difference between the extent of the protection ensured by the EUCFR compared to the ECHR. In fact, the EUCFR expressly refers both to the right to private and family life and to the right to data protection, whereas the ECHR concentrates the relevant protection within Article 8 ECHR, which formally speaking only deals with the right to privacy. Therefore, at least from a formal and textual point of view, the EUCFR apparently affords broader protection to the interests at stake.

The European personal data fortress resulting from the amplification of judicial momentum is also built on an extension of the reach of EU law. While the jurisdictional issue is less relevant in *Digital Rights Ireland*, in *Google Spain* and *Schrems I* the CJEU applied EU provisions in light of the fundamental rights enshrined in the EUCFR beyond the borders of Europe, thus claiming its digital sovereignty. In *Google Spain*, by expansively interpreting the notion of establishment, it limited the power of search engines, as private actors, to perform their digital business on a global scale without being subject to the regulations of the country in which they operate.[123] Likewise, in *Schrems I*, the CJEU's assessment of the safe harbour was primarily driven by the need to ensure that the formal notion of territory and jurisdiction would not substantially undermine effective protection for fundamental rights in the digital domain.

That said, it is worth considering whether this judicial activism might change in the light of the GDPR's territorial scope. Before focusing on the GDPR in Chapter 4, it will be interesting to consider a decision of the Supreme Court of British Columbia of 2014, which was handed down[124] before the CJEU adopted a new stance in 2019 in *Google v CNIL*[125] to clarify that the right to be forgotten enshrined in Article 17 GDPR cannot be enforced outside the EU. Here, the Supreme Court of British Columbia – which was expressly quoted by the CJEU decision in *Google Spain* – addressed the problem of the extraterritorial application of the domestic protection afforded to personal data and, more generally, the lack of effectiveness of solutions designed only on a local (and not necessarily a national) basis.

The plaintiff had sought an interim injunction preventing Google from displaying search results linking to a website, which was alleged to violate the plaintiff's intellectual property rights. Google had complied with the order, although the removal only affected the Canadian version of the search engine (google.ca). Therefore, links to the relevant website were still being provided by the other non-Canadian search engines operated by Google. The Canadian Supreme Court of British Columbia, thus, ordered Google to delete certain web pages from its search results not only from the national search engine, but worldwide. The case

[123] On the consequences of these judgments on this specific field see Christopher Docksey, 'The EU Approach to the Protection of Rights in the Digital Environment: Today and Tomorrow – State Obligations and Responsibilities of Private Parties – GDPR Rules on Data Protection, and What to Expect from the Upcoming ePrivacy Regulation' in Council of Europe (ed), *Human Rights Challenges in the Digital Age: Judicial Perspectives* (Strasbourg, Council of Europe Publishing, 2020) 47.

[124] *Equustek Solutions Inc v Jack* [2014] BCSC 1063.

[125] Case C-507/17 *Google v CNIL*, ECLI:EU:C:2019:772.

therefore involved an order for removal worldwide, which most likely constituted an attempt to respond to the problems of fragmentation of legal protection, which are inherently connected to the local nature of the enforcement jurisdiction.

Google not only brought an appeal against the decision, but also applied for a partial stay of the order while the appeal was pending, arguing that compliance with the court order would have resulted in irreparable harm to it.

The British Columbia Court of Appeal dismissed Google's appeal, finding that the court had territorial jurisdiction to issue that decision not only in Canada, but also outside its territory.[126] Google argued in particular that, since it operates online, the territorial jurisdiction of the Canadian court does not apply. Here, it is particularly interesting to observe how the court relied on the *Google Spain* decision, where the same argument used by Google was not upheld by the CJEU. Indeed, as the British Columbia Court of Appeal observed:

> Google submits that it merely offers a passive website to residents of British Columbia who wish to search the internet. It argues that its programs automatically generate search results without Google being actively involved in the particular search … I conclude that Google's internet search websites are not passive information sites. As a user begins to type a few letters or a word of their query, Google anticipates the request and offers a menu of suggested potential search queries … Google sells advertising to British Columbia clients. Indeed, Google entered into an advertising contract with the defendants and advertised their products up to the hearing of this application.[127]

Having established the reasons why the Canadian court was competent to issue its decision in the case in question, the British Columbia Court of Appeal focused on the issue of extraterritoriality. In a similar manner to *Google Spain*, the issue was to grant effective protection to the plaintiff and to prevent the law from being circumvented through the online environment. While the focus in *Google Spain* was on the protection of the fundamental rights of EU citizens, here the Canadian courts focused on equity considerations:[128]

> [T]he process was wholly unsatisfactory from the plaintiffs' perspective. In place of the de-indexed websites, a whole host of new websites moved up the rankings to take their place. Websites can be generated automatically, resulting in an endless game of 'whac-a-mole' with the plaintiffs identifying new URLs and Google deleting them. The plaintiffs argue that any scheme that depends on the deletion of individual URLs is ineffective … I conclude that the Court has authority to grant an injunction against a non-party resident in a foreign jurisdiction in appropriate circumstances. The fact that an injunction has not before been made against an internet search provider such as Google is reason to tread carefully, but does not establish that the Court does not have subject matter competence.[129]

[126] *Equustek Solutions Inc v Google Inc* [2015] BCCA 265.

[127] ibid paras 47–48 and 50.

[128] The argument of the BC courts was based on s 39 of the Law and Equity Act. According to this law, injunctions may be issued 'in all cases in which it appears to the court to be just or convenient that the order should be made … on terms and conditions the court thinks just'.

[129] *Equustek Solutions Inc v Jack* (n 126) paras 72 and 133.

Although Google argued that the Canadian courts did not have the power to impose the delisting of searches worldwide since Google could be put in the situation of having to violate foreign law, the Supreme Court of British Columbia nonetheless also dismissed this argument, showing a deep understanding of how the online environment functions, and held that

> although Google has a website for each country to which searches made within that country default, users can override that default and access other country's Google websites. For example, even if the defendants' websites were blocked from searches conducted through www.google.ca, Canadian users can go to www.google.co.uk or www.google.fr and obtain results including the defendants' websites. On the record before me it appears that to be effective, even within Canada, Google must block search results on all of its websites.[130]

However, these reasons of the British Columbia courts were not enough for Google, which decided to appeal to the Supreme Court of Canada. In 2017 the ruling of the Supreme Court of Canada can be considered as a landmark decision since it recognised that Canadian courts, by virtue of their jurisdiction, can order global de-indexing against search engines.[131] In particular, such orders on search engines are intended to address unlawful online activities, which, in the case in question, consisted in the sale of products created by using misappropriated trade secrets.

Even during this phase, Google tried to argue, inter alia, that the courts enjoy limited jurisdiction within their own territory and cannot impose extraterritorial orders on search engines. In addition, it argued more broadly that a worldwide order would violate the principle of comity as well as freedom of speech. Focusing in particular on the possibility for the courts to impose orders with extraterritorial effects, by following a path similar to the British Columbia courts, the Supreme Court of Canada explained why such an order could be justified according to the circumstances of the case:[132]

> The problem in this case is occurring online and globally. The Internet has no borders – its natural habitat is global. The only way to ensure that the interlocutory injunction attained its objective was to have it apply where Google operates – globally. As Fenlon J. found, the majority of Datalink's sales take place outside Canada. If the injunction were restricted to Canada alone or to google.ca, as Google suggests it should have been, the remedy would be deprived of its intended ability to prevent irreparable harm … There is no equity in ordering an interlocutory injunction which has no realistic prospect of preventing irreparable harm.

In this case, the imposition of an injunction sought to avoid irreparable damage associated with the data flows facilitated by Google's services. Otherwise, Datalink's business on the Internet would be commercially impossible.

[130] ibid para 148.
[131] *Google Inc v Equustek Solutions Inc* [2017] SCC 34.
[132] ibid para 41.

Focusing on the principle of comity and freedom of expression, Google complained that the imposition of an extraterritorial order would violate the principle of comity since Google could be forced in some cases to violate the law of other states. Even with regard to freedom of speech, Google observed that this kind of injunction risks compromising freedom of expression on the Internet. However, in this case, the Supreme Court of Canada also rejected these arguments.

First, the Supreme Court of Canada observed that the violation of the principle of comity is only theoretical since Google had not provided sufficient evidence of the impact of a global delisting order on the legal orders of other states. Secondly, the right to freedom of expression cannot justify the facilitation of unlawful activities occurring online. These are the two main reasons that led the Supreme Court of Canada to state that

> [i]n the absence of an evidentiary foundation, and given Google's right to seek a rectifying order, it hardly seems equitable to deny Equustek the extraterritorial scope it needs to make the remedy effective, or even to put the onus on it to demonstrate, country by country, where such an order is legally permissible. We are dealing with the Internet after all, and the balance of convenience test has to take full account of its inevitable extraterritorial reach when injunctive relief is being sought against an entity like Google. This is not an order to remove speech that, on its face, engages freedom of expression values, it is an order to de-index websites that are in violation of several court orders. We have not, to date, accepted that freedom of expression requires the facilitation of the unlawful sale of goods.[133]

The decision in question is relevant since, as previously addressed in Chapter 1, the fundamental issue at stake was the relationship between technology and the courts. The increasing development of online activities has inevitably created new threats and risks, in addition to establishing new opportunities and channels for a variety of activities. Within this framework, the victims of such illegal conduct may have limited scope for enforcing their rights against various offenders. Furthermore, since online conduct usually involves multiple jurisdictions, it is becoming increasingly crucial to define remedies with extraterritorial effects in order to avoid individuals being forced to bring legal proceedings in every country where such illicit conduct occurs.

As will also be addressed in Chapter 4, the extraterritorial scope of the GDPR codifies the judicial attempts by the CJEU to ensure effective protection for the rights of their citizens from a transnational perspective. In particular, Article 3(2) GDPR can be considered as the result of the high-level standard of protection for privacy in the EU, which, in the information society, can no longer be limited to the EU territory but needs to be ensured globally. In particular, according to Article 3(2) GDPR:

> This Regulation applies to the processing of personal data of data subjects who are in the Union by a controller or processor not established in the Union, where the processing

[133] ibid paras 47–48.

> activities are related to: (a) the offering of goods or services, irrespective of whether a payment of the data subject is required, to such data subjects in the Union; or (b) the monitoring of their behaviour as far as their behaviour takes place within the Union.

The consequence of such a rule is twofold. On the one hand, this provision concerns the issue of jurisdiction. In particular, all cases involving the processing of personal data that fall within the scope of Article 3(2) GDPR will be subject to EU jurisdiction. This approach will overcome the doctrine of establishment developed by the CJEU in *Google Spain* since even those entities that are not established in the EU will be subject to the GDPR. Even more importantly, the main consequence is essentially to extend EU privacy rules to the global context – and this is more a matter of digital sovereignty. While, as noted above, the CJEU dealt with the standard of protection of US measures for processing the personal data of EU citizens in the *Schrems I* case, now the operative parameter will be the EU one as established by the GDPR.

V. Conclusions

The cases considered in the above overview seem to be the most critical point of the process of judicial Europeanisation of the Internet, the transnational nature of which seems to be incompatible with attempts to 'regionalise' protection, even if this process is inspired by the purpose of increasing the degree of such protection. This process of regionalisation, as an example of the amplification of judicial momentum, is likely to result in the fragmentation and, perhaps, the balkanisation of the Internet and the related legal instruments for protection.

It goes without saying that the contrast between the territorial limits of the enforcement jurisdiction and the global nature of the digital service could entail risks of a race to the bottom in the protection of the rights at issue and a lack of effectiveness in the respective mechanisms for protection. It is a further expression of the conflict between local and global law that characterises judicial globalisation.

The case law analysis reveals a migration of legal (or constitutional) ideas across the Atlantic.[134] Thus far, the migration has been almost exclusively unidirectional. European judges 'export' European ideas outside Europe. Put differently, EU courts' rulings, which are extensively quoted in an attempt to increase the legitimacy and persuasiveness of their own rulings, inspire and influence non-EU judges, as occurred in Canada. Any reverse treatment appears to be largely off the judicial agenda for the time being. The European courts seem more inclined 'to teach' rather than 'to learn' when discussing the protection, *erga omnes*, of European constitutional values, even beyond the reaches of Europe. In other words, European judicial dialogue remains European-value based even when it is globalised.

[134] Krystyna Kowalik-Bańczyk and Oreste Pollicino, 'Migration of European Judicial Ideas Concerning Jurisdiction Over Google on Withdrawal of Information' (2016) 17(3) *German Law Journal* 315.

Once we observe such a unidirectional migration of ideas, it is worth focusing on which European ideas are migrating. The CJEU's reasoning in *Google Spain* possibly asserts that the main idea is to adapt the right to privacy to the characteristics of the digital world. Warren and Brandeis depicted this, looking at the world of atoms. Some doubt remains as to whether the CJEU may have taken too seriously the issue of the definition and protection of this new right. As a result, it may have overseen the consequences that are likely to result from this new approach, which was most probably brought about by the scandal surrounding the NSA case. Two negative consequences should be carefully considered.

The first consequence of this new approach is the possible underestimation of the implications of offering such an extreme degree of protection to personal data vis-à-vis the protection of other constitutional values – for example, other fundamental rights. Above all, this concerns freedom of expression. Furthermore, there is a risk that such an extreme approach may result in an excess of 'Europeanisation' of Internet regulation. The European courts may be victims, in other words, of a self-referential attitude.

With regard to the first risk, freedom of expression receives less protection in the digital world. As was noted above, the absence of any express reference to Article 11 EUCFR in *Google Spain* is only one of the signals confirming that the balance seems to be skewed in favour of the right to digital privacy. A consequence of this overbalancing is that it results in a degree of protection for freedom of expression on the Internet that is lower than the standard of protection granted by the courts within non-digital freedom of expression cases. Such a trend is also visible in the ECtHR, which, as seen in Chapter 2, while using different arguments, seems to reach the same conclusions as the CJEU, downgrading protection for freedom of expression when it is exercised on the Internet, as it is concerned more with the threats that its exercise may determine than about the opportunities it may entail.

With respect to the second risk, there are at least two indications that point towards possible detrimental consequences, especially in terms of an excessive 'Europeanisation' of Internet regulation.

The first signal is the rapidly increasing inclination to apply EU law on data protection whenever a case involves European citizens, especially if the citizen is resident in the EU. First, courts apply EU law regardless of the circumstances surrounding the processing of personal data. If the effects were not felt in Europe, the analysis takes into account the place where the controller is established and not solely the place where the relevant equipment is located. Secondly, the courts apply EU law regardless of where the process servers are located. The broad interpretation given to the notion 'context of the activities' of an establishment brings the CJEU to the same conclusion that it would most likely have reached by applying Article 3(2) GDPR. In fact, the CJEU has adopted an expansive interpretation of this expression by taking it to mean that a controller is not necessarily the same subject that actually processes personal data.

The second signal concerns the issue of the physical location at which personal data are stored. This forms part of the alarming trend toward the excessive

'Europeanisation' of the Internet by the EU courts. This approach can be seen in *Digital Rights Ireland* in which the CJEU invalidated the Data Retention Directive. The problems of determining the applicable law and the place of data storage are two aspects within the same project of the EU courts, which seeks to turn European law, and the territory of Europe, into a possible data protection fortress. It is a fortress that, even if otherwise considered impregnable, might lack the necessary flexibility to ensure the actual extraterritorial application of EU law, which is necessary in order to adequately protect the right to digital privacy. This is the most critical point within the process of the judicial Europeanisation of the Internet. The Internet's transnational nature makes it incompatible with attempts to regionalise protection, despite the fact that such attempts are inspired by the aim to increase the degree of that protection.

The contrast between the territorial limits of enforcement jurisdiction and the global nature of the service could lead to a 'race to the bottom' in the protection of the rights at issue and of a lack of enforcement mechanisms for such protection. Indeed, it is a further expression of the conflict between local law and global law that characterises judicial globalisation, of which Internet law constitutes a privileged field for investigation.

The decision of the CJEU seemed to be aimed at ensuring the highest degree of protection for privacy and personal data from a transnational standpoint. However, it is worth stressing that the extension of European judicial power that is making Europe, almost paradoxically, a data protection fortress does not consider the political and also the legal impacts of this decision with regard to relations with third countries. This political choice made by the EU can be read as an attempt to codify the right to digital privacy which the CJEU has contributed to defining over recent years since the *Digital Rights Ireland* case. Nonetheless, the role of courts in relation to the transnational protection of privacy and data protection is only just beginning, as stressed in Chapters 4 and 5.

4

The Judicial Bridges of Privacy and Speech in the Information Society

I. Judicial Momentum at the Intersection

We are now aware of how the amplification of judicial momentum in the transition from the world of atoms to the world of bits has affected fundamental rights, as the case law of US and European courts has shown. By adopting different judicial frames and approaches to territorial boundaries (ie jurisdictional issues), courts across the Atlantic have adapted their approaches to face the new challenges raised by the Internet.

In Chapters 2 and 3, we focused respectively on the adaptation of judicial protection for freedom of expression, and privacy and data protection in Europe and the US. In this chapter, I stress the role of courts in substantially extending constitutional values to the digital environment beyond formal geographical boundaries. I consider this phenomenon as a judicial expression of digital sovereignty. We have already observed this phenomenon in Chapter 3 when describing the path towards digital privacy. In this chapter, by looking at expressions and data on a global scale, I shall examine how courts have extended the scope of these fundamental rights from a transatlantic judicial perspective.

The linkage between these two rights seems to have acquired a broader dimension within the digital environment. The implication for, and connections of data with, political speech, and thus not only freedom of information as highlighted in *Google Spain*, were made clear in the Cambridge Analytica case. It is no coincidence that the former European Data Protection Supervisor, Giovanni Buttarelli, stressed on various occasions that, in the digital world, freedom of expression and the right to privacy are two sides of the same coin.[1] The intimate relationship between privacy and free speech has been present since the outset within the balancing processes suggested by Warren and Brandeis, where freedom of expression could be limited due to privacy considerations.[2] Today, it is even clearer how these two rights, which might prima facie seem different, are in fact quite

[1] Giovanni Buttarelli, 'Privacy in an age of hyperconnectivity, Keynote speech to the Privacy and Security Conference (2016)' at https://edps.europa.eu/sites/edp/files/publication/16-11-07_speech_gb_austria_en.pdf.

[2] Samuel D Warren and Louis D Brandeis, 'The Right to Privacy' (1890) 4 *Harvard Law Review* 193.

connected in the digital world. Besides, '[t]here is a saying in Silicon Valley that "Big Data is the new oil"'.[3] Moreover, the interconnection between data and speech is even clearer when one focuses on the challenges raised by algorithms, as will be addressed in Chapter 5, which discusses the new challenges for judicial power.[4]

This close connection between privacy and freedom of expression online is not merely theoretical or factual. This linkage has also involved the role of courts across the Atlantic. In Europe, the ECtHR and CJEU have dealt with the scope of these two fundamental rights in the information society. On the other hand, the US Supreme Court seems to be stuck in a different type of path, or rather to be rooted to a different judicial frame underlying these two rights, as is evident from a consideration of the cases involving online platforms. More specifically, this becomes even clearer when some of the landmark decisions are considered, which point towards a new trend of assessing the scope of free speech, privacy and data protection in the information society.

Although the judicial enforcement of digital privacy is a paradigmatic case study for analysing the European migration of constitutional values on the Internet, it is not the only angle to understand the scope of protection of speech and privacy in the information society. Even, the absolutist approach of the US to free speech can be seen as an expression of digital sovereignty. Within this context, it is worth mentioning that the migration of technological and constitutional values does not only involve Europe or the US. Other countries, such as China, play a critical role in regulating the digital environment.[5] Nonetheless, as was explained in the Introduction, our attention is focused on the US and European area, as two constitutional, democratic orders that have experienced the role of courts in dealing with digital technologies.

Therefore, the issue of the 'Europeanisation' of data protection represents a critical challenge to the digital sovereignty of third countries,[6] including first and foremost the US. In fact, we use this expression not only to refer to the harmonisation of data protection law in the EU but also to describe the tendency to extend the territorial scope of EU law. The term will be used in this chapter with the latter meaning. From this point of view, as far as the recent case law of the

[3] Jack M Balkin, 'Free Speech in the Algorithmic Society: Big Data, Private Governance, and New School Speech Regulation' (2018) 51 *UC Davis Law Review* 1149, 1154. The first author credited to have introduced such formula is Clive Humby, a mathematician, back in 2006. However, this metaphor recently regained attention after the publication of the report 'The world's most valuable resource is no longer oil, but data' by *The Economist* in 2017.

[4] Article 19, 'Privacy and Freedom of Expression in the Age of Artificial Intelligence', *Article 19* (11 May 2018) at www.article19.org/wp-content/uploads/2018/04/Privacy-and-Freedom-of-Expression-In-the-Age-of-Artificial-Intelligence-1.pdf.

[5] Nicholas F Palmieri, 'Data Protection in an Increasingly Globalized World' (2019) 94 *Indiana Law Journal* 297. See also Griffin Drake, 'Navigating the Atlantic: Understanding EU Data Privacy Compliance Amidst a Sea of Uncertainty' (2017) 91 *Southern California Law Review* 163; Paul M Schwartz, 'The EU-U.S. Privacy Collision: A Turn to Institutions and Procedures' (2013) 126 *Harvard Law Review* 1966.

[6] See Orla Lynskey, 'The "Europeanisation" of Data Protection Law' (2017) 19 *Cambridge Yearbook of European Legal Studies* 1.

CJEU is considered, it is possible to stress how the process developed by the CJEU for balancing rights has been impacting on third countries' constitutional values. However, this problem is also emerging in the ECHR system, albeit in a different way, and was in some sense inherent in the very origins of the debate concerning the role played by US-based companies in the digital world.

Within this framework, the first part of this chapter will address the European judicial approach to (and intersection with) freedom of expression, privacy and data protection, which is becoming increasingly projected onto a global scale. The second part will, on the other hand, present the opposing approach of the US in relation to the protection of fundamental rights in the digital environment, underlining an omissive approach to the transnational challenges for freedom of expression and privacy in the information society.

II. The Drawbridge of the European Fortress

The case law of the European courts has already shown how the ECtHR and the CJEU have played a critical role in the constitutionalisation of the European environment in light of the new technological paradigm. Nonetheless, European courts have still not exhausted their role, especially as the transnational dimension to freedom of expression, privacy and data protection is becoming increasingly intertwined with and challenging for political power.

The judicial connection between freedom of expression, privacy and data protection and the limits of their scope can be introduced first of all by focusing on some decisions of the ECtHR. The Strasbourg court adopted different approaches. In *Arlewin v Sweden*[7] the ECtHR designed a specific approach for a case involving defamation in satellite broadcasting, while extending constitutional values in *Perrin v UK*,[8] even underlining the potential legal drawbacks in *Williamson v Germany*.[9] Within this framework, the case *Big Brother Watch v UK* is particularly relevant.[10] The decision concerned three joined cases involving mass surveillance: the regime of bulk interception; the sharing of data with foreign agencies and governments; and data requests to communications service providers.

In the wake of the revelations by Edward Snowden, the applicants asserted that their communications were intercepted by UK intelligence services, or by foreign intelligence services that may have shared information with the British services, or alternatively that their communications may have been violated by a request by British authorities to communications service providers. Some of the applicants sought to launch domestic proceedings before the Investigatory Powers Tribunal (IPT),

[7] *Arlewin v Sweden*, App no 22302/10, judgment of 1 June 2016.

[8] *Perrin v UK*, App no 5446/03, judgment of 18 October 2005.

[9] *Williamson v Germany*, App no 64496/17, admissibility decision, 8 January 2019.

[10] *Big Brother Watch and Others v The United Kingdom*, App nos 58170/13, 62322/14 and 24960/15, judgment of 13 September 2018, Referral to the Grand Chamber 4 February 2019, para 9.

a special tribunal created under the Regulation of Investigatory Powers Act 2000, which dismissed the cases in part, while others alleged that there was no effective domestic remedy.

First of all, it is important to stress that this type of mass surveillance has been made possible by digital technologies and is strictly connected to data and communication obtained through online platforms, as was stressed by the ECtHR in the first decision on the case. What is interesting in this first decision is how freedom of expression and privacy intersect with each other.[11] Indeed, while the infringement in all three applications concerned the right to privacy as guaranteed by Article 8 ECHR,[12] the last two also involved a violation of freedom of expression as enshrined in Article 10 ECHR.

With regard to data protection and privacy issues, the ECtHR analysed the compatibility with Article 8 ECHR of the regime of the bulk interception of communications, intelligence sharing, and the acquisition of communications data.

In relation to the first issue, the applicants alleged that there was no legal basis for the operations carried out under the bulk interception regime, that there was no clarity concerning the distinction between external and internal communications – also given the fact that modern technological developments had made the distinction between the two meaningless – and a range of issues concerning the data processing and the management of data acquired from intercepted communications in breach of their right to privacy, such as the duration of surveillance, filtering procedures, the storage and analysis of data and information, disclosed arrangements and, finally, the absence of any effective guarantees against the disproportionate retention and processing of data. In analysing these complaints, the starting point of this decision can be framed in terms of the internal perspective, which the ECtHR has traditionally adopted when dealing with Internet issues:

> [I]n view of the current threats facing many Contracting States (including the scourge of global terrorism and other serious crime, such as drug trafficking, human trafficking, the sexual exploitation of children and cybercrime), advancements in technology which have made it easier for terrorists and criminals to evade detection on the Internet, and the unpredictability of the routes via which electronic communications are transmitted, the Court considers that the decision to operate a bulk interception regime in order to identify hitherto unknown threats to national security is one which continues to fall within States' margin of appreciation.[13]

However, the ECtHR also developed a regime for assessing the proportionality of measures of mass surveillance.[14] Within this perspective, according to the

[11] Neil Richards, *Intellectual Privacy: Rethinking Civil Liberties in the Digital Age* (Oxford, Oxford University Press, 2015).

[12] *Big Brother Watch* (n 10) para 269.

[13] ibid para 314.

[14] 'Nevertheless, as indicated previously, it is evident from the Court's case-law over several decades that all interception regimes (both bulk and targeted) have the potential to be abused, especially where the true breadth of the authorities' discretion to intercept cannot be discerned from the relevant

plaintiffs, the test developed by the Strasbourg court in its case law should have been updated in view of technological evolutions in more recent years.[15] However, the ECtHR did not change its test, but took into account all aspects of the phenomenon analysed, such as, for instance, automated processes:

> However, while the Court does not doubt the impact of modern technology on the intrusiveness of interception, and has indeed emphasised this point in its case-law, it would be wrong automatically to assume that bulk interception constitutes a greater intrusion into the private life of an individual than targeted interception, which by its very nature is more likely to result in the acquisition and examination of a large volume of his or her communications. In any event, although the Court would agree that the additional requirements proposed by the applicants might constitute important safeguards in some cases, for the reasons set out below it does not consider it appropriate to add them to the list of minimum requirements in the case at hand.[16]

It could be observed that, in adopting this decision, the ECtHR normalised the mass surveillance regime, implicitly overruling its past decisions.[17] Moreover, regarding this aspect, the nature of the digital world and new technological evolutions seem to have played a very important role:

> With regard to the proportionality of the bulk interception regime, the Court notes that the Independent Reviewer of Terrorism Legislation, examined a great deal of closed material and concluded that bulk interception was an essential capability: first, because terrorists, criminals and hostile foreign intelligence services had become increasingly sophisticated at evading detection by traditional means; and secondly, because the nature of the global Internet meant that the route a particular communication would travel had become hugely unpredictable.[18]

In this sense, the lack of oversight over bulk interception processes and the absence of any real safeguards against arbitrary actions were the two primary reasons that led the Strasbourg court to rule that Article 8 ECHR had been infringed.

legislation … Therefore, while States enjoy a wide margin of appreciation in deciding what type of interception regime is necessary to protect national security, the discretion afforded to them in operating an interception regime must necessarily be narrower. In this regard, the Court has identified six minimum requirements that both bulk interception and other interception regimes must satisfy in order to be sufficiently foreseeable to minimise the risk of abuses of power …', ibid para 315.

[15] 'In their view, such changes would reflect the fact that due to recent technological developments the interception of communications now has greater potential than ever before to paint an intimate and detailed portrait of a person's private life and behaviour. However, while the Court does not doubt the impact of modern technology on the intrusiveness of interception, and has indeed emphasised this point in its case-law, it would be wrong automatically to assume that bulk interception constitutes a greater intrusion into the private life of an individual than targeted interception, which by its very nature is more likely to result in the acquisition and examination of a large volume of his or her communications', ibid para 316.

[16] ibid para 316.

[17] Marko Milanovic, 'ECtHR Judgment in Big Brother Watch v. UK', *EJIL: Talk* (23 September 2018) at www.ejiltalk.org/ecthr-judgment-in-big-brother-watch-v-uk/.

[18] *Big Brother Watch* (n 10) para 384.

From this point of view, it is quite important to stress how the ECtHR treated metadata as equivalent to communication:

> [T]he Court is not persuaded that the acquisition of related communications data is necessarily less intrusive than the acquisition of content. For example, the content of an electronic communication might be encrypted and, even if it were decrypted, might not reveal anything of note about the sender or recipient. The related communications data, on the other hand, could reveal the identities and geographic location of the sender and recipient and the equipment through which the communication was transmitted. In bulk, the degree of intrusion is magnified, since the patterns that will emerge could be capable of painting an intimate picture of a person through the mapping of social networks, location tracking, Internet browsing tracking, mapping of communication patterns, and insight into who a person interacted with.[19]

Turning to the second issue in the case, ie the sharing of intercepted communications, and thus access to data of citizens from other countries, the applicants complained that Article 8 ECHR had been violated only as regards the requesting and acquisition of data from other countries, and did not allege that data were being shared in any other manner.[20] In this regard, the ECtHR ruled that the evolution of the Internet and technologies would require a regime for sharing intercepted communications:

> Due to the nature of global terrorism, and in particular the complexity of global terror networks, the Court accepts that taking such a stand – and thus preventing the perpetration of violent acts endangering the lives of innocent people – requires a flow of information between the security services of many countries in all parts of the world. As, in the present case, this 'information flow' was embedded into a legislative context providing considerable safeguards against abuse, the Court would accept that the resulting interference was kept to that which was 'necessary in a democratic society'.[21]

The court argued in relation to this point that, considering the procedure governing and the supervision of this type of acquisition, Article 8 ECHR had not been violated.

As regards the third issue, the data acquisition regime under chapter II RIPA was held to infringe Article 8 ECHR. In fact, the absence of any prior review by a court or an independent authority in order to allow access to stored data led the ECtHR to stress the role of domestic law, as interpreted by the domestic authorities in the light of the recent judgments of the CJEU, in allowing the authorities to access stored data, while also limiting access for the purpose of combating 'serious crime' and subjecting it to prior review by a court or independent administrative body.[22]

[19] ibid para 356.
[20] ibid para 416.
[21] ibid para 446.
[22] ibid para 467.

From the perspective of freedom of expression, it should be stressed how most of the issues alleged by the applicants were also linked to Article 10 ECHR. This is interesting, not in terms of the traditional relationship between free speech and privacy, ie the balancing process between the two rights, but because it underlines the interconnection between these two rights in the new digital society.

Nonetheless, only the journalist's complaint was ruled admissible, specifically as regards the journalistic interest in protecting sources of information. This is because, for instance,

> obtaining of communications data which constituted confidential journalistic material was as intrusive as obtaining content, since a single piece of communications data could reveal the identity of a journalist's source, and when aggregated and subjected to modern data-mining technology, it could reveal an enormous range of (journalistically privileged) information.[23]

In fact, according to the applicants, the regime was in some way undermining the foundation of the journalist's work. As regards the regime of bulk interception, the ECtHR assumed a deep link between data and free speech, and claimed:

> Nevertheless, in view of the potential chilling effect that any perceived interference with the confidentiality of their communications and, in particular, their sources might have on the freedom of the press and, in the absence of any 'above the waterline' arrangements limiting the intelligence services' ability to search and examine such material other than where 'it is justified by an overriding requirement in the public interest', the Court finds that there has also been a violation of Article 10 of the Convention.[24]

Consequently, the ECtHR considered that the regime could not be '"in accordance with the law" for the purpose of the Article 10 complaint'.[25] As noted above, the analysis of the issue even in a case that was more focused on data and the right to privacy, such as that examined, cannot be read separately from the consequences for the free speech clause, given the close connection between these two aspects in the digital world.

As far as the issue of extraterritorial effect is concerned, it is somehow recalled under a hypothetical violation of the principle of non-discrimination in the different treatment of and safeguards for non-British citizens as regards their freedom of speech and digital privacy.[26] The ECtHR held that the allegation had not been adequately proved and that, owing to the fact that those whose communications were intercepted were not present in British territory, Article 14 ECHR, read in conjunction with Articles 8 and 10 ECHR, had not been violated.

[23] ibid para 480.
[24] ibid para 495.
[25] ibid para 499.
[26] 'The applicants in the third of the joined cases further complained under Article 14 of the Convention, read together with Articles 8 and 10, that the section 8(4) regime was indirectly discriminatory on grounds of nationality because persons outside the United Kingdom were disproportionately likely to have their private communications intercepted; and section 16 of RIPA provides additional safeguards only to persons known to be in the British Islands', ibid para 514.

In this judgment, the ECtHR declined to take a view concerning one of the most complicated issues within the digital world, namely the scope of fundamental rights on the Internet and the resulting risk of clashes with constitutional values.[27] As mentioned above, the case was referred to the Grand Chamber of the ECtHR, which will be able to explore these issues more deeply. What is interesting in this preliminary decision is how the ECtHR started to analyse the issue of privacy in the digital world as being deeply connected with free speech, and how this aspect cannot be separated by the implications for fundamental and human rights, namely freedom of expression and information.

Adopting a different focus, it is worth noting how the German Constitutional Court extended privacy rights to foreign nationals living abroad, thus asking the government to review the law on foreign intelligence agencies,[28] clarifying specifically the legal grounds for monitoring individuals' data abroad. Indeed, such a law allows the intelligence services to process the data of non-German citizens outside the country in order to tackle potential threats. In other words, the primary issue concerned the lack of safeguards for processing these data, such as protection for journalists.

A group of journalists and civil society organisations that brought the case before the German Constitutional Court claimed that the law violated their privacy rights, in the wake of the outrage and reaction to the Snowden disclosures. The decision established that the right to privacy should apply to any means of communication and to any individual. This case offers another example of the intersection between the right to privacy and free speech in the processing of data. However, even more importantly, such an extension of constitutional values on a global scale represents a step forward in the judicial protection of fundamental rights in the information society.

Moving to the EU framework, the CJEU added another piece of the puzzle in the Schrems saga. We have already seen in Chapter 3 how the *Schrems I* decision was a cornerstone in the path towards digital privacy. In *Schrems II*, the CJEU reinforced its approach, and consolidated its power across the Atlantic, by invalidating the Privacy Shield.[29] Already in its report on the annual joint reviews of the Privacy Shield, the European Data Protection Board (EDPB) questioned the compliance with the data protection principles of necessity and proportionality

[27] On which see Oreste Pollicino and Marco Bassini, 'The Law of the Internet between Globalization and Localization' in Miguel Maduro, Kaarlo Tuori and Suvi Sankari (eds), *Transnational Law – Rethinking Law and Legal Thinking* (Cambridge, Cambridge University Press, 2014) 346 regarding the trade-off between globalisation and localisation; and see Oreste Pollicino and Marco Bassini, 'Free Speech, Defamation and the Limits to Freedom of Expression in the EU: A Comparative Analysis' in Andrej Savin and Jan Trzaskowski (eds), *Research Handbook on EU Internet Law* (Cheltenham, Edward Elgar, 2014) 508 regarding the applicable standard of protection of freedom of speech on the Internet.

[28] German Constitutional Court, judgment of 19 May 2020, 1 BvR 2835/17.

[29] Case C-311/18 *Data Protection Commissioner v Facebook Ireland Limited and Maximillian Schrems*, ECLI:EU:C:2020:559 (*Schrems II*).

in the application of US law.[30] As Chuches and Zalnieriute wrote on the day on which the *Schrems II* decision was published, reading the judgment gives more than a simple feeling of déjà vu; rather it looks like a full-blown Groundhog Day.[31]

Following the first judgment, the domestic court annulled the rejection of the applicant's complaint and referred the decision about the prohibition to transfer personal data back to the Data Protection Commissioner (Ireland). Facebook Ireland explained that a large part of personal data was transferred based on the Standard Contractual Clauses (SCCs) and, therefore, the Commissioner asked the applicant to reformulate his complaint.[32] The second claim concerned, inter alia, the possibility of surveillance and law enforcement authorities accessing data from Facebook and using this information in monitoring programmes, thus interfering with Articles 7, 8 and 47 EUCFR.

In 2016 the Data Protection Commissioner (Ireland) agreed with this position, observing that SCCs found that the standard data protection clauses in the annex to the SCCs Decision are not capable of remedying that defect since they confer only contractual rights on data subjects against the data exporter and importer, without, however, binding the US authorities. The Commissioner decided to bring an action before the Irish High Court, which then made the reference for a preliminary ruling before the CJEU.

The shift (and manipulation) was easier in this case than it was first time around (*Schrems I*) because of recital 104 of the GDPR, which states that '[t]he third country should offer guarantees ensuring an adequate level of protection essentially equivalent to that ensured within the Union, in particular where personal data are processed in one or several specific sectors'.[33] However, Article 45 GDPR still clarifies that such cases only involve an evaluation as to the adequacy of the level of protection, and not a comparison. It should not therefore be any surprise when the CJEU asserted that

> [t]he first sentence of Article 45(1) of the GDPR provides that a transfer of personal data to a third country may be authorised by a Commission decision to the effect that that third country, a territory or one or more specified sectors within that third country, ensures an adequate level of protection. In that regard, although not requiring a third country to ensure a level of protection identical to that guaranteed in the EU legal

[30] See EDPB, 'EU-U.S. Privacy Shield – Second Annual Joint Review report' (22 January 2019) at https://edpb.europa.eu/our-work-tools/our-documents/other/eu-us-privacy-shield-second-annual-joint-review-report-22012019_en; EDPB, 'EU-U.S. Privacy Shield – Third Annual Joint Review report' (12 November 2019) at https://edpb.europa.eu/our-work-tools/our-documents/eu-us-privacy-shield-third-annual-joint-review-report-12112019_en.

[31] Genna Chuches and Monika Zalnieriute, 'A Groundhog Day in Brussels. Schrems II and International Data Transfers', *Verfassungsblog.de* (16 July 2020) at https://verfassungsblog.de/a-groundhog-day-in-bruessels.

[32] Commission Decision of 5 February 2010 on standard contractual clauses for the transfer of personal data to processors established in third countries under Directive 95/46/EC of the European Parliament and of the Council.

[33] Oreste Pollicino, 'Diabolical Persistence. Thoughts on the Schrems II Decision' *Verfassungsblog.de* (25 July 2020) at https://verfassungsblog.de/diabolical-persistence/.

> order, the term 'adequate level of protection' must, as confirmed by recital 104 of that regulation, be understood as requiring the third country in fact to ensure, by reason of its domestic law or its international commitments, a level of protection of fundamental rights and freedoms that is essentially equivalent to that guaranteed within the European Union by virtue of the regulation, read in the light of the Charter.[34]

Advocate General Saugmandsgaard Øe's Opinion had already paved the way for the CJEU's decision.[35] Already when focusing on the extension of the assessment to national surveillance, AG Saugmandsgaard Øe underlined that, when adopting an adequacy decision, the EU Commission is to take account of, inter alia, the legislation of the third country concerned relating to national security.[36] Despite such an extensive trend, AG Saugmandsgaard Øe underlined that the resolution of the dispute in the case in question would not have required the CJEU to rule on the validity of the 'privacy shield' decision since the dispute concerned only the validity of the SCCs Decision. Nonetheless, AG Saugmandsgaard Øe raised doubts about whether the US legal framework met the standard of protection required to transfer personal data beyond the EU territory. He expressly clarified:

> I doubt, as do Mr Schrems and the EPIC, that EO 12333, like PPD 28, which sets out guarantees applicable to all signals intelligence activities, are sufficiently foreseeable to have the 'quality of law'. Those instruments expressly state that they do not confer legally enforceable rights on the persons concerned. The latter cannot therefore rely on the guarantees set out in PPD 28 before the courts. The Commission considered, moreover, in the 'privacy shield' decision, that although the guarantees set out in PPD 28 have binding force for the intelligence services, they are 'not phrased in … legal terms'. EO 12333 and PPD 28 bear more resemblance to internal administrative instruction that can be revoked or amended by the President of the United States. The ECtHR has already held that internal administrative directives do not constitute 'law'.[37]

At the same time, looking also at the case of the ECtHR, AG Saugmandsgaard Øe observed that the very essence of Articles 7 or 8 ECHR was not compromised. Indeed, security is one of the reasons justifying potential restrictions to the right to privacy and data protection. According to AG Saugmandsgaard Øe:

> I shall merely observe, on that subject, that the ECtHR has not had recourse, in its case-law relating to Article 8 of the ECHR, to the concept of violation of the essential content, or the very essence, of the right to respect for private life. It has not thus far considered that regimes that allow the interception of electronic communications, even on a mass scale, exceeded as such the margin of appreciation of the Member States. The ECtHR considers that such regimes are compatible with Article 8(2) of the ECHR provided that they are accompanied by a number of minimum guarantees. In those

[34] *Schrems II* (n 29) para 94.
[35] AG Opinion, *Data Protection Commissioner v Facebook Ireland Limited and Maximillian Schrems*, ECLI:EU:C:2019:1145.
[36] ibid para 108.
[37] ibid paras 266–67.

> circumstances, it does not seem appropriate to me to conclude that a surveillance regime such as that provided for by EO 12333 would exceed the margin of appreciation of the Member States without undertaking any examination whatsoever of any guarantees that accompany it.[38]

Concerning the safeguards, AG Saugmandsgaard Øe underlined his concerns due to lack of prior review. With specific regard to the first point, he observed:

> I have already pointed out that PPD 28 does not create rights for individuals. Next, I doubt that the requirement to guarantee surveillance 'as tailored as feasible' is formulated in sufficiently clear and precise terms to forewarn the data subjects adequately against the risks of abuse. Last, the 'privacy shield' decision does not establish that the surveillance based on EO 12333 would be subject to prior review by an independent body or might be the subject of post factum judicial review.[39]

Similar concerns were expressed about the lack of effective remedies and the inadequacy of the ombudsperson mechanism.[40] All these doubts led AG Saugmandsgaard Øe to observe:

> In the light of all of the foregoing considerations, I entertain certain doubts as to the conformity of the 'privacy shield' decision to Article 45(1) of the GDPR, read in the light of Articles 7, 8 and 47 of the Charter and of Article 8 of the ECHR.[41]

The decision of the CJEU shed light on AG Saugmandsgaard Øe's concerns. The CJEU firstly underlined that the GDPR applies to the transfer of personal data for commercial purposes by an economic operator established in a Member State to another economic operator established in a third country, even if, at the time of that transfer or thereafter, that data may be processed by the authorities of the third country in question for the purposes of public security, defence and State security.

As in *Schrems I*, the CJEU underlined that personal data can be transferred only pursuant to an essentially equivalent standard of protection. The CJEU underlined that the essentially equivalent level of protection applies not only to an adequacy decision by the EU Commission, but also to the use of SCCs.[42] Precisely, by interpreting Article 46(1) and 46(2)(c) with Article 45(2) GDPR, transfers of personal data based on SCCs have to take into consideration any access by the public authorities of that third country to the personal data transferred and the relevant aspects of the legal system of that third country, in particular those set out, in a non-exhaustive manner, in Article 45(2) GDPR.

The CJEU did not invalidate the SCCs Decision. Indeed, the CJEU underlined the role of economic operators to set additional safeguards when contractual

[38] ibid para 282.
[39] ibid para 307.
[40] ibid paras 332 and 339.
[41] ibid para 342.
[42] ibid paras 104 and 137.

clauses cannot ensure the aforementioned level of protection. According to the CJEU:

> [T]he standard data protection clauses adopted by the Commission on the basis of Article 46(2)(c) of the GDPR are solely intended to provide contractual guarantees that apply uniformly in all third countries to controllers and processors established in the European Union and, consequently, independently of the level of protection guaranteed in each third country. In so far as those standard data protection clauses cannot, having regard to their very nature, provide guarantees beyond a contractual obligation to ensure compliance with the level of protection required under EU law, they may require, depending on the prevailing position in a particular third country, the adoption of supplementary measures by the controller in order to ensure compliance with that level of protection.[43]

Since SCCs are not capable of binding the authorities of that third country,[44] the controller established in the EU and the recipient of personal data have to verify, prior to any transfer, whether the level of protection required by EU law is respected in the third country concerned.[45]

On the one hand, the CJEU seems to underline the role of economic operators to assess the compliance of the SCCs. In a way, as observed by Daskal, companies can do even more since

> they can ensure that all the data is encrypted in transit, applying the strongest encryption protocols possible – so that it cannot be deciphered if acquired as it crosses underseas cables. They can challenge – and demand individual reviews of – all intelligence community demands for EU citizen and resident data.[46]

However,

> there is no guarantee that the companies will win such challenges; they are, after all, ultimately bound by U.S. legal obligations to disclose. And even more importantly, there is absolutely nothing that companies can do to provide the kind of back-end judicial review that the Court demands.[47]

On the other hand, the CJEU underlined the primary role of the national competent authority in the context of third-country transfers of data. The CJEU clarified the primary role of supervisory authorities in case of the lack of a valid EU Commission adequacy decision. The CJEU underlined that these authorities are required to suspend or prohibit a transfer of personal data to a third country on a case-by-case assessment, precisely if, in its view and in the light of all the circumstances of that transfer, contractual clauses are not or cannot be complied with in

[43] ibid para 133.
[44] ibid para 136.
[45] ibid paras 135, 137 and 142.
[46] Jennifer Daskal, 'What Comes Next: The Aftermath of European Court's Blow to Transatlantic Data Transfers', *Just Security* (17 July 2020) at www.justsecurity.org/71485/what-comes-next-the-aftermath-of-european-courts-blow-to-transatlantic-data-transfers/.
[47] ibid.

that third country and the protection of the data transferred that is required by EU law cannot be ensured by other means, where the controller or a processor has not itself suspended or put an end to the transfer.[48] The assessments focus on whether data protection clauses can be respected in that country and whether the protection of the data transferred that is required by EU law can be ensured by other means.

Once the CJEU had underlined the application of EU law to the case in question and the validity of the SCC system, it moved to the assessments of the validity of the Privacy Shield. The CJEU focused on appropriate safeguards, namely enforceable rights and effective legal remedies in light of the fundamental rights, with a specific focus on privacy and data protection. The CJEU recognised that US law does not meet the standard of protection which should be essentially equivalent to the protection of EU law, precisely the principle of proportionality, since US surveillance programmes are not limited to what is strictly necessary. The CJEU underlined that

> neither Section 702 of the FISA, nor E.O. 12333, read in conjunction with PPD-28, correlates to the minimum safeguards resulting, under EU law, from the principle of proportionality, with the consequence that the surveillance programmes based on those provisions cannot be regarded as limited to what is strictly necessary. In those circumstances, the limitations on the protection of personal data arising from the domestic law of the United States on the access and use by US public authorities of such data transferred from the European Union to the United States, which the Commission assessed in the Privacy Shield Decision, are not circumscribed in a way that satisfies requirements that are essentially equivalent to those required, under EU law, by the second sentence of Article 52(1) of the Charter.[49]

According to the CJEU, these surveillance programmes do not limit the power which US authorities can exercise in implementing them or targeting non-US citizens. Even if formally US authorities have to comply with some safeguards, data subjects cannot rely on actionable rights before the courts against the US authorities. This is particularly relevant for ensuring the protection of Article 47 EUCFR. It is not by chance that recital 104 of the GDPR states, in that regard, that the third country 'should ensure effective independent data protection supervision and should provide for cooperation mechanisms with the Member States' data protection authorities' and adds that 'the data subjects should be provided with effective and enforceable rights and effective administrative and judicial redress'. According to the CJEU:

> [T]he very existence of effective judicial review designed to ensure compliance with provisions of EU law is inherent in the existence of the rule of law. Thus, legislation not providing for any possibility for an individual to pursue legal remedies in order to have access to personal data relating to him or her, or to obtain the rectification or erasure

[48] *Schrems II* (n 29) para 146.
[49] ibid paras 184–85.

> of such data, does not respect the essence of the fundamental right to effective judicial protection, as enshrined in Article 47 of the Charter.[50]

Besides, even the ombudsperson mechanism does not provide enough guarantees from two perspectives. First, the CJEU recognised the lack of independence of the ombudsperson provided for by that mechanism. Secondly, the CJEU underlined that the ombudsperson could not adopt decisions that are binding on the US intelligence services. Regarding the first point, the CJEU observed:

> In the letter referred to in paragraph 193 above, the Privacy Shield Ombudsperson, although described as 'independent from the Intelligence Community', was presented as '[reporting] directly to the Secretary of State who will ensure that the Ombudsperson carries out its function objectively and free from improper influence that is liable to have an effect on the response to be provided'. Furthermore, in addition to the fact that, as found by the Commission in recital 116 of that decision, the Ombudsperson is appointed by the Secretary of State and is an integral part of the US State Department, there is, as the Advocate General stated in point 337 of his Opinion, nothing in that decision to indicate that the dismissal or revocation of the appointment of the Ombudsperson is accompanied by any particular guarantees, which is such as to undermine the Ombudsman's independence from the executive.[51]

Together with the lack of independence, data subjects have no cause of action before a body which offers guarantees substantially equivalent to those required by EU law. Indeed,

> although recital 120 of the Privacy Shield Decision refers to a commitment from the US Government that the relevant component of the intelligence services is required to correct any violation of the applicable rules detected by the Privacy Shield Ombudsperson, there is nothing in that decision to indicate that that ombudsperson has the power to adopt decisions that are binding on those intelligence services and does not mention any legal safeguards that would accompany that political commitment on which data subjects could rely.[52]

These were the primary reason leading the CJEU to declare the Privacy Shield invalid. This decision, as also welcomed by the EDPB,[53] can be considered another expression of the path of the CJEU towards digital privacy. Nonetheless, the consequences of this decision are far from just an expression of digital sovereignty. As observed by Irion, '[t]he judgment is emblematic of the formal strength of the EU's fundamental rights approach to personal data protection but also its limits in the age of digital interdependency'.[54] The increasing digital connection in

[50] ibid para 187.
[51] ibid para 195.
[52] ibid para 196.
[53] EDPB, 'Statement on the Court of Justice of the European Union Judgment in Case C-311/18 – Data Protection Commissioner v Facebook Ireland and Maximillian Schrems' (17 July 2020) at https://edpb.europa.eu/sites/edpb/files/files/file1/edpb_statement_20200717_cjeujudgmentc-311_18_en.pdf.
[54] Kristina Irion, 'Schrems II and Surveillance: Third Countries' National Security Powers in the Purview of EU Law', *EU Law Blog* (24 July 2020) at https://europeanlawblog.eu/2020/07/24/schrems-ii-and-surveillance-third-countries-national-security-powers-in-the-purview-of-eu-law/. See also

the flow of personal data has clear consequences for the balance between security and the protection of fundamental rights online. Unlike the Opinion of AG Saugmandsgaard Øe, which took a more moderate view, the CJEU recognised the lack of safeguards in the balancing assessment between privacy and security.

The effects of this extension of European values is important even as a limit against surveillance regulatory schemes which could undermine the principle of the rule of law and fundamental rights in the information society. Bignami stressed that

> the unstable geopolitics and the illiberal developments of the past couple of years highlight the many competing considerations – combating election interference based on the unlawful manipulation of personal data is one of the important activities of national security agencies, yet at the same time expansive surveillance laws threaten rights and, in the case of democratic-backsliding, can be used to consolidate authoritarian rules.[55]

In this scenario, the *Schrems II* decision is a clear example of how the CJEU is trying to use the drawbridge of the European fortress opening to avoid disproportionate interferences in a transnational digital environment.

The judicial extension of EU values beyond national borders is also evident in the CJEU's approach to the territorial scope of national orders to remove statements or data. As was examined in Chapter 3, in Europe the CJEU has started to extend the geographical scope of EU law in the area of privacy and data protection. The EU system has created a *sui generis* system, an innovative and pervasive right to data protection and privacy that has transfigured the Internet and deeply influenced other legal systems, causing a new migration in relation to this right.[56]

However, this migration was preceded by extensive CJEU case law that sought to apply the European vision of the right to digital privacy and thus to build a European 'fortress'. From *Digital Rights Ireland*,[57] where the physical atomic infrastructure became a crucial criterion for assessing the invalidity of the Data Retention Directive, to *Google Spain* and *Schrems I* and *II*, where the CJEU expanded its scope to clashes between the US and European legal paradigms, the CJEU has provided a model for the codification of Article 3(2) GDPR. In this way, the court has ensured extraterritorial protection for the European right to privacy and data protection online *ante litteram*.

Marc Rotenberg, 'Schrems II: From Snowden to China, the Evolution of Data Protection as a Fundamental Right' (2020) *European Law Journal*, forthcoming.

[55] Francesca Bignami, 'Schrems II: The Right to Privacy and the New Illiberalism', *Verfassungsblog.de* (29 July 2020) at https://verfassungsblog.de/schrems-ii-the-right-to-privacy-and-the-new-illiberalism/?fbclid=IwAR1wXiMQ1HL_KwaOTw3TzTIFOGRBtNzTaTMrd3mVMGovHyLonTjvNye-vMk.

[56] Krystyna Kowalik-Bańczyk and Oreste Pollicino, 'Migration of European Judicial Ideas Concerning Jurisdiction over Google on Withdrawal of Information' (2016) 17(3) *German Law Journal* 315.

[57] Joined Cases C-293/12 and C-594/12 *Digital Rights Ireland Ltd v Minister for Communications, Marine and Natural Resources, Minister for Justice, Equality and Law Reform, The Commissioner of the Garda Síochána, Ireland and the Attorney General and Kärntner Landesregierung, Michael Seitlinger, Christof Tschohl and Others* [2014] ECR I-238.

Nonetheless, the CJEU approach to privacy and data protection as well as freedom of expression is not just directed to extend EU law beyond the EU territorial boundaries. As we will see in the next section, the CJEU has also shown itself to be aware of the consequences for other legal systems and the international legal framework.

III. Judicial Protection of Speech and Data on a Global Scale

Territory and sovereignty still matter in the digital world. The European data protection fortress for its residents is founded on two pillars: European law and the EU 'territory'. The digital territory seems to be the most critical aspect of this account: the transnational nature of the Internet appears to be irreconcilable with attempts at regionalising data protection online. Therefore, Articles 7 and 8 EUCFR become trump cards for ensuring greater protection and for extending the 'territorial scope' of EU law online.

Within this framework, the cases of *CNIL v Google*[58] and *Glawischnig-Piesczek v Facebook*[59] are paradigmatic examples of the CJEU approach to constitutional values on a global scale at the intersection between speech and privacy.[60] Both decisions show how the judicial frame adopted by the CJEU has been seeking to adapt protection for fundamental rights in line with global challenges where the jurisdictional issue is now a matter of digital sovereignty rather than the attribution of judicial power within a certain territory. Whereas this relationship was more traditionally limited to striking a balance between these rights as conflicting interests, as in *Google Spain*, it is now possible to observe a new interconnection between the two 'faces of the same coin'. The above decisions opened up a new route for this path: judicial linkage between the regimes governing these two rights in the digital environment.

Within this framework, in *Google v CNIL* the CJEU considered a preliminary reference concerning the territorial scope of the right to be forgotten online. The case arose out of a formal notice by which the President of the CNIL ordered Google to delist information concerning data subjects from all of its domain name extensions. Despite the proposal by Google to adopt geo-blocking measures, the CNIL nevertheless decided to sanction Google for a failure to comply with the order. Before the Conseil d'État, the point raised by Google concerning the vague boundaries within the *Google Spain* case led the administrative court to send a

[58] Case C-507/17 *Google v CNIL*, ECLI:EU:C:2019:772.

[59] Case C-18/18 *Eva Glawischnig-Piesczek v Facebook Ireland Limited*, ECLI:EU:C:2019:821.

[60] On the connection between these judgments see Giovanni De Gregorio, 'Google v. CNIL and Glawischnig-Piesczek v. Facebook: Content and Data in the Algorithmic Society' (2020) 1 *Rivista di diritto dei media* 249.

preliminary reference to the CJEU concerning the scope of search engine delisting obligations.

Starting from the Opinion of AG Szpunar in *Google v CNIL*, it is possible to observe an approach characterised by self-restraint. According to AG Szpunar, neither the EU law nor the CJEU case law engaged with the territoriality of de-referencing within the context of protection for rights under Articles 7 and 8 EUCFR.[61] In other words, neither EU lawmakers nor the EU courts provided any answers for dealing with the results of searches made outside the EU's physical borders. As a consequence, the main question was:

> If the provisions of Directive 95/46 are thus intended to protect the fundamental rights, on the basis of Articles 7 and 8 of the Charter, of the person 'searched' and subsequently 'referenced', they are silent, however, on the question of the territoriality of the de-referencing. By way of example, neither those provisions nor the judgment in Google Spain and Google make clear whether a search request made from Singapore must be treated differently from a search request made from Paris or from Katowice.[62]

From this point of view, AG Szpunar argued that there should be no potential expansion of the territorial scope of fundamental rights beyond the EU's borders. Indeed, he both rejected the argument that the EUCFR has extraterritorial effects and asserted that the right to be forgotten did not have the status of a super-right not subject to any balancing process, thus clarifying an approach marked by self-restraint in relation to the jurisdictional issue. According to AG Szpunar:

> If worldwide de-referencing were admitted, the EU authorities would not be in a position to define and determine a right to receive information, still less to strike a balance between that right and the other fundamental rights to data protection and to private life, *a fortiori* because such a public interest in having access to information will necessarily vary, depending on its geographic location, from one third State to another.[63]

This point concerns not only the 'invasion' of third countries' sovereignty in striking their own balances between fundamental rights, but also the increasing risk of triggering a counter-response:

> If an authority within the European Union could order de-referencing on a worldwide scale, an inevitable signal would be sent to third countries, which could also order de-referencing under their own laws. Let us suppose that, for whatever reason, third countries interpret certain of their rights in such a way as to prevent persons located in a Member State of the European Union from having access to information which they sought. There would be a genuine risk of a race to the bottom, to the detriment of freedom of expression, on a European and worldwide scale.[64]

This is why AG Szpunar's proposal was more focused on geo-blocking technologies applied within the EU.

[61] AG Opinion, Case C-507/17, *Google v CNIL*, ECLI:EU:C:2019:15, para 45.
[62] ibid.
[63] ibid para 60.
[64] ibid para 61.

Having reasserted that EU law applies to the activities of search engines and noting that the CNIL had rejected the proposed geo-blocking application as formulated by Google, the CJEU analysed the questions proposed for a preliminary ruling: whether according to Articles 12(b) and 14 of the Data Protection Directive and Article 17(1) GDPR, de-referencing is due either on all the versions of the search engine, or only on the versions of that search engine corresponding to all the Member States, or even only on the version corresponding to the Member State where the de-referencing was requested. The global nature of the Internet and the claims of the right to digital privacy and data protection seemed to open the door on a new phase in the extraterritoriality saga:

> Such considerations are such as to justify the existence of a competence on the part of the EU legislature to lay down the obligation, for a search engine operator, to carry out, when granting a request for de-referencing made by such a person, a de-referencing on all the versions of its search engine.[65]

However, by embracing AG Szpunar's Opinion, in contrast to what happened in the *Google Spain* case, the CJEU highlighted the different approach to the right to privacy and data protection in other legal systems as well as the relative nature of this fundamental right. Two of the pillars underlying the extraterritoriality effect seem to have fallen: on the one hand, the limited digital sovereignty of the EU has been recognised, or rather the presence of different sovereignties also within the digital world has been recognised. On the other hand, the trump card of the absolute right to data protection and privacy online appears, in part, to have become less powerful. As a result, even if, in light of the precedents, the coherent solution would have been to extend the right to be forgotten to a global scale, the CJEU opted for a self-restraint approach, motivated by the risk of a kind of European legal colonisation in the name of cultural hegemony.

However, this decision seems to be more a tactical retreat than a surrender to criticism against the Europeanisation of Internet regulation. It appears to amount more to self-restraint on the part of the judiciary, pending a decision by politicians. In fact, the CJEU held that

> [w]hile the EU legislature has, in Article 17(3)(a) of Regulation 2016/679, struck a balance between that right and that freedom so far as the Union is concerned (see, to that effect, today's judgment, GC and Others (De-referencing of sensitive data), C-136/17, paragraph 59), it must be found that, by contrast, it has not, to date, struck such a balance as regards the scope of a de-referencing outside the Union.[66]

Aside from these considerations, the obligation to delist seems to be restricted to the EU Member States,[67] while national authorities may be free to require global removal.

[65] *CNIL v Google* (n 58) para 58.

[66] ibid para 61.

[67] 'The EU legislature has now chosen to lay down the rules concerning data protection by way of a regulation, which is directly applicable in all the Member States, which has been done, as is emphasised

In this sense, it should be considered that the CJEU is also engaging in dialogue with Member State courts, as the last two decisions of the German Constitutional Court on the right to be forgotten have shown.[68] The two decisions concern partially and fully harmonised areas of EU law. In the first case, the right to privacy had to be balanced against freedom of the press,[69] and in this field the court reasserted its right to apply national fundamental rights, whereas in the second case[70] the court claimed that it could have the power to review a hypothetical infringement of EU fundamental rights.[71] The most significant aspects of these decisions are, first of all, the attention given to the technological dimension and, secondly, the more careful balancing by the German Constitutional Court between the right to be forgotten and free speech.[72] The court stressed that conflicting fundamental rights must be weighed up equally, and there is no presumption that the right to personality must prevail in all cases.[73]

From the first point of view, the technological dimension played an important role in the German Constitutional Court's considerations, showing how courts are being continuously called upon to update their reasoning in line with technological evolution.[74] From the second point of view, on the other hand, the first case showed careful consideration for freedom of the press,[75] while the second did not appear to consider search engines' freedom of expression, but rather limited the analysis to their economic interests by holding that a search engine operator cannot invoke freedom of the press and freedom of opinion and media prerogatives

by recital 10 of Regulation 2016/679, in order to ensure a consistent and high level of protection throughout the European Union and to remove the obstacles to flows of personal data within the Union, that the de-referencing in question is, in principle, supposed to be carried out in respect of all the Member States', ibid para 66.

[68] German Constitutional Court, Judgment of 06 November 2019, 1 BvR 16/13 and Judgment of 06 November 2019, 1 BvR 276/17. See also Eva M Herzog, 'Dialogue and Diversity. The "Right to Be Forgotten" – Decisions of the Federal Constitutional Court' (2020) 1 *Rivista di diritto dei media* 285.

[69] German Constitutional Court, Judgment no 1 BvR 16/13 (n 68) para 45.

[70] German Constitutional Court, Judgment no 1 BvR 276/17 (n 68) para 50.

[71] See on this point, Dana Burchardt, 'Backlash against the Court of Justice of the EU? The Recent Jurisprudence of the German Constitutional Court on EU Fundamental Rights as a Standard of Review' (2020) 21 *German Law Journal* 1.

[72] German Constitutional Court, Judgment no 1 BvR 276/17 (n 68) para 120.

[73] ibid para 121.

[74] 'Die sich gegenüberstehenden Grundrechte sind miteinander abzuwägen. Als Grundlage der Abwägung ist zunächst ihr jeweiliger Gewährleistungsgehalt zu erfassen. Hierbei ist insbesondere auch den Kommunikationsbedingungen des Internets Rechnung zu tragen', German Constitutional Court, Judgment no 1 BvR 16/13 (n 68) para 96. But above all the court claimed 'Angesichts der fortschreitenden technischen Entwicklung und der damit verbundenen Ungewissheit, wie und wieweit ein Inhalteanbieter die Verbreitung im Internet im Wechselspiel mit den Suchmaschinen beeinflussen kann, werden die Fachgerichte die Konturen wirksamer und zumutbarer Schutzmaßnahmen fortlaufend fortzuschreiben haben. Soweit zumutbar, können sie den Akteuren auch die Entwicklung neuer Instrumente aufgeben. Bei alledem haben sie einen erheblichen Wertungsspielraum', ibid para 142.

[75] 'Die Bereitstellung von Onlinearchiven dient nicht nur den Interessen der Presseverlage, sondern ist zugleich von öffentlichem Interesse', ibid para 113.

in general.[76] However, the important point appears to be the less absolute nature of the right to digital privacy.[77] According to the German Constitutional Court:

> Thus, in the present case – in contrast to some of the cases decided by the CJEU, which concerned different scenarios – it cannot be presumed that protecting the right of personality takes precedence; rather the conflicting fundamental rights must be balanced on an equal basis. It is not for the individual to determine unilaterally what information may be disseminated about them in the course of public communication processes, neither vis-à-vis the media nor vis-à-vis the search engine operators.[78]

A similar approach can be discerned in relation to freedom of expression. Specifically, in *Glawischnig-Piesczek v Facebook*, the CJEU addressed the territorial scope of national orders concerning the removal of content, thus configuring the impact of EU law, especially freedom of expression, on a global scale. In contrast to the previous case, this case did not concern a non-harmonised framework of EU law.[79] As was stressed by AG Szpunar in this case:

> The situation at issue in the main proceedings is, prima facie, different from that which constituted the starting point of my analysis concerning the territorial scope of a de-referencing of the results of a search engine in *Google (Territorial scope of de-referencing)*, cited by Facebook Ireland and the Latvian Government. That case concerns Directive 95/46/EC, which harmonises, at Union level, certain material rules on data protection. It was, notably, the fact that the applicable material rules are harmonised that led me to conclude that a service provider had to be required to delete the results displayed following a search carried out not only from a single Member State but from a place within the European Union. However, in my Opinion in that case I did not exclude the possibility that there might be situations in which the interest of the Union requires the application of the provisions of that directive beyond the territory of the European Union.[80]

[76] As stressed by the German Constitutional Court, search engines cannot be considered as the press. German Constitutional Court, Judgment no 1 BvR 276/17 (n 68) para 9. And additionally, search engines cannot be considered as holding an independent and autonomous right to freedom of expression, ibid para 105.

[77] Even recognising that 'Soweit die Charta der Grundrechte der Europäischen Union anwendbar sei, sei die vom Europäischen Gerichtshof in der Entscheidung Google Spain gewählte Formulierung, dass die durch Art. 7, Art. 8 GRCh geschützten Rechte der betroffenen Person im Allgemeinen gegenüber dem Interesse der Internetnutzer überwiegen, nicht über den damals entschiedenen Fall hinaus verallgemeinerbar. Eine derartige Prädisposition für den Datenschutz anstelle einer offenen Grundrechtsabwägung würde sich im deutlichen Gegensatz zur Judikatur des Bundesverfassungsgerichts, aber auch des Europäischen Gerichtshofs für Menschenrechte sowie des Europäischen Gerichtshofs selbst bewegen. Der vom Oberlandesgericht entschiedene und der der Entscheidung Google Spain des Europäischen Gerichtshofs zugrundeliegende Sachverhalt wiesen sachliche Unterschiede auf. Ferner sei zu überlegen, inwiefern die Medienfreiheiten in solchen Fällen zu berücksichtigen seien', ibid para 21.

[78] German Constitutional Court, Judgment no 1 BvR 276/17 (n 68), Press Release No 84/2019 of 27 November 2019.

[79] AG Opinion, Case C-18/18, *Eva Glawischnig-Piesczek v Facebook Ireland Limited*, ECLI:EU:C:2019:458, para 79.

[80] ibid.

Freedom of expression is not regulated by a harmonised set of provisions at supranational level, such as those contained in the GDPR. Nonetheless, even though the matter is not fully harmonised and Member States grant different degrees of protection to freedom of expression, it is worth emphasising how the EU has intervened in the area of freedom of expression.[81] The willingness of the EU institutions to create a *droit acquis communautaire* in relation to freedom of expression may be due to various factors, which cannot be analysed in this chapter, such as furthering the political integration of the EU or responding to populist challenges. The EU's actions in the area of freedom of expression have also recently included measures such as the amendments to the Audiovisual Media Service Directive or the Copyright Directive.[82] Besides, it is worth mentioning here also the Code of Conduct on countering illegal hate speech online,[83] which seeks to combat hate speech online, as well as the Code of Practice on Disinformation,[84] which enshrined the first attempt to regulate online platforms with reference to disinformation and misinformation.[85]

As is the case in relation to digital privacy, fundamental rights are balanced quite differently in Europe than they are in the US.[86] Whereas in the US legal system the doctrine of the marketplace of ideas considers state intervention within public discourse to be inconsistent with the First Amendment, Europe has embraced a different balancing process for establishing the limits of free speech. It was noted in Chapter 1 that, under Article 10 ECHR and Article 11 EUCFR, not all forms of speech enjoy the same form of protection, and this is particularly evident in the fields of hate speech and fake news. Consequently, another clash of digital sovereignties could potentially break out online. In this regard, it must be

[81] See, for instance, Directive (EU) 2011/93 on combating the sexual abuse and sexual exploitation of children and child pornography; Directive (EU) 2017/541 on combating terrorism; Commission Recommendation (EU) 2018/334 on measures to effectively tackle illegal content online C/2018/1177; Proposal for a Regulation of The European Parliament and of the Council on preventing the dissemination of terrorist content online, COM/2018/640 final.

[82] Directive (EU) 2018/1808 of the European Parliament and of the Council of 14 November 2018 amending Directive 2010/13/EU on the coordination of certain provisions laid down by law, regulation or administrative action in Member States concerning the provision of audiovisual media services (Audiovisual Media Services Directive) in view of changing market realities; Directive (EU) 2019/790 of the European Parliament and of the Council of 17 April 2019 on copyright and related rights in the Digital Single Market and amending Directives 96/9/EC and 2001/29/EC.

[83] Code of Conduct on countering illegal hate speech online (2016) at https://ec.europa.eu/info/policies/justice-and-fundamental-rights/combatting-discrimination/racism-and-xenophobia/eu-code-conduct-countering-illegal-hate-speech-online_en.

[84] Code of Practice on Disinformation (2018) at https://ec.europa.eu/digital-single-market/en/news/code-practice-disinformation.

[85] Even if – according to some authors – this soft legal instrument can be ascribed to a logic that delegates the balancing process of fundamental rights to private powers, which entails some risks of privatisation of the censorship: Matteo Monti, 'The EU Code of Practice on Disinformation and the Risk of the Privatisation of Censorship' in Serena Giusti and Elisa Piras (eds), *Democracy and Fake News: Information Manipulation and Post-Truth Politics* (Abingdon, Routledge, forthcoming, 2020).

[86] See Frederick Schauer, 'Freedom of Expression Adjudication in Europe and America: A Case Study in Comparative Constitutional Architecture' in Georg Nolte (ed), *European and US Constitutionalism* (Cambridge, Cambridge University Press, 2005) 49.

stressed that judicial protection for freedom of expression in Europe has not been particularly broad. On the other hand, as was stressed in Chapter 2, the rise of new technologies has led European courts to narrow protection for freedom of expression in order to protect other conflicting interests online.

In this context, the decision in *Glawischnig-Piesczek v Facebook* considered the compatibility with the e-Commerce Directive (most notably with the absence of a general obligation to monitor) of the removal of defamatory content from Facebook. In this case, a former Member of the Austrian Parliament complained that her honour had been impugned following the publication of a defamatory content, which was accessible to all Facebook users. Nonetheless, the social network refused to remove the comments. In view of the conflicting views adopted by the domestic courts, the Austrian Supreme Court of Justice decided to refer some questions to the CJEU, asking whether Facebook should be required to remove expressions that are identical and equivalent to hosted content as ordered by the national courts, as well as the territorial reach of such an order.

The two main issues in play in the decision were the type of content that can be removed and the scope of EU law in this field. The issue of the removal of identical allegations and/or 'equivalent content' will not be considered with reference to the privatisation of censorship, which will be addressed in Chapter 5. Here, the analysis will focus on the territorial application of EU law in the area of freedom of expression.

The challenges raised by this new decision are already apparent from the choice made by the CJEU not to limit removal to identical content but also to equivalent content, thus broadening content-based control over the information disseminated. This seems to be the first problematic aspect of the decision. To allow the removal of more content that is considered to be equivalent in nature to banned content could increase the likelihood of a different balance of rights being struck in a third country as regards expressions that are not covered by free speech clauses. For instance, the clash between the balancing processes becomes clearly evident where the balance struck by the US Supreme Court in the defamatory cases is compared with the Austrian position.[87]

Furthermore, as in *Google v CNIL*, AG Szpunar proposed geographical limits to the application of national law in the digital world. Once again, the problem concerned other states' digital sovereignty:

> [A]s regards defamatory infringements, the imposition in one Member State of an obligation consisting in removing certain information worldwide, for all users of an electronic platform, because of the illegality of that information established under an applicable law, would have the consequence that the finding of its illegality would have effects in other States. In other words, the finding of the illegal nature of the information in question would extend to the territories of those other States. However, it is

[87] On the *probatio diabolica* of the 'actual malice' in the US legal system, see Kyu Ho Youm, '"Actual Malice" in U.S. Defamation Law: The Minority of One Doctrine in the World?' (2011) 4 *Journal of International & Entertainment Law* 1.

> not precluded that, according to the laws designated as applicable under those States' national conflict rules, that information might be considered legal.[88]

Stressing the lack of harmonisation in defamation law and how European law does not preclude a removal order with global reach, AG Szpunar emphasised that

> in the interest of international comity … that court should, as far as possible, limit the extraterritorial effects of its junctions concerning harm to private life and personality rights. The implementation of a removal obligation should not go beyond what is necessary to achieve the protection of the injured person. Thus, instead of removing the content, that court might, in an appropriate case, order that access to that information be disabled with the help of geo-blocking.[89]

On this basis, the CJEU held that no EU provisions impose a territorial limitation in this area.

> However, it is apparent from recitals 58 and 60 of that directive that, in view of the global dimension of electronic commerce, the EU legislature considered it necessary to ensure that EU rules in that area are consistent with the rules applicable at international level.[90]

As in *Google v CNIL*, the CJEU decision could be read as a green light for national courts to impose a global reach to their decisions on the removal of online content.[91] Indeed, in *Glawischnig-Piesczek v Facebook*, the CJEU did not deny the possibility that EU Member States' laws might have extraterritorial effect. Its approach sought to leave open the issue of the extraterritorial scope of EU law. Besides, the recent request for a preliminary ruling referred by the Belgian Constitutional Court including 10 preliminary questions on the obligation to transfer passenger information could allow the CJEU to clarify the issue of the third countries' digital sovereignty.[92]

In the light of the European approach to fundamental rights on a global scale, as resulting from these decisions, and the growing convergence of the principles regulating freedom of expression and data protection online,[93] it appears possible to discern a broader trend: the Europeanisation of Internet regulation as an expression of digital sovereignty through judicial power. In addition, it has to be stressed that a 'sword of Damocles' is hanging over this apparently self-restrained approach of the CJEU. By not excluding the possibility that the territorial reach of

[88] AG opinion, *Google v CNIL* (n 61) para 80.

[89] ibid para 100.

[90] *Glawischnig-Piesczek v Facebook* (n 59) para 51.

[91] As stressed by Thomas Hughes, Executive Director of Article 19 in Article 19, 'CJEU judgment in Facebook Ireland case is threat to online free speech', *Article 19* (3 October 2019) at www.article19.org/resources/cjeu-judgment-in-facebook-ireland-case-is-threat-to-online-free-speech/.

[92] Belgian Constitutional Court, Judgment no 135, 10 October 2019.

[93] Giovanni De Gregorio, 'The e-Commerce Directive and GDPR: Towards Convergence of Legal Regimes in the Algorithmic Society?' (2019) *Robert Schuman Centre for Advanced Studies Research Paper No. RSCAS 2019/36.*

EU fundamental rights may be global, the CJEU leaves margins for politicians to decide on the territorial scope of EU law.

The EU path towards digital privacy is peculiar but it is not the only approach to digital sovereignty in the information society. When moving to the other side of the Atlantic, it is worth observing the lack of a tendency towards judicial activism but towards stagnation. As we will examine in the next section, the US judicial approach still provides almost absolute protection to the right to free speech online while leaving privacy and data protection to play a secondary role in the information society.

IV. The Stagnation in the US

The European approach to fundamental rights online is not the general rule across the Atlantic. While Europe has been extending the scope of 'its' fundamental rights online, the US system seems stuck in a 'constitutional stagnation'. It has become mired in the quicksand of the definition of the right to privacy,[94] granting a right to data protection only in some specific fields,[95] while protecting the right to free speech online without any change in the last 20 years. From a general point of view, it seems that the First Amendment remains the lodestar against which all balancing processes of fundamental rights must be aligned.[96]

Under these circumstances, it is possible to identify a clash between the US and European perspectives. When looking at privacy and data protection, the approach followed by the US Supreme Court has been quite different. It has been characterised by the so-called 'third-party doctrine' according to which any person who gives information voluntarily to third parties, including Internet service providers, has no reasonable expectation of privacy. Besides, in the US, the main role in protecting users' data is played – at federal level – by the FTC (Federal Trade Commission),[97] and not by the US Supreme Court.

This paradigm has only been partially challenged in the last few years. The case of *United States v Jones*[98] involved an arrest for drug possession after police had used a tracker without judicial approval for one month. The primary question was therefore whether the warrantless use of a tracking device to monitor

[94] Neil M Richards, 'The Puzzle of Brandeis, Privacy, and Speech' (2010) 63 *Vanderbilt Law Review* 1295.

[95] Francesca Bignami and Giorgio Resta, 'Transatlantic Privacy Regulation: Conflict and Cooperation' (2015) 8 *Law and Contemporary Problems* 231. On the 'third-party doctrine' and the general idea of privacy in the US, see Daniel J Solove, 'Fourth Amendment Pragmatism' (2010) 51 *Boston College Law Review* 1511.

[96] See also Eugene Volokh, 'Freedom of Speech, Information Privacy, and the Troubling Implications of a Right to Stop People from Speaking About You' (2000) 52 *Stanford Law Review* 1049.

[97] Woodrow Hartzog and Daniel J Solove, 'The Scope and Potential of FTC Data Protection' (2015) 83 *George Washington Law Review* 2230.

[98] *United States v Jones* 565 US ____ (2012).

the defendant's movements on public streets violated the Fourth Amendment. The US Supreme Court rejected the government's argument concerning the lack of reasonable expectation of privacy and upheld the judgment of the lower court, holding that the use of a GPS tracking device on the defendant's vehicle without a warrant constituted an unlawful search under the Fourth Amendment. Even more importantly, in this case, Justice Sotomayor stressed the need to reconsider the premise that an individual has no reasonable expectation of privacy in relation to information voluntarily disclosed to third parties:

> This approach is ill suited to the digital age, in which people reveal a great deal of information about themselves to third parties in the course of carrying out mundane tasks. People disclose the phone numbers that they dial or text to their cellular providers; the URLs that they visit and the e-mail addresses with which they correspond to their Internet service providers; and the books, groceries, and medications they purchase to online retailers.[99]

Even more importantly, this decision has led to the emergence of the so-called 'mosaic theory'.[100] Before this decision, we have seen in Chapter 3 how courts addressed violations of the Fourth Amendment by looking at the specific individual step within the investigation. By contrast, the approach adopted in this case results in a focus on governmental activity as collective or aggregate behaviour when reviewing compliance with Fourth Amendment safeguards. In other words, when small pieces of information are collected, there should not be any problem as a warrant should only be required for bulk surveillance. Any given piece within a mosaic cannot reveal the overall picture without adding the other tiles. It is only the aggregation of the tiles that enables the full picture to be established.

Some years later, it became possible to enshrine this framework in law in one of the most important steps in the field of digital privacy in the US. In *Carpenter v United States*,[101] after the police arrested four men for a series of armed robberies, the FBI accessed transactional records, including geo-location, from the telephone of one of them and discovered that Mr Carpenter was responsible for aiding and abetting a robbery that affected interstate commerce. The defendant claimed a violation of his Fourth Amendment rights due to failure to obtain a warrant. Therefore, the question was whether a warrantless search and seizure of mobile telephone records violates the Fourth Amendment.

A majority ruled that, in order for police to access cell site location information or 'tower dumps', it is necessary to obtain a search warrant in order to avoid infringing Fourth Amendment rights. This is perhaps one of the rare decisions in which the US Supreme Court applied an internal perspective:

> The Government's position fails to contend with the seismic shifts in digital technology that made possible the tracking of not only Carpenter's location but also everyone else's,

[99] Concurring opinion of Justice Sotomayor, ibid 5.
[100] Orin S Kerr, 'The Mosaic Theory of the Fourth Amendment' (2012) 111 *Michigan Law Review* 311.
[101] *Carpenter v United States*, 585 US ____ (2018).

> not for a short period but for years and years. Sprint Corporation and its competitors are not your typical witnesses. Unlike the nosy neighbour who keeps an eye on comings and goings, they are ever alert, and their memory is nearly infallible. There is a world of difference between the limited types of personal information addressed in Smith and Miller and the exhaustive chronicle of location information casually collected by wireless carriers today. The Government thus is not asking for a straightforward application of the third-party doctrine, but instead a significant extension of it to a distinct category of information.[102]

However, the US Supreme Court stressed that it amounted to a 'narrow decision', which did not affect other aspects of the third-party doctrine.[103]

It is clear that, in the US framework, privacy and data protection are locked in a judicial frame of full trust in digital technologies. Indeed, aside from the exceptions mentioned above, there are no concerns regarding the new challenges raised by new digital technologies. This also applies in relation to the digital world and, owing to the considerable difference in the paradigm for balancing fundamental rights, may even result in some of them being considered as fundamental rights.

The US Supreme Court did not subject the use of data and the infringement of privacy to safeguards since the system is still based on a narrow notion of reasonable expectation of privacy. Such a liberal judicial approach to digital privacy is evident in the field of free speech. This is a general trend, which can be described as a decision to favour economic freedoms over fundamental rights, or better to focus only on the vertical dimension to fundamental rights in the digital world rather than the horizontal one.

As noted in Chapter 2, by enforcing Section 230 of the Communications Decency Act, the federal courts have left broad scope for action to moderate online speech.[104] This liberal approach led online platforms to establish their standard of protection of free speech online. This judicial approach can be considered as an expression of the US constitutional model, in contrast with the position on the other side of the Atlantic, which aims to limit forms of absolute protection.

Some scholars have tried to argue that it is necessary to apply the so-called state action doctrine to mitigate such situation of freedom and horizontally extend First Amendment rights against property rights.[105] However, federal circuit courts have rejected this doctrine, and in a recent case the US Supreme Court confirmed a viewpoint that restricted the scope of the state action doctrine to specific cases.

[102] ibid 15.

[103] 'Our decision today is a narrow one. We do not express a view on matters not before us: real-time CSLI or "tower dumps" (a download of information on all the devices that connected to a particular cell site during a particular interval). We do not disturb the application of *Smith* and *Miller* or call into question conventional surveillance techniques and tools, such as security cameras. Nor do we address other business records that might incidentally reveal location information. Further, our opinion does not consider other collection techniques involving foreign affairs or national security', ibid 17.

[104] Kate Klonick, 'The New Governors: The People, Rules, and Processes Governing Online Speech' (2018) 131 *Harvard Law Review* 1599.

[105] See, in particular, Jonathan Peters, 'The "Sovereigns of Cyberspace" and State Action: The First Amendment's Application (or Lack Thereof) to Third-Party Platforms' (2017) 32 *Berkeley Technology Law Journal* 989.

In *Manhattan Community Access Corp v Halleck*[106] the US Supreme Court ruled in favour of a very strict application of the state action doctrine, declining to apply it to a public access television network serving New York City. The case specifically concerned the refusal to broadcast a television documentary by Manhattan Community Access Corp, the private actor controlling the public access television network 'Manhattan Neighborhood Network'.

It is worth pointing out that the US Supreme Court did not refer to online platforms or focus on the effects of censorship caused by a refusal to broadcast. It still looked at an older framework.[107] Nonetheless, if this decision is framed in the digital environment where private actors provide digital spaces for the online exercise of freedom of expression, the consequence of this decision can be appreciated. Indeed, according to the US Supreme Court:

> Under the Court's cases, a private entity may qualify as a state actor when it exercises 'powers traditionally exclusively reserved to the State' … It is not enough that the federal, state, or local government exercised the function in the past, or still does. And it is not enough that the function serves the public good or the public interest in some way. Rather, to qualify as a traditional, exclusive public function within the meaning of our state-action precedents, the government must have traditionally and exclusively performed the function.[108]

This passage seems to leave no potential for broadening the scope of the state action doctrine to online platforms.[109] Furthermore, this consideration could be framed in terms of the frequently adopted external perspective of the US Supreme Court when addressing cases involving new technologies. On the other hand, the technological aspect seems to be quite significant in Justice Sotomayor's dissenting opinion. In fact, the dissenting opinion of the four remaining justices concludes that

> [w]hile the majority emphasizes that its decision is narrow and factbound, *ante*, at 15, that does not make it any less misguided. It is crucial that the Court does not continue to ignore the reality, fully recognized by our precedents, that private actors who have been delegated constitutional responsibilities like this one should be accountable to the Constitution's demands.[110]

The effects of this decision were immediately felt in the case law of the lower courts, which concluded that online platforms did not have the status of public forums.[111]

[106] *Manhattan Community Access Corp v Halleck* 587 US ___ (2019).

[107] 'The same principle should operate in this higher tech realm. Just as if the channels were a billboard, the City obtained rights for exclusive use of the channels by the public for the foreseeable future; no one is free to take the channels away, short of a contract renegotiation', ibid 8.

[108] ibid 6.

[109] 'The Hudgens decision reflects a commonsense principle: Providing some kind of forum for speech is not an activity that only governmental entities have traditionally performed. Therefore, a private entity who provides a forum for speech is not transformed by that fact alone into a state actor … In short, merely hosting speech by others is not a traditional, exclusive public function and does not alone transform private entities into state actors subject to First Amendment constraints', ibid 9.

[110] ibid 20.

[111] See, in particular, *Prager University v Google LLC* No 18-15712 (9th Cir 2020); *Mishiyev v Alphabet, Inc et al* No 3:2019cv05422 (ND Cal 2020) – Document 38.

In *PragerU*[112] the US Court of Appeals for the Ninth Circuit expressly referred to *Manhattan Community Access Corp v Halleck*, observing that

> [j]ust last year, the Court held that 'merely hosting speech by others is not a traditional, exclusive public function and does not alone transform private entities into state actors subject to First Amendment constraints.' … The Internet does not alter this state action requirement of the First Amendment. We affirm the district court's dismissal of PragerU's complaint.[113]

These decisions show how the approach of the US courts has become stagnant. The silence of the US Supreme Court could be interpreted as the result of the difference between the judicial frames adopted across the Atlantic. This is the case at any rate not only for the so-called third-party doctrine in the field of digital privacy, but also when focusing on challenges to free speech, such as disinformation and hate speech.[114] Over the last few years, it has been possible to observe a migration of the US model around the world on the wings of online platforms, rather than just from the dialogue between courts.[115] The hegemonic role played by online companies has led European courts to adapt their judicial frames and their approach to sovereignty and territory online. From this point of view, the US has in some way exported its paradigm of protection for fundamental rights through online platforms, the terms and conditions of which were heavily influenced, at least at least initially, by First Amendment lawyers.[116] This was already evident from the case law analysed in Chapters 2 and 3, where both the US Supreme Court and national courts showed their liberal approach to freedom of expression and privacy.

Unlike in Europe, where a new regulatory approach is rising also as a result of the European case law, the US system still continues to discuss or propose reforms that have not yet seen the light of day, even though the recent decision by President Trump to issue Executive Order 13925 on 28 May 2020 with a view to amending the scope of the broad liability exemption enshrined in Section 230 CDA may give rise to further moves in this respect. As already observed, this is primarily because most of the leading online companies are based in the US. Nonetheless, the Europeanisation of this system would be hard to avoid since the European market plays a critical role for these companies.[117] Besides, even though these cases mainly concerned US-based web giants such as Google or Facebook,[118] the extraterritorial

[112] *Prager University v Google LLC* (n 111) 5.
[113] ibid.
[114] On which see Giovanni Pitruzzella and Oreste Pollicino, *Disinformation and Hate Speech: A European Constitutional Perspective* (Milan, Bocconi University Press, 2020).
[115] Kowalik-Bańczyk and Pollicino (n 56).
[116] Klonick (n 104) 1621. *Cf* Marvin Ammori, 'The "New" New York Times: Free Speech Lawyering in the Age of Google and Twitter' (2014) 127 *Harvard Law Review* 2259, 2263. See also Dawn C Nunziato, 'The Death of the Public Forum in Cyberspace' (2007) 20 *Berkeley Technology Law Journal* 1115 and Tarleton Gillespie, *Custodians of the Internet Platforms, Content Moderation, and the Hidden Decisions That Shape Social Media* (New Haven, CT, Yale University Press, 2018).
[117] Daniel J Solove, *Understanding Privacy* (Cambridge, MA, Harvard University Press, 2008) 2–6.
[118] Kimberly A Houser and W Gregory Voss, 'GDPR: The End of Google and Facebook or a New Paradigm in Data Privacy' (2018) 25 *Richmond Journal of Law & Technology* 1.

scope can also affect other sectors such as newspapers and publishers.[119] From this viewpoint, it must also be stressed that the US Supreme Court has not had the opportunity to rule on the acquisition of data stored in other countries, declaring one case moot due to the enactment of the so-called CLOUD Act.[120]

Within this framework, Executive Order 13925 issued by President Trump targeting social media companies would seem to be an exceptional move on that side of the Atlantic.[121] This turning point was triggered by Twitter's response to the false and inflammatory claims made by President Trump (during a global pandemic). Specifically, Twitter added a fact-checking link to President Trump's tweet. By accusing social media platforms of 'invoking inconsistent, irrational, and groundless justifications to censor or otherwise punish Americans' speech here at home',[122] the order aims to dismantle immunity based on Section 230 CDA. According to the order:

> When an interactive computer service provider removes or restricts access to content and its actions do not meet the criteria of subparagraph (c)(2)(A), it is engaged in editorial conduct. It is the policy of the United States that such a provider should properly lose the limited liability shield of subparagraph (c)(2)(A) and be exposed to liability like any traditional editor and publisher that is not an online provider.[123]

Nonetheless, in *Gomez v Zuckenburg*,[124] the US District Court for the Northern District of New York underlined the limits of Executive Order 13925 by observing that

> EO 13925 was not intended to – and specifically precluded – a private right of action for individuals who assert an online platform targeted their accounts. To that end, EO 13925, Section 8(c) provides '[t]his order is not intended to, and does not, create any right or benefit, substantive or procedural, enforceable at law or in equity by any party against the United States, its departments, agencies, or entities, its officers, employees, or agents, or any other person.'[125]

In any case, it is worth observing that Executive Order 13925 concerns politicians (and not judges) that dealt with the activities of social media companies. Indeed, acting outside the realm of the judiciary, the government has tried to alter the system of social media immunity mentioned above. As has been observed, Executive Order 13925 can be considered as a 'constitutional paradox'.[126] We have

[119] And how this would be inconsistent with the First Amendment: Kurt Wimmer, 'Free Expression and EU Privacy Regulation: Can the GDPR Reach U.S. Publishers' (2018) 68 *Syracuse Law Review* 547.

[120] *United States v Microsoft Corp* 584 US ___ (2018).

[121] Executive Order on Preventing Online Censorship (28 May 2020) at www.whitehouse.gov/presidential-actions/executive-order-preventing-online-censorship/.

[122] ibid.

[123] ibid.

[124] *Gomez v Zuckenburg* No 5:20-CV-633 (NDNY 2020).

[125] ibid 5.

[126] Giovanni De Gregorio and Roxana Radu, 'Trump's Executive Order: Another Tile in the Mosaic of Governing Online Speech', *MediaLaws* (6 June 2020) at www.medialaws.eu/trumps-executive-order-another-tile-in-the-mosaic-of-governing-online-speech/.

seen how the US Supreme Court has protected the right to free speech online while limiting any attempt to regulate online intermediaries in the last 20 years. Executive Order 13925 indeed clashes not only with the constitutional stagnation of the US approach from a legislative perspective,[127] but also with the judicial protection of the right to free speech online.

Along with this reaction from political authorities, and aside from this exceptional case, it is worth observing that even the European approach influences the US environment as freedom of expression and privacy are highly interconnected in today's digital world. In addition, the new EU regulatory approach could influence the business of US online platforms. If online platforms' policies are to be subject to a process of Europeanisation, even the US digital marketplace of ideas will be transformed to a greater extent than before.[128] This trend is supported by the European judicial approach, which has embraced a common rulebook for regulating online speech and data, which could result in a new clash between values and digital sovereignty claims across the Atlantic.

V. Digital Sovereignty Across the Atlantic and Beyond

The transatlantic framework of protection of free speech and privacy shows how the judicial approach of the EU and US have focused on different strategies precisely when those fundamental rights purport to extend their effects to a global scale. In this perspective, there is an evident contrast between the territorial limits of enforcement jurisdiction and the global nature of the Internet. Only two solutions appear to be possible: tolerating the lack of effectiveness of mechanisms for protecting fundamental rights on the Internet that rely on technological architecture (eg geo-blocking), or alternatively imposing its own constitutional rules on other players.

The stance adopted by the CJEU has proved to be mixed, even though the adoption of the GDPR offers a strong model for data protection and privacy rights online (including in particular the right to be forgotten), which has already influenced some third countries, which have started to take account of the CJEU case law,[129] or to enact laws incorporating similar rights.[130] It is thus clear how the new

[127] However, see the proposal for the Platform Accountability and Consumer Transparency (PACT) Act (2020).

[128] Danielle K Citron and Helen Norton, 'Intermediaries and Hate Speech' (2011) 91 *Boston University Law Review* 1435, 1456.

[129] See *ex multis* the Canadian case, *Equustek Solutions Inc v Jack* [2014] BCSC 1063.

[130] It is possible to enumerate some examples, between them: Canada, Colombia, Chile, Israel, Peru, Mexico, Kenya, Russia and Indonesia. See Oskar J Gstrein, 'The Judgment That Will Be Forgotten. How the ECJ Missed an Opportunity in Google vs CNIL (C-517/17)', *Verfassungsblog* (25 September 2019) at https://verfassungsblog.de/the-judgment-that-will-be-forgotten/; David Erdos and Krzysztof Garstka, 'The "Right to be Forgotten" Online within G20 Statutory Data Protection Frameworks' (2019) *University of Cambridge Faculty of Law Research Paper No. 31/2019*.

interpretation of fundamental rights and the new balance between the right to digital privacy and other rights have indirectly paved the way for manipulating the standard of adequate protection for personal data in order to require substantially equivalent protection in third countries.

Against this background, the last decision of the CJEU seems to have changed the data-centric judicial approach, resulting in quite uncharacteristic self-restraint, which could be interpreted either as a silent overruling of previous judgments or a slowing down of development in the law, waiting for further steps to be legitimised by political authorities. After all, even in the *Schrems* saga, the CJEU recognised the role of the EU Commission in checking on equivalent protection for EU citizens' rights in third countries by issuing adequacy decisions or SCCs. It cannot be excluded that the CJEU will exercise greater judicial restraint not only in the light of technological developments, but also due to the broader scenario on which its decisions are likely to have an impact. Moreover, from this perspective, while it is likely that this trend will give rise to a new horizontal dialogue across the Atlantic, this phenomenon could help to build a more shared model of protection for fundamental rights beyond Europe's borders.

With this in mind, it is necessary to mention briefly the Guidelines 3/2018 on the territorial scope of the GDPR.[131] The European Data Protection Board has confirmed the broad application of the GDPR whenever the data processing involves a person resident in the EU. Even though the report does not concern chapter five of the GDPR, it is possible to identify several considerations for understanding the implications of EU law for third countries: first of all, confirmation of GDPR territorial scope with a broad interpretation of the provisions on 'establishment' and the processing of personal data resulting from targeting or other operations, regardless of where data are processed and even whether the processor chosen by the controller is situated outside the EU. Among these provisions, letter (e) on 'Interaction with other GDPR provisions and other legislations' is of particular interest. It restates the requirement for controllers or processors not established in the EU to comply with both EU law and the third country's law, which seems to imply that all foreign legislation grants a lower degree of protection to the right to data protection compared to European law, and thus that contradictions could only arise vis-à-vis broader protection under EU law. Consequently, these contradictions can be simply resolved by applying the more protective law, ie European law.

However, conversely, a kind of extraterritorial effect could arise in the area of free speech, where EU law is constantly expanding. European courts have already expressed their dissatisfaction with the so-called 'deconstitutionalisation

[131] Guidelines 3/2018 on the territorial scope of the GDPR (Article 3) (12 November 2019) at https://edpb.europa.eu/our-work-tools/our-documents/riktlinjer/guidelines-32018-territorial-scope-gdpr-article-3-version_it. Dan Jerker B Svantesson, 'European Union Claims of Jurisdiction over the Internet – an Analysis of Three Recent Key Developments' (2018) 9 *Journal of Intellectual Property, Information Technology and Electronic Commerce Law* 112.

of freedom of expression' imposed by online platforms.[132] From this perspective, moreover, European courts not only seem to have started embracing Balkin's idea of 'Free Speech as a Triangle',[133] but are also more aware of the implications of its balancing processes in the digital world. This evolution seems once again to set the increasingly active European courts against a rather static US Supreme Court.[134]

There is no doubt that the issue of the territorial scope of fundamental rights is an expression of a broader conflict between local law and global law, which characterises (judicial) globalisation. Similarly, the extraterritorial effect brought about by the GDPR and CJEU case law is also indisputable. However, according to the last decisions of the CJEU, the process of expanding European fundamental rights to a global scale seems to be slowing down in the area of privacy, while new trends are arising in the area of free speech, which could inject a new vibrancy into the perennial conflict between different views of digital sovereignty across the Atlantic. Therefore, the question is whether the European fortress of data privacy could face up to the castle of freedom of expression in US constitutional law.

In the light of this background, the courts have helped to extend constitutional values far beyond their national boundaries. Developments in Europe and the US provide examples of the role of judicial power in the information society, specifically in expressing a form of digital sovereignty which sees the European concept of privacy and data protection opposed to absolute protection for free speech on the other side of Atlantic.

Nonetheless, the COVID-19 pandemic has shown how models for protecting fundamental rights in the digital age should also be considered beyond democratic borders and outside judicial scrutiny. I am referring to the attempts around the world to provide a map of the virus through different technological systems of contact tracing. Since the outbreak of the pandemic, Asian countries such as China and South Korea have shown how technology can help to provide a map of the virus.[135] But what is the (constitutional) price paid for this? Before we even think about the law, we must compare different cultural models. On the one hand there is the Asian model rooted in collectivism, where the term 'private sphere' does not feature, which thus does not represent any obstacle for the establishment of surveillance infrastructure. On the other hand, there is the individualist European

[132] Damian Tambini, Danilo Leonardi and Chris T Marsden, *Codifying Cyberspace: Communications Self-Regulation in the Age of Internet Convergence* (London, Routledge, 2007) 275.

[133] Jack M Balkin, 'Free Speech Is a Triangle' (2012) 118 *Columbia Law Review* 2011.

[134] 'In the age of metadata, privacy constitutes a kind of precondition to speech, just as assembly constitutes a necessary antecedent activity to petitioning. At the macro level, privacy and speech are both essential conditions for the maintenance and functioning of a democratic polity. The CJEU seems to have recognised this important link in Digital Rights Ireland and has acted to secure privacy in order to safeguard speech. The U.S. federal courts should strongly consider following the CJEU's lead on this important question'. Ronald J Krotoszynski, 'Reconciling Privacy and Speech in the Era of Big Data: A Comparative Legal Analysis' (2015) 56 *William and Mary Law Review* 1279, 1335.

[135] Yasheng Huang, Meicen Sun and Yuze Sui, 'How Digital Contact Tracing Slowed Covid-19' *Harvard Business Review* (15 April 2020) at https://hbr.org/2020/04/how-digital-contact-tracing-slowed-covid-19-in-east-asia.

model, where a systemic and uncontrolled use of data is simply not compatible with the European constitutional matrix for protecting fundamental rights.

The narrative concerning the cultural difference between those two models is well founded as regards their legal implications, while at the same time being entirely misleading in terms of the ultimate idea that it seems to suggest. A trade-off must be made between the degree of precision of the virus map and the need to respect the quite demanding European data protection rules.

As far as the allegedly less effective (in terms of the fight against the virus) European contact tracing model is concerned, the main strength of European constitutionalism could lie precisely in what might appear to be an obstacle from a Far Eastern perspective. Even the most necessary and important goal (such as in this case ensuring safety and, ultimately, protecting life) cannot be achieved by interfering with the essence of contrasting fundamental rights. And the rights at issue, in this case the right to privacy and to personal data, should not be violated in a disproportionate manner. At the end of the day, this is the spirit (and the letter) of Article 52 EUCFR.

In other words, even without the legendary GDPR, it would already be sufficient to read Article 52 EUCFR carefully in order to assert that the EU Bill of Rights does not allow for digital surveillance systems, but rather only anonymous digital alerting systems. It is no coincidence that, since the very first call by the European Data Protection Supervisor for a pan-European approach and the European Commission Recommendation of April 8, proposing a common Union toolbox, Bluetooth technology was the suggested option and GPS technology was essentially excluded. The question of 'with whom' (if the answer is anonymised) is much less intrusive than the question about 'where'.

Before returning to the EU responses to the pandemic as far as the (apparent) trade-off between public health and privacy is concerned, it should be added that, while the framers of the GDPR might not exactly have predicted the pandemic, they did get quite close. Recital 46 of the GDPR states, among other things, that

> Some types of processing may serve both important grounds of public interest and the vital interests of the data subject of public interest and the vital interests of the data subject as for instance when processing is necessary for humanitarian purposes, including for monitoring epidemics.

This means that European constitutional law and the EU legislative compass are sufficiently solid and precise to provide a point of reference during the pandemic. If the Constitution is to act as our general compass, the relevant provisions of the EUCFR and the GDPR are the specific guides for identifying the limits to contact tracing in Europe.

The primary European constitutional principles that must be taken into consideration are freedom, individual choice, dignity and solidarity, which lie at the root of the recommendation that usage of the app should be voluntary. The 'binding suggestion' was confirmed by the initial responses that followed, starting with the joint statement of the EU Commission and the President of the European Council proposing a European Roadmap for lifting COVID-19 containment measures, the EU Commission guidance paper on COVID-19 apps and the release of a Common EU Toolbox for Member States by the EU's eHealth Network, an EU Commission-established body comprised of Member State authorities responsible for eHealth matters, as well as a letter by the EDPB in response to the guidance.

According to one view, adoption of the app should be voluntary and based on individual trust; at the same time, however, it must also be a choice made by individuals as a token of collective responsibility. However, voluntary adoption does not mean that the legal basis for processing should be consent. This message has been clearly stressed from the outset in the responses from the European Institutions mentioned above, and also in even greater detail in the more recent EDPB Guidelines 03/2020. It must be clearly stressed, as the EDPB has done many times, that the fact that use of the contact tracing app is voluntary does not mean that the processing of personal data by public authorities must necessarily be based on consent. When public authorities provide a service, based on a mandate assigned by and in line with requirements laid down by law, it would appear that the most significant legal basis for processing is necessity for the performance of a task in the public interest (Article 6(1)(e) GDPR). As regards health data, Article 9(2)(i) GDPR clearly states that it is even possible to process health data where it is 'necessary for reasons of public interest in the area of public health, such as protecting against serious cross-border threats to health'.

As is stated in the first recommendation referred to above, the idea of a pan-European app would entail Member State authorities, represented in the EU's eHealth Network, establishing a process for exchanging information and ensuring the interoperability of apps in cross-border scenarios. In other words, even if there is no common technological framework of contact tracing apps in the EU, the idea is to find a common legal language for a European app, which can generate results based on the main ingredients of: voluntary adoption, temporary retention of data, Bluetooth technology, as well as open source and decentralised storage systems in which the data controller is a public authority.

There are essentially two main challenges for a real EU interoperable language: one from below and one from above.

As regards the first challenge, Member States could, for example, have relied on the operating model that is already functioning well on electronic identification and trust services for electronic transactions in the internal market (eIDAS Regulation), as adopted on 23 July 2014. It creates an EU internal market for electronic trust services – namely electronic signatures, electronic seals, time stamps, electronic delivery services and website authentication – by ensuring that they will operate across borders and have the same legal status as traditional paper-based processes. They did not follow this model. Hence, the risk of national fragmentation is particularly high. There are no indications at the moment that the Member States have any desire to truly seek to set up a pan-European model, and this situation could also frustrate the idea of a common legal framework for contact tracing apps in context.

Considering the risk from above, the key issue is the global strategy adopted by Apple and Google, which are cooperating in order to launch a system 'to assist in enabling contact tracing', whereby apps can notify smartphone users if they have come close to people infected with COVID-19. It is very tempting to follow the path proposed by the two web giants. The proposal seems to be entirely consistent with the European approach mentioned earlier.

However, if the contact tracing system is to be based on trust, it should come as no surprise that a degree of digital distrust has been displayed by some states, including in particular France, towards the new private powers, which are now competing with the public authorities in the digital domain and which, in the recent past, have been (in)famously known in Brussels for their abuses of dominant positions.

Besides, adopting such a model would require not only users, but also EU institutions to trust these private actors without having any opportunity to check how personal data are subsequently stored, processed or used, thus transforming a global health emergency into an opportunity to grow and enhance their political and economic power.

In a way, there are fears that, once Apple and Google have done the hard work, they will then also decide on the rules of the game: it is not clear whether or not this is being taken seriously by Member State and European institutions. However, this perhaps should be in the light of Pasquale's suggestion that there has been a shift from territorial sovereignty to functional sovereignty, under which digital platforms fall into the hands of private powers, competing with and taking over public powers.[136]

It is obviously possible to comment on the beauty of European constitutional law in relation to the protection of contrasting fundamental rights, even in the throes of the pandemic, and the difficulty in speaking a pan-European language as regards app interoperability. However, it is also worth observing the dominant narrative according to which a trade-off must be made between the degree of precision of the virus map and the need to respect the quite demanding European data protection legal regime. This essentially focuses on the proportionality test only and not, as Article 52 EUCFR, Article 23 GDPR and Article 15 of the e-Privacy Directive show, on the necessity of the limitations on privacy. In other words, it is taken for granted that the app will be effective in combating the virus, and it is consequently taken for granted that it will be necessary. This is a typical expression of, in Morozovian terms, technology solutionism, according to which every problem must find an almost immediate technological solution. In this case, the solution should be the digital contact tracing system.

[136] Frank Pasquale, 'From Territorial to Functional Sovereignty: The Case of Amazon, Law and Political Economy', *Law and Political Economy blog* (6 December 2017) at https://lpeblog.org/2017/12/06/from-territorial-to-functional-sovereignty-the-case-of-amazon/. In Europe, according to some authors, this shift has been strengthened by a common trend, among the Member States, the EU Commission (for instance with the EU Code of Practice on Disinformation) and sometimes the CJEU, to delegate important content-based choices to the Internet platforms: see Monti (n 85).

The truth is that we do not have any empirical evidence that this is the solution – at least where app downloading is voluntary there will be no penalties for those who choose to do otherwise (the ABC of a liberal democracy model). Even in Singapore, which is far from having such a model and where there is a high degree of digitalisation and an even higher degree of trust in public authorities, the app (TraceTogether) has been downloaded by a low percentage of the population and does not appear to have had any significant impact on reducing infections. Finally, even in Europe, doubts concerning its necessity (effectiveness) are rising.[137]

These responses represent an alarm bell that is not ringing: if we cannot be reasonably certain that a digital tracing model that is compliant with European constitutional law will be effective and hence necessary, then even minimum restrictions on privacy become problematic. The alternative shifts from a European model of exposure notification to an Asiatic model based on digital surveillance or, in the best scenario, on walking and scary robots in parks.[138] I would be inclined to exclude that option outright. Otherwise, it would represent an unforgivable betrayal of the roots of European constitutionalism.

The case of contact tracing is a paradigmatic example of the challenges which courts will likely face in the next years. Judicial frames and the jurisdictional issue will continue to play a predominant role in the evolution of the judicial protection of fundamental rights and freedoms in the information society.

VI. Conclusions

The digital domain has called traditional legal categories into question. In some circumstances, the global nature of the Internet has allowed the sovereignty of a legal order to be extended beyond its own boundaries.

Nonetheless, this occurs in different ways. We have seen that the US approach to the transnational protection of fundamental rights looks stagnant when looking at the European judicial activism. Freedom of expression seems to enjoy an almost absolute protection, while the right to privacy does not enjoy protection at a federal level and risks being locked into the mosaic theory. Such a liberal approach to the digital environment nonetheless conceals a common denominator between online privacy and free speech regimes under US law. The omissive strategy characterised by a lack of influence on the part of courts and lawmakers is

[137] For instance, Belgium plans to continue with traditional contact tracing as it does not consider that there is sufficient evidence that the instrument will be effective. In Austria only 4% of the population has downloaded the app, despite pressure from the government. In the Netherlands, the supervisory authority has stated that it will not be in a position to approve it unless it is confirmed as being effective. Finally, in France, the CNIL will only approve it after a parliamentary debate has been held and studies have been completed showing it to be effective.

[138] Edgar Su, 'Roaming "Robodog" Politely Tells Singapore Park Goers to Keep Apart', *Reuters* (8 May 2020) at www.reuters.com/article/us-health-coronavirus-singapore-robot/roaming-robodog-politely-tells-singapore-park-goers-to-keep-apart-idUSKBN22K1S6.

a specific characteristic of the US courts' judicial frame and their approach to the jurisdictional issue.

On the other side of the Atlantic, European courts have proved willing to go beyond the limits of interpretation. They have contributed to the rise of a sort of super fundamental right to privacy online and broadened the territorial scope of that right. By creating a continental fortress around the right to privacy and data protection online, the CJEU has sometimes lowered the drawbridge, allowing extraterritorial effectiveness for the European rules on the protection of digital privacy. Indeed, while the case law of the CJEU turns the EU into a fortress for personal data, it does not appear to consider the political and legal impact of its decisions with regard to relations with third countries. However, we have seen how this process of extending constitutional values outside the borders of the EU has been mitigated by the need to respect other principles of the international legal framework. Therefore, the EU approach cannot be considered imperialistic but, rather, as being focused on ensuring the effective protection of fundamental rights in the information society.

From a global perspective, it is worth observing how the judicial protection of fundamental rights in democratic States is not the only model. There are increasing concerns at the migration of technological (rather than constitutional) ideas from the East that could find fertile ground for implementation in the West as the need to find technological instruments to resolve the pandemic crisis has shown. Therefore, digital sovereignty is not expressed in the same way across the globe but reflects the political and (constitutional) values extended to the information society.

5

The Courts and Private Powers in the World of Bits: Towards Digital Constitutionalism?

I. The Rise and Amplification of Judicial Activism

As was mentioned in the Introduction, this chapter aims to reconnect the judicial language of protection of fundamental rights in the digital age with the terms of the emerging debate on a new round of modern constitutionalism in the information society, so-called 'digital constitutionalism'.[1] I believe in fact that the increasing role of courts in matters involving digital technologies has been one of the reasons for the emergence of a new round of modern constitutionalism in the information society. In other words, judicial activism has been playing a critical role in incorporating the relevance of constitutional law into the framework of the information society.

In order to contextualise this perspective within this study, it is worth observing the general increase in judicial momentum, which has led to an emerging imbalance between judicial and political actors in facing the new challenges associated with the protection of fundamental rights online. Nonetheless, in order to understand why the increasing relevance of judicial power is simply an amplification of a pre-existing phenomenon, it is important to step back and try to understand how the transformation of the form of state (ie the vertical relationship between rulers and the governed) affect the different (but related) issue of the institutional balance from a horizontal perspective, that is between constitutional branches of state (ie the legislative, executive and judiciary branches).

A tentative answer could be that it has been possible to observe a corresponding gradual strengthening of the role of judiciary over politics from the

[1] Giovanni De Gregorio, 'The Rise of Digital Constitutionalism in the European Union' (2020) *International Journal of Constitutional Law*, forthcoming; Edoardo Celeste, 'Digital Constitutionalism: A New Systematic Theorization' (2019) 33(1) *International Review of Law, Computers and Technology* 76; Dennis Redeker, Lex Gill and Urs Gasser, 'Towards Digital Constitutionalism? Mapping Attempts to Craft an Internet Bill of Rights' (2018) 80 *International Communication Gazette* 302; Mauro Santaniello, Nicola Palladino, Maria Carmela Catone and Paolo Diana, 'The Language of Digital Constitutionalism and the Role of National Parliaments' (2018) 80 *International Communication Gazette* 320; Nicolas Suzor, 'Digital Constitutionalism: Using the Rule of Law to Evaluate the Legitimacy of Governance by Platforms' (2018) 4(3) *Social Media + Society* 1.

nineteenth-century liberal state, through the consolidation of the welfare state, to the present post-modern globalised governance. It is well known that, as far as the horizontal division of powers is concerned, the state of the nineteenth century was characterised by the absolute predominance of the Parliament over the executive and the judicial branches, which were considered to be ancillary to the representative body vested with popular sovereignty.[2] This parliamentary hegemony manifested itself, within the hierarchy of sources of law, in the absolute predominance of the 'legal rule', which, according to a pure 'rule of law' logic, prevailed also over constitutional (flexible) rules.

To use Montesquieu's metaphor, judicial power was considered to be nothing more than the 'bouche de la loi'.[3] It is well known that this expression underscores the element of pure and mechanical logic within judicial decision making, while neglecting, or concealing, the voluntary and discretionary element of choice. This is the main reason why, during the historical period under scrutiny, judicial power could be defined, only apparently paradoxically, as a 'not power' because it was not expected to express its own will but rather only to apply clear and precise rules created by the legislature.

In the twentieth century, the executive branch replaced Parliament in taking the leading role within modern welfare societies. The welfare state could no longer be based on the exercise of traditional punitive functions or a limited role in the protection of negative freedoms. On the contrary, this new paradigm promised active and positive protection for citizens. Such an attitude involves, by definition, planning policies and actions for future developments, while formulating social aims and principles broadly, leaving the courts with the task of giving tangible meaning to these principles in context as well as defining their extent and limits.

It is evident that this kind of legislation has encouraged judicial creativity and the amplification of their *marge de manoeuvre*.[4] The significant growth in state intervention in areas previously left to private self-regulation has led to a corresponding increase in judicial activity.[5] In the social state, through a process involving the 'judicialisation' of politics, the distance between institutions and citizens has become narrower and opportunities for exchanging views between those

[2] Gustavo Zagrebesky, *Il diritto mite* (Turin, Einaudi, 1992); Giovanni Bognetti, *La divisione dei Poteri* (Milan, Giuffrè, 2001).

[3] Charles-Louis Montesquieu, *De l'Esprit des Lois* (1758).

[4] It was no coincidence that, at the beginning of the twentieth century, in parallel with the above change in the institutional balance between the state's constitutional powers, a cultural and juridical movement called 'revolt against the formalism' was born to 'fight' the excessive legalism of the post-codification era. According to this movement, deciding a case cannot be limited to simply 'applying' formal rules to facts in a mechanical way pursuant to the rule of law. In consonance with this view, the judgment itself will be added to the interpretation of the rule to be applied and may thus help to define its meaning. See François Gény, *Méthode d'interprétation et Sources en Droit Privé Positif* (Paris, LGDJ, 1899).

[5] See Mauro Cappelletti, 'The Law-Making Power of Judges and Its Limits' (1981) 8 *Munich University Law Review* 15; Oreste Pollicino, 'The Legal Reasoning of the Court of Justice in the Context of the Principle of Equality' (2004) 5(3) *German Law Journal* 283.

actors have become more frequent. In other words, in this context, courts can be defined as a privileged meeting place.[6]

Concluding this brief overview, in the current era of legal and economic globalisation, it is worth observing that traditional constitutional governance is altering the characteristics that marked the process of its development in previous centuries. In particular, it is possible to observe a definitive decline in the historical constellation that featured the simultaneous presence, within the same national borders, of state, sovereignty and economy.[7] Post-modern constitutionalism is characterised by a process of fragmentation in terms of sovereignty, followed by a parallel process of reconfiguration within a multilevel and polycentric system.[8] Within this context, it is essential to establish the correct and fastest interconnections between the different constitutional centres that frame the new polycentric global order at national, supranational and international level. It is a commonly held opinion that the multilevel network of judicial decisions provides the best pathway for interconnections.[9]

The 'road to juristocracy' is thus one of the main trends within post-modern constitutionalism in the era of judicial globalisation.[10] In other (more convincing) words, judicial power has moved from being the 'weak link' in the chain to become the strong one.[11] Judge-made law seems to be better placed than legislative or administrative acts, in terms of flexibility and its pragmatic approach, to face the challenge of legal systems as they become increasingly more interdependent, while subject to constant and unforeseen transformation. To put it blandly, global governance seems to prefer the language of the 'law in action' rather than the ink of the 'law in the books'.[12]

[6] See, for a similar point of view, Maria Rosaria Ferrarese, *Il Diritto al Presente* (Bologna, Il Mulino, 2002) 208.

[7] Habermas identifies a different kind of triangle (ie, state, society, economy) that would be the basis of the classical constitutional governance. See Jürgen Habermas, *The Postnational Constellation: Political Essays* (Cambridge, MA, MIT Press, 2001).

[8] Gunther Teubner, 'Societal Constitutionalism: Alternatives to State-Centered Constitutional Theory?' in Christian Joerges, Inge-Johanne Sand and Gunther Teubner (eds), *Constitutionalism and Transnational Governance* (Oxford, Hart Publishing, 2004) 3.

[9] Claire L'Heureux-Dube, 'The International Judicial Dialogue: When Domestic Constitutional Courts Join the Conversation' (2001) 114 *Harvard Law Review* 2049; Anne-Marie Slaughter, 'A Global Community of Courts' (2003) 44(1) *Harvard International Law Journal* 191; Anne-Marie Slaughter, *A New World Order* (Princeton, NJ, Princeton University Press, 2004); Sujit Choudry, 'Globalization in Search of Justification: Towards a Theory of Comparative Constitutional Interpretation' (1999) 74(3) *Indiana Law Journal* 821; Christopher McCrudden, 'A Common Law of Human Rights? Transnational Judicial Conversations on Constitutional Rights' (2000) 20(4) *Oxford Journal of Legal Studies* 499; Martin Shapiro and Alec Stone Sweet, *On Law, Politics and Judicialization* (Oxford, Oxford University Press, 2002); Alec Stone Sweet, *Governing with Judges: Constitutional Politics in Europe* (Oxford, Oxford University Press, 2000).

[10] Anne-Marie Slaughter, 'Judicial Globalization' (2000) 40 *Virginia Journal of International Law* 1103; Ran Hirschl, *Towards Juristocracy: The Origins and Consequences of the New Constitutionalism* (Cambridge, MA, Harvard University Press, 2004); C Neale Tate and Torbjörn Vallinder (eds), *The Global Expansion of the Judicial Power* (New York, New York University Press, 1995).

[11] Ralf Dahrendorf, *Dopo la democrazia* (Rome-Bari, Laterza, 2003) 65.

[12] The dichotomy between 'law in action' and 'law in the book' was originally underlined by Roscoe Pound, 'Law in Books and Law in Action' (1910) 44 *American Law Review* 12.

If this is true, before returning to the added value that digital technologies provide in order to enhance the language of the law in action in a globalised information society, it is important to add one further point to clarify a stereotype which unavoidably appears whenever discourse on judicial globalisation addresses the relationship between the European legal framework and the national constitutional dimension.[13] Indeed, in order to avoid the mistake made by those who, when looking at a finger pointing at the moon, focus on the finger and not on the moon, it should be noted that the notion of judicial dialogue is nothing but a signal of the presence of something else behind it, which is often particularly problematic.[14]

It is thus not a substantive goal in itself but rather a procedural tool for improving the status quo that is not entirely satisfactory. In particular, the debate seems to show that, if there is something called European judicial dialogue,[15] it very often arises due to a (real or presumed) risk of constitutional collision between the domestic and European levels, especially as regards the standard of protection for fundamental rights.[16] It may also occur due to the willingness on the part of national constitutional courts to clarify what appears to be unclear in relation to the interpretation (or validity) of EU law by sending a reference to the CJEU, rather than (more poetically but less realistically) aspiring to belong to different, but interacting, constitutional jurisdictions in order to build a judicial '*Harmonia Caelestis*'.[17]

[13] Esin Orucu, *Judicial Comparativism in Human Rights Cases* (London, British Inst of Intl & Comparative Law, 2003); Francesco Francioni, 'International Law as a Common Language for National Courts' (2001) 36(3) *Texas International Law Journal* 587; Vassilios Skouris, 'The Position of the European Court of Justice in the EU Legal Order and its Relationship with National Constitutional Courts' (2005) *Zeitshrift für öffentliches Recht* 323; Alec Stone Sweet, 'Constitutional Dialogue in the European Community' in Anne-Marie Slaughter, Alec Stone Sweet and Joseph Weiler (eds), *The European Court and National Courts. Doctrine and Jurisprudence: Legal Change in its Social Context* (Oxford, Hart, 2004) 304.

[14] It is perhaps worth making clear that the term 'judicial dialogue' is used here in a twofold way. First, the reference is only to judicial relations between interconnected 'vertically' legal orders situated at different, not hierarchically based, levels (national, European and international); secondly the reference is only to the direct relationship between courts and not to the broader situation of constitutional cross-fertilisation and judicial borrowing between legal systems where the judges generally conduct a form of dialogue through mutual citations. See Francis G Jacobs, 'Judicial Dialogue and the Cross Fertilization of Legal System: The European Court of Justice' (2003) 38(3) *Texas International Law Journal* 547; Allan Rosas, 'The European Court of Justice in Context: Forms and Pattern of Judicial Dialogue' (2007) 1(2) *European Journal of Legal Studies* 1.

[15] Martin Belov (ed), *Judicial Dialogue* (The Hague, Eleven International Publishing, 2019); Amrei Müller (ed), *Judicial Dialogue and Human Rights* (Cambridge, Cambridge University Press, 2017); Giuseppe Martinico and Oreste Pollicino, *The Interaction Between Europe's Legal Systems: Judicial Dialogue and the Creation of Supranational Laws* (London, Edward Elgar, 2012); Rosas (n 14).

[16] Neil MacCormik, 'Risking Constitutional Collision in Europe?' (1998) 18(3) *Oxford Journal of Legal Studies* 517.

[17] Péter Esterházy, *Harmonia Caelestis* (Milan, Feltrinelli, 2003). Along the same lines, in a broader and philosophically based context, Jürgen Habermas and Jacques Derrida argue that 'the image of a peaceful cooperative Europe, open toward other cultures and capable of dialogue, floats like a mirage before all of us'. See Jürgen Habermas and Jacques Derrida, 'February 15, or What Binds Europeans Together: A Plea for a Common Foreign Policy, Beginning in the Core of Europe' (2003) 10(3) *Constellations* 291, 293.

Therefore, the involvement of interconnecting jurisdictions in European judicial dialogue is, generally speaking, a reaction, and very rarely a spontaneous action, to either a lack of legal clarity regarding the interpretation and application within national law of EU law or the (risk of a) collision between EU law and Member States' constitutional systems.

Therefore, the need to maintain a symmetrical balance between judicial and political powers in the digital era may not come from either hyper-activism on the part of the courts or inertia on the part of the legislator, but perhaps from the judicial ability to promptly react. Since judges appear to be best placed to identify the possible collision between fundamental rights online and, consequently, to be the bodies best equipped to provide an initial answer, the systemic answer (but not the final answer, as the last word is always left to the constitutional court) should come from the legislative branch by responding *lato sensu* and codifying the relevant case law. In other words, if it is the case, as has been said, that the new round of judicial globalisation constitutes a response to a pre-existing problem involving a possible contrast between fundamental rights, a further response, after the initial judicial response, should come from the legislature.

This twofold response has been engaged, for instance, in relation to European protection for fundamental rights in the information society, such as within the GDPR, and has worked quite well. Nonetheless, the challenges ahead raised by new technologies require us to reconsider the relationship between political and judicial power under the lens of digital constitutionalism, which, as has been stressed,[18] tends to focus on the rise of private powers implementing algorithmic technologies, and, secondly, the constitutional remedies arising out of the mix between judicial and political instruments respectively in terms of the horizontal application of fundamental rights and the possible adoption of a new set of rights as a consolidation of existing charters and Bills of Rights.

II. The Courts and Private Power in the Digital Era

This book has examined how courts across the Atlantic have reacted to technology by restricting or amplifying the frame of protection for fundamental rights, while, at the same time, addressing jurisdictional issues. Nonetheless, the role of courts in the information society is still at the dawn of a new phase characterised by the rise of digital constitutionalism, addressing questions relating to automated technologies as well as attempts by lawmakers to codify new guarantees, the boundaries of which need still to be shaped by the courts.

Since the advent of the Internet at the end of the last century, lawmakers, courts and scholars have tried to re(interpret) the classic models of protection for

[18] Giovanni De Gregorio, 'From Constitutional Freedoms to Power. Protecting Fundamental Rights Online in the Algorithmic Society' (2019) 11(2) *European Journal of Legal Studies* 65.

fundamental rights as free speech and privacy in the light of the impact of digital technologies. It is no coincidence that the debate has started to question consolidated concepts such as sovereignty and territory.[19] The case of *Yahoo v Licra* provided a paradigmatic example of the new challenges that were on the horizon at that time.[20] This also touched on the liberal idea of a digital world free from any form of regulation based on geographical boundaries.[21] Under the cyber-anarchic view, the rise of Internet law caused the disintegration of state sovereignty over cyberspace, thus potentially rendering any regulatory attempt irrelevant for the digital environment.

As was stressed in Chapter 1, these positions have revealed their fallacies, and scholars have emphasised how states are instead seeking to regulate the digital environment in different ways,[22] and also how to solve the problem of enforcement in the digital domain.[23] Nonetheless, this was not the end of the story. Indeed, in recent years new concerns have been raised as a result of the increasing economic power that some business actors have acquired in the digital environment, especially online platforms. This economic power has resulted primarily from the potential of new digital technologies and the high degree of freedom recognised by constitutional democracies to the private sector.[24] The shift from the world of atoms to the world of bits has led to the emergence of previously unknown players, which now act as information gatekeepers and hold significant economic power, with direct effects on individuals' everyday lives.[25]

At the dawn of the digital era, it was possible to regard the emergence of these new actors merely as a consequence of freedom to conduct business. The main legal (but also economic) issue was thus to protect that freedom, while at the same time preventing any possible abuse. In fact, Section 230 CDA and the e-Commerce Directive set out liability exemptions for illegal content, which apply to Internet service providers with a view to facilitating the further development of these services and the flow of content.[26] Therefore, in the EU the e-Commerce Directive encapsulates the approach that inspired lawmakers and regulators (most notably in the US) during the initial years of the Internet: *minimum* regulation

[19] John P Barlow, 'A Declaration of the Independence of Cyberspace', *Electronic Frontier Foundation* (8 February 1996) at https://projects.eff.org/~barlow/Declaration-Final.html.

[20] High Court of Paris, *UEJF et LICRA v Yahoo! Inc. Et Yahoo! France* [2000] no RG:00/0538. See Joel R Reidenberg, 'Yahoo and Democracy on the Internet' (2001/2002) 42 *Jurimetrics* 261; *Yahoo!, Inc v La Ligue Contre le Racisme et L'Antisemitisme* 169 F Supp 2d 1182 (ND Cal 2001).

[21] David R Johnson and David G Post, 'Law and Borders. The Rise of Law in Cyberspace' (1996) 48 *Stanford Law Review* 1367.

[22] Lawrence Lessig, *Code 2.0* (New York, Basic Books, 2006).

[23] Joel R Reidenberg, 'States and Internet Enforcement' (2004) 1 *University of Ottawa Law & Technology Journal* 213.

[24] De Gregorio (n 18).

[25] Emily B Laidlaw, 'A Framework for Identifying Internet Information Gatekeepers' (2012) 24(3) *International Review Law, Computers and Technology* 263.

[26] Directive 2000/31/EC of the European Parliament and of the Council of 8 June 2000 on certain legal aspects of information society services, in particular electronic commerce, in the Internal Market ('e-Commerce Directive').

with a view to maintaining the freedom to conduct business (while not burdening ISPs in connection with third-party illegal content), while preventing abuses of that freedom (in cases in which ISPs exercised editorial responsibility instead of performing a merely neutral and passive role vis-à-vis content). Likewise, even competition law turned out to be a privileged tool in this respect.[27]

Thanks to the minimum level of intervention in the digital domain, the factor of technology played a crucial role once again. In the meantime, the development of algorithmic technologies to process data and profit from the vast amount of information has come into play. Nonetheless, it is no longer exclusively a matter of profits. The involvement of the market with automated decision-making technologies has led to the transformation of economic freedoms into something that resembles the exercise of powers vested in public authorities. This power can be observed from many different perspectives, such as the field of competition law in terms of economic and data power.[28] In other words, the development of new digital and algorithmic technologies has led to the rise of new opportunities for fostering freedoms, but also to the consolidation of powers embodying a private model of protection of rights and users' governance. Beyond public powers, the freedom to conduct business has now developed into a new dimension, namely private power. It goes without saying that this entails significant challenges to the role and tools of constitutional law and, consequently, the instrument on which courts can rely in order to address emerging threats. In fact, competition law and regulation are no longer sufficient to engage with the operations of these actors where fundamental rights adjudication is directly involved and affected. It was noted in Chapters 2 and 3 how judicial activism has led courts to deal with the new challenges raised by the implementation of new technologies.

One might actually wonder what the connection is between algorithms and courts, which are seemingly so distant, and yet in effect so close. In order to explain the link between the two, it could be argued that the large-scale implementation of automated technologies has the potential to cause a further transmutation in protection of fundamental rights and, consequently, the role of courts in overcoming legislative inertia. In addition to the changes already caused by the shift from the world of atoms to the world of bits,[29] where constitutionalism becomes 'digital constitutionalism' and power is relocated among different actors in the information society,[30] this relationship between algorithms and court leads judicial activism to play a critical role in the information society. It should not come as any surprise if courts continue to be the best-equipped bodies to address these challenges. Therefore, it is possible that judicial power may increasingly become predominant over politics in the field of digital technologies.

[27] Angela Daly, *Private Power, Online Information Flows and EU Law: Mind the Gap* (Oxford, Hart Publishing, 2016).

[28] Inge Graef, *EU Competition Law, Data Protection and Online Platforms: Data as Essential Facility* (Alphen aan den Rijn, Wolters Kluwer, 2016).

[29] Nicholas Negroponte, *Being Digital* (New York, Alfred A Knopf Inc, 1995).

[30] De Gregorio (n 1); Suzor (n 1).

The emergence of private powers in the information society is causing the most disruptive challenges to the modern constitutional state, while questioning the various policy options for facing technological transformations. Private actors other than the traditional public authorities are now vested with some forms of power that is no longer merely economic in nature. This is not a trivial point. As is well known, constitutional theory has historically framed power as vested in public authorities, which *by default* hold the monopoly on violence under the social contract.[31] It is no coincidence that constitutional law has been built around the functioning of public authorities. The original mission of constitutionalism was to set out certain mechanisms for restricting governmental power through self-binding principles, including by providing different arrangements for the separation of powers and constitutional review.

For our present purposes, judicial activism may be a solution for legislative inertia, but may also trigger new challenges for the rule of law in times of digital constitutionalism. In fact, algorithms enable activities of various types to be carried out that may significantly affect individuals' rights and freedoms. Individuals may not notice that many decisions are carried out in an automated manner without, at least prima facie, any opportunity for control of them. A broad range of decision-making activities are increasingly being delegated to algorithms, which can advise, and in some cases make decisions, based on the data they process.[32] As scholars have observed, 'how we perceive and understand our environments and interact with them and each other is increasingly mediated by algorithms'.[33] In other words, algorithms are not necessarily driven by the pursuit of public interests and are instead sensitive to business needs. These concerns are even more serious in the light of the learning capabilities of algorithms, which – by introducing a degree of autonomy and hence unpredictability – are likely to undermine 'accountability' and human understanding of the decision-making process. For instance, the opacity of algorithms is regarded by scholars as a possible cause of discrimination or differentiation between individuals with regard to activities such as profiling and scoring.[34]

The COVID-19 pandemic has highlighted the relevance of online platforms in the information society. For instance, Amazon provided deliveries during the lockdown phase, while Google and Apple offered their technology for contact tracing apps.[35] These actors have played a critical role in providing services which other businesses or, even the state, failed to deliver promptly. The COVID-19 crisis

[31] Thomas Hobbes, *Leviathan* (1651).

[32] Brent D Mittelstadt, Patrick Allo, Mariarosaria Taddeo, Sandra Wachter and Luciano Floridi, 'The Ethics of Algorithms: Mapping the Debate' (2016) 3(2) *Big Data & Society* 1.

[33] ibid 1.

[34] Danielle K Citron and Frank Pasquale, 'The Scored Society: Due Process for Automated Predictions' (2014) 89 *Washington Law Review* 1; Tal Z Zarsky, 'Transparent Predictions' (2013) 4 *University of Illinois Law Review* 1507.

[35] 'Privacy-Preserving Contact Tracing', *apple.com* at www.apple.com/covid19/contacttracing.

has led these actors to become increasingly involved in our daily lives, becoming part of our social structure. In other words, their primary role during the pandemic has resulted in these actors being thought of as public utilities.

Nonetheless, commentary has not been exclusively positive. The model of the contact tracing app proposed by these tech giants aroused various privacy and data protection concerns.[36] The pandemic has also shown how artificial intelligence can affect fundamental rights online without human oversight. Once Facebook and Google sent their moderators home, the effect of these measures extended to the process of content moderation, resulting in the suspension of various accounts and the removal of some content even though there was no specific reason for this.[37] This situation has not only affected users' right to freedom of expression, but has also led to discriminatory results and the spread of disinformation. Generally speaking, it is worth observing that the solidarity expressed during the pandemic has also been mediated by the role of online platforms at the heart of individuals' lives and relationships.

This does not mean that the pandemic has only revealed the opportunities and challenges raised by online platforms. Indeed, as was underlined in Chapter 4, the pandemic has offered an excuse for authoritarian regimes to foster their regime of surveillance, as has occurred in Singapore. At the same time, democratic states have paid greater attention to the risks that contact tracing apps may entail for the rights and freedoms of citizens. In other words, the balancing between the right to health and the right to privacy on the one hand, and respect for the rule of law on the other, has blocked the adoption of certain measures with the potential to increase public surveillance. Here, too, courts have played a critical role. For instance, the Israeli Supreme Court banned electronic contact tracing without statutory authorisation.[38]

Therefore, the role of courts in addressing these challenges has not lost any significance, even during the pandemic, in its ability to resist interference from the public and private sectors. The question is whether courts will adopt new judicial frames or new strategies for dealing with the jurisdictional issue in order to address the increasing and troubling legal uncertainty surrounding new technologies. The next subsections provide an insight into the future challenges which courts will face in the field of freedom of expression and data protection.

[36] Jennifer Daskal and Matt Perault, 'The Apple-Google Contact Tracing System Won't Work. It Still Deserves Praise', *Slate* (22 May 2020) at https://slate.com/technology/2020/05/apple-google-contact-tracing-app-privacy.html.

[37] Elizabeth Dwoskin and Nitasha Tiku, 'Facebook Sent Home Thousands of Human Moderators due to the Coronavirus. Now the Algorithms are in Charge', *The Washington Post* (24 March 2020) at www.washingtonpost.com/technology/2020/03/23/facebook-moderators-coronavirus/.

[38] Israeli Supreme Court, *Ben Meir v Prime Minister*, HC 2109/20, 26 April 2020. See Elena Chachko, 'The Israeli Supreme Court Checks COVID-19 Electronic Surveillance', *Lawfare* (5 May 2020) at www.lawfareblog.com/israeli-supreme-court-checks-covid-19-electronic-surveillance.

A. Algorithms and Freedom of Expression

The way in which we express opinions and ideas online has changed over the last 20 years. Courts have proved to have different approaches to the protection of freedom of expression online, as was noted in Chapter 2. The Internet has been considered either as an opportunity by the US Supreme Court or as a threat by European courts (CJEU and ECtHR). This is no coincidence. The digital environment has indeed been a crucial vehicle for fostering democratic values such as freedom of expression.[39] At the same time, new threats have appeared on the horizon, leading courts to react to technology-driven changes.

At first glance, the characteristics of the Internet should have not entailed any risk for accessing information since pluralism was originally concerned with the scarcity of resources. On the other hand, in the world of atoms, one of the priorities in the media sector is to protect pluralism of information. On the Internet, however, legal rules (and especially public law) were supposed to rely on the alleged self-corrective capacity of the market for information. Nonetheless, the evolution of the digital environment has challenged this paradigm.[40] Recently, the implementation of automated decision-making systems online has given cause for concern in terms of protection for freedom of expression.

The increasing implementation of these technologies by private actors such as search engines and social networks has led to questions as to how and to what extent automated decision-making technologies affect (or even determine) the paradigm of protection for freedom of expression online. This is not a neutral activity for the principle of the rule of law and the role of the courts as the actors called upon to express the last word when defining the boundaries of protection for rights and freedoms in the digital realm. The setting of a global private standard of protection of fundamental rights tends to create a hybrid paradigm, thus engaging the role of courts as mediators of the boundaries between law and technology.

In order to understand how automation influences freedom of expression, it would be sufficient to consider closely the way in which information flows online. One example is particularly insightful in this context: enforcement of the right to be forgotten online. Search engines rely on automated decision-making systems, which help to organise and delist the vast amount of information they host. These private (and automated) systems create a need for data protection rights to be balanced against other fundamental rights, including, in particular, freedom of expression, as was made clear in the landmark decision by the CJEU in the *Google Spain* case.[41] As already stressed in Chapter 3, this decision recognised the role of

[39] Yochai Benkler, *The Wealth of Networks: How Social Production Transforms Markets and Freedom* (New Haven, CT, Yale University Press, 2006).

[40] Peggy Valcke, Miklos Sukosd and Robert Picard (eds), *Media Pluralism and Diversity: Concepts, Risks and Global Trend* (London, Palgrave, 2015).

[41] Case C-131/12 *Google Spain SL and Google Inc v Agencia Española de Protección de Datos and Mario Costeja González*, ECLI:EU:C:2014:317. See Orla Lynskey, 'Control over Personal Data in a Digital Age: Google Spain v AEPD and Mario Costeja Gonzalez' (2015) 78 *Modern Law Review* 522.

a private actor managing a search engine to make decisions in relation to personal data, and especially to expressions. Google enjoys broad margins of discretion in deciding whether to delist information. In fact, when search engines receive a request from a data subject, they are required to decide whether to uphold or dismiss it, thus balancing and enforcing fundamental rights online.[42] The primary issue is that this balancing is usually performed by artificial intelligence systems, which decide to organise and delist content. The involvement of these technologies in this field establishes another layer of complexity for freedom of expression since this fundamental right is not only balanced by a private actor like a search engine, but is also subject to decision making by automated systems, the outcome of which is not always reasonable.

These considerations could also be extended beyond the right to be forgotten online. Artificial intelligence systems help to interpret legal protection for freedom of expression by de facto setting a private standard of protection for fundamental rights in the digital environment.[43] It would be sufficient to focus on social media such as Facebook or YouTube in order to understand how freedom of expression and artificial intelligence are intertwined in the information society.[44] In fact, in order to organise and moderate billions of items of content every day, platforms rely on artificial intelligence to decide whether to remove content or to signal certain expressions to human moderators.[45] The lack of transparency and accountability within decisions concerning freedom of expression online means that what happens away from screen cannot be measured. The implementation of machine learning technologies does not allow decisions taken in relation to expressions that are still private but that involve the public at large to be scrutinised. Absent any regulation establishing legal safeguards, online platforms will continue to be free to assess and remove speech according to their own opaque purposes.[46]

Nonetheless, while US law still ensures a broad frame of protection for the Internet in general, and social media in particular, as seen in *Packingham* (although aside from the Executive Order mentioned in Chapter 4),[47] these challenges have instead led EU lawmakers to react against the power held by online platforms. By codifying some of the safeguards which the CJEU has identified in recent years in cases concerning freedom of expression online, the EU has tried to provide an initial answer to this dilemma. The adoption of the Copyright Directive can be taken as an example of a paradigm shift in that it not only considers platform liability,

[42] Marco Bassini, 'Fundamental Rights and Private Enforcement in the Digital Age' (2019) 25(2) *European Law Journal* 182.

[43] Kate Klonick, 'The New Governors: The People, Rules, and Processes Governing Online Speech' (2018) 131 *Harvard Law Review* 1599.

[44] Jack M Balkin, 'Free Speech in the Algorithmic Society: Big Data, Private Governance, and New School Speech Regulation' (2018) 51 *UC Davis Law Review* 1149.

[45] Tarleton Gillespie, *Custodians of the Internet Platforms, Content Moderation, and the Hidden Decisions That Shape Social Media* (New Haven, CT, Yale University Press, 2018).

[46] Giovanni De Gregorio, 'Democratising Content Moderation: A Constitutional Framework' (2019) 36 *Computer Law and Security Review* 1.

[47] *Packingham v North Carolina* 582 US ___ (2017).

but also takes on board the lessons of the CJEU.[48] It is no coincidence that the Copyright Directive has emphasised how obligations towards online content sharing service providers cannot overcome the ban on general monitoring,[49] which was firmly asserted in *Scarlet* and *Netlog*.[50] Likewise, the creation of an economic threshold as a prerequisite for applicability constitutes another important example of proportionality, which also resulted from the need to protect the freedom to conduct business on the internal market.

These examples of codification can also be noticed in soft-law documents adopted by the EU Commission in recent years in the field of hate speech and disinformation for example.[51] It would be sufficient to focus on the Recommendation on measures to effectively tackle illegal content online as well as the EU Code of Conduct on countering illegal hate speech online in order to understand how freedom of expression online has been taken more seriously also by lawmakers.[52] Specifically, the Recommendation encourages Member States and hosting service to

> take effective, appropriate and proportionate measures to tackle illegal content online, in accordance with the principles set out in this Recommendation and in full compliance with the Charter, in particular the right to freedom of expression and information, and other applicable provisions of Union law, in particular as regards the protection of personal data, competition and electronic commerce.[53]

Within this framework, the Digital Services Act will contribute to the codification of new rules and safeguards, which are also derived from EU case law.

This change of approach might at first glance suggest a new appropriation of control over the technological factor by politicians. The new content curation safeguards should limit the role of courts in extending or narrowing the boundaries of the legal system. On the other hand, the new standards of protection are likely to result in another phase of judicial activism due to the need to fill the gaps within a legal framework, which, in the meantime, has already been superseded by new automated technologies. In other words, the courts have been far from marginalised, at least in Europe.

Nonetheless, the potential of artificial intelligence to challenge protection for fundamental rights is not limited to freedom of expression. The next subsection

[48] Directive (EU) 2019/790 of the European Parliament and of the Council of 17 April 2019 on copyright and related rights in the Digital Single Market and amending Directives 96/9/EC and 2001/29/EC.

[49] ibid Art 17.

[50] Case C-70/10 *Scarlet Extended SA v SABAM* [2011] ECR I-11959; Case C-360/10 *Belgische Vereniging van Auteurs, Componisten en Uitgevers CVBA (SABAM) v Netlog NV* [2012] ECR I-0000.

[51] Giovanni Pitruzzella and Oreste Pollicino, *Hate Speech and Disinformation: A European Constitutional Perspective* (Milan, Bocconi University Press, 2020).

[52] Code of Conduct on countering illegal hate speech online (2016) at https://ec.europa.eu/info/policies/justice-and-fundamental-rights/combatting-discrimination/racism-and-xenophobia/eu-code-conduct-countering-illegal-hate-speech-online_en.

[53] Recommendation of 1 March 2018 on measures to effectively tackle illegal content online (C(2018) 1177 final) para 1(1).

shows even more clearly how automated decision-making systems raise comparable challenges in the field of data protection and, consequently, encourage courts to shape protection for fundamental rights.

B. Algorithms and Data Protection

The *Google Spain* case could be taken as a relevant example also in the field of data protection. Indeed, as has already been observed, this case involves not only speech, but also personal data. Nonetheless, a closer look at the field of data protection can reveal other challenges for constitutional law in the information society, mainly due to the challenges for legal certainty and the unpredictability in relation to automated decision-making processes.

Over the last few years, unlike the US Supreme Court, the CJEU has shown that it clearly intends to take data protection seriously in the light of new challenges by building a European data protection fortress, as noted in Chapters 3 and 4. Aside from *Google Spain*, as already discussed, the CJEU has had other opportunities to highlight the role of fundamental rights online.

In *Digital Rights Ireland*[54] the CJEU stressed the relevance of the principle of the rule of law in avoiding the retention of personal data by public authorities for the purposes of fighting serious crime and its role in guaranteeing the limits and safeguards recognised by EU constitutional law. This was the reason why the CJEU invalidated the Data Retention Directive.[55] The disproportionate effects of its measures and the lack of safeguards in relation to data processing could result in the surveillance of the 'entire European population'.[56]

Likewise, in the Schrems saga,[57] the CJEU went even further in order to ensure that the need to respect EU law is not negated due to the transnational exchange of personal data across the Atlantic. It is possible to consider how the parameter of adequacy is interpreted in two ways. First of all, moving from adequacy to essential equivalence could be considered as a threat to the rule of law, as an extensive interpretation may reach beyond the literal wording of the provision. Nonetheless, it could also be argued that the need to ensure effective protection for the fundamental rights of privacy and personal data in the information society has led the

[54] Joined Cases C-293/12 and C-594/12 *Digital Rights Ireland Ltd v Minister for Communications, Marine and Natural Resources, Minister for Justice, Equality and Law Reform, The Commissioner of the Garda Síochána, Ireland and the Attorney General and Kärntner Landesregierung, Michael Seitlinger, Christof Tschohl and Others* [2014] ECR I-238.

[55] Directive 2006/24/EC of the European Parliament and of the Council of 15 March 2006 on the retention of data generated or processed in connection with the provision of publicly available electronic communications services or of public communications networks and amending Directive 2002/58/EC.

[56] *Digital Rights Ireland* (n 54) 56.

[57] Case C-311/18 *Data Protection Commissioner v Facebook Ireland Limited and Maximillian Schrems*, ECLI:EU:C:2020:559; Case C-362/14 *Maximillian Schrems v Data Protection Commissioner*, ECLI:EU:C:2015:650.

CJEU to extend the boundaries of fundamental rights' protection in order to avoid frustrating constitutional values and, de facto, to set aside the principle of the rule of law.

Nonetheless, the CJEU has not solved all of the issues. As is the case in the field of freedom of expression, it is possible to consider the codification of judicial advice. More specifically, the GDPR constituted a new step in the evolution of EU data protection law.[58] In contrast to its approach under the Data Protection Directive adopted in 1995, which sought to achieve minimum harmonisation, the EU shifted towards full harmonisation by adopting the GDPR, as already stressed in Chapter 1. This was not simply a formal change since the adoption of the GDPR not only avoids (potentially divergent) national implementation and fragmentation, but also extends its effects horizontally into the private sector. Nonetheless, the GDPR still maintains a certain degree of discretion for Member States, which have led some to question the overall nature of the GDPR as a regulation.[59] Besides, the adoption of the GDPR does not imply that codification has solved the problem in the field of data protection and that the courts have no other roles that could be applied in place of the new EU data protection law framework. On the contrary, the courts will play a critical role in shaping a legal framework, the boundaries of which are still flexible and indirectly call for (judicial) interpretation.

This becomes evident if one focuses on issues arising in relation to new forms of automated processing that affect legal certainty and undermine the democratic safeguards that EU data protection law aims to protect. The lack of transparency and accountability in automated decision making naturally challenges the aim of EU data protection law to ensure a transparent and fair framework for data subjects in relation to the processing of their data. Artificial intelligence is in fact proving to limit the possibilities for data controllers and subjects to carry out checks in relation to decision-making processes.[60] It is no coincidence that this system clashes with the general principles of the GDPR.[61] Specifically, the principles of lawfulness, fairness and transparency require that personal data are processed lawfully, fairly and in a transparent manner in relation to the data subject.[62] Nonetheless, the implementation of machine learning systems does not always allow data controllers to respect this principle. The black box effect limits the ability to look inside and understand how data inputs result in a particular output.[63] Besides, the principles of purpose limitation and data minimisation clash with the potential reuse of personal data for different goals by automated systems.[64]

58 Regulation (EU) 2016/679 of the European Parliament and of the Council of 27 April 2016 on the protection of natural persons with regard to the processing of personal data and on the free movement of such data, and repealing Directive 95/46/EC (General Data Protection Regulation).

59 See, in particular, GDPR Arts 6, 9.

60 Frank Pasquale, *The Black Box Society: The Secret Algorithms That Control Money and Information* (Cambridge, MA, Harvard University Press, 2015).

61 Tal Z Zarsky, 'Incompatible: The GDPR in the Age of Big Data' (2017) 47 *Seton Hall Law Review* 995.

62 GDPR Art 5.

63 Pasquale (n 60).

64 GDPR Art 5(1)(a), 5(1)(b).

Even more importantly, the principle of accountability introduced by the GDPR requires data controllers to demonstrate compliance with the general principles mentioned above.[65] For instance, the GDPR expressly requires data controllers to adopt appropriate technical and organisational measures that are designed to implement EU data protection principles in an effective manner and to integrate the necessary safeguards into processing. In addition, data controllers are also obliged to implement appropriate technical and organisational measures to ensure that, by default, only personal data that are necessary for each specific purpose are processed.[66] Nonetheless, the GDPR also clarifies that, when assessing these obligations, it is necessary to take account of 'the state of the art, the cost of implementation and the nature, scope, context and purposes of processing as well as the risks of varying likelihood and severity for rights and freedoms of natural persons posed by the processing'.[67]

The EU principles of privacy by design and by default are clear examples of the margins of discretion that a data controller can exercise in order to implement legal safeguards. Even if the data controller's responsibility is considered, the GDPR stresses that the implementation of technical and organisational measures that are capable of demonstrating compliance with the GDPR should still be read taking into account the nature, scope, context and purposes of the processing activities of data as well as the risks of varying likelihood and severity for the rights and freedoms of natural persons.[68] Within this context, the courts will play a crucial role in adjudicating on claims that seek to scrutinise data controllers' accountability, which would otherwise be free to decide to what extent they comply with the GDPR.

With this in mind, it is likely that the courts will play a critical role in interpreting the relationship between the GDPR's principles and norms and the implementation of artificial intelligence technologies. Similarly, the role of courts can also be understood by focusing on the rights of data subjects, especially the right of individuals not to be subject to a decision based solely on automated processing, including profiling, which produces legal effects concerning him or her or similarly significantly affects him or her.[69] This right of data subjects has been analysed primarily from the perspective of the right to explanation.[70] Scholars have pointed

[65] ibid Art 5(2).
[66] ibid Art 25(1).
[67] ibid.
[68] ibid Art 24.
[69] ibid Art 22.
[70] Margot E Kaminski, 'The Right to Explanation, Explained' (2019) 34(1) *Berkeley Technology Law Journal* 189; Antoni Roig, 'Safeguards for the Right Not to Be Subject to a Decision Based Solely on Automated Processing (Article 22 GDPR)' (2017) 8(3) *European Journal of Law and Technology* 1; Sandra Wachter, Brent D Mittelstadt and Luciano Floridi, 'Why a Right to Explanation of Automated Decision-Making does not Exist in the General Data Protection Regulation' (2017) 7 *International Data Privacy Law* 76; Gianclaudio Malgieri and Giovanni Comandé, 'Why a Right to Legibility of Automated Decision-Making Exists in the General Data Protection Regulation' (2017) 7 *International Data Privacy Law* 243; Bryce Goodman and Seth Flaxman, 'European Union Regulations on Algorithmic Decision-Making and a "Right to Explanation"' (2017) 38(3) *AI Magazine* 50.

out possible bases for the right to explanation, such as those provisions requiring that data subjects receive meaningful information concerning the logic involved, as well as the significance, and the envisaged consequences of, processing according to Articles 13–15 GDPR. In addition, the new rights provided for under the GDPR (including data portability and right to erasure) have been pinpointed as offering some legal grounds for broader control by individuals over the automated processing of personal data. This catalogue of guarantees can be better framed having regard to Recital 71 of the GDPR, which provides as follows:

> In order to ensure fair and transparent processing in respect of the data subject, taking into account the specific circumstances and context in which the personal data are processed, the controller should use appropriate mathematical or statistical procedures for the profiling, implement technical and organisational measures appropriate to ensure, in particular, that factors which result in inaccuracies in personal data are corrected and the risk of errors is minimised, secure personal data in a manner that takes account of the potential risks involved for the interests and rights of the data subject, and prevent, inter alia, discriminatory effects on natural persons … or processing that results in measures having such an effect.

Within this context, transparency and accountability play a pivotal role. Since ensuring full transparency may prove to be difficult in this context, due to the protection afforded by legal systems to algorithms (eg through the legal protection ensured for trade secrets), courts (and data protection authorities) are likely to shape the meaning of transparency and accountability within automated decision-making systems. More specifically, this right of data subjects raises various interpretative issues, even beyond the debate on the right to explanation. Indeed, it is not easy to ensure legal certainty within this framework where there is no definition of the expression 'solely on automated processing' or of 'legal effects concerning him or her or similarly significantly affects him or her', as affirmed by the same Recital 71 of the GDPR.

The lack of clear definitions constitutes a clear challenge, which the courts will need to deal with, considering the extensive implementation of artificial intelligence technologies and the multiplicity of situations in which these systems can have legal effects on individuals. The GDPR has tried to establish some limits to the application of this right. Specifically, data controllers can rely on various exceptions where a processing is necessary for entering into, or performance of, a contract between the data subject and a data controller; is authorised by Union or Member State law to which the controller is subject and which also lays down suitable measures to safeguard the data subject's rights and freedoms and legitimate interests; or is based on the data subject's explicit consent.[71] Nonetheless, the GDPR also allows Member States to limit the application of this right of data subjects.[72] This is an issue that reaches beyond technology and affects the entire

[71] GDPR Art 22(2).
[72] ibid Art 23.

structure of the GDPR. Despite its status as a regulation, it leaves the Member States broad margins of discretion at the domestic level.[73] Within this framework, the role of judicial interpretation is likely to provide assistance in making policy decisions, leading to a further extension of judicial power over political power.

III. Digital Constitutionalism in Action: Which Remedies can be Invoked against the Emergence of Digital Private Powers?

In the light of the context set out above, in which the judicial enforcement of fundamental rights is strictly connected with the new challenges of digital constitutionalism, one particular question needs to be addressed (and possibly answered): which remedies should be available to achieve the aims of this new round of modern constitutionalism, with specific regard to the rise of new private powers in competition with public authorities?

Two possible remedies can be identified. The first concerns the possible horizontal application of fundamental rights vis-à-vis private parties. The second focuses instead on the path that could be followed in the new season of digital constitutionalism and will explore, in particular, the possibility that a constellation of new rights could be identified to deal with the new challenge posed by algorithms. In other words, the Easterbrook dilemma between the 'law of animals' and the 'law of horses', which we examined in Chapter 1, will be considered from both sides. On the one hand, the horizontal effects doctrine focuses on existing instruments applied to new (digital) legal challenges. On the other hand, calls for the introduction of new rights arise out of the opposite trend, which seeks to rethink categories by providing new substantive and procedural safeguards.

The suitability of these two remedies will be assessed by considering each of them in turn, starting with the issue of the possible horizontal application of fundamental rights. It is evident that, in order to understand the feasibility of such remedies in the context of new digital challenges, it is important to take a step back and to explore briefly the theoretical foundations of the issue.

A good starting point could be Alexy's assumption that the issue of the horizontal effect of fundamental rights protected by Constitutions (and Bills of Rights) cannot be detached in theoretical terms from the more general issue of the direct effect of the same rights.[74] In other words, according to the German legal theorist,

[73] Gianclaudio Malgieri, 'Automated Decision-making in the EU Member States: The Right to Explanation and Other "Suitable Safeguards" in the National Legislations' (2019) 35(5) *Computer Law and Security Review* 1.

[74] Robert Alexy, *A Theory of Constitutional Rights* (Oxford, Oxford University Press, 2002) 570–71. See Graziella Romeo, 'Building Integration Through the Bill of Rights? The European Union at the Mirror' (2018) 47 *Georgia Journal of International & Comparative Law* 21.

once it is recognised that a fundamental right has direct effect, that recognition must be characterised by a dual dimension. The first, vertical dimension concerns the classic relationship of 'public authority vs individual freedom', while the second, horizontal dimension focuses on the relationship between private actors, but also, as mentioned above, the much less classic relationship between new private powers and individuals/users.

The problem with Alexy's assumption, which is quite convincing from a theoretical point of view, is that the shift from the Olympus of the legal theorist to the arena of the law in action risks neglecting the fact that the approach of courts from different jurisdictions might be quite different as far as the concrete recognition of the horizontal effect of fundamental rights is concerned. This should not come as any surprise because the forms and limits of that recognition depend on the cultural and historical crucible in which a specific constitutional order is cultivated.

As far as the US is concerned, the state action doctrine apparently precludes any possibility to apply the US Federal Bill of Rights between private parties and consequently any ability for individuals to rely on such horizontal effects, and accordingly to enforce fundamental rights vis-à-vis private actors.[75] The reason for this resistance to accepting any general horizontal effect to the rights protected by the US Federal Bill of Rights is obviously that the cultural and historical basis for US constitutionalism is rooted in the values of liberty, individual freedom and private autonomy. The state action doctrine is critical to understanding the scope of the rights enshrined in the US Constitution. Indeed, were the fundamental rights protected by the US Constitution to be extended to non-public actors, this would result in an inevitable compression of the sphere of freedom of individuals and, more generally, private actors. For instance, such friction is evident when focusing on the right to free speech, which can only be directly enforced vis-à-vis public actors.

Historically, the state action doctrine owes its origins to the civil rights cases, a series of rulings dating back to 1883 in which the US Supreme Court recognised the power of the US Congress to prohibit racially based discrimination by private individuals in the light of the Thirteenth and Fourteenth Amendments.

Even in the area of freedom of expression, the US Supreme Court extended the scope of the First Amendment to include private actors on the grounds where they are substantially equivalent to a state actor. In *Marsh v Alabama*[76] the US Supreme Court held that the State of Alabama had violated the First Amendment by prohibiting the distribution of religious material by members of the Jehovah's Witness community within a corporate town, which, although privately owned, could be

[75] Stephen Gardbaum, 'The "Horizontal Effect" of Constitutional Rights' (2003) 102 *Michigan Law Review* 388; Mark Tushnet, 'The Issue of State Action/Horizontal Effect in Comparative Constitutional Law' (2003) 1 *International Journal of Constitutional Law* 79; Wilson R Huhn, 'The State Action Doctrine and the Principle of Democratic Choice' (2006) 84 *Hofstra Law Review* 1380.

[76] *Marsh v Alabama* 326 US 501 (1946).

considered to perform a substantially recognisable 'public function' in spite of the fact that, formally speaking, it was privately owned. In *Amalgamated Food Emps Union Local 590 v Logan Valley Plaza*,[77] the US Supreme Court considered a shopping centre similar to the corporate town in *Marsh*. In *Jackson v Metropolitan Edison*,[78] the US Supreme Court held that equivalence should be assessed in the exercise of powers traditionally reserved exclusively to the state. Nonetheless, as noted in Chapter 4, in *Manhattan Community Access Corp v Halleck*,[79] the US Supreme Court more recently adopted a narrow approach to the state action doctrine, recalling in particular its precedent in *Hudgens v NLRB*.[80]

This narrow approach is also the standard for protecting fundamental rights in the digital domain and, consequently, the US Supreme Court would seem to restrict the possibility to enforce the free speech protection enshrined in the First Amendment against digital platforms, as new private powers.[81] More specifically, and more convincingly, it has been observed by Berman that the need to call into question the implications of a radical state action doctrine[82] can lead, in the digital age, to the transformation of cyberspace into a totally private 'constitution free zone'.[83] Balkin has recently highlighted a shift in the well-established paradigm of free speech, described as a triangle involving nation states, private infrastructure, and speakers.[84] In particular, digital infrastructure companies must be regarded as governors of social spaces instead of mere conduit providers or platforms. This new scenario, in Balkin's view, leads to a new school of speech regulation triggered by the dangers of abuse by the privatised bureaucracies that govern end users arbitrarily and without due process and transparency; it also entails a danger of digital surveillance that facilitates manipulation.[85]

Despite the proposal that a 'functional approach' be adopted,[86] partial attempts to reveal the limits on fully embracing the state action doctrine in the digital age, the US Supreme Court recently confirmed in its case law the classic view of the intangibility of the state action doctrine.[87] However, even one of the US scholars who is more keenly aware of the de facto public functions carried out by the digital platforms concedes that

> however important Facebook or Google may be to our speech environment, it seems much harder to say that they are acting like the government all but in name. It is true

[77] *Amalgamated Food Emps Union Local 590 v Logan Valley Plaza* 391 US 308 (1968).

[78] *Jackson v Metropolitan Edison Co* 419 US 345 (1974).

[79] *Manhattan Community Access Corp v Halleck* 587 US ___ (2019).

[80] *Hudgens v NLRB* 424 US 507 (1976).

[81] Jonathan Peters, 'The "Sovereigns of Cyberspace" and State Action: The First Amendment's Application (or Lack Thereof) to Third-Party Platforms' (2017) 32 *Berkeley Technology Law Journal* 989.

[82] Paul S Berman, 'Cyberspace and the State Action Debate: The Cultural Value of Applying Constitutional Norms to "Private" Regulation' (2000) 71 *University of Colorado Law Review* 1263.

[83] Bassini (n 42) 182.

[84] Jack M Balkin, 'Free Speech Is a Triangle' (2012) 118 *Columbia Law Review* 2011.

[85] Balkin (n 44).

[86] Peters (n 81) 1022–24.

[87] *Manhattan Community Access Corp v Halleck* (n 79).

> that one's life may be heavily influenced by these and other large companies, but influence alone cannot be the criterion for what makes something a state actor; in that case, every employer would be a state actor, and perhaps so would nearly every family.[88]

Shifting from the US to Europe, the relevant historical, cultural and consequently constitutional milieu is clearly very different. The constitutional keyword is *Drittwirkung*, a legal concept originally developed in the 1950s by the German Constitutional Court,[89] which presumes that an individual plaintiff can rely on a national Bill of Rights to sue another private individual alleging the violation of those rights. In other words, it can be defined as a form of horizontality in action or a total Constitution.[90] It is a legal concept that, as mentioned, has its roots in Germany and then subsequently migrated to many other constitutional jurisdictions, exerting a strong influence even on the case law of the CJEU and ECtHR.[91]

It should not come as any surprise that a difference emerged between US and European constitutional practice as regards the recognition of horizontal effect to fundamental rights. As noted above, individual freedom and private autonomy are not constitutionally compatible with such recognition. On the other hand, however, human dignity as a super-constitutional principle supports such recognition, at least in theory.[92] The very concept of the abuse of rights, which is not recognised under US constitutional law, while instead being explicitly codified in the ECHR and the EUCFR,[93] seems to reflect the same Euro-centric approach.

In the light of this scenario, it is no coincidence that, as early as 1976, the CJEU decided in *Defrenne II* to acknowledge and enforce the obligation for private employers (and the corresponding right of employees) to ensure equal pay for equal work, in relation to a provision of the former Treaty establishing the European Economic Community.[94] Article 119 of the EC Treaty was unequivocally and exclusively addressed at the Member States. It provided that 'each Member State shall ensure that the principle of equal pay for male and female

[88] Tim Wu, 'Is the First Amendment Obsolete?' in Lee C Bollinger and Geoffrey R Stone (eds), *Free Speech Century* (Oxford, Oxford University Press, 2019) 272.

[89] The *Lüth* case concerned a *querelle* about the distribution of the anti-Semitic movie *Jüd Jüss* in a private location. Following the conviction, Lüth appealed to the German Constitutional Court complaining of the violation of her freedom of expression. The German Constitutional Court, therefore, addressed a question relating to the extension of constitutional rights in a private relationship. In this case, for the first time, the German court argued that constitutional rights not only constitute individual claims against the state, but also constitute a set of values that apply in all areas of law by providing axiological indications to the legislative power, executive, and judicial. In the present case, the protection of freedom of expression develops not only vertically towards the state, but also horizontally since civil law rules must be interpreted according to the spirit of the German Constitution. German Constitutional Court, judgment of 15 January 1958, 1 BvR 400/51.

[90] Mattias Kumm, 'Who is Afraid of the Total Constitution? Constitutional Rights as Principles and the Constitutionalization of Private Law' (2006) 7(4) *German Law Journal* 341.

[91] *X and Y v The Netherlands*, App no 8978/80, Judgment of 26 March 1985.

[92] Catherine Dupré, *The Age of Dignity. Human Rights and Constitutionalism in Europe* (Oxford, Hart Publishing, 2016).

[93] Art 17 ECHR; Art 54 EUCFR.

[94] Case C-43/75 *Defrenne v Sabena* [1976] ECR 455.

workers for work of equal value is applied'. When compared to the wording of that provision, it could be observed that each provision of the EUCFR is more detailed and, therefore, more amenable to potential horizontal direct effect. It is no coincidence that, in 2014, while in *AMS* the CJEU adopted a minimalist approach to the possible horizontal direct effect only of those provisions of the EUCFR from which it could derive a legal right for individuals and not simply a principle, it also applied Articles 7 and 8 EUCFR in relation to the enforcement of digital privacy rights, specifically in relation to search engines in *Google Spain*.[95]

Several years later, the CJEU had the opportunity to further develop the horizontal application of the EUCFR. More specifically, in four judgments from 2018 – *Egenberger*,[96] *IR v JQ*,[97] *Bauer*,[98] and *Max Planck*[99] – the CJEU definitively clarified the horizontal scope of Articles 21, 31(2) and 47 EUCFR within disputes between private parties.[100] In the light of the emerging scenario, it seems clear that a potential initial answer to the new challenges for constitutional law in the age of new private powers could be found in the brave horizontal enforcement of fundamental rights, especially in the field of freedom of expression and privacy and data protection.

However, as mentioned above, it is also worth reaching beyond the debate on horizontal/vertical effects of fundamental rights in the digital age in order to propose an alternative weapon for the challenges that will need to be faced during the new round of digital constitutionalism. Most notably, it is necessary to propose a frame that describes the relationship between the three parties that Balkin puts at the heart of the information society: platforms, states and individuals.[101] In other words, a digital habeas corpus of substantive and procedural rights should be identified, which can be enforced by the courts as they are inferred from existing rights protected under current digital constitutionalism.[102] While substantive rights concern the status of individuals as subjects of a kind of sovereign power that is no longer exclusively vested in public authorities, procedural rights stem from the expectation that individuals have to claim and enforce their rights before bodies

[95] *Google Spain* (n 41).

[96] Case C-414/16 *Vera Egenberger v Evangelisches Werk für Diakonie und Entwicklung eV*, ECLI:EU:C:2018:257.

[97] Case C-68/17 *IR v JQ*, ECLI:EU:C:2018:696.

[98] Joined Cases C-569/16 and C-570/16 *Stadt Wuppertal v Maria Elisabeth Bauer and Volker Willmeroth v Martina Broßonn*, ECLI:EU:C:2018:871.

[99] Case C-684/16 *Max-Planck-Gesellschaft zur Förderung der Wissenschaften eV v Tetsuji Shimizu*, ECLI:EU:C:2018:874.

[100] Aurelia Colombi Ciacchi, 'The Direct Horizontal Effect of EU Fundamental Rights: ECJ 17 April 2018, Case C-414/16, Vera Egenberger v Evangelisches Werk für Diakonie und Entwicklung e.V. and ECJ 11 September 2018, Case C-68/17, IR v JQ' (2019) 15(2) *European Constitutional Law Review* 294; Eleni Frantziou, *The Horizontal Effect of Fundamental Rights in the European Union. A Constitutional Analysis* (Oxford, Oxford University Press, 2019); Sonya Walkila, *Horizontal Effect of Fundamental Rights in EU Law* (Groningen, Europa Law Publishing, 2016).

[101] Balkin (n 84).

[102] De Gregorio (n 1).

other than traditional jurisdictional bodies, which employ methods different from judicial discretion, such as technological and horizontal due process.

With regard to new rights,[103] consideration should be given at least to the right to explanation (meaning the right of an individual to obtain information about the way his/her data are being processed) although also the right to easy access (right to accessibility) and the right to obtain a translation from the language of technology into the language of human beings. While the first of these rights is meant as the right to be allowed the opportunity to interact with algorithms and digital platforms implementing their use, the right to easy access requires that simple, clear and understandable information be used; moreover, it entitles users to receive not only the reasons, for example, for the removal of online content, but also to exercise their rights more effectively before a judicial or administrative body.

Both rights already have constitutional roots in the existing framework for the protection of fundamental rights, which clearly starts from a theological and technology-oriented interpretation of Article 10 ECHR, Article 11 EUCFR and the First Amendment of the US Constitution. If some basis within constitutional theory is sought, this gap can perhaps be filled or reduced by leveraging the value of human dignity as a cornerstone of human rights protection. If this holds true, a new set of fundamental rights can be derived from the protection of human dignity: more broadly, a right that decisions impacting the legal and political sphere of individuals be made by human beings and not exclusively by machines, even the most advanced and efficient ones, and a requirement that minim safeguards be protected.

However, these rights, and more specifically the right to explanation,[104] can establish another solid constitutional root in the right to data protection as enshrined in the EUCFR and in the GDPR. In particular, as mentioned above, the GDPR introduces, inter alia, a new safeguard guaranteeing individuals the right not to be subject to a decision taken by a machine based on the processing of their data, including profiling, that results in legal consequences for them. Regardless of whether the GDPR already provides grounds for such a right to explanation to be enforced, the assumption is that the time is ripe for a new *pactum subjectionis*. Due to the significant shift that individuals are witnessing in their relationship with power, it is necessary to revisit their status and to focus on a set of rights that can be enforced vis-à-vis not only governmental powers, but also private actors.

The assumption here is that these substantive rights are justified by the hidden price that individual users pay to digital platforms while enjoying their service apparently free of charge, a cost that is not limited to personal data. Moreover, from an anthropological perspective, human behaviour, feelings, emotions and political choices have a value for algorithms, most notably insofar as they help

[103] De Gregorio (n 18); Citron and Pasquale (n 34); Kate Crawford and Jason Schultz, 'Big Data and Due Process: Toward a Framework to Redress Predictive Privacy Harms' (2014) 55 *Boston College Law Review* 93.

[104] See footnote 70.

machines to learn something about individuals' reactions based on a certain input. The new catalogue of rights seems to respond to Pasquale's questions concerning the transparency gap between users and digital platforms:

> Without knowing what Google actually *does* when it ranks sites, we cannot assess when it is acting in good faith to help users, and when it is biasing results to favor its own commercial interests. The same goes for status updates on Facebook, trending topics on Twitter, and even network management practices at telephone and cable companies. All these are protected by laws of secrecy and technologies of obfuscation.[105]

If, on the one hand, this new digital *pactum subjectionis* requires new rights to be recognised and protected, it is also necessary to understand how their enforcement can be effective, how they can actually be put into practice. In other words, it is necessary to couple the claim for a new catalogue of substantive rights with the need for certain procedural guarantees that allow individuals to ensure that these 'quasi-legal' expectations can actually be met. Therefore, it is necessary to speculate also on the 'procedural counterweight' to the creation of new substantive rights, focusing on the fairness of the *process* by which individuals can enforce them. In fact, since speculation has hitherto focused on the exercise of powers, there is no reason to exclude from the scope of procedural guarantees those situations in which powers are vested in private bodies charged with the performance of certain public functions.[106]

Digital platforms can be said to exercise administrative powers that are normally vested in public authorities. However, considering how rights can be exercised vis-à-vis these new actors, vagueness and opacity can still be discerned within the relevant procedures. Among others, the right to be forgotten clearly shows the lack of appropriate procedural safeguards, since steps such as the evaluation of a delisting request and the adoption of the relevant measures (whether consisting of the removal of a link or confirming that it is lawful) rely on an entirely discretionary assessment, supported by the use of algorithms. Therefore, the merely horizontal application to the fundamental right to data protection enshrined in Article 8 EUCFR does not prove to be satisfactory. Moreover, the notification and take down mechanisms implemented by platforms hosting user-generated content do not entirely fulfil the requirements of transparency and fairness so as to render the status of the user/individual enforcing his/her rights vis-à-vis these platforms comparable to the status of citizens exercising their rights against public authorities. It is argued that the time is ripe for filling this gap.

Procedural rights will play a pivotal role in ensuring that these new substantive rights are actually protected and rendered enforceable vis-à-vis emerging private actors. Within the context of research into big data and predictive privacy violations

[105] Pasquale (n 60) 9.

[106] Giacinto della Cananea, *Due Process of Law Beyond the State* (Oxford, Oxford University Press, 2016).

(including those caused by the use of predictive algorithms), Crawford and Schultz have stressed the need to frame a form of 'procedural data due process'.[107]

The application of such a form of technological due process would also have an impact on substantive rights as the same should preserve, in accordance with the Redish and Marshall model of due process, values such as accuracy; the appearance of fairness; equality of inputs; predictability, transparency and rationality; participation; revelation; and privacy-dignity.[108] The traditional function of due process of keeping powers separate must be fine-tuned to the specific context of algorithms, where interactions occur between various actors (algorithm designers, adjudicators and individuals). Citron has pointed out some of the requirements that automated systems should meet in order to fulfil procedural due process requirements, including (a) adequate notice to be given to individuals affected by the decision-making process; (b) opportunity for individuals to be heard before the decision is released; and (c) record, audits or judicial review.[109] According to Crawford and Schultz's model of procedural data[110] due process, the requirement of notice can be fulfilled by providing individuals with 'an opportunity to intervene in the predictive process' and to know about (ie to obtain an explanation concerning) the type of predictions and the sources of data. On the other hand, the right to be heard is seen as a tool for ensuring that, once data are disclosed, individuals have the opportunity to challenge the fairness of the predictive process. The right to be heard thus implies having access to a computer program's source code or to the logic on which a computer program's decision is based. Finally, this model requires guarantees of the impartiality of the 'adjudicator', including judicial review, in order to ensure that individuals do not suffer from any bias when subject to predictive decisions.

IV. Conclusions

Within this framework, both the horizontal effect doctrines and new substantive and procedural rights seem to be promising candidates among the available remedies. In the face of these challenges, it is likely that the courts will by no means lose the predominant role over political power acquired in recent years. The challenges raised by new automated technologies are likely to operate as a new call for courts to protect fundamental rights in the information society once again.

As noted in the Introduction, this response, and consequently the further amplification of judicial power, is amplified in the digital age by procedural and substantial issues, which are related, in the second instance, to the obvious yet

[107] Crawford and Schultz (n 103).

[108] Martin H Redish and Lawrence C Marshall, 'Adjudicatory Independence and the Values of Procedural Due Process' (1986) 95(3) *Yale Law Journal* 455.

[109] Danielle K Citron, 'Technological Due Process' (2008) 85(6) *Washington University Law Review* 1249.

[110] Crawford and Schultz (n 103).

somehow banal awareness that legal reforms tend to lag behind technological advances. Therefore, the answer to the question 'Does a change in the relevant technological environment have a significant impact on judicial protection for fundamental rights?' would be that it does. We have seen how the newness of technologies has encouraged courts to respond to new challenges in order to ensure protection for fundamental rights in the context of new technology. This has led to an increasing amplification of judicial momentum, which we have observed in this study under the lens of the judicial frame and jurisdictional issue in the transition from the world of atoms to bits on both sides of the Atlantic.

However, there cannot be just a single answer to the second (related) question 'Does this impact enhance or reduce the level of protection for fundamental rights?' As noted above, there is no doubt that courts today are the institutions best equipped to identify the risk of a constitutional collision. However, this does not mean that judges should act in splendid isolation. The fact that they are the best-placed institutions does not mean that they are the only ones. Moreover, the comparative analysis carried out above has made clear how the specific individual judicial frame can have a crucial impact on the court's final decision, not only between different courts, but also within the same court at different times and comprised of different judges. We have seen above how the rise of the Internet has resulted in increasing protection for the right to free speech in the US, while leading to the consolidation and emancipation of the right to data protection in the EU. At the same time, this extension in protection for these fundamental rights has led to the rolling back of protection for other constitutional interests. Besides, this approach clearly entails fragmenting existing protection, and the unpredictable nature of the relevant case law, thus causing clear harm for the principle of legitimate expectations and legal certainty. However, those reasons are not the only reasons why the judicial activism of the (especially) European courts needs to be compensated due to inertia and a lack of political will.

This leads us to third and fourth questions arising in relation to the judicial approach to freedom of expression, privacy and data protection across the Atlantic. 'How does Internet technology affect the models of judicial protection when freedom of expression and data protection are at stake?' More specifically, 'What are the consequences on the case law of, on the one hand, the European courts and, on the other hand, the US Supreme Court?' As already observed, the rise of the Internet has led courts to face new challenges, which have affected the judicial protection for freedom of expression, privacy and data protection. However, this is more evident in Europe, where, as seen in the previous chapter, judicial interpretation of the relevant provisions has shifted towards judicial manipulation. The same provisions have been essentially rewritten by the courts in light of the new digital context. Does it mean that we still need, quoting again Easterbrook,[111] a new law of the horse for every technological change? Not at all.

[111] Frank H Easterbrook, 'Cyberspace and the Law of the Horse' (1996) *University of Chicago Legal Forum* 207.

For instance, we do not need ad hoc new charters of fundamental rights on the Internet[112] considering, as was seen in Chapters 2 and 3, how the ECtHR and the US Supreme Court have been able to update judicial protection for free speech and privacy in line with technological developments, while relying on provisions written decades ago (in the former case) or centuries ago (in the latter case). With specific reference to the US framework, the US Supreme Court has adopted a different approach to protection of free speech and privacy. Nonetheless, this does not mean that Internet technologies have not affected judicial protection for fundamental rights. On the contrary, the Internet has highlighted different judicial frames and approaches to the territorial boundaries that underscore constitutional differences across the Atlantic.

The role of the judicial frame and the jurisdictional issue as examples of judicial amplification are the two paradigmatic examples of how digital technology has affected the judicial protection for fundamental rights. Accordingly, the answer to the question 'What is the relationship between metaphorical language, jurisdiction and the judicial protection of fundamental rights on the Internet?' could already be apparent from the considerations mentioned above. The analysis of judicial frames across the Atlantic has shown how the courts have adapted constitutional values in line with new technologies. We have seen how the ECtHR and CJEU have adopted a frame of distrust towards new technologies, which has led to a fostering of protection for privacy and data protection, while containing the boundaries of freedom of expression. In the US, on the other hand, the frame of trust has resulted in protection for free speech online in a quasi-absolute manner, having been perceived as an enabler for fostering democracy.

Likewise, when looking at the jurisdictional issue, it is possible to observe its effects on judicial protection for fundamental rights online. The courts have indeed played a critical role in dealing with the cross-border nature of the Internet. On both sides of the Atlantic, we have seen how both the CJEU and US Supreme Court have dealt with defining their jurisdiction. Nonetheless, this is only part of the jurisdictional issue, which has resulted in the extension of constitutional values on a global scale. In Chapter 3 we saw how the CJEU has extended protection for privacy and personal data far beyond the territory of the EU, while in Chapter 4 the same approach was mitigated to take into account the impact on other interests at international level, such as the protection for freedom of expression. On the other side of the Atlantic, the approach pursued by the US Supreme Court in protecting free speech has not formally led to the extension of such a value, but

[112] Different attempts to define new constitutional instruments relating to the Internet have failed. See, in particular, Redeker, Gill and Gasser (n 1). In Italy, for instance, there was a debate about the opportunity to adopt a sort of Internet bill of rights, which however was not considered a necessary step to fill the apparent constitutional gap when framing fundamental rights in the digital environment. See Marco Bassini, *Internet e libertà di espressione. Prospettive costituzionali e sovranazionali* (Roma, Aracne, 2020) forthcoming; Oreste Pollicino and Marco Bassini, *Verso un Internet Bill of Rights* (Roma, Aracne, 2015).

has empowered private actors operating on a global scale to extend certain values beyond the boundaries of the US.

In the light of such a predominant role of courts, the answer to the question 'What is the impact of digital technologies on the relationship between judicial power and political power?' could not be anything other than 'deep and vast'. I started in Chapter 1 to stress the amplification of the judicial momentum in the information society, and the following chapters appear to have provided a clear picture of judicial activism in order to deal with legislative inertia. As far as digital technologies are concerned, the courts have proved to be the primary actors in bridging the gap between law and technology. Over the last 20 years, regulation of the digital environment across the Atlantic has been limited by the need to ensure protection for freedom of expression and the development of digital services. While this is almost the prevalent narrative, in the US, the role of political power in the EU has changed, where the effects of the role of new technologies on other fundamental rights have thus also been considered. And this is closely related to the new round of digital constitutionalism in Europe.[113]

This does not mean that the role of courts will be rebalanced by the emergence of political power in the technological domain. On the contrary, it is likely that the courts will continue to adapt protection for fundamental rights in the information society in line with new technology. While there is no doubt that technology clearly develops much more quickly than the law, at the same time it is important to point out that legislative inertia, and the resulting judicial activism, has not only been caused by the inability of the legislator to keep pace with technological evolution. Indeed, sometimes inertia is simply a political choice. More specifically, it has often been chosen to charge the courts with responsibility for identifying the precise formula for balancing between contrasting fundamental rights in the digital era.[114]

The final research question of this book is 'What are the specific expressions of this momentum in the age of digital constitutionalism in light of the pandemic?' The answer to this question is multifaceted. We have seen in this book how the courts play a role in providing the grounds for a new round of modern constitutionalism, which considers the opportunities and challenges associated with digital technologies in the information society. It is conceivable that, despite the codification of new safeguards, the role of courts in interpreting the challenges raised by new technologies is far from being exhausted, also due to the role of online platforms. Indeed, artificial intelligence technologies have raised different questions for protecting fundamental rights, which still have not been answered

[113] De Gregorio (n 1).

[114] Defining the balancing between conflicting fundamental rights has always been critical and not univocal since there is not a unique formula. Courts usually rely on precedents or the advice of experts for technical matters. It is the work of Robert Alexy in 2002 on the 'weight formula' for fundamental rights which inspired Mart Susi and his 'internet balancing formula'. See Mart Susi, 'The Internet Balancing Formula' (2019) 25(2) *European Law Journal* 198; Alexy (n 74).

through the political process. We have seen how constitutional law can provide some solutions to these new challenges. Nonetheless, absent any regulation, the role of courts is likely to be predominant. The COVID-19 pandemic has only amplified this dynamic. It has confirmed the role of legislative inertia in the face of the new challenges associated with the implementation of technology and the increasing role of online platforms in providing services and new solutions to combat the virus.

Therefore, the amplification of the judicial momentum does not seem to be destined to fall, but to expand its boundaries for interpreting and enforcing fundamental rights in the algorithmic society.

BIBLIOGRAPHY

Abel, Nikolas, 'United States vs. Mehanna, the First Amendment, and Material Support in the War on Terror' (2013) 54 *Boston College Law Review* 711

Albert, Richard and Yaniv Roznai (eds), *Constitutionalism Under Extreme Conditions* (New York, Springer, 2020)

Alexy, Robert, *A Theory of Constitutional Rights* (Oxford, Oxford University Press, 2002)

—— *A Theory of Legal Argumentation* (Oxford, Oxford University Press, 1989)

Allard, Julie and Antoine Garapon, *Les juges dans le mondialisation. La nouvelle révolution du droit* (Paris, Seuil, 2005)

Ammori, Marvin, 'The "New" New York Times: Free Speech Lawyering in the Age of Google and Twitter' (2014) 127 *Harvard Law Review* 2259

Apa, Ernesto and Oreste Pollicino, *Modeling the Liability of Internet Service Providers: Google vs. Vivi Down* (Milan, Egea, 2013)

Article 19, 'CJEU judgment in Facebook Ireland case is threat to online free speech' *Article 19* (3 October 2019)

—— 'Privacy and Freedom of Expression in the Age of Artificial Intelligence', *Article 19* (11 May 2018)

Ausloos, Jef, *The Right to Erasure in EU Data Protection Law. From Individual Rights to Effective Protection* (Oxford, Oxford University Press, 2020)

Austin, Lisa M, 'Technological Tattletales and Constitutional Black Holes: Communications Intermediaries and Constitutional Constraints' (2016) 17 *Theoretical Inquiries in Law* 451

Avbelj, Matej, Filippo Fontanelli and Giuseppe Martinico (eds), *Kadi on Trial: A Multifaceted Analysis of the Kadi Trial* (Abingdon, Routledge, 2014)

Balkin, Jack M, 'Free Speech in the Algorithmic Society: Big Data, Private Governance, and New School Speech Regulation' (2018) 51 *UC Davis Law Review* 1149

—— 'Free Speech Is a Triangle' (2012) 118 *Columbia Law Review* 2011

Ballanco, Michael, 'Searching for the First Amendment: An Inquisitive Free Speech Approach to Search Engine Rankings' (2013) 24 *George Mason University Civil Rights Law Journal* 89

Baran, Paul, *Communications, Computers and People* (Santa Monica, CA, The RAND Corporation, 1965)

Barlow, John P, 'A Declaration of the Independence of Cyberspace', *Electronic Frontier Foundation* (8 February 1996)

Barsotti, Vittoria, *L'arte di tacere. Strumenti e tecniche di non decisione della Corte suprema degli Stati Uniti* (Turin, Giappichelli, 1999)

Bassini, Marco, 'Fundamental Rights and Private Enforcement in the Digital Age' (2019) 25(2) *European Law Journal* 182

—— *Internet e libertà di espressione. Prospettive costituzionali e sovranazionali* (Rome, Aracne, forthcoming 2020)

Belov, Martin (ed), *Judicial Dialogue* (The Hague, Eleven International Publishing, 2019)

Benkler, Yochai, *The Wealth of Networks: How Social Production Transforms Markets and Freedom* (New Haven, CT, Yale University Press, 2006)

Berger, Linda L, 'Metaphor and Analogy: The Sun and the Moon of Legal Persuasion' (2013) 22 *Journal of Law and Policy* 176

Berman, Paul S, 'Cyberspace and the State Action Debate: The Cultural Value of Applying Constitutional Norms to "Private" Regulation' (2000) 71 *University of Colorado Law Review* 1263

Bernal, Paul, *Internet Privacy Rights: Rights to Protect Autonomy* (Cambridge, Cambridge University Press, 2014)

Besselink, Leonard FM, 'The Parameters of Constitutional Conflict after Melloni' (2014) 39 *European Law Review* 531

Bignami, Francesca, 'Protecting Privacy Against the Police in the European Union: The Data Retention Directive' (2007) 8 *Chicago Journal of International Law* 233

—— 'Schrems II: The Right to Privacy and the New Illiberalism', *Verfassungsblog.de* (29 July 2020)

Bignami, Francesca and Giorgio Resta, 'Transatlantic Privacy Regulation: Conflict and Cooperation' (2015) 8 *Law and Contemporary Problems* 231

Black, Max, 'Metaphor' (1954) 55 *Proceedings of the Aristotelian Society* 273

—— *Models and Metaphors. Studies in Languages and Philosophy* (Ithaca, NY, Cornell University Press, 1962)

Blavin, Jonathan H and I Gleen Cohen, 'Gore, Gibson, and Goldsmith: The Evolution of Internet Metaphors in Law and Commentary' (2002) 16 *Harvard Journal of Law & Technology* 265

Boehm, Franziska and Mark D Cole, 'Data retention after the Judgement of the Court of Justice of the European Union' (2014) report commissioned by Greens/EFA, European Parliament

Bognetti, Giovanni, *La divisione dei Poteri* (Milan, Giuffrè, 2001)

Bollinger, Lee C, *The Tolerant Society: Freedom of Speech and Extremist Speech in America* (New York, Oxford University Press, 1988)

Bosmajian, Haig, *Metaphor and Reason in Judicial Opinions* (Carbondale, IL, Southern Illinois University Press, 1992)

Bracha, Oren, 'The Folklore of Informationalism: The Case of Search Engine Speech' (2014) 82 *Fordham Law Review* 1630

Brems, Eva (ed), *Conflicts Between Fundamental Rights* (Cambridge, Intersentia, 2008)

Brousseau, Eric, Meryem Marzouki and Cécile Méadel (eds), *Governance, Regulation and Powers on the Internet* (Cambridge, Cambridge University Press, 2012)

Burchardt, Dana, 'Backlash against the Court of Justice of the EU? The Recent Jurisprudence of the German Constitutional Court on EU Fundamental Rights as a Standard of Review' (2020) 21 *German Law Journal* 1

Buttarelli, Giovanni, 'Privacy in an age of hyperconnectivity, Keynote speech to the Privacy and Security Conference 2016'

Bygrave, Lee A and Jon Bing, *Internet Governance: Infrastructure and Institutions* (Oxford, Oxford University Press, 2009)

Cannie, Hannes and Dirk Voorhoof, '*The Abuse Clause and Freedom of Expression in the European Human Rights Convention*: An Added Value for Democracy and Human Rights Protection?' (2011) 29 *Netherlands Quarterly of Human Rights* 54

Cappelletti, Mauro, 'The Law-Making Power of Judges and Its Limits' (1981) 8 *Munich University Law Review* 15

Cavallone, Giulia, 'European Arrest Warrant and Fundamental Rights in Decisions Rendered in Absentia: The Extent of Union Law in the Case C-399/11 Melloni v Ministerio Fiscal' (2014) 4 *European Criminal Law Review* 19

Celeste, Edoardo, 'Digital Constitutionalism: A New Systematic Theorization' (2019) 33(1) *International Review of Law, Computers and Technology* 76

Chachko, Elena, 'The Israeli Supreme Court Checks COVID-19 Electronic Surveillance' *LawfareBlog* (5 May 2020)

Choudry, Sujit, 'Globalization in Search of Justification: Towards a Theory of Comparative Constitutional Interpretation' (1999) 74(3) *Indiana Law Journal* 821

Chuches, Genna and Monika Zalnieriute, 'A Groundhog Day in Brussels. Schrems II and International Data Transfers', *verfassungsblog.de* (16 July 2020)

Citron, Danielle K, 'Technological Due Process' (2008) 85(6) *Washington University Law Review* 1249

Citron, Danielle K and Helen Norton, 'Intermediaries and Hate Speech' (2011) 91 *Boston University Law Review* 1435

Citron, Danielle K and Frank Pasquale, 'The Scored Society: Due Process for Automated Predictions' (2014) 89 *Washington Law Review* 1

Citron, Danielle K and Benjamin Wittes, 'The Internet Will Not Break: Denying Bad Samaritans § 230 Immunity' (2017) 86 *Fordham Law Review* 401

Cocq, Céline and Francesca Galli, 'Comparative Paper on Data Retention Regulation in a Sample of EU Member States', *Surveille.eui.eu* (2013)

Cohn, Cindy and Rainey Reitman, 'USA Freedom Act Passes: What We Celebrate, What We Mourn, and Where We Go From Here' *Electronic Frontier Foundation* (2 June 2015)

Cole, David, '39 Ways to Limit Free Speech' *The New York Review of Books* (2012)

Colombi Ciacchi, Aurelia, 'The Direct Horizontal Effect of EU Fundamental Rights: ECJ 17 April 2018, Case C-414/16, Vera Egenberger v Evangelisches Werk für Diakonie und Entwicklung e.V. and ECJ 11 September 2018, Case C-68/17, IR v JQ' (2019) 15(2) *European Constitutional Law Review* 294

Contini, Annamaria, 'La forza cognitiva della metafora' (2016) 1 *I castelli di Yale online* 14.

Costello, Cathryn, 'The Bosphorus Ruling of the European Court of Human Rights: Fundamental Rights and Blurred Boundaries in Europe' (2006) 6 *Human Rights Law Review* 87

Council of Europe, *Human Rights Challenges in the Digital Age: Judicial Perspectives* (Strasbourg, Council of Europe Publishing, 2020)

Cover, Robert M, 'Violence and the Word' (1986) 95(8) *Yale Law Journal* 1601

Crawford, Kate and Jason Schultz, 'Big Data and Due Process: Toward a Framework to Redress Predictive Privacy Harms' (2014) 55 *Boston College Law Review* 93

Dahrendorf, Ralf, *Dopo la democrazia* (Rome-Bari, Laterza, 2003)

Daly, Angela, *Private Power, Online Information Flows and EU Law: Mind the Gap* (Oxford, Hart Publishing, 2016)

Daskal, Jennifer, 'What Comes Next: The Aftermath of European Court's Blow to Transatlantic Data Transfers' *Just Security* (17 July 2020)

Daskal, Jennifer and Matt Perault, 'The Apple-Google Contact Tracing System Won't Work. It Still Deserves Praise', *Slate* (22 May 2020)

De Gregorio, Giovanni, 'Democratising Content Moderation: A Constitutional Framework' (2019) 36 *Computer Law and Security Review* 1

—— 'From Constitutional Freedoms to Power. Protecting Fundamental Rights Online in the Algorithmic Society' (2019) 11(2) *European Journal of Legal Studies* 65

—— 'Google v. CNIL and Glawischnig-Piesczek v. Facebook: Content and Data in the Algorithmic Society' (2020) 1 *Rivista di diritto dei media* 249

—— 'The e-Commerce Directive and GDPR: Towards Convergence of Legal Regimes in the Algorithmic Society?' (2019) *Robert Schuman Centre for Advanced Studies Research Paper No. RSCAS 2019/36*

—— 'The Rise of Digital Constitutionalism in the European Union' (2020) *International Journal of Constitutional Law*, forthcoming

De Gregorio, Giovanni and Roxana Radu, 'Trump's Executive Order: Another Tile in the Mosaic of Governing Online Speech', *MediaLaws* (6 June 2020)

De Gregorio, Giovanni and Nicole Stremlau, 'Internet Shutdowns and the Limits of the Law' (2020) *International Journal of Communication*, forthcoming

De Hert, Paul and Pedro C Bocos, 'Case of Roman Zakharov v Russia: The Strasbourg follow up to the Luxembourg Court's Schrems judgment', *Strasbourg Observers* (23 December 2015)

della Cananea, Giacinto, *Due Process of Law Beyond the State* (Oxford, Oxford University Press, 2016)

Del Mar, Maksymilian, *Artefacts of Legal Inquiry: The Value of Imagination in Adjudication* (Oxford, Hart Publishing, 2020)

De Visser, Maartje, 'Dealing with Divergences in Fundamental Rights Standards' (2013) 20 *Maastricht Journal of European and Comparative Law* 576

Dickie, John, *Internet and Electronic Commerce Law in the European Union* (Oxford, Hart Publishing, 1999)

Docksey, Christopher, 'The EU Approach to the Protection of Rights in the Digital Environment: Today and Tomorrow – State Obligations and Responsibilities of Private Parties – GDPR rules on Data Protection, and What to Expect from the Upcoming ePrivacy Regulation' in Council of Europe (ed), *Human Rights Challenges in the Digital Age: Judicial Perspectives* (Strasbourg, Council of Europe Publishing, 2020) 47

Doffman, Zak, 'Forget Apple and Google: Contact-Tracing Apps Just Dealt Serious New Blow', *Forbes* (12 May 2020)
Drake, Griffin, 'Navigating the Atlantic: Understanding EU Data Privacy Compliance Amidst a Sea of Uncertainty' (2017) 91 *Southern California Law Review* 163
Dupré, Catherine, *The Age of Dignity. Human Rights and Constitutionalism in Europe* (Oxford, Hart Publishing, 2016)
Dwoskin, Elizabeth and Nitasha Tiku, 'Facebook Sent Home Thousands of Human Moderators due to the Coronavirus. Now the Algorithms are in Charge', *The Washington Post* (24 March 2020)
Easterbrook, Frank H, 'Cyberspace and the Law of the Horse' (1996) *University of Chicago Legal Forum* 207
EDPB, 'EU-U.S. Privacy Shield – Second Annual Joint Review report' (22 January 2019)
—— 'EU-U.S. Privacy Shield – Third Annual Joint Review report' (12 November 2019)
—— 'Statement on the Court of Justice of the European Union Judgment in Case C-311/18 – Data Protection Commissioner v Facebook Ireland and Maximillian Schrems' (17 July 2020)
Edwards, Lilian, 'Defamation and the Internet' in Lilian Edwards and Charlotte Waelde (eds), *Law and Internet-regulating Cyberspace* (Oxford, Hart Publishing, 1997)
Edwards, Lilian and Charlotte Waelde (eds), *Law and Internet-regulating Cyberspace* (Oxford, Hart Publishing, 1997)
Erdos, David and Krzysztof Garstka, 'The "Right to be Forgotten" Online within G20 Statutory Data Protection Frameworks' (2019) *University of Cambridge Faculty of Law Research Paper No. 31/2019*
Esterházy, Péter, *Harmonia Caelestis* (Milan, Feltrinelli, 2003)
Fabbrini, Federico, 'The European Court of Justice Ruling in the Data Retention Case and its Lessons for Privacy and Surveillance in the U.S.' (2015) 28 *Harvard Human Rights Journal* 65
Ferrarese, Maria Rosaria, *Il Diritto al Presente* (Bologna, Il Mulino, 2002)
Feteris, Eveline T (ed), *Fundamentals of Legal Argumentation. A Survey of Theories on the Justification of Judicial Decisions* (Dordrecht, Springer, 2017)
Ficsor, Mihály J, *The Law of Copyright and the Internet: The 1996 WIPO Treaties, Their Interpretation and Implementation* (Oxford, Oxford University Press, 2002)
Flauss, Jean-François, 'The European Court of Human Rights and the Freedom of Expression' (2009) 84 *Indiana Law Journal* 809
Floridi, Luciano, 'The Fight for Digital Sovereignty: What It Is, and Why It Matters, Especially for the EU' (2020) 33 *Philosophy & Technology* 369
—— *The Fourth Revolution: How the Infosphere Is Reshaping Human Reality* (Oxford, Oxford University Press, 2014)
—— (ed), *The Onlife Manifesto: Being Human in a Hyperconnected Era* (Cham, Springer, 2015)
Francioni, Francesco, 'International Law as a Common Language for National Courts' (2001) 36(3) *Texas International Law Journal* 587
Frantziou, Eleni, *The Horizontal Effect of Fundamental Rights in the European Union. A Constitutional Analysis* (Oxford, Oxford University Press, 2019)
Froomkin, Michael A, 'The Internet as a Source of Regulatory Arbitrage' in Brian Kahin and Charles Nesson (eds), *Borders in Cyberspace* (Cambridge, MA, MIT Press, 1997) 129
Gardbaum, Stephen, 'The "Horizontal Effect" of Constitutional Rights' (2003) 102 *Michigan Law Review* 388
Gény, François, *Méthode d'intérpretation et Sources en Droit Privé Positif* (Paris, LGDJ, 1899)
Gillespie, Alisdair, 'Hate and Harm: The Law on Hate Speech' in Andrej Savin and Jan Trzaskowski (eds), *Research Handbook on EU Internet Law* (Cheltenham, Edward Elgar, 2014) 488
Gillespie, Tarleton, *Custodians of the Internet Platforms, Content Moderation, and the Hidden Decisions That Shape Social Media* (New Haven, CT, Yale University Press, 2018)
Goldman, Eric, 'The Ten Most Important Section 230 Rulings' (2017) 20 *Tulane Journal of Technology & Intellectual Property* 1
Goldsmith, Jack L, 'Against Cyberanarchy' (1999) 65 *University of Chicago Law Review* 1199
—— 'The Internet and the Abiding Significance of Territorial Sovereignty' (1998) 5 *Indiana Journal of Global Legal Studies* 475

—— 'Unilateral Regulation of the Internet: a Modest Defence' (2000) 11 *European Journal of International Law* 135

Goldsmith, Jack L and Tim Wu, *Who Controls the Internet? Illusions of a Borderless World* (New York, Oxford University Press, 2008)

Goodman, Bryce and Seth Flaxman, 'European Union Regulations on Algorithmic Decision-Making and a "Right to Explanation"' (2017) 38(3) *AI Magazine* 50

Graef, Inge, *EU Competition Law, Data Protection and Online Platforms: Data as Essential Facility* (Alphen aan den Rijn, Wolters Kluwer, 2016)

Gstrein, Oskar J, 'The Judgment That Will Be Forgotten. How the ECJ Missed an Opportunity in Google vs CNIL (C-517/17)', *Verfassungsblog* (25 September 2019)

Habermas, Jürgen, *The Postnational Constellation: Political Essays* (Cambridge, MA, MIT Press, 2001)

Habermas, Jürgen and Jacques Derrida, 'February 15, or What Binds Europeans Together: A Plea for a Common Foreign Policy, Beginning in the Core of Europe' (2003) 10(3) *Constellations* 291

Hart, Herbert LA, *The Concept of Law* (Oxford, Oxford University Press, 1961)

Hartzog, Woodrow, *Privacy's Blueprint: The Battle to Control the Design of New Technologies* (Cambridge, MA, Harvard University Press, 2018)

Hartzog, Woodrow and Daniel J Solove, 'The Scope and Potential of FTC Data Protection' (2015) 83 *George Washington Law Review* 2230

Herzog, Eva M, 'Dialogue and Diversity. The "Right to be forgotten" – decisions of the Federal Constitutional Court' (2020) 1 *Rivista di diritto dei media* 285

Hirschl, Ran, *Comparative Matters: The Renaissance of Comparative Constitutional Law* (Oxford, Oxford University Press, 2014)

—— *Towards Juristocracy: The Origins and Consequences of the New Constitutionalism* (Cambridge, MA, Harvard University Press, 2004)

Hobbes, Thomas, *Leviathan* (1651)

Hörnle, Julia, 'The Jurisdictional Challenge of the Internet' in Lilian Edwards and Charlotte Waelde (eds), *Law and The Internet* (Oxford, Hart Publishing, 2009) 121

Houser, Kimberly A and W Gregory Voss, 'GDPR: The End of Google and Facebook or a New Paradigm in Data Privacy' (2018) 25 *Richmond Journal of Law & Technology* 1

Huang, Yasheng, Meicen Sun and Yuze Sui, 'How Digital Contact Tracing Slowed Covid-19' *Harvard Business Review* (15 April 2020)

Huhn, Wilson R, 'The State Action Doctrine and the Principle of Democratic Choice' (2006) 84 *Hofstra Law Review* 1380

Hunter, Dan, 'Cyberspace as Place and the Tragedy of the Digital Anticommons' (2003) 91 *California Law Review* 439

Irion, Kristina, 'Schrems II and Surveillance: Third Countries' National Security Powers in the Purview of EU Law', *EU Law Blog* (24 July 2020)

Jacobs, Francis G, 'Judicial Dialogue and the Cross Fertilization of Legal System: The European Court of Justice' (2003) 38(3) *Texas International Law Journal* 547

Johnson, David R and David G Post, 'Law and Borders. The Rise of Law in Cyberspace' (1996) 48 *Stanford Law Review* 1367

Johnson, Mark, *The Aesthetics of Meaning and Thought: The Bodily Roots of Philosophy, Science, Morality, and Art* (Chigago, IL, Chigago University Press, 2018)

Joo, Thomas W, 'Contract, Property, and the Role of Metaphor in Corporations Law' (2001) 35 *U.C. Davis Law Review* 779

Jorgensen, Rikke F (ed), *Human Rights in the Age of Platforms* (Cambridge, MA, MIT Press, 2019)

Kahn, Robert A, 'Why Do Europeans Ban Hate Speech? A Debate Between Karl Lowenstein and Robert Post' (2013) 41 *Hofstra Law Review* 545

Kaminski, Margot E, 'The Right to Explanation, Explained' (2019) 34(1) *Berkeley Technology Law Journal* 189

Kerr, Orin S, 'The Mosaic Theory of the Fourth Amendment' (2012) 111 *Michigan Law Review* 311

Klonick, Kate, 'The Facebook Oversight Board: Creating an Independent Institution to Adjudicate Online Free Expression' (2020) 129 *Yale Law Journal* 2418

—— 'The New Governors: The People, Rules, and Processes Governing Online Speech' (2018) 131 *Harvard Law Review* 1599
Knox, John H, 'Horizontal Human Rights Law' (2008) 102(1) *American Journal of International Law* 1
Kohl, Uta, *Jurisdiction and the Internet. Regulatory Competence over Online Activity* (Cambridge, Cambridge University Press, 2007)
Kokott, Juliane and Christoph Sobotta, 'The Kadi Case – Constitutional Core Values and International Law – Finding the Balance?' (2012) 23 *European Journal of International Law* 1015
Koltay, András, *New Media and Freedom of Expression. Rethinking the Constitutional Foundations of the Public Sphere* (Oxford, Hart Publishing, 2019)
Kosseff, Jeff, *The Twenty-Six Words That Created the Internet* (Ithaca, NY, Cornell University Press, 2019)
Kosta, Eleni, 'The Way to Luxembourg: National Court Decisions on the Compatibility of the Data Retention Directive with the Right to Privacy and Data Protection' (2013) 10 *scritpted* 339
Kowalik-Bańczyk, Krystyna and Oreste Pollicino, 'Migration of European Judicial Ideas Concerning Jurisdiction over Google on Withdrawal of Information' (2016) 17(3) *German Law Journal* 315
Kranenborg, Herke, 'Article 8 Protection of Personal Data' in Steve Peers, Tamara Hervey, Jeff Kenner and Angela Ward (eds), *The EU Charter of Fundamental Rights:A Commentary* (Oxford, Hart Publishing, 2014) 223
Krotoszynski, Ronald J, 'Reconciling Privacy and Speech in the Era of Big Data: A Comparative Legal Analysis' (2015) 56 *William And Mary Law Review* 1279
Kumm, Mattias, 'Who is Afraid of the Total Constitution? Constitutional Rights as Principles and the Constitutionalization of Private Law' (2006) 7(4) *German Law Journal* 341
Kumm, Mattias and Victor Ferreres Comella, 'What Is So Special about Constitutional Rights in Private Litigation? A Comparative Analysis of the Function of State Action Requirements and Indirect Horizontal Effect' in Andras Sajó and Renata Uitz (eds), *The Constitution in Private Relations: Expanding Constitutionalism* (The Hague, Eleven International Publishing, 2005) 241
Kuner, Christopher, 'Reality and Illusion in EU Data Transfer Regulation Post Schrems' (2017) 18(4) *German Law Journal* 881
Laidlaw, Emily B, 'A Framework for Identifying Internet Information Gatekeepers' (2012) 24(3) *International Review Law, Computers and Technology* 263
Lakoff, George, *Women, Fire, and Dangerous Things. What Categories Reveal about the Mind* (Chicago, IL, University Chicago Press, 1987)
Lakoff, George and Mark Johnson, *Metaphors We Live By* (Chicago, IL, University of Chicago Press, 1980)
Larkin, John F, 'Strasbourg or Luxembourg: A Right to Truth or *Suppressio Veri*?' in *Human Rights Challenges in the Digital Age: Judicial Perspective* (Strasbourg, Council of Europe Publishing, 2020) 79
Larsson, Stefan, *Conceptions in the Code. How Metaphors Explain Legal Challenges in Digital Times* (Oxford, Oxford University Press, 2017)
Lemley, Mark A, Peter S Menell, Robert P Merges and Pamela Samuelson, *Software and Internet Law* (New York, Aspen Law & Business, 2000)
Lessig, Lawrence, *Code 2.0* (New York, Basic Books, 2006)
—— *Code and Other Laws of Cyberspace* (New York, Basic Books, 1999)
—— 'Reading the Constitution in Cyberspace' (1996) 45 *Emory Law Journal* 869
L'Heureux-Dube, Claire, 'The International Judicial Dialogue: When Domestic Constitutional Courts Join the Conversation' (2001) 114 *Harvard Law Review* 2049
Lutzi, Tobias ',Internet Cases in EU Private International Law – Developing a Coherent Approach' (2017) 66 *International and Comparative Law Quarterly* 687
Lynskey, Orla, 'Control over Personal Data in a Digital Age: Google Spain v AEPD and Mario Costeja Gonzalez' (2015) 78 *Modern Law Review* 522
—— 'Deconstructing Data Protection: The "Added-Value" of a Right to Data Protection in the EU Legal Order' (2014) 63 *International & Comparative Law Quarterly* 569
—— 'The "Europeanisation" of data protection law' (2017) 19 *Cambridge Yearbook of European Legal Studies* 1

MacCormick, Neil, 'Argumentation and Interpretation in Law' (1995) 9 *Argumentation* 467
—— *Legal Reasoning and Legal Theory* (Oxford, Oxford University Press, 1978)
—— 'Risking Constitutional Collision in Europe?' (1998) 18(3) *Oxford Journal of Legal Studies* 517
Madsen, Mikael R, 'Judicial Independence: Online Public Talk by Robert Spano, President of the ECtHR' *Københavns Universitet Video Portal* (2 June 2020)
Malgieri, Gianclaudio, 'Automated Decision-making in the EU Member States: The Right to Explanation and Other "Suitable Safeguards" in the National Legislations' (2019) 35(5) *Computer Law and Security Review* 1
Malgieri, Gianclaudio and Giovanni Comandé, 'Why a Right to Legibility of Automated Decision-Making Exists in the General Data Protection Regulation' (2017) 7 *International Data Privacy Law* 243
Martinico, Giuseppe and Oreste Pollicino, *The Interaction Between Europe's Legal Systems: Judicial Dialogue and the Creation of Supranational Laws* (London, Edward Elgar, 2012)
McCrudden, Christopher, 'A Common Law of Human Rights? Transnational Judicial Conversations on Constitutional Rights' (2000) 20(4) *Oxford Journal of Legal Studies* 499
Menendez, Agustín J and Erik O Eriksen (eds), *Arguing Fundamental Rights* (London, Springer, 2006)
Menthe, Darrel C, 'Jurisdiction in Cyberspace: A Theory of International Spaces' (1998) 4 *Michigan Telecommunication & Technology Law Review* 69
Milanovic, Marko, 'ECtHR Judgment in Big Brother Watch v. UK', *EJIL: Talk* (23 September 2018)
Mittelstadt, Brent D, Patrick Allo, Mariarosaria Taddeo, Sandra Wachter and Luciano Floridi, 'The Ethics of Algorithms: Mapping the Debate' (2016) 3(2) *Big Data & Society* 1
Montesquieu, Charles-Louis, *De l'Esprit des Lois* (1758)
Monti, Matteo, 'The EU Code of Practice on Disinformation and the Risk of the Privatisation of Censorship' in Serena Giusti and Elisa Piras (eds), *Democracy and Fake News – Information Manipulation and Post-Truth Politics* (Abingdon, Routledge, forthcoming, 2020)
Moore, Martin and Damian Tambini (eds), *Digital Dominance: The Power of Google, Amazon, Facebook, and Apple* (Oxford, Oxford University Press, 2018)
Morelli, Alessandro and Oreste Pollicino, 'Metaphors, Judicial Frames and Fundamental Right in Cyberspace' (2020) *American Journal of Comparative Law*, forthcoming
Müller, Amrei (ed), *Judicial Dialogue and Human Rights* (Cambridge, Cambridge University Press, 2017)
Negroponte, Nicholas, *Being Digital* (New York, Alfred A Knopf Inc, 1995)
Nicola, Fernanda and Oreste Pollicino, 'The Balkanization of Data Privacy Regulation' (2020) *West Virginia Law Review*, forthcoming.
Nunziato, Dawn C, 'The Death of the Public Forum in Cyberspace' (2007) 20 *Berkeley Technology Law Journal* 1115
Orucu, Esin, *Judicial Comparativism in Human Rights Cases* (London, British Inst of Intl & Comparative Law, 2003)
Palmieri, Nicholas F, 'Data Protection in an Increasingly Globalized World' (2019) 94 *Indiana Law Journal* 297
Pasquale, Frank, 'From Territorial to Functional Sovereignty: The Case of Amazon, Law and Political Economy', *Law and Political Economy blog* (6 December 2017)
—— *The Black Box Society: The Secret Algorithms That Control Money and Information* (Cambridge, MA, Harvard University Press, 2015)
Paul, Greig, 'Contact-tracing apps: Apple dictating policies to nations won't help its EU anti-trust probe', *The Conversation* (24 June 2020)
Peers, Steve, 'Bosphorus – European Court of Human Rights: Limited Responsibility of European Union Member States for Actions within the Scope of Community Law Judgment of 30 June 2005, Bosphorus Airways v Ireland, Application No. 45036/98' (2006) 2 *European Constitutional Law Review* 443
Peters, Jonathan, 'The "Sovereigns of Cyberspace" and State Action: The First Amendment's Application (or Lack Thereof) to Third-Party Platforms' (2017) 32 *Berkeley Technology Law Journal* 989
Petkova, Bilyana, 'Privacy as Europe's First Amendment' (2019) 25(2) *European Law Journal* 140

Pistor, Katharina, *Law in the Time of COVID-19* (New York, Columbia Law School, 2020)
Pitruzzella, Giovanni and Oreste Pollicino, *Disinformation and Hate Speech: A European Constitutional Perspective* (Milan, Bocconi University Press, 2020)
Pochon, Christopher, 'Applying the Holder Standard to Speech That Provides Material Support to Terrorism in United States v. Mehanna, No. 09-10017-GAO (D. MASS. 2012)' (2013) 36 *Harvard Journal of Law & Public Policy* 375
Pollicino, Oreste, 'Diabolical Persistence. Thoughts on the Schrems II Decision', *Verfassungsblog.de* (25 July 2020)
—— 'The Legal Reasoning of the Court of Justice in the Context of the Principle of Equality' (2004) 5(3) *German Law Journal* 283
Pollicino, Oreste and Marco Bassini, 'Free Speech, Defamation and the Limits to Freedom of Expression in the EU: A Comparative Analysis' in Andrej Savin and Jan Trzaskowski (eds), *Research Handbook on EU Internet Law* (Cheltenham, Edward Elgar, 2014) 508
—— and —— 'Reconciling Right to Be Forgotten and Freedom of Information: Past and Future of Personal Data Protection in Europe' (2014) 2 *Diritto pubblico comparato ed europeo* 641
—— and —— 'The Law of the Internet between Globalization and Localization' in Miguel Maduro, Kaarlo Tuori and Suvi Sankari (eds), *Transnational Law – Rethinking Law and Legal Thinking* (Cambridge, Cambridge University Press, 2014) 346
—— and —— *Verso un Internet Bill of Rights* (Rome, Aracne, 2015)
Pollicino, Oreste and Graziella Romeo (eds), *The Internet and Constitutional Law: The Protection of Fundamental Rights and Constitutional Adjudication in Europe* (London, Routledge, 2016)
Pollicino, Oreste and Mart Susi, 'Internet and Human Rights Law: Introduction' (2019) 25(2) *European Law Journal* 120
Posner, Richard A, *How Judges Think* (Cambridge, MA, Harvard University Press, 2008)
—— 'The Law of the Beholder', *New Republic* (16 October 2000)
Post, Robert C, 'Data Privacy and Dignitary Privacy: Google Spain, the Right To Be Forgotten, and the Construction of the Public Sphere' (2018) 67 *Duke Law Journal* 981
Pound, Roscoe, 'Law in Books and Law in Action' (1910) 44 *American Law Review* 12
Price, Monroe E, *Media and Sovereignty: The Global Information Revolution and Its Challenge to State Power* (Cambridge, MA, MIT Press, 2002)
—— 'The Newness of New Technology' (2001) 22(5–6) *Cardozo Law Review* 1885
Redeker, Dennis, Lex Gill and Urs Gasser, 'Towards Digital Constitutionalism? Mapping Attempts to Craft an Internet Bill of Rights' (2018) 80 *International Communication Gazette* 302
Redish, Martin H and Lawrence C Marshall, 'Adjudicatory Independence and the Values of Procedural Due Process' (1986) 95(3) *Yale Law Journal* 455
Reed, Chris, *Internet Law: Text and Materials* (Cambridge, Cambridge University Press, 2004)
Reidenberg, Joel R, 'States and Internet Enforcement' (2004) 1 *University of Ottawa Law & Technology Journal* 213
—— 'Technology and Internet Jurisdiction' (2005) 153 *University of Pennsylvania Law Review* 1951
—— 'Yahoo and Democracy on the Internet' (2001/2002) 42 *Jurimetrics* 261
Richards, Ivor A, *The Philosophy of Rhetoric* (Oxford, Oxford University Press, 1936)
Richards, Neil, *Intellectual Privacy: Rethinking Civil Liberties in the Digital Age* (Oxford, Oxford University Press 2015)
Richards, Neil M, 'The Puzzle of Brandeis, Privacy, and Speech' (2010) 63 *Vanderbilt Law Review* 1295
Riley, Chris, 'The Rite of Rhetoric: Cognitive Framing in Technology Law' (2009) 9(3) *Nevada Law Journal* 495
Robertson, Adi, 'The Supreme Court Live-Streamed its First Phone Hearing, and (Almost) Everything Worked' *The Verge* (5 May 2020)
Roig, Antoni, 'Safeguards for the Right Not to Be Subject to a Decision Based Solely on Automated Processing (Article 22 GDPR)' (2017) 8(3) *European Journal of Law and Technology* 1
Romeo, Graziella, 'Building Integration Through the Bill of Rights? The European Union at the Mirror' (2018) 47 *Georgia Journal of International & Comparative Law* 21

Ronsenfeld, Michel and András Sajó, 'Spreading Liberal Constitutionalism: An Inquiry into the Fate of Free Speech in New Democracies' in Sujit Choudhry (ed), *The Migration of Constitutional Ideas* (Cambridge, Cambridge University Press, 2006) 142

Rosas, Allan, 'The European Court of Justice in Context: Forms and Patterns of Judicial Dialogue' (2007) 1(2) *European Journal of Legal Studies* 1

Ross, Catherine J, 'Incredible Lies' (2018) 89 *University of Colorado Law Review* 377

Rotenberg, Marc, 'Schrems II: From Snowden to China, the Evolution of Data Protection as a Fundamental Right' (2020) *European Law Journal*, forthcoming

Sacco, Rodolfo, 'Legal Formants: A Dynamic Approach To Comparative Law' (1991) 39(1) *The American Journal of Comparative Law* 1

Sachdeva, Amit M, 'International Jurisdiction in Cyberspace: A Comparative Perspective' (2007) 13(8) *Computer and Telecommunication Law Review* 245

Sajó, András, *Limiting Government. An Introduction to Constitutionalism* (Budapest, Central European University Press, 1999)

Sajó, András and Clare Ryan, 'Judicial Reasoning and New Technologies: Framing, Newness, Fundamental Rights and the Internet' in Oreste Pollicino and Graziella Romeo (eds), *The Internet and Constitutional Law: The Protection of Fundamental Rights and Constitutional Adjudication in Europe* (London, Routledge, 2016) 3

Sajó, András and Renáta Uitz, *The Constitution of Freedom: An Introduction to Legal Constitutionalism* (Oxford, Oxford University Press, 2017)

Santaniello, Mauro, Nicola Palladino, Maria Carmela Catone and Paolo Diana, 'The Language of Digital Constitutionalism and the Role of National Parliaments' (2018) 80 *International Communication Gazette* 320

Schauer, Frederick, 'Freedom of Expression Adjudication in Europe and America: A Case Study in Comparative Constitutional Architecture' in Georg Nolte (ed), *European and US Constitutionalism* (Cambridge, Cambridge University Press, 2005) 49

Schorkopf, Frank, 'The European Court of Human Rights' Judgment in the Case of Bosphorus Hava Yollari Turizm v Ireland' (2005) 6 *German Law Journal* 1255

Schwartz, Paul M, 'The EU-U.S. Privacy Collision: A Turn to Institutions and Procedures' (2013) 126 *Harvard Law Review* 1966

Schwartz, Paul M and Karl-Nikolaus Peifer, *Transatlantic Data Privacy Law* (2017) 106 *Georgetown Law Journal* 115

Shapiro, David L, 'In Defense of Judicial Candor' (1986–1987) 100 *Harvard Law Review* 731

Shapiro, Martin and Alec Stone Sweet, *On Law, Politics and Judicialization* (Oxford, Oxford University Press, 2002)

Skouris, Vassilios, 'The Position of the European Court of Justice in the EU Legal Order and its Relationship with National Constitutional Courts' (2005) *Zeitshrift für öffentliches Recht* 323

Slaughter, Anne-Marie, 'A Global Community of Courts' (2003) 44(1) *Harvard International Law Journal* 191

—— *A New World Order* (Princeton, NJ, Princeton University Press, 2004)

—— 'Judicial Globalization' (2000) 40 *Virginia Journal of International Law* 1103

Smith, Graham JH, *Internet Law and Regulation* (London, Sweet and Maxwell, 2002)

Smith, Peter J, 'New Legal Fictions' (2006–2007) 95 *Georgetown Law Journal* 1484

Solove, Daniel J, 'Fourth Amendment Pragmatism' (2010) 51 *Boston College Law Review* 1511

—— *Understanding Privacy* (Cambridge, MA, Harvard University Press, 2008)

Spanó, Róbert, 'Intermediary Liability for Online User Comments under the European Convention on Human Rights' (2017) 17(4) *Human Rights Law Review* 665

—— 'Summary of the Issues Discussed During the Seminar: An Aerial View' in Council of Europe, *Human Rights Challenges in the Digital Age: Judicial Perspectives* (Strasbourg, Council of Europe Publishing, 2020) 201

—— 'Universality or Diversity of Human Rights? Strasbourg in the Age of Subsidiarity' (2014) 14(3) *Human Rights Law Review* 487

Stonebridge, Lyndsey, *The Judicial Imagination: Writing After Nuremberg* (Edinburgh, Edinburgh University Press, 2011)

Stone Sweet, Alec, 'Constitutional Dialogue in the European Community' in Anne-Marie Slaughter, Alec Stone Sweet and Joseph Weiler (eds), *The European Court and National Courts. Doctrine and Jurisprudence: Legal Change in Its Social Context* (Oxford, Hart Publishing, 2004)

—— *Governing with Judges: Constitutional Politics in Europe* (Oxford, Oxford University Press, 2000)

Su, Edgar, 'Roaming "Robodog" Politely Tells Singapore Park Goers to Keep Apart', *Reuters* (8 May 2020)

Sunstein, Cass R, 'Constitutional Caution the Law of Cyberspace' (1996) *University of Chicago Legal Forum* 361

Susi, Mart (ed), *Human Rights, Digital Society and the Law. A Research Companion* (London, Routledge, 2019)

—— 'The Internet Balancing Formula' (2019) 25(2) *European Law Journal* 198

Suzor, Nicolas, 'Digital Constitutionalism: Using the Rule of Law to Evaluate the Legitimacy of Governance by Platforms' (2018) 4(3) *Social Media + Society* 1

Svantesson, Dan Jerker B, 'European Union Claims of Jurisdiction over the Internet – an Analysis of Three Recent Key Developments' (2018) 9 *Journal of Intellectual Property, Information Technology and Electronic Commerce Law* 112

—— *Private International Law and the Internet* (Alphen aan den Rijn, Wolters Kluwer, 2007)

—— *Solving the Internet Jurisdiction Puzzle* (Oxford, Oxford University Press, 2017)

Taddeo, Mariarosaria and Luciano Floridi (eds), *The Responsibilities of Online Service Providers* (Berlin, Springer Verlag, 2017)

Tambini, Damian, Danilo Leonardi and Chris T Marsden, *Codifying Cyberspace: Communications Self-Regulation in the Age of Internet Convergence* (London, Routledge, 2007)

Tate, C Neale and Torbjörn Vallinder (eds), *The Global Expansion of the Judicial Power* (New York, New York University Press, 1995)

Teubner, Gunther, 'Societal Constitutionalism: Alternatives to State-Centered Constitutional Theory?' in Christian Joerges, Inge-Johanne Sand and Gunther Teubner (eds), *Constitutionalism and Transnational Governance* (Oxford, Hart Publishing, 2004) 3

Tomuschat, Christian, 'Primacy of the United Nations Law. Innovation Features in the Community Legal Order' (2006) 43 *Common Market Law Review* 537

Trachtman, Joel P, 'Cyberspace, Sovereignty, Jurisdiction and Modernism' (1998) 5 *Indiana Journal of Global Legal Studies* 561

Tulkens, Françoise, 'Freedom of Expression and Hate Speech in the Case-law of the European Court of Human Rights' in Josep Casadevall, Egbert Myjer and Michael O'Boyle (eds), *Freedom of Expression. Essays in Honour of Nicolas Bratza* (Oisterwijk, Wolf Legal Publishers, 2012) 349

Tushnet, Mark, 'The Issue of State Action/Horizontal Effect in Comparative Constitutional Law' (2003) 1 *International Journal of Constitutional Law* 79

Valcke, Peggy, Miklos Sukosd and Robert Picard (eds), *Media Pluralism and Diversity: Concepts, Risks and Global Trend* (London, Palgrave, 2015)

Van Loo, Rory, 'The Corporation as Courthouse' (2016) 33 *Yale Journal on Regulation* 548

Vedaschi, Arianna and Valerio Lubello, 'Data Retention and Its Implications for the fundamental Right to Privacy: A European Perspective' (2014) 20 *Tilburg Law Review* 14

Volokh, Eugene, 'Freedom of Speech, Information Privacy, and the Troubling Implications of a Right to Stop People from Speaking About You' (2000) 52 *Stanford Law Review* 1049

Volokh, Eugene and Donald Falk, 'First Amendment Protection for Search Engine Search Results: White Paper Commissioned by Google' (2012) *UCLA School of Law Research Paper* no 12–22

Voorhoof, Dirk, 'Freedom of Expression under the European Human Rights System. From Sunday Times (n° 1) v. U.K. (1979) to Hachette Filipacchi Associés ("Ici Paris") v. France (2009)' (2009) 1–2 *Inter-American and European Human Rights Journal/Revista Interamericana y Europa de Derechos Humanos* 3

—— 'Same Standards, Different Tools? The ECtHR and the Protection and Limitations of Freedom of Expression in the Digital Environment' in Council of Europe, *Human Rights Challenges in the Digital Age: Judicial Perspectives* (Strasbourg, Council of Europe Publishing, 2020)

Wachter, Sandra, Brent D Mittelstadt and Luciano Floridi, 'Why a Right to Explanation of Automated Decision-Making does not Exist in the General Data Protection Regulation' (2017) 7 *International Data Privacy Law* 76

Wagner, Ben, Matthias C Kettemann and Kilian Vieth (eds), *Research Handbook on Human Rights and Digital Technology: Global Politics, Law and International Relations* (Cheltenham, Edward Elgar, 2019)

Waldron, Jeremy (ed), *Theories of Rights* (Oxford, Oxford University Press, 1984)

Walkila, Sonya, *Horizontal Effect of Fundamental Rights in EU Law* (Groningen, Europa Law Publishing, 2016)

Warren, Samuel D and Louis D Brandeis, 'The Right to Privacy' (1890) 4 *Harvard Law Review* 193

West, Sonja R, 'Press Exceptionalism' (2014) 127 *Harvard Law Review* 2434

White, James B, *The Legal Imagination* (Chicago, IL, University of Chicago Press, 1985)

Wimmer, Kurt, 'Free Expression and EU Privacy Regulation: Can the GDPR Reach U.S. Publishers' (2018) 68 *Syracuse Law Review* 547

Woods, Lorna, 'Article 11 Freedom of Expression and Information' in Steve Peers, Tamara Hervey, Jeff Kenner and Angela Ward (eds), *The EU Charter of Fundamental Rights A Commentary* (Oxford, Hart Publishing, 2014) 311

—— 'Zakharov v Russia: Mass Surveillance and the European Court of Human Rights', *EU Law Analysis* (16 December 2015)

Wu, Tim, 'Is the First Amendment Obsolete?' (2018) 547 *Michigan Law Review* 117

—— 'Is the First Amendment Obsolete?' in Lee C Bollinger and Geoffrey R Stone (eds), *Free Speech Century* (Oxford, Oxford University Press, 2019) 272

Youm, Kyu Ho, '"Actual Malice" in U.S. Defamation Law: The Minority of One Doctrine in the World?' (2011) 4 *Journal of International & Entertainment Law* 1

Yuhas, Alan, 'NSA reform: USA Freedom Act passes first surveillance reform in decade – as it happened' *The Guardian* (2 June 2015)

Zagrebesky, Gustavo, *Il diritto mite* (Turin, Einaudi, 1992)

Zarsky, Tal Z, 'Incompatible: The GDPR in the Age of Big Data' (2017) 47 *Seton Hall Law Review* 995

—— 'Transparent Predictions' (2013) 4 *University of Illinois Law Review* 1507

Zittrain, Jonathan L, Robert Faris, Helmi Noman, Justin Clark, Casey Tilton and Ryan Morrison-Westphal, 'The Shifting Landscape of Global Internet Censorship', *Berkman Klein Center for Internet & Society Research Publication* (2017)

Zoller, Elisabeth, 'The United States Supreme Court and the Freedom of Expression' (2009) 84 *Indiana Law Journal* 885

Zuboff, Shoshana, 'Big Other: Surveillance Capitalism and the Prospects of an Information Civilization' (2015) 30(1) *Journal of Information Technology* 75

Zucca, Lorenzo, *Constitutional Dilemmas – Conflicts of Fundamental Legal Rights in Europe and the US* (Oxford, Oxford University Press, 2007)

INDEX

www.ingramcontent.com/pod-product-compliance
Ingram Content Group UK Ltd.
Pitfield, Milton Keynes, MK11 3LW, UK
UKHW021037150926
475561UK00003B/154

9 781509 947225